Knowledge and Space

Volume 6

Knowledge and Space

This book series entitled "Knowledge and Space" is dedicated to topics dealing with the production, dissemination, spatial distribution, and application of knowledge. Recent work on the spatial dimension of knowledge, education, and science; learning organizations; and creative milieus has underlined the importance of spatial disparities and local contexts in the creation, legitimation, diffusion, and application of new knowledge. These studies have shown that spatial disparities in knowledge and creativity are not short-term transitional events but rather a fundamental structural element of society and the economy.

The volumes in the series on Knowledge and Space cover a broad range of topics relevant to all disciplines in the humanities and social sciences focusing on knowledge, intellectual capital, and human capital: clashes of knowledge; milieus of creativity; geographies of science; cultural memories; knowledge and the economy; learning organizations; knowledge and power; ethnic and cultural dimensions of knowledge; knowledge and action; and the spatial mobility of knowledge. These topics are analyzed and discussed by scholars from a range of disciplines, schools of thought, and academic cultures.

Knowledge and Space is the outcome of an agreement concluded by the Klaus Tschira Foundation and Springer in 2006.

Series Editor:

Peter Meusburger, Department of Geography, Heidelberg University, Germany

For further volumes:
http://www.springer.com/series/7568

Learning Organizations

Ariane Berthoin Antal • Peter Meusburger
Laura Suarsana
Editors

Learning Organizations

Extending the Field

 Springer

Editors
Ariane Berthoin Antal
Research Unit "Cultural Sources of Newness"
Social Science Research Center Berlin (WZB)
Berlin, Germany

Peter Meusburger
Department of Geography
Heidelberg University
Heidelberg, Germany

Laura Suarsana
Department of Geography
Heidelberg University
Heidelberg, Germany

Technical Editor
David Antal, Berlin

ISSN 1877-9220
ISBN 978-94-007-7219-9   ISBN 978-94-007-7220-5 (eBook)
DOI 10.1007/978-94-007-7220-5
Springer Dordrecht Heidelberg New York London

Library of Congress Control Number: 2013954708

Printed on acid-free paper

Springer is part of Springer Science+Business Media (www.springer.com)

Acknowledgments

The editors thank the Klaus Tschira Foundation for funding our enterprise (symposia and book series on Knowledge and Space). The staff of the Klaus Tschira Stiftung, Beate Spiegel, Renate Ries, Jana Brinkmann, and Sylke Peters always contribute a great deal to the success of the symposia. Together with all the authors in this volume, we are especially grateful to David Antal for his tireless dedication to quality as technical editor of all the chapters and as translator for some of them. Volker Schniepp at the Department of Geography at Heidelberg University has been an enormous support in ensuring that the figures and maps meet the high standards of publication. We also thank the students of Heidelberg University's Department of Geography who helped to organize the 6th symposium and prepare this publication, especially Amadeus Barth, Julia Brasche, Helen Dorn, Claudia Kämper, Melanie Kudermann, Inga Labuhn, Martina Ries, and Tina Thiele.

Contents

1   The Importance of Knowledge Environments and Spatial Relations
    for Organizational Learning: An Introduction   1
    Ariane Berthoin Antal, Peter Meusburger, and Laura Suarsana

2   Learning from Screens: Does Ideology Prevail over Lived
    Experience? The Example of ERP Systems   17
    François-Régis Puyou

3   Organizational Design for Knowledge Exchange:
    The *Hau-Ba* Model   29
    Ahmed Bounfour and Gwénaëlle Grefe

4   Command or Conviction? Informal Networks and the Diffusion
    of Controversial Innovations   49
    Johannes Glückler and Robert Panitz

5   Collaboration and Knowledge Gains in Organizations   69
    Wolfgang Scholl

6   Organizing Relational Distance: Innovation as the Management
    of Sociocultural and Time-spatial Tensions   85
    Oliver Ibert

7   Organizational Learning and Physical Space—How Office
    Configurations Inform Organizational Behaviors   103
    Kerstin Sailer

8   The Unexpected Neighbor: Learning, Space, and the Unconscious
    in Organizations   129
    Russ Vince

9   Can Social Space Provide a Deep Structure for the Theory
    and Practice of Organizational Learning?   143
    Victor J. Friedman and Israel J. Sykes

10   Learning in Temporary Organizations: The Case of UN Global Conferences.. 157
Kathrin Böhling

11   When Arts Enter Organizational Spaces: Implications for Organizational Learning 177
Ariane Berthoin Antal

12   Research-based Theater as a Facilitator of Organizational Learning... 203
Anne Pässilä and Tuija Oikarinen

13   Creative Space in Organizational Learning and Leadership: 21st-Century Shapeshifting.. 223
Shaun McNiff

The Klaus Tschira Foundation 239

Index... 243

Contributors

Ariane Berthoin Antal Research Unit "Cultural Sources of Newness," Social Science Research Center Berlin (WZB), Berlin, Germany

Kathrin Böhling TUM School of Management, Chair of Forest and Environmental Policy, Freising, Germany

Ahmed Bounfour European Chair On Intellectual Capital Management & PESOR, Université Paris-Sud, Sceaux, France

Victor J. Friedman Department of Sociology and Anthropology/Department of Behavioral Sciences, Max Stern Yezreel Valley College, Jezreel Valley, Israel

Johannes Glückler Department of Geography, Heidelberg University, Heidelberg, Germany

Gwénaëlle Grefe Granem (Groupe de recherches angevin en économie et management), Université Angers, Angers Cedex 01, France

Oliver Ibert Forschungsabteilung 1 Dynamiken von Wirtschaftsräumen, Leibniz-Institut für Regionalentwicklung und Strukturplanung e.V. (IRS), Erkner, Germany

Institut für Geographische Wissenschaften [Institute for Geographical Sciences], Freie Universität Berlin, Malteserstr 74-100, D-12249, Berlin, Germany

Shaun McNiff Lesley University, Cambridge, MA, USA

Peter Meusburger Department of Geography, Heidelberg University, Heidelberg, Germany

Tuija Oikarinen LUT Lahti School of Innovation, Lappeenranta University of Technology, Lahti, Finland

Robert Panitz Department of Geography, Heidelberg University, Heidelberg, Germany

Anne Pässilä LUT Lahti School of Innovation, Lappeenranta University of Technology, Lahti, Finland

François-Régis Puyou Département Comptabilité, Contrôle de Gestion, Audit, Audencia Nantes School of Management, Nantes Cedex 3, France

Kerstin Sailer The Bartlett School of Graduate Studies, University College London (UCL), London, UK

Wolfgang Scholl Sozial- und Organisationspsychologie & Ingenieurpsychologie, Humboldt-Universität zu Berlin, Wolfgang Köhler–Haus, Berlin, Germany

Laura Suarsana Department of Geography, Heidelberg University, Heidelberg, Germany

Israel J. Sykes Independent Consultant, Jerusalem, Israel

Russ Vince School of Management, University of Bath, Bath, North East Somerset, UK

The Importance of Knowledge Environments and Spatial Relations for Organizational Learning: An Introduction

Ariane Berthoin Antal, Peter Meusburger, and Laura Suarsana

The birthplace of the field of organizational learning can be traced back to management scholars in the United States who were interested in organizational behavior. Over the years it has attracted researchers from diverse disciplines and from all around the world. This line of inquiry is particularly apt to address the way interest in the field has spread and how it has been populated so far, given that the current edited volume is appearing in the series Knowledge and Space, an intellectual venture launched by the department of geography at Heidelberg University.

The first book dedicated to organizational learning grew out of the collaborative relationship between Chris Argyris (Harvard University) and Don Schön (MIT) in Boston, Massachusetts. They published it in 1978 then revised it significantly in 1996, both times with the Massachusetts-based publisher Addison-Wesley. The year 1996 saw the appearance of two edited volumes (Cohen & Sproull, 1996; Moingeon & Edmondson, 1996), both of whose contents show that scholars from other parts of the United States as well as some Europeans had become engaged in the field. The internationalization appears to have started with visiting fellowships of U.S. scholars in Europe. In the 1970s the young Swede Bo Hedberg worked at the International Institute of Management of the Social Science Research Center Berlin (WZB) in Germany with the American scholar Bill Starbuck, who was a senior fellow there, and one outcome was the landmark chapter on organizational unlearning (Hedberg, 1981) in the first volume of the *Handbook of Organizational Design* (Nystrom & Starbuck, 1981). Later, Europeans went to work in the United

A. Berthoin Antal (✉)
Research Unit "Cultural Sources of Newness," Social Science Research
Center Berlin (WZB), Reichpietschufer 50, D-10785 Berlin, Germany
e-mail: ariane.berthoin.antal@wzb.eu

P. Meusburger • L. Suarsana
Department of Geography, Heidelberg University,
Berliner Strasse 48, D-69120 Heidelberg, Germany
e-mail: peter.meusburger@geog.uni-heidelberg.de;
laura.suarsana@geog.uni-heidelberg.de

A. Berthoin Antal et al. (eds.), *Learning Organizations: Extending the Field*,
Knowledge and Space 6, DOI 10.1007/978-94-007-7220-5_1,
© Springer Science+Business Media Dordrecht 2014

States. In the 1990s the French scholar Bertrand Moingeon became involved in the field while he was at Harvard with Chris Argyris and Amy Edmondson, a working relationship that grew into a coeditorship (Moingeon & Edmondson). Another landmark book in the field came from Japan. Ikujiro Nonaka and Hirotaka Takeuchi shifted the discussion both geographically and conceptually by drawing on experiences in Japanese organizations and by introducing "the SECI[1] model of knowledge creation" as a different way of framing processes of learning in organizations (Nonaka & Takeuchi, 1995). In 2006 three researchers from Israel (one of whom had studied with Argyris and Schön in the early 1980s) wrote a book to offer readers help in "demystifying organizational learning" because the field had meanwhile become highly complex and its ideas appeared too complicated to apply in organizations (Lipshitz, Friedman, & Popper, 2007).

At the turn of the millennium the maturation of the field was marked by the appearance of the first handbooks, both with international editorial teams and contributions from Asia, Europe, and North America (Dierkes, Berthoin Antal, Child, & Nonaka, 2001; Easterby-Smith & Lyles, 2003). The internationalization of this area of inquiry received additional impetus from the translation of the handbook by Dierkes et al. (2001) into Mandarin for publication by the Peoples' Publishing House in Shanghai (also in 2001). The field's spread into multiple disciplines was explicitly documented in that handbook, with scholars from anthropology, economics, management science, political science, psychology, and sociology reviewing the contributions that their disciplines had made. Geographers and environmental psychologists were absent in those compendia, probably more because the disciplinary networks of editors and authors did not yet overlap with them than because of a lack of geographical interest in the phenomena connected to organizational learning.

Shared Interests and Different Approaches

Organizational Learning from the Perspective of Geography

Geographers have a long-standing interest in the organization and coordination of social systems in space. Indeed, the term *region* has the same etymological root as the words *rex* (king), regulate, regime, regiment, or the German verb *regieren* (to rule, to govern). Originally, region meant a space that was organized, coordinated, controlled, and influenced by a power center or a social system's authority. In the context of this volume, the term *space* is understood as relative space, which is a product of interrelations and interactions. Relative space is never a closed system; it is always "in a process of becoming, always being made" (Massey, 1999, p. 28). The term *place* has a multidimensional meaning. First, it denotes a location characterized by specific configurations, facilities, and resources, enabling or impeding certain actions. Second, it signifies a position in a hierarchy

---

[1] SECI is an acronym for socialization, externalization, combination, internalization.

or network, that is, in relation to other positions. Third, it can be defined as a "discursively constructed setting" (Feld & Basso, 1996, p. 5) having a symbolic and emotional meaning, providing an identity, and communicating a complex history of events, cultural memories, and emotional attachments (Canter, 1977, 1985; Manzo, 2005; Rowles, 2008a, 2008b; Scannel & Gifford, 2010). Places can be studied from a broad variety of philosophical perspectives. They are "known, imagined, yearned for, held, remembered, voiced, lived, contested, and struggled over ... and metaphorically tied to identities" (Feld & Basso, p. 11). People are rooted in and attached to places.

In the 1960s and 1970s geographers became interested in spatial disparities of educational achievement (Geipel, 1965), the exchange of knowledge within and between organizations, the spatial concentration of knowledge and power, and in central-peripheral disparities in the distribution of jobs for high- and low-skilled employees (for an overview see Meusburger, 1980, 1998, 2000, 2007a, 2007b). They studied the importance of face-to-face contacts and telecommunication for the acquisition and diffusion of various types of knowledge and inquired into the importance of office locations for the communication process. The Swedish geographers Bertil Thorngren (1970) and Gunnar Törnqvist (1970) analyzed the spatial dimension of contact systems and their impact on regional development. The American geographer John R. Borchert (1978) studied the major control points in the American economy. The British geographer John B. Goddard and his colleagues focused for many years on office communication and office location, the communications factor in office decentralization, office linkages and location, and the impact that new technologies of telecommunication have on office location (Goddard, 1971, 1973; Goddard & Gillespie, 1986; Goddard, Gillespie, Thwaites, & Robinson, 1986; Goddard & Morris, 1976; Goddard & Pye, 1977). The Oxford geographer Jean Gottmann (1979, 1980a, 1980b, 1982, 1983) wrote about the symbolic meaning of centrality, relations between centers and peripheries, the organizing and reorganizing of space, the impact of telecommunication on urban settlements, and transactions as the main function of cities. These early studies on office locations, office linkages, and spatial concentration of knowledge and power were designed to explain why the headquarters of many large companies tended to concentrate on large cities rather than take advantage of modern telecommunication technologies and incentives to move to smaller towns or rural areas.

As of the 1980s geographers of science turned their attention to the spatiality of science and research and to the places and spaces of knowledge production, the networks and spatial mobility of scholars (Jöns, 2003, 2007; Livingstone, 1995, 2002, 2003; Withers, 2002), knowledge environments and scientific milieus (Matthiesen, 2013; Meusburger, 2012), and the regional mobility of various categories of knowledge (Meusburger, 2009b).

Key research areas for economic and social geographers in recent decades have included the transfer of knowledge in and between organizations, the learning and decision-making procedures in organizations, the role of places as knowledge environments, the coordination and governance of spatially distributed system elements, the role of proximity and distance in learning processes, the spatial concentration of knowledge and power, and the asymmetric relationships between center and periphery. However, the authors of most of these early geographical studies did not use the concept of organizational learning. They preferred other expressions, such as diffusion of knowledge in organizations or knowledge-sharing in organizations or adaptation of organizational structures to internal needs and external pressure.

Additional research areas relating to learning processes and knowledge sharing in and between organizations, particularly companies, have emerged in geography since the late 1980s. They include the geography of the firm or of enterprises (Dicken, 1990; Dicken & Thrift, 1992; Hayter, Patchell, & Rees, 1999; Hayter & Watts, 1983; Krumme, 1969; Maskell, 2001; McNee, 1960; Walker, 1989), studies on processes of knowledge work and the division of labor in organizations (Glückler, 2008a, 2008b, 2010, 2013), models of organizational structures and dynamics in geographic perspective (Hayter et al., 1999; Hayter & Watts; Taylor, 1987, 1995; Taylor & Thrift, 1982, 1983), project ecologies and projects as new models of organization (e.g., Grabher, 2001, 2002; Chap. 6 by Ibert in this volume), and organized corporate networks and network organizations (e.g., Glückler, Dehning, Janneck, & Armbrüster, 2012).

Geographers have been quite familiar with key issues of organization theory and organizational learning, and they have indisputably profited a great deal from organization theory (e.g., Argyris & Schön, 1978, 1996; Mintzberg, 1979; Nonaka & Takeuchi, 1995), systems theory (Bertalanffy, 1950, 1968, 1976), and environmental psychology (Graumann, 1978, 2002a, 2002b; Graumann & Kruse, 2003). But what can a geographical perspective offer to organization theory and to organizational learning and knowledge in particular? Learning processes and scientific research do not take place in a social, political, or economic vacuum. They are influenced by a multitude of factors whose local interaction results in a spatial context, action-setting, milieu or environment (for details see Meusburger, 2008, 2009a, 2012). Each place, milieu, or spatial context affords an organization or its parts a particular knowledge environment, a unique access to important networks and research facilities, a different degree of reputation and attractiveness, and a distinctive potential for spontaneous high-level interactions. In the field of research Meusburger (2012) described these mechanisms:

> The possibilities for discussing contested ideas and conducting expensive experiments, for becoming part of important networks, for hearing promptly of crucial developments or for receiving access to restricted data, and the likelihood of meeting with agreement or criticism upon airing new ideas or of having to grapple with controversial theoretical concepts are not equally distributed in space. The success of research projects or the intellectual development and academic careers of young scholars are thus contingent not only on the goals, talents, and creativity of the people involved, but also on existing structures. Each university location affords a scientist a different knowledge environment, which, in turn, has a bearing on whether and how soon new scientific concepts, practices, or technical innovations are accepted and acted upon or how that scientist is able to develop. (p. 12)

Geographers have a long tradition of studying the relation between structure and action (Werlen, 1993, 2010a, 2010b) and the impact that social environments can[2] have on learning processes on various scales, of analyzing the reasons for regional economic and social disparities, and of discussing the applicability of various concepts of space and place in the social sciences.

Success in a competitive society is not based on knowledge or information per se but rather on advantage or a lead in knowledge, expertise, professional skills and competence, or early access to crucial information. The skills, experience, training, and knowledge needed by top managers and high-level experts of large and complex organizations acting in an uncertain environment will always be scarce. From a geographer's point of view, therefore, there are several crucial questions: Where does one locate the scarce knowledge, the high-level decision-making, and the key responsibilities in the architecture of a social system and in the spatial dimension? How can the internal and external formal structures of communication be organized? How is it possible to create a milieu that fosters learning processes and creativity and facilitates interactions between top managers and specialized experts of different organizations and domains? And how are the effects of new communication technologies, new external pressures (e.g., economic competition and high degree of uncertainty), new internal dynamics (e.g., acquisition of new expertise) or a change of the organization's goals translatable into new structures? Under which circumstances are steep hierarchies and centralization of expertise and decision-making more efficient than flat hierarchies and decentralized networks of expertise? In which cases is the opposite true? Which functions of an organization depend heavily on frequent and spontaneous face-to-face contacts with those in power or a certain type of knowledge environment? Which functions are more or less place-independent?

The increasing availability of telecommunication may have reduced the functional necessity of proximity in learning processes in some cases, especially within trustful relationships between administrators, communities of practice, and scientists, but the symbolic meaning of places and the importance of spatiality for representation of authority and construction of difference have not diminished in recent history (Meusburger, Koch, & Christmann, 2011). A location can still be a symbol for prestige, reliability, credit-worthiness, institutional power, repression, and social control; another may suggest untrustworthiness, low reputation, backwardness, or criminality. Place names can stand for specific and unique knowledge environments. Meusburger (2012) describes the reciprocal projection of scientific reputation between scholars and institutions (places) as follows:

> The achievements of scientists who have worked successfully for a long time in a department or at a university are transferred to the institution, places, or milieu of that period. Place names such as Berkeley, Cambridge, and Heidelberg serve as a kind of shorthand for complex and now arcane circumstances surrounding the practice and standards of science. Such projections may be unjustified, erroneous, or controversial, but they must be taken seriously because people make them in every aspect of daily life. When projecting scientific

---

[2] A social environment or knowledge environment is not an independent variable that has a direct effect on human agency. It is rather a potential or offer that some actors will use and others will ignore.

prestige onto places, institutions, or even entire universities, one assumes from past experience that superb science is being practiced now and will be in the future, a supposition that, in turn, attracts top scientists. Historically less-successful universities can wind up with the stigma of being below average and of having produced or attracted few important scholars. Interestingly, this projection reflects back onto the scientists working there. The scientific prestige of an institution and that of its academics is thus reciprocal. (p. 14)

In the view of geographers, the center of a social system or a domain (e.g., chemical industry, diamond trade, or scientific discipline) is the place where its most powerful authority is located. Theoretically, each domain and each organization can have its own center. If a firm or industry in a small town grows to become an international market leader (e.g., the chemical company BASF in Ludwigshafen), then this small town represents a worldwide center of that industry. However, small towns may become the center of only one or two domains, whereas high-ranking large cities may attract the centers of dozens of different domains (politics, economics, science, media, and culture). Such places offer a multidimensional network centrality, which is much more attractive for top managers of large, multinational companies than a one-dimensional location. Nevertheless, geographers recognize that innovations are also often generated from the periphery, and they point out that it is important to distinguish between "imagined" and "real" (i.e., historically proven) centrality. Boden's differentiation between psychological creativity and historical creativity is useful in this context (Boden, 1994; see also Meusburger, 2009a). Recently, some geographers have been stepping into the breach between imagined and real centralities by exploring "diverse economies" with the intention of "putting forward a new economic ontology that could contribute to novel economic performances" (Gibson-Graham, 2008, p. 615).

Summing up, geographers have shown that the interpretation of spatial patterns, the study of knowledge environments, spatial relations, spatial diffusion processes, and positioning of functions in space allow deeper insights into organizations and their "power-geometries" (Massey, 1999) than a space-blind approach does. Since early human history, partitioning of space and positioning in space have been used to display gradations of authority and status. In all types of societies, the varying degrees of power and authority are expressed by the separation and demarcation of spaces, and by exclusion and positioning in space. Geographers have also explained why the spatial mobility (diffusion) of various categories of knowledge is not as simple as traditional communication models (sender-receiver) suggest.

From the Perspective of Organization Studies

Scholars of organizational behavior, for their part, have addressed spatial considerations for many decades without asking geographers for their input. The relevance appears self-evident: "Is not social organization a product, a function of the space it inhabits?" (Kornberger & Clegg, 2004, p. 1103). Perhaps the most attention has gone to location decisions and their implications, ranging from the global to the very local in scale. Adler's textbook, *International Dimensions of Organizational Behavior*, which first appeared in 1986 and is now in its fifth revised edition (2008), illustrates particularly well the multiple issues that management scholars (and managers) think about when expanding operations abroad (Adler, 1986, 2008). Spatial considerations matter not only because "organizations can be understood as spatially embedded at various levels" (Taylor & Spicer, 2007, p. 326) but also because organizations themselves create spaces in which people live and work. For example, "one of the first things a newcomer to any organization has to learn is how to navigate within this new spatial environment: what are the cues which signal territorial boundaries, and whether such territories are functional or hierarchical" (Turner, 1971, p. 50).

Given the longstanding omnipresence of spatial issues in organization studies, it is interesting that there are both calls for and evidence of a "spatial turn" in organization studies over the past decade or so. Sydow (2002), for instance, associates the recognition of this need partly with the rise in organizational network analysis, whereas van Marrewijk and Yanow (2010) draw attention to the material experience of workspaces. Rousseau and Fried (2001) explain the growing need for researchers to attend to the context in which the organizational phenomena they are studying are set:

> Contextualization is more important in contemporary organizational behavior research than it has been in the past. Two reasons in particular motivate this editorial. First, the domain of organizational research is becoming more international, giving rise to challenges in transporting social science models from one society to another. Second, the rapidly diversifying nature of work and work settings can substantially alter the underlying causal dynamics of worker-organizational relations. (p. 1)

The communication gap between organization scholars and their peers in human geography, science studies, and environmental psychology had costs. The spatial turn came 10–20 years later in organization studies than in other disciplines, and some wheels were invented a second or third time. For the purposes of this volume, it is significant that scholars in the subfield of organization studies concerned with organizational learning and knowledge have also identified the need to address spatial dimensions. "The increasingly accepted perception that organizational learning (OL) does not only involve abstract, cognitive processes has triggered researchers' interest in the relationship between the physical settings and individuals' cognitive skills" (Edenius & Yakhlev, 2007, p. 193).

Some organizational scholars are seeking input from colleagues in disciplines that have expertise in dealing with spatial issues. The need is nicely illustrated by the title of Ford and Harding's (2004) article, "We went looking for an organization but could find only the metaphysics of its presence." The fact that the disciplines of management and architecture are positioned in professional schools in some universities may help explain why their scholars seem to have started working together to address spatiality and organizations before bringing geographers on board (especially if their universities have no geography department). For instance, MIT's School of Architecture and Planning in Boston created "The Space and

Organization Workgroup" (SPORG) to explore the interdependence of physical space and organizational behavior. However, Kornberger and Clegg (2004) observe with some concern that "the main focus is on optimizing the use of space. Critically, this could be interpreted as conventional business process re-engineering with a spatial dimension added—indeed, almost a marriage between Taylor and Le Corbusier" (p. 1097).

Organizational scholars admit that their field has problems addressing spatial phenomena because of "fragmented contributions" (Taylor & Spicer, 2007, p. 326) and the "ongoing controversy around differentiating the concepts of space and place" (p. 326). Attempts to resolve the problems of fragmentation and conceptual distinctions with help from sociologists have not been completely successful: "the discipline chops up the phenomena into incommunicado bits: urban sociology, rural sociology, suburban sociology, home, the environment, neighbourhood, workplaces, ecology" (Gieryn, 2000, p. 464).

How This Volume Enriches the Conversation

One of the objectives of our book is to advance the field by bringing the voices of geographers into conversations with those of other disciplines. It is therefore high time to join forces with geographers! This volume also seeks to expand the conversation by including learning spaces that were not addressed in the two handbooks that marked the state of the art at the turn of the millennium. The field originally focused on processes *within* organizations, then expanded to include *interorganizational* learning, not only in multinationals (Macharzina, Oesterle, & Brodel, 2001), strategic alliances (Child, 2001), and joint ventures (Lyles, 2001) but also in supplier networks (Lane, 2001) and global and local networks (Tsui-Auch, 2001). In this volume we expand the scope by addressing organizational learning in temporary organizations at the international level (Chap. 10 by Böhling, in this volume), an organizational phenomenon that appears to be becoming more prevalent than in the past and that may be particularly important for the learning processes of other kinds of organizations. At the other end of the size spectrum, we draw attention to the space of computer screens that display abstract representations of the organization (Chap. 2 by Puyou, in this volume). Indeed, a strength of organizational learning theories is the multilevel analysis that they enable—individuals, groups, units, and communities of practice in and between organizations, and whole organizations. The potential strength in the field is not always realized, because it is difficult to connect the different levels and there is the risk of mistakenly applying individual-level concepts to organizations. This volume addresses the potential and the difficulties head on in the contribution by Friedman and Sykes (Chap. 9), who offer a model that also encompasses systemic learning.

Although it is not our intention to redress the imbalance in the field that has tended to underexpose barriers to organizational learning, this volume indeed provides ample evidence of unsuccessful learning and knowledge sharing in organizations. For example, Scholl finds multiple cases of information pathologies in organizations, and Glückler and Panitz document the frequently encountered problem of top-down management models generating resistance in innovation processes. However, it is not only senior managers who are at risk of being out of touch with reality in modern organizations; new technologies, too, can filter out information provided in the lived environment of employees at all levels of the organization, leading to Mad-Hatter-like situations, as Puyou shows in Chap. 2. The distances that people need to bridge in order to share and create knowledge in organizations are multiple and entangled, as illustrated by the contributions in this volume. In addition to the gaps between top management and other employees (Glückler & Panitz), they include relational distance in professional mindsets and values, such as that between researchers and business (Ibert), between experienced workers and new recruits (Bounfour & Grefe), and between civil society and national representatives in the United Nations system (Böhling). Furthermore, there are physical distances between headquarters and sales units (Puyou) and between offices in a building complex (Sailer). The chapters offer various concepts to characterize the multidimensionality of spaces that interconnect physical, social unconscious, and mental aspects. For example, Pässilä and Oikarinen describe polyphonic spaces, Friedman and Sykes draw on the works of Lewin (1948, 1951) and Bourdieu (1985, 1989, 1998) to refer to life space and social space, Vince evokes relational space, and McNiff treats creative spaces. Sometimes these spaces are ephemeral by definition, such as the interspaces afforded by exercises in class-rooms (Vince), artistic interventions in organizations (Berthoin Antal), and United Nations Global Conferences (Böhling). The temporary nature of these spaces makes it possible to suspend established rules and codes, to express the unsayable, and to try out new behaviors. The organizational learning challenge is then how to re-embed the new ways of doing things and change the organizational context—in other words, to sustain the learning.

The analyses also show how the existence of such distances and of different kinds of spaces in and between organizations can also be resources for innovation. For example, the movement between "cold" and "hot" spaces in a foundry affords different kinds of learning *ba*, as Bounfour and Grefe reveal when they apply the SECI model and enrich it with the concept of *hau* from gift theory. Building on Stark's (2009) concept of dissonance, Ibert points out how valuable for innovation processes the confrontation of different ways of seeing and doing things is. McNiff reinforces the argument for maintaining distinct mindsets and practices in organizational entities and subunits (silos) while offering suggestions for how to enhance the organization's capacity to benefit from the unavoidable tensions and conflicts that arise.

The multidisciplinarity that has characterized the field of organizational learning from its early years is expanded in this volume not only the perspectives of geographers about spatial aspects of organizational learning and knowledge but also by concepts and practices of inquiry from the world of the arts. They offer the potential to enrich the analysis of organizational learning processes by addressing the role of aesthetics and the senses, which have been neglected in the field so far because "traditional views of OL have privileged Cartesian Perspectivalism, abstract thinking, cultural, and cognitive processes as the modalities of learning" (Edenius & Yakhlev, 2007, p. 207). By contrast, the physical bodies that human beings inhabit as they move into and out of organizational spaces with their knowledge, and the sensations they experience in situations of learning and change, receive explicit attention from the arts. There the human body is valued for its capacity to express beyond words and to integrate knowing tacitly, as well as for its role as a source of energy for action. The inclusion of art-based perspectives offers glimpses into new ways of managing and learning in organizations (in this volume see Chap. 11 by Berthoin Antal; Chap. 13 by McNiff; and Chap. 12 by Pässilä & Oikarinen). The mix of disciplines represented in the chapters of this book may have the additional advantage of shifting the tenor of the conversation. The language of management research has recently been criticized as "dehydrated" (Adler, 2010), so it may surprise readers to find that many of the contributions about the spatiality of organizational learning make use of terminology with emotional, spiritual, and sensual tones. Bounfour and Grefe refer to the spirit of the gift, *hau*, as the essential element enabling intergenerational sharing of trade secrets and co-creation of new knowledge. The theoretical physicists in Sailer's study seek out the sunny rooms for their meetings rather than limiting themselves to the practical choice of the closest office. Scholl's analysis of innovation failures reveals that the absence of sympathy was a key factor. In the Finnish forestry industry, which is beset by downsizing, Pässilä and Oikarinen describe processes designed to move toward polyphony and joy.

The Structure of This Volume

There are many ways to organize knowledge, and as editors we had to choose how to structure the knowledge offered by the contributors. One option would have been to take a disciplinary approach, but we wanted the readers to enter into a space in which the voices of the different disciplines come together on equal footing rather than fencing them off and implying a hierarchy of importance. We are all-too aware of the risk in academia of the "aggrandizement effect" that leads members of departments and disciplines to overrate the importance of their work (Caplow & McGee, 1958, p. 45).[3] An alphabetical ordering of authors would have been an option free of all interpretation, but we felt that this route would have meant an abdication of editorial responsibility for providing some guidance through the multivocal, multiperspec-tival space that this book offers. Organizing the chapters according to the research methods used by the authors was not an option because almost all the studies in this volume are based on mixed methods (i.e., different combinations of methods such as individual interviews, focus groups, participant observation, action learning, and surveys). In keeping with the theme of the book, we opted for a spatial organization and started by clustering together the chapters that treat similar settings.

---

[3] Studies found that raters overestimated the prestige of their own organization eight times more frequently than they underestimated it (Caplow & McGee, 1958, p. 105).

Chapters 2 and 3 explore examples of organizational learning processes and barriers in companies. Francois-Régis Puyou conducted his research in the Paris headquarters of a retail chain and its airport shops. He zoomed in on the representation of reality created on computer screens by a software package for ERP (enterprise resource planning). The next chapter, by Ahmed Bounfour and Gwénaëlle Grefe, stays in France but shifts to an organization with a completely different kind of work setting, namely, a foundry. The researchers follow workers as they move between "cold" zones and "hot" zones of production at the furnace and show how the way they share and create knowledge changes in the different places and over time. Chapters 4 and 5 are set in Germany. The case study at the heart of the chapter by Johannes Glückler and Robert Panitz is a medium-sized ophthalmological engineering firm. The authors examine the introduction of an organizational innovation and highlight the barriers encountered by top-down approaches to knowledge communication. Wolfgang Scholl's contribution expands the scope of analysis by shifting from a single-case approach to drawing on 16 firms, where he and his team analyzed 21 successful and 21 unsuccessful cases of innovation.

Chapters 6 and 7 are located in publicly funded research labs in Germany. Oliver Ibert traces the dynamics of knowledge creation in the development of a technological innovation (a sensor system for the detection of biological molecules in small quantities) across several dimensions: relational and physical space and time. Kerstin Sailer measures the distances that scientists from around the world cross within a building in order to share knowledge when they are temporarily colocated in an institute.

The final three contributions shift to different countries and domains. Chapters 8 and 9 relate to learning in educational contexts; Chap. 10, to organizational learning in the international system. Russ Vince describes action learning experiments in the use of space in an executive education classroom in the United Kingdom, bringing out the unconscious in the process. Victor Friedman and Israel Sykes develop a model of social space in which learning is understood as patterns of change in the structure of the field. They specify five learning patterns, which they then illustrate by applying them to possible ways of changing how learning is conceived and organized in the Israeli education system. Chapter 10, by Kathrin Böhling, extends the perspective up a level by addressing how Global Conferences, which she treats as temporary organizations, can serve as a space for organizational learning in the United Nations system.

The organizing principle for the last three chapters in this volume is not based on a type of organization or a particular location but rather on the movement between worlds. They are clustered around art-based innovations in organizational learning. The contribution by Ariane Berthoin Antal (Chap. 11) offers a panoramic view of how the world of the arts can contribute to organizational learning. She outlines different kinds of artistic interventions into the spaces, routines, and mindsets of public and private organizations of all sizes and industries. Her chapter is followed by the experimental research-based theater intervention that Anne Pässilä and Tuja Oikarinen conducted in a Finnish forestry company to help employees make sense of the significant changes they were experiencing (Chap. 12).

Shaun McNiff (Chap. 13) invites the reader to follow him back and forth between his practice in the art studio and his leadership roles in a university in the United States, showing how the movement between the two very different worlds can open creative spaces for organizational learning.

We hope that this book will contribute to intensifying communication and the creation of knowledge between the disciplines interested in organizational learning and organization theory. The whole "Knowledge and Space" series is intended to bring together scholars from various disciplines, schools of thought, and cultures and to provide a platform for creative discussions. Concepts of place and space or the spatial dimension of human agency can serve as a common denominator connecting the research interests of various disciplines.

References

Adler, N. J. (1986). *International dimensions of organizational behavior*. Boston MA: Kent Publishing.

Adler, N. J. (2010). Going beyond the dehydrated language of management: Leadership insight. *Journal of Business Strategy, 31*(4), 90–99.

Adler, N. J. (with Gundersen, A.). (2008). *International dimensions of organizational behavior* (5th ed.). Mason, OH: Cengage.

Argyris, C., & Schön, D. (1978). *Organizational learning: A theory of action perspective*. Reading, MA: Addison-Wesley.

Argyris, C., & Schön, D. (1996). *Organizational learning II: Theory, method, and practice*. Reading, MA: Addison Wesley.

Bertalanffy, L. (1950). An outline of general system theory. *The British Journal for the Philosophy of Science, 1*, 139–164.

Bertalanffy, L. (1968). *General system theory: Foundations, development, applications*. New York: George Braziller.

Bertalanffy, L. (1976). General systems theory: A critical review. In J. Beishon & G. Peters (Eds.), *Systems behavior* (2nd ed., pp. 30–50). London: Open University Set Book.

Boden, M. A. (1994). What is creativity? In M. A. Boden (Ed.), *Dimensions of creativity* (pp. 75–117). Cambridge, MA: MIT Press.

Borchert, J. R. (1978). Major control points in American economic geography. *Annals of the Association of American Geographers, 68*, 214–232.

Bourdieu, P. (1985). Social space and the genesis of groups. *Theory and Society, 14*, 723–744.

Bourdieu, P. (1989). Social space and symbolic power. *Sociological Theory, 7*, 14–25.

Bourdieu, P. (1998). *Practical reason: On the theory of action* (R. Johnson, Trans.). Stanford, CA: Stanford University Press.

Canter, D. (1977). *The psychology of places*. London: Architectural Press.

Canter, D. (1985). Putting situations in their place: Foundations for a bridge between social and environmental psychology. In A. Furnham (Ed.), *Social behavior in context* (pp. 208–239). London: Allyn and Bacon.

Caplow, T., & McGee, R. J. (1958). *The academic market place*. New York: Basic Books.

Child, J. (2001). Learning through strategic alliances. In M. Dierkes, A. Berthoin Antal, J. Child, & I. Nonaka (Eds.), *Handbook of organizational learning and knowledge* (pp. 657–680). Oxford, UK: Oxford University Press.

Cohen, M. D., & Sproull, L. S. (Eds.). (1996). *Organizational learning*. Thousand Oaks, CA: Sage.

Dicken, P. (1990). The geography of enterprise: Elements of a research agenda. In M. de Smidt & E. Wever (Eds.), *The corporate firm in a changing world economy: Case studies in the geography of enterprise* (pp. 234–244). London: Routledge.

Dicken, P., & Thrift, N. (1992). The organization of production and the production of organization: Why business enterprises matter in the study of geographical industrialization. *Transactions of the Institute of British Geographers, New Series, 17*, 279–291.

Dierkes, M., Berthoin Antal, A., Child, J., & Nonaka, I. (Eds.). (2001). *Handbook of organizational learning and knowledge*. Oxford, UK: Oxford University Press.

Easterby-Smith, M., & Lyles, M. A. (Eds.). (2003). *The Blackwell handbook of organizational learning and knowledge management*. Oxford, UK: Blackwell.

Edenius, M., & Yakhlef, A. (2007). Space, vision and organizational learning: The interplay of incorporating and inscribing practices. *Management Learning, 38*, 193–210.

Feld, S., & Basso, K. H. (1996). Introduction. In S. Feld & K. H. Basso (Eds.), *Senses of place* (pp. 3–11). Santa Fe, NM: School of American Research Press.

Ford, J., & Harding, N. (2004). We went looking for an organization but could find only the metaphysics of its presence. *Sociology, 38*, 815–830.

Geipel, R. (1965). *Sozialräumliche Strukturen des Bildungswesens. Studien zur Bildungsökonomie und zur Frage der gymnasialen Standorte in Hessen* [Sociospatial structures of the educational system: Studies on the economics of education and the siting of secondary schools in Hesse]. Frankfurt am Main, Germany: Diesterweg.

Gibson-Graham, J. K. (2008). Diverse economies: Performative practices for 'other worlds'. *Progress in Human Geography, 32*, 613–632.

Gieryn, T. F. (2000). A space for place in sociology. *Annual Review of Sociology, 26*, 463–496.

Glückler, J. (2008a). Die Chancen der Standortspaltung: Wissensnetze im globalen Unternehmen [The opportunities of location-splitting: Knowledge networks in a global enterprise]. *Geographische Zeitschrift, 96*, 125–139.

Glückler, J. (2008b). Service Offshoring: globale Arbeitsteilung und regionale Entwicklungschancen [Service offshoring: Global division of labor and opportunities for regional development]. *Geographische Rundschau, 60*(9), 36–42.

Glückler, J. (2010). The creation and diffusion of controversial innovations in the organizational periphery. *SPACES online: Spatial Aspects Concerning Economic Structures* (Vol. 8, Issue 2010–06). Marburg, Germany: Philipps-University Marburg, Department of Geography. Retrieved from http://www.spaces-online.uni-hd.de/include/SPACES%202010-06%20Glueckler.pdf

Glückler, J. (2013). The problem of mobilizing expertise at a distance. In P. Meusburger, J. Glückler, & M. El Meskioui (Eds.), *Knowledge and the economy* (pp. 95–109). Knowledge and Space: Vol. 5. Dordrecht, The Netherlands: Springer.

Glückler, J., Dehning, W., Janneck, M., & Armbrüster, T. (Eds.). (2012). *Unternehmensnetzwerke. Architekturen, Strukturen und Strategien* [Network organizations: Architectures, structures, and strategies]. Heidelberg, Germany: Springer Gabler.

Goddard, J. B. (1971). Office communications and office location: A review of current research. *Regional Studies, 5*, 263–280.

Goddard, J. B. (1973). *Office linkages and location: A study of communication and spatial patterns in central London*. Progress in planning: Vol. 1 (part 2). Oxford, UK: Pergamon Press.

Goddard, J. B., & Gillespie, A. (1986). Advanced telecommunications and regional economic development. *The Geographical Journal, 152*, 383–397.

Goddard, J. B., Gillespie, A., Thwaites, A., & Robinson, F. (1986). The impact of new information technology on urban and regional structure in Europe. *Land Development Studies, 11*, 19–30.

Goddard, J. B., & Morris, D. (1976). *The communications factor in office decentralization*. Progress and planning: Vol. 6 (part 1). Oxford, UK: Pergamon Press.

Goddard, J. B., & Pye, R. (1977). Telecommunications and office location. *Regional Studies, 11*, 19–30.

Gottmann, J. (1979). Office work and the evolution of cities. *Ekistics: The Problems and Science of Human Settlements, 46*(274), 4–7.

Gottmann, J. (1980a). Confronting centre and periphery. In J. Gottmann (Ed.), *Centre and periphery: Spatial variation in politics* (pp. 11–25). Beverly Hills, CA: Sage.

Gottmann, J. (1980b). Organizing and reorganizing space. In J. Gottmann (Ed.), *Centre and periphery: Spatial variation in politics* (pp. 217–224). Beverly Hills, CA: Sage.

Gottmann, J. (1982). Urban settlements and telecommunications. *Ekistics: The Problems and Science of Human Settlements, 50*(302), 411–416.

Gottmann, J. (1983). *The coming of the transactional city.* Monograph series no. 2. Institute of Urban Studies, College Park, MD: University of Maryland.

Grabher, G. (2001). Ecologies of creativity: The village, the group, and the heterarchic organization of the British advertising industry. *Environment and Planning A, 33*, 351–374.

Grabher, G. (2002). The project ecology of advertising: Talents, tasks, and teams. *Regional Studies, 36*, 245–262.

Graumann, C. F. (Ed.). (1978). *Ökologische Perspektiven in der Psychologie* [Ecological perspectives in psychology]. Berne, Switzerland: Huber.

Graumann, C. F. (2002a). The phenomenological approach to people–environment studies. In R. B. Bechtel & A. Churchman (Eds.), *Handbook of environmental psychology* (pp. 95–113). New York: Wiley.

Graumann, C. F. (2002b). Zwischen den Disziplinen. Dilemma und Chancen der Umweltpsychologie [Between the disciplines: Dilemmas and opportunities of environmental psychology]. *Umweltpsychologie, 6*, 154–161.

Graumann, C. F., & Kruse, L. (2003). Räumliche Umwelt. Die Perspektive der humanökologisch orientierten Umweltpsychologie. [Spatial environment: The perspective of an environmental psychology oriented to human-ecology]. In P. Meusburger & T. Schwan (Eds.), *Humanökologie. Ansätze zur Überwindung der Natur-Kultur-Dichotomie.* (pp. 239–256). Erdkundliches Wissen: Vol. 135. Stuttgart, Germany: Franz Steiner.

Hayter, R., Patchell, J., & Rees, K. (1999). Business segmentation and location revisited: Innovation and the terra incognita of large firms. *Regional Studies, 33*, 425–442.

Hayter, R., & Watts, H. D. (1983). The geography of enterprise: A reappraisal. *Progress in Human Geography, 7*, 158–181.

Hedberg, B. (1981). How organizations learn and unlearn. In P. Nystrom & W. Starbuck (Eds.), *Handbook of organizational design* (Vol. 1, pp. 3–27). Oxford, UK: Oxford University Press.

Jöns, H. (2003). *Grenzüberschreitende Mobilität und Kooperation in den Wissenschaften. Deutschlandaufenthalte US-amerikanischer Humboldt-Forschungspreisträger aus einer erweiterten Akteursnetzwerkperspektive* [Cross-boundary mobility and cooperation in the sciences: U.S. Humboldt Research Award winners in Germany from an expanded actor–network perspective]. Heidelberger Geographische Arbeiten No. 116. Heidelberg, Germany: Heidelberg University, Department of Geography.

Jöns, H. (2007). Transnational mobility and the spaces of knowledge production: A comparison of global patterns, motivations and collaborations in different academic fields. *Social Geography, 2*, 97–114. doi:10.5194/sg-2-97-2007

Kornberger, M., & Clegg, S. R. (2004). Bringing space back in: Organizing the generative building. *Organization Studies, 25*, 1095–1114.

Krumme, G. (1969). Toward a geography of enterprise. *Economic Geography, 45*, 30–40.

Lane, C. (2001). Organizational learning in supplier networks. In M. Dierkes, A. Berthoin Antal, J. Child, & I. Nonaka (Eds.), *Handbook of organizational learning and knowledge* (pp. 699–715). Oxford, UK: Oxford University Press.

Lewin, K. (1948). *Resolving social conflicts.* New York: Harper & Row.

Lewin, K. (1951). In D. Cartwright (Ed.), *Field theory in social science: Selected theoretical papers.* New York: Harper & Row.

Lipshitz, R., Friedman, V. J., & Popper, M. (2007). *Demystifying organizational learning.* Thousand Oaks, CA: Sage.

Livingstone, D. N. (1995). The spaces of knowledge: Contributions towards a historical geography of science. *Environment and Planning D: Society and Space, 13*, 5–34.

Livingstone, D. N. (2002). Knowledge, space and the geographies of science. In D. N. Livingstone, *Science, space and hermeneutics* (pp. 7–40). Hettner-Lecture: Vol. 5. Heidelberg, Germany: Heidelberg University, Department of Geography.

Livingstone, D. N. (2003). *Putting science in its place: Geographies of scientific knowledge.* Chicago: University of Chicago Press.

Lyles, M. (2001). Organizational learning in international joint ventures: The case of Hungary. In M. Dierkes, A. Berthoin Antal, J. Child, & I. Nonaka (Eds.), *Handbook of organizational learning and knowledge* (pp. 681–698). Oxford, UK: Oxford University Press.

Macharzina, K., Oesterle, M.-J., & Brodel, D. (2001). Learning in multinationals. In M. Dierkes, A. Berthoin Antal, J. Child, & I. Nonaka (Eds.), *Handbook of organizational learning and knowledge* (pp. 631–656). Oxford, UK: Oxford University Press.

Manzo, L. C. (2005). For better or worse: Exploring multiple dimensions of place meaning. *Journal of Environmental Psychology, 25,* 67–86.

Maskell, P. (2001). The firm in economic geography. *Economic Geography, 77,* 329–344.

Massey, D. (1999). Philosophy and politics of spatiality: Some considerations. In D. Massey, *Power-geometries and the politics of space-time* (pp. 27–42). Hettner-Lecture: Vol. 2. Heidelberg, Germany: Heidelberg University, Department of Geography.

Matthiesen, U. (2013). KnowledgeScapes: A new conceptual approach and selected empirical findings from research on knowledge milieus and knowledge networks. In P. Meusburger, J. Glückler, & M. El Meskioui (Eds.), *Knowledge and the economy* (pp. 173–203). Knowledge and Space: Vol. 5. Dordrecht, The Netherlands: Springer.

McNee, R. B. (1960). Toward a more humanistic economic geography: The geography of enterprise. *Tijdschrift voor Economische en Sociale Geografie, 51,* 201–205.

Meusburger, P. (1980). *Beiträge zur Geographie des Bildungs- und Qualifikationswesens. Regionale und soziale Unterschiede des Ausbildungsniveaus der österreichischen Bevölkerung* [Contributions to the geography of knowledge and education: Regional and social disparities of educational attainment of the Austrian population]. Innsbrucker Geographische Studien: Vol. 7. Innsbruck, Austria: Innsbruck University, Department of Geography.

Meusburger, P. (1998). *Bildungsgeographie. Wissen und Ausbildung in der räumlichen Dimension* [Geography of education: Knowledge and education in the spatial dimension]. Heidelberg, Germany: Spektrum Akademischer Verlag.

Meusburger, P. (2000). The spatial concentration of knowledge: Some theoretical considerations. *Erdkunde, 54,* 352–364.

Meusburger, P. (2007a). Macht, Wissen und die Persistenz von räumlichen Disparitäten [Power, knowledge, and the persistence of spatial disparities]. In I. Kretschmer (Ed.), *Das Jubiläum der Österreichischen Geographischen Gesellschaft. 150 Jahre (1856–2006)* (pp. 99–124). Vienna, Austria: Österreichische Geographische Gesellschaft.

Meusburger, P. (2007b). Power, knowledge and the organization of space. In J. Wassmann & K. Stockhaus (Eds.), *Experiencing new worlds* (pp. 111–124). New York: Berghahn Books.

Meusburger, P. (2008). The nexus of knowledge and space. In P. Meusburger, M. Welker, & E. Wunder (Eds.), *Clashes of knowledge: Orthodoxies and heterodoxies in science and religion* (pp. 35–90). Knowledge and Space: Vol 1. Dordrecht. The Netherlands: Springer.

Meusburger, P. (2009a). Milieus of creativity: The role of places, environments, and spatial contexts. In P. Meusburger, J. Funke, & E. Wunder (Eds.), *Milieus of creativity: An interdisciplinary approach to spatiality of creativity* (pp. 97–153). Knowledge and Space: Vol. 2. Dordrecht, The Netherlands: Springer.

Meusburger, P. (2009b). Spatial mobility of knowledge: A proposal for a more realistic communication model. *disP—The Planning Review, 177*(2), 29–39.

Meusburger, P. (2012). Wissenschaftsatlas of Heidelberg University: An introduction. In P. Meusburger & T. Schuch (Eds.), *Wissenschaftsatlas of Heidelberg University: Spatio-temporal relations of academic knowledge production* (pp. 12–17). Knittlingen, Germany: Bibliotheca Palatina.

Meusburger, P., Koch, G., & Christmann, G. B. (2011). Nähe- und Distanz-Praktiken in der Wissenserzeugung. Zur Notwendigkeit einer kontextbezogenen Analyse [Practices of proximity and distance in knowledge generation: The need for contextual analysis]. In O. Ibert & H. J. Kujath (Eds.), *Räume der Wissensarbeit. Zur Funktion von Nähe und Distanz in der Wissensökonomie* (pp. 221–249). Wiesbaden, Germany: VS Verlag für Sozialwissenschaften.

Mintzberg, H. (1979). *The structuring of organizations: A synthesis of the research.* Englewood Cliffs, NJ: Prentice Hall.

Moingeon, B., & Edmondson, A. (Eds.). (1996). *Organizational learning and competitive advantage.* London: Sage.

Nonaka, I., & Takeuchi, H. (1995). *The knowledge-creating company: How Japanese companies create the dynamics of innovation.* New York: Oxford University Press.

Nystrom, P., & Starbuck, W. (Eds.). (1981). *Handbook of organizational design: Vol. 1. Adapting organizations to their environments.* Oxford, UK: Oxford University Press.

Rousseau, D. M., & Fried, Y. (2001). Location, location, location: Contextualizing organizational research [Editorial]. *Journal of Organizational Behavior, 22,* 1–13.

Rowles, G. D. (2008a). The meaning of place. In E. B. Crepeau, E. S. Cohn, & B. A. Boyt Schell (Eds.), *Willard and Spackman's occupational therapy* (11th ed., pp. 80–89). Philadelphia PA: Wolters Kluwer/Lippincott Williams & Wilkins.

Rowles, G. D. (2008b). Place in occupational science: A life course perspective on the role of environmental context in the quest for meaning. *Journal of Occupational Science, 15,* 127–135.

Scannel, L., & Gifford, R. (2010). Defining place attachment: A tripartite organizing framework. *Journal of Environmental Psychology, 30,* 1–10.

Stark, D. (2009). *The sense of dissonance: Accounts of worth in economic life.* Princeton, NJ: Princeton University Press.

Sydow, J. (2002). *Towards a spatial turn in organization science?—A long wait* (SECONS Discussion Forum, Contribution No. 8). Bonn, Germany: Free University of Berlin, Institute of Business Administration. Retrieved from http://www.wiwiss.fu-berlin.de/institute/management/sydow/media/pdf/Sydow-Towards_a_Spatial_Turn_in_Organization_Science.pdf

Taylor, M. (1987). Enterprise and the product-cycle model: Conceptual ambiguities. In G. A. Knaap & E. Wever (Eds.), *New technology and regional development* (pp. 75–93). London: Croom Helm.

Taylor, M. (1995). The business enterprise, power and patterns of geographical industrialisation. In S. Conti, E. J. Malecki, & P. Oinas (Eds.), *The industrial enterprise and its environment: Spatial perspectives* (pp. 99–122). Aldershot, UK: Ashgate.

Taylor, S., & Spicer, A. (2007). Time for space: A narrative review of research on organizational spaces. *International Journal of Management Reviews, 9,* 325–346.

Taylor, M., & Thrift, N. (1982). Industrial linkage and the segmented economy, Part 1. Some theoretical proposals. *Environment and Planning A, 14,* 1601–1613.

Taylor, M., & Thrift, N. (1983). Business organization, segmentation and location. *Regional Studies, 17,* 445–465.

Thorngren, B. (1970). How do contact systems affect regional development? *Environment and Planning A, 2,* 409–427.

Törnqvist, G. (1970). *Contact systems and regional development.* Lund Studies in Geography, Ser. B, no. 35. Lund, Sweden: Lund University Press.

Tsui-Auch, L.-S. (2001). Learning in global and local networks: Experience of Chinese firms in Hong Kong, Singapore, and Taiwan. In M. Dierkes, A. Berthoin Antal, J. Child, & I. Nonaka (Eds.), *Handbook of organizational learning and knowledge* (pp. 716–732). Oxford, UK: Oxford University Press.

Turner, B. (1971). *Exploring the industrial subculture.* London: Macmillan.

van Marrewijk, A., & Yanow, D. (Eds.). (2010). *Organizational spaces: Rematerializing the workaday world.* Cheltenham, UK: Edward Elgar.

Walker, R. (1989). A requiem for corporate geography: New directions in industrial organization, the production of place and the uneven development. *Geografiska Annaler Series B, Human Geography, 71,* 43–68.

Werlen, B. (1993). *Society, action and space: An alternative human geography* (G. Walls, Trans.). London: Routledge.

Werlen, B. (2010a). *Gesellschaftliche Räumlichkeit 1. Orte der Geographie* [Societal spatiality 1: Places of geography]. Stuttgart, Germany: Franz Steiner.

Werlen, B. (2010b). *Gesellschaftliche Räumlichkeit 2. Konstruktion geographischer Wirklichkeiten* [Societal spatiality 2: Construction of geographical realities]. Stuttgart, Germany: Franz Steiner.

Withers, C. W. J. (2002). The geography of scientific knowledge. In N. A. Rupke (Ed.), *Göttingen and the development of the natural sciences* (pp. 9–18). Göttingen, Germany: Wallstein.

Learning from Screens: Does Ideology Prevail over Lived Experience? The Example of ERP Systems

2

François-Régis Puyou

> *"For instance, suppose it were nine o'clock in the morning, just time to begin lessons: you'd only have to whisper a hint to Time, and round goes the clock in a twinkling! Half-past one, time for dinner!"* ...
> *"That would be grand, certainly," said Alice thoughtfully; "but then—I shouldn't be hungry for it, you know."*
> *"Not at first, perhaps," said the Hatter: "but you could keep it to half past one as long as you liked."*
> *"Is that the way you manage?" Alice asked.*
>
> (Carroll, 1865/2006, p. 71)

The development of information technology (IT) over recent decades has dramatically increased the number of listings, graphs, charts, and other images and documents that attract the daily attention of millions of employees worldwide.[1] The computer mouse has certainly become a most common tool for people to arrange, store, and retrieve all sorts of texts, icons, signs, and figures that stand for objects, individuals, and projects difficult to grasp or handle in their material form. Indeed, software and hardware are necessary auxiliaries for most people in work relations that are now to a large extent mediated by screens. The fundamental issue of this chapter is to improve the understanding of how far we users of IT in a work environment have distorted our directly experiential knowledge of the social world for the expediency of getting on with the task at hand—or rather at a click's distance.

My claim is that the possibilities offered by information systems in a context of the "scientification" of management have legitimized the mediation of the

---

[1] The terms *employee* and *worker* are synonymous in this chapter.

F.-R. Puyou (✉)
Département Comptabilité, Contrôle de Gestion, Audit, Audencia Nantes School of Management, 8 route de la Jonelière, 44312 Nantes Cedex 3, France
e-mail: frpuyou@audencia.com

A. Berthoin Antal et al. (eds.), *Learning Organizations: Extending the Field*, Knowledge and Space 6, DOI 10.1007/978-94-007-7220-5_2, © Springer Science+Business Media Dordrecht 2014

computer interface for acting upon organizations. Drawing on the research of
the phenomenologist Michel Henry (1983, 2003), I argue that such management
practices are part of an ideology that overemphasizes abstract representation to the
detriment of lived experience. Of course, IT is necessary to coordinate complex
organizations, and I certainly do not advocate a technological U-turn. The aim is
rather to heighten awareness of the limitations of the current use of IT systems
such as Enterprise Resource Planning (ERP)[2] when they are applied to project
management. More specifically, I argue that managing through computers prevents
managers from being in touch with the consequences of their actions, makes them
indifferent to others, and leads to gross simplifications of situations that favor
routine behavior. My analysis of a promotional video from the website of Systems,
Applications and Products in Data Processing (SAP) and of a case study on Airshop
(a fictitious name) is consistent with the fact that ERP systems support ideological
management techniques. Wide discrepancies between the reality of work experienced
on site and the representations of that reality as circulated at headquarters restrict,
for example, the possibilities for learning from situations. I argue that abstract
models and experiences from the field contribute most to innovative learning
processes only when these two sources of knowledge are articulated together.

SAP Vision: "Make Every Customer a Best-run Business"

A promotional video from the SAP website illustrates the types of services currently
feasible through ERP systems. This "demo" is a carefully designed marketing device
made to convince prospective users of the benefits of SAP xRPM applications.[3]
It flatteringly illustrates the software potentialities for structuring complex situations
in organizations. The video puts the viewer into the shoes of various employees at
Viper Corporation (a fictitious firm) and shows, as if through their eyes, the work
being done in real time. Several short sequences[4] show managers successfully complete their tasks by availing themselves of the diverse functionalities. In each clip
the visual display constitutes their fieldwork, the mouse is their tool to take action,
and the elements to be planned and managed are representations of people, resources,
and projects on the screen. Red, yellow, and green signals indicate explicitly where

[2] Since the initial coining of the term *ERP* in the early 1990s, integrated software solutions for
management have spread to all activity sectors and continents. For many organizations, the
judiciousness of purchasing an ERP system is no longer questioned. Because its primary focus is
to improve communication and the sharing of information, it is difficult to claim to be against
the use of ERP (Hansen & Mouritsen, 1999). Major actors on this market have become world-
class players, such as the German company SAP and the American company Oracle. Famous
newcomers—Microsoft, for example—are making a move into this lucrative business.
[3] This video is a fantasy (from *phantazein,* "to make visible") that pictures an ideal situation
illustrating SAP xRPM's ability to solve all sorts of organizational problems.
[4] The video is 8 min long and has five sections: "Analyse," "Prioritize," "Plan," "Manage," and
"Execute."

the attention of the viewers is required. The project manager, for instance, learns from a yellow alert that she has no senior programmer to staff her project team. She scrolls down the online human resources (HR) database, from which she retrieves the name of every member of the company workforce who possesses the necessary expertise to meet the requirements of the mission. She clicks, drags, and drops the name of the desired programmer from the HR database into her project roster. By the time the programmer receives an e-mail with his new appointment, the yellow alert has turned into a green signal again!

Not all employees operating SAP xRPM have access to the same functionalities. The division of labor is incorporated into the software that can equip each employee with the information and options relating to his or her specific position. Every screen is designed to meet the needs of specific jobs, some of them calling for delays; others, for profits; still others, for inventory, and so on. The knowledge required to fulfill each person's tasks is distributed to the appropriate desktop. The employees coordinate themselves through the software. Because every manager has access to the others' agendas, the distribution of work can be done without any intermediary. All the processes related to a project are managed from only a few workstations, and the face-to-face contacts or telephone discussions are dispensable. SAP xRPM creates a common time frame and shared workplace that enforces a temporal and spatial arrangement of people, actions, and events.

Townley (2002) has shown the simplistic nature of "abstract" management based on technologies that ignore the ambivalence of situations, take no account of the contextual character of measurement and knowledge, and enable managers to accomplish their tasks while saving the effort of face-to-face management. ERP contributes to "abstract management" to the extent that "the entire cognitive apparatus is an apparatus for abstraction and simplification, not directed at knowledge but at the control of things" (Nietzsche as quoted in Townley, p. 560). What is to be considered important is instantly clear to the system's operators. The world is already interpreted and selected for them, and the data displayed is unambiguous (Introna & Ihlarco, 2004). Color coding directs these people to where action is needed, with green indicating "normal" or "success"; yellow, "attention required"; and red, "immediate danger" or "top priority." The visual display greatly reduces the necessity for workers to engage in collective sense-making through dialogue (Introna, 1997).

The users' knowledge about the actual activities is easily obtained and remains simple and superficial. ERP systems come across as instruments "to be practiced" (Quattrone, 2009), not as tools with which to gain new knowledge. Indeed, not only does the visual display synthesize the situation and depict the tasks at hand, it also drives the users to action. The software contains "ready-to-use" modes of action that require little prior understanding of the context. The organization appears in its entirety as a complete system at peace, structured and acted upon with a few clicks based on immediate rational and aesthetic criteria.[5] There is no longer a need for

---

[5] I am not contrasting rationality and aesthetics. The Latin origin of the word *ratio* also means "schema" (Carruthers, 1998). Rationality is also visual, for red lights urge action that will turn them into green lights.

face-to-face meetings, for it is much easier and just as legitimate to act through the software. Workers at Viper Corporation meet virtually and organize their respective contributions to common objectives through representations only. In this model of organization, members communicate but do not meet. The difficulty of giving meaning is collectively overcome by technologies for "packaging data" (Boland, 1987, p. 372) and simplifying reality. The screen is the workplace where information circulates; it is the depository of knowledge from which access to all necessary data is granted. The SAP xRPM video shows "ideal" management as it is generally presented with a commercial objective. This demo effectively suggests the possibility of finally making the myth of "management at a distance" come true in a way that is all the more credible and convincing in that it takes place "live" before one's eyes. The video advocates a form of utopia—in the first sense of the term: "absence of a place"—insofar as Viper is a virtual organization where physical space for meetings has no purpose.

Michel Henry and the Two Modes of Perception

Husserl (1936/1970), in his critique of European sciences, condemns the primacy that ideal forms abstracted from experience are accorded in the establishment of scientific criteria for truth. The numerous tables, graphs, organizational charts, and other diagrams in companies clearly indicate that the world of management, like western sciences, has adopted the apparent rigor and quasi-mathematical exactitude of abstract representations as a means to gain knowledge from situations. Phenomenology, the focus of which is the study of the ways things appear to be, therefore facilitates an understanding of this evolution's impact. Henry (1963, 1973) distinguishes two modes of perception: the ideology of abstract representations and the reality of auto-affection. A scene from the novel *Alice's Adventures in Wonderland* by Lewis Carroll (1865/2006) sketches the tensions between those two modes of perception and helps draw a parallel between the ideal situation of the SAP xRPM video and the situation in Wonderland, where inhabitants rely so much on instruments that they are mad.

In the chapter entitled "A Mad Tea Party," Carroll (1865/2006) sets the scene with the Mad Hatter, the March Hare, and a dormouse drinking tea around a large table. The piles of dirty dishes and the many seats left vacant intrigue Alice, who at length discovers that the Hatter's watch, which is stuck at 6:00 p.m., explains the characters' obsession with drinking tea.

> "Is that the reason so many tea-things are put out there?" she asked.
> "Yes, that's it," said the Hatter with a sigh: "it's always tea-time, and we've no time to wash the things between whiles."
> "Then you keep moving round, I suppose?" said Alice.
> "Exactly so," said the Hatter: "as the things get used."
> "But what happens when you come to the beginning again?" Alice ventured to ask.
> "Suppose we change the subject," the March Hare interrupted, yawning. (p. 72)

For the Hatter and the Hare, it is never time to wash the dishes. Changing one's place between each cup is the only way to have a clean place for the following cup of tea. To them, the space between the hands of the watch is the sole relevant indicator of the passage of time. Alice immediately perceives the limitations of this narrow understanding of time and rapidly concludes that her interlocutors are fools, too focused on their immediate business to reflect upon their behavior.

In Henry's terminology, the Hatter and the March Hare would have been considered to have a "theoretical" (etymologically, "a world *vision*") perception of time. They know time through images and ideas based on the relative position of the hands on the face of the watch. Time is made visible, but it is not experienced and the sensitive qualities of the characters other than Alice are excluded. They perceive the world by way of ideal representations and abstract models only. They are distanced from phenomena, which appear to them to be external because of the conscious representations they have of them.

Alice, on the other hand, is certainly capable of reading time, but, as is evident from the present chapter's epigraph, she simultaneously experiences the passage of time through fatigue, boredom, or the need to eat. She illustrates the second mode of perception defined by Henry (1983) as auto-affection, which everyone (except some literary characters) inevitably and constantly experiences. This mode of access to the world owes nothing to representations. Instead of knowing time by an ideal geometry only, Alice perceives it through the whole range of affects from joy to pain, including need and hunger. Lived experience gives access to the always subjective reality of situations.

The relationship of each person with the world is complex, combining reflexive perception and lived experience. Human beings certainly cannot think without representations that instill understanding through categories like language or images upon which the exercise of reason rests. Yet neither can one live in a social world without auto-affection, and the two modes of perception are not equal or symmetric. Henry (1983) deems "Real" only "that which cannot be represented" (p. 160), as opposed to "Ideology," defined as "the whole of the representations of human consciousness in the sense of mere representations—the whole of the images, memories, ideas, notions, arguments, categories and theoretical or practical schemata that this very consciousness is capable of forming" (p. 161). There exists for Henry an unbeatable primacy of real experience as the source of the categories constitutive of each person's ideology. To paraphrase Henry: It is an illusion of ideology to posit sets of representations as autonomous totalities possessing their own stability and authority. Their origin lies in reality, and all representations flow from the praxis of which they are the expression and the language. Therefore, ideology is not autonomous or independent and is primarily determined by actual practices of individuals.[6] The reverse is not true, and the ambition to modify reality by changing the representations of it can be nothing but illusory (Henry, 2003). As far as reality is concerned, the manipulation of representations changes nothing.

Normally, only in Wonderland do representations possess their own indisputable authority. The characters drink tea because it is tea time, not because they feel the

---

[6]Commenting on Karl Marx, Henry (1983, p. 176) insists that a peasant thinks what he thinks not because he belongs to a class and participates in its ideology but rather because he does what he does.

need for it or because they enjoy drinking tea together. Having tea permanently focuses their attention so much that it is difficult for The Hatter or the March Hare to take others into account. They do not listen to each other, they ceaselessly interrupt one another to change places, and they ignore each other to the point that the Hatter utilizes the Dormouse as an armrest. This imaginary episode illustrates what Henry (1990) calls "barbarism" (p. 207) insofar as the signals of the instrument "take a life of their own to the detriment of real life" (p. 207, my translation). The face of the watch is given priority over the faces of the characters who, with the exception of Alice, are subjugated to representations. In such dire situations, abstract prescriptions impose themselves on activities.

Paradoxically, the situation in Wonderland is not very different from the one depicted in the SAP video. The Hatter's pathological relation to the world is close to the model of managers in the demo, who are entirely absorbed by the stream of tasks imposed on them in the form of indicators, objectives, and e-mails communicated by intermediary screens. What was a fantasy to entertain the readers in Lewis Carroll's mind has gradually become a fantasy many managers are longing for.[7]

It is now time to turn to field observations to grasp the extent to which the fascination with ERP interfaces and ideologies drives (or does not drive) "real" managers in organizations to abstract management.

Learning (or Not) from Reality

A selective review of recent empirical studies conducted in France and the United Kingdom show that ERP applications, far from being the standard solutions denounced at the beginning, are now also seen as highly flexible tools (Quattrone & Hopper, 2005, 2006; Segrestin, 2003, 2004). Saturated with myths as diverse as panoptic surveillance, the standardization of practices, empowerment, and real time management, ERP systems are described as tools that are particularly "ambiguous" (Segrestin, 2004, p. 317, my translation) and likely to support contradictory objectives. They simultaneously appear as inexhaustible sources of organizational innovations and as auxiliaries of injunctions derived from standardizations. Lastly, when it comes to actual implementation, local negotiations are the norm, and only end users actually decide between the possible orientations.

The Airshop case study illustrates that practices at times very much like those in the ideal model described by the video coexist with others that conform to those identified in the studies cited above. In various situations the same managers deliberately ignore discomfort, joy, pain, and effort involved in their actions or, conversely, permit themselves to be affected and amend their behavior accordingly. It is the impact that these dynamics of ERP have on innovation and routine that prompts me to offer my own findings from the field.

---

[7] Fantasies can be defined as imaginary tales, but they are also "strong, imaginative devices that powerfully shape the images that are so central to the way we impose order and give meaning to the world" (Boland, 1987, p. 367).

The Airshop Case Study

Airshop is a company specialized in the distribution of luxury products (mostly perfumes, alcohol, and tobacco) in French airports. From February to June 2004, 35 interviews were conducted with managers working in the head office or airport terminals. At the time of the study, Airshop had been drawing on SAP to support financial, commercial, and logistic activities for more than 2 years. By systematically allowing for comparison between actual and forecasted data, SAP has become a major component of the performance evaluation process for all managers in the organization. It is part of a sophisticated reporting system that precisely monitors transactions of the 140 boutiques and compares their actual results with expected figures. All respondents, be they management controllers, administrative directors, terminal managers, or sales managers, pay attention to the information circulating on SAP. The issue is of substantial importance when results match the forecast; they lead to large financial incentives, whereas the opposite situation increases the control from the hierarchy.

The perpetual reference to figures from the software for assessing individual performances has given rise to subtle games around the calculation of forecasted values. All the interviews highlight that numbers are subjected to arbitrations, upward or downward, that do not relate to operational aspects. Estimations ventured by operational managers regarding future trends are, for example, followed by numerous adjustments decided upon in closed-door discussions during which management authorities reserve the right to stipulate targeted increases. These modifications give forecasts a goal-oriented turn. Not infrequently, managers discover that their forecasts have been revised unannounced.

> It is always Finance that has the last word[.] … [W]e make the necessary changes without consulting anyone. (Management controller, Airshop)
> Then we hear on the grapevine that the budget has been changed. It's a pity we weren't told over the phone first. (Manager, Airshop)

Top-down modifications blur the links between the figures and the elements they were originally based on. Arbitrations at the top disconnect numbers from operational situations and render them meaningless. "Last time, after the operational manager's proposal, we had to make a few quick overall corrections which weren't realistic for the sales outlets. If we make too many corrections, we get lost" (Management controller, Airshop).

Moreover, management controllers are overwhelmed by daily reporting duties and dedicate all their attention to feeding in the system. Confronted by a never ending flow of tasks, they prefer not to get into touch with the operational staff, for such avoidance saves time to cope with the demands from top management.

> There is not much time to analyze, and yet analysis is supposed to be the heart of our work. It is more like the mass production of numbers. (Management controller, Airshop)
> We hardly have any contact with the operational staff[.] … The process of reporting is so cumbersome and absorbing that we do not have the time to respond to the directors and the operational staff; we do not go to see them. (Management controller, Airshop)

> We work on a bundle, and we absolutely want to pass off the 150 pages and that's it! If five minutes after the dispatch somebody asks for the turnover of a particular subsidiary, it is no longer remembered. (Management controller, Airshop)

All management controllers and operational managers mention their uneasiness about a gap between the representations of activities and the activities themselves. With no other choice but to keep referring to the figures when dealing with their colleagues, they experience a form of malaise (Faÿ, Introna, & Puyou, 2010). When figures and abstract considerations dictate their behavior, most of the management controllers and operational managers have a sense of resignation or keep a distance from their work.

> Sometimes I am told to bring the forecast up to a point with which I do not agree, but I do it all the same. (Management controller, Airshop)
> When people ask us to be more optimistic, we have no choice. We just get on with it. We don't have any qualms about it. We say, "Oh dear, it's going to be tough," because we thought the first version was the right one; but we do it. … We keep quiet and just take it because it's our job, (Manager, Airshop)
> Sometimes I prepare something for the budget, and they do things differently. And sometimes I don't agree, and in that case I become very detached from what I've done. (Management controller, Airshop)

Lastly, most managers anticipate adjustments from the top and minimize their estimates. The most common strategy consists in communicating intentionally lowered forecasts to save margins of autonomy and ensure that objectives are attainable in the end. "The management is pessimistic in the budgets, since they want to do better than the budget" (Management controller, Airshop). All the attention is therefore focused on the game around numbers at the expense of management-related issues. Exchanges are more about accounting innovations than about operational ones: "Anyway, we always make the profits we said we would make because if profits are higher, part of this is put aside; and if profits are lower than expected, we use former provisions" (Managing director at Airshop). Not much information about what actually happens to the periphery is then communicated to the top. SAP and other tools that have been developed to control distributed operations turn out to be the instruments of strategic interactions in which people try to outwit each other. The actors make a great effort to manage figures on their activities even though the data in circulation is largely bereft of operational meaning and relevance.

Reconciling Different Sources of Knowledge for Learning and Innovation

It also happens at Airshop that interlocutors are genuinely concerned with maintaining the links between figures from SAP and actual practices. Colleagues willing to meet and share with each other the constraints of their activities are likely to ignore temporarily the pressure exerted by the ideology embedded in the software.

Joint efforts enable management controllers to experience the reality of operational managers and take a critical stance toward models and representations.

> I work directly with the operational managers. It's a team effort, and we rely on one another a great deal. … I try to go to the airport once a month to visit the shops, give them a hand setting up. Next Tuesday, a remodeled shop is opening, so everyone's coming to lend a hand moving, which will be a good way of getting to know everyone as well as the sales outlet. (Management controller, Airshop)
>
> There is an operational side to this job, because even though we do spend days pouring over figures, we see the buyers and the operational managers and so are still involved at an operational level, which means we're not just dealing with abstract ideas all day. (Management controller, Airshop)

Figures are used in a way that complements lived experience and facilitates the development of new knowledge through collective interpretation of information. The learning goes both ways, with employees in the airports also realizing the intimate relationships between their activities and those carried out at headquarters. The representations sensitize them, for instance, to the financial issues and expectations.

> If we go way over, I call my director to explain that—let's say–that with the mobile perfume shop, I had to hire a few more temps, and that's really exciting for the table. We didn't use to have that. It's interesting to see what room for maneuver he has. We look at all the costs. (Manager, Airshop)
>
> It's really interesting because we have discussions going with Management Controllers to increase sales as quickly as possible. (Manager, Airshop)

Managers are concerned not just for their own sake but also for the sake of improving the understanding of situations. Targets and objectives are central and are continuously assessed with operational settings in mind. Regular discussions maintain a link between practices and reporting.

> I watch the turnover on the terminal every day[.] … My manager and I telephone each other every day to discuss the turnover, and we know why there are variations. We do not wait until the end of the month to talk. (Manager, Airshop)

It is in these situations that innovation may emerge and bring about the simultaneous evolution of the reporting system and the operational practices. A few weeks before this study began, Airshop finally decided to take into account the impact of the distance between the boutiques and the customs counters in the performance evaluation process. For some time the sales managers had been complaining of what they perceived to be unequal treatment resulting from the different locations of their boutiques. They argued that sales points placed further from the main stream of passengers had *de facto* poorer results than those placed near the exit of customs areas. It was not until a controller and a terminal manager decided that they would jointly investigate the performance variations between sales points and bear in mind the experience of the sales people onsite that the flaw in the performance evaluation process was recognized by top management. This formalization based on actual practices supported the decision to launch new boutiques "on wheels" in order to better capture the major stream of passengers. Reflexive thinking on the discrepancies between representations and the lived experience of work did allow for unexpected new developments.

Learning from Conflicting Sources of Knowledge

This case study shows how, in certain circumstances, ERP interfaces create a distance between individuals, who therefore remain indifferent to each other. During the performance evaluation process, for example, individuals are no longer thought of as qualitatively determined living beings but rather as mere means of quantitatively evaluated production. Managers who work at a distance from each other mutually demand extra effort of themselves regardless of the context and knowledge of the actual local situations. Imperatives of accountability and reactivity make the employees scrutinize their monitors for virtual solutions to ideological matters while being indifferent to the material situation experienced by others.

The diversity of the situations reported by the employees from Airshop underlines nonetheless that the complexity of work relations cannot be explained by the distance imposed by technical interfaces only. Most managers in Airshop do not exclusively use the software interfaces. It is certainly easier, faster, and very legitimate to manage through representations, but it also drives actors to uneasiness. All the individuals interviewed in the study experience their work through the ERP representations and through their praxis simultaneously. Some make special effort to meet coworkers and have regular face-to-face discussions about the interpretations of representations. They do not content themselves with following the injunctions of ERP at all times and in all matters. The confrontation between knowledge drawn from individual praxis and lived experience and knowledge made accessible through representations gives rise to a potentially rich and innovative dialogue. The concerns communicated by groups of actors who signal the inappropriateness of figures and images standing for their activities are a major source of new learning. The limitations of the tools for taking those concerns into account lead to ways of improving not only the software but also the conduct of activities. Unsurprisingly, it is when sources of knowledge have the opportunity to clash that important sources of innovation are to be tamed (Meusburger, 2008). The effort to link representations with lived experiences reveals the limits of ideologies and opens new paths for innovation. When discussed, ERP flaws and limitations are drivers of interpersonal communication and are most helpful for collective action.

Deadlines and management by objectives are examples of software-embedded imperatives that reinforce abstract management as the main mode of action. Workers tied up with constant solicitations from instruments are urged to take action immediately. The taste for abstract management is further reinforced by visual understanding of gross simplifications of reality, which requires only linear and superficial knowledge of the operations and the social context. The software yields powerful images that influence ideas and mobilize people "to follow as true believers" (Boland, 1987, p. 367). Having only limited time, pragmatic individuals are tempted to rely extensively on the powerful tools readily available to them. Paradoxically, behaving like the Hatter in Wonderland might become the preferred option. As ambiguity is gradually cleared up, routines emerge and flexibility decreases.

The primacy of virtual communication and the lack of face-to-face interaction are harmful, for they leave no room for actual cooperation, confrontation, and motivation (Segrestin, 2004). Representations are dangerous when they no longer map reality but rather create a world of their own with little connection to practice. Many people are attracted by the security offered by the software to manage a budget, an activity, or a project and prefer clicking on resources that are neatly defined and easily at hand rather than meeting with interlocutors and tackling messy situations. Certainly, the computer's responses are anticipated less apprehensively than those of coworkers. Yet innovation, new knowledge, and original developments come from the shared endeavor to link abstract representations to actual lived experience, which can be harnessed only when the users themselves critically assess the abstract working space of the screen with their own knowledge of operations gained from their work spaces in offices, warehouses, factories, and other places.

References

Boland, R. J. (1987). The in-formation of information systems. In R. J. Boland & R. Hirschheim (Eds.), *Critical issues in information systems research* (pp. 363–394). New York: Wiley.

Carroll, L. (2006). *Alice's adventures in wonderland*. Harmondsworth, UK: Penguin Books. (Original work published 1865)

Carruthers, M. (1998). *The craft of thought: Meditation, rhetoric and the making of images, 400–1200*. Cambridge, UK: Cambridge University Press.

Faÿ, E., Introna, L., & Puyou, F.-R. (2010). Living with numbers: Accounting for subjectivity in management accounting systems. *Information and Organization, 20*, 21–43.

Hansen, A., & Mouritsen, J. (1999). Managerial technology and netted networks. *Organization, 6*, 451–471.

Henry, M. (1963). *L'Essence de la manifestation*. Paris: PUF.

Henry, M. (1973). *The essence of manifestation* (G. Etzkorn, Trans.). The Hague, The Netherlands: Nijhoff.

Henry, M. (1983). *Marx: A philosophy of human reality* (K. McLaughlin, Trans). Bloomington, IN: Indiana University Press.

Henry, M. (1990). *Du communisme au capitalisme: Théorie d'une catastrophe* [From communism to capitalism: Theory of a catastrophe]. Paris: Editions Odile Jacob.

Henry, M. (2003). *Phénoménologie de la vie* [Phenomenology of life]. Paris: PUF.

Husserl, E. (1970). *The crisis of European sciences and transcendental phenomenology* (D. Carr, Trans.). Evanston, IL: Northwestern University Press. (German original work published 1936)

Introna, L. (1997). *Management, information and power*. London: Macmillan.

Introna, L., & Ihlarco, F. M. (2004). The ontological screening of contemporary life: A phenomenological analysis of screens. *European Journal of Information Systems, 13*, 221–234.

Meusburger, P. (2008). The nexus of knowledge and space. In P. Meusburger, M. Welker, & E. Wunder (Eds.), *Clashes of knowledge: Orthodoxies and heterodoxies in science and religion* (pp. 35–90). Knowledge and Space: Vol. 1. Dordrecht, The Netherlands: Springer.

Quattrone, P. (2009). Books to be practiced: Memory, the power of the visual and the success of accounting. *Accounting, Organizations and Society, 34*, 85–118.

Quattrone, P., & Hopper, T. (2005). A 'time-space odyssey': Management control systems in two multinational organisations. *Accounting, Organizations and Society, 30*(7–8), 735–764.

Quattrone, P., & Hopper, T. (2006). What is IT? SAP, accounting, and visibility in a multinational organisation. *Information and Organization, 16*, 212–250.

Segrestin, D. (2003). Les nouveaux horizons de la régulation en organisation: Le cas des progiciels de gestion intégrés [The new horizons for regulation in organizations: The case of ERP]. In G. De Tersac (Ed.), *La théorie de la régulation sociale de Jean-Daniel Reynaud: Débat et prolongement* (pp. 61–77). Paris: La Découverte.

Segrestin, D. (2004). *Les chantiers du manager* [The manager's tasks]. Paris: Armand Colin.

Townley, B. (2002). Managing with modernity. *Organization, 9*, 549–564.

Organizational Design for Knowledge Exchange: The *Hau-Ba* Model

3

Ahmed Bounfour and Gwénaëlle Grefe

Exploring Space and Spirit in Knowledge-Sharing

The key role of knowledge in today's economy has made the creation and transfer of knowledge the focus of many recent approaches. Among them, the fundamental Japanese concept of *ba* (Nonaka & Konno, 1998) affords an innovative perspective on how the different dimensions of knowledge can be connected to a spiral of transformations in which knowledge is created. The concept makes it possible to take both tacit and explicit knowledge into account, depending on the context and quality of the interactions between the individuals involved. The places that host and sustain these interactions are called *ba*, and they define the proper physical, mental, and virtual spaces, or any combination of them, that make specific knowledge transformations possible.

However, this model is not totally clear when it comes to addressing the issue of *ba* sequences. Depending on the nature of the knowledge before and after transformation, four kinds of functional *ba* (originating, interacting, cyber and exercising) figure in the SECI[1] matrix (Nonaka, 1994; Nonaka & Takeuchi, 1995), but none of them have been examined analytically. Moreover, something beyond transfer—an exchange—is entailed between an individual who gives knowledge and one who receives it. Authors of several articles dealing with the concept of knowledge

---

[1] SECI is the acronym for the four parts of the knowledge creation cycle: Socialization, Externalization, Combination, and Internalization (Nonaka, 1994; Nonaka & Takeuchi, 1995).

A. Bounfour (✉)
European Chair on Intellectual Capital Management & PESOR,
Université Paris-Sud, 54, Boulevard Desgranges, 92330 Sceaux, France
e-mail: ahmed.bounfour@u-psud.fr

G. Grefe
Granem (Groupe de recherches angevin en économie et management),
Université Angers, 13, allée François Mitterrand,
BP 13633, 49100 Angers Cedex 01, France
e-mail: gwenaelle.grefe@univ-angers.fr

A. Berthoin Antal et al. (eds.), *Learning Organizations: Extending the Field*,
Knowledge and Space 6, DOI 10.1007/978-94-007-7220-5_3,
© Springer Science+Business Media Dordrecht 2014

transfer (Berthon, 2003; Habib, 2008; Monnier-Sénicourt, 2005) have attempted to analyze its process within each interaction, but very few researchers have considered the global-exchange approach (Ferrary, 2003). And none have provided an explanation of the relationship between the dynamics of knowledge transfer and the "spirit" of exchange that governs the actors.

Our research originates in the lack of clarification about the connection between knowledge exchanges and the force that drives them. To explore how organizational communities grow and how they develop their own memory, we question the logic of individuals' input to that transfer knowledge. By analyzing the interactions within occupational communities, we hope to offer new leverage to managers seeking incentives for knowledge transfer. This research can aid management by suggesting ways to design or foster spaces for ad hoc knowledge transfer. It can also highlight how to identify and increase the motivation of exchangers. To advance research in this area, we propose an enriched version of the *ba* concept that does not divorce knowledge from its owners, the individuals. It is between the two concepts of knowledge and knowledge giver that the *hau* comes in: the spirit in which a gift is given, the strength of the circulating gift.

The *Hau-Ba* Model

From the Concept of *Ba* to the Community-Order Perspective

The concept of *ba* has been prominent in the Japanese way of creating knowledge and now has its place in the language of knowledge management. The imprint of Japanese culture on this concept makes it difficult to understand in western languages. Translated as "strategic knowledge community" (Fayard, 2003), the concept loses its very first characteristic, that of being a "space" rather than a governance mode. Nevertheless, the term does clearly retain the idea that such a place hosts the members of a *community* who interact and exchange knowledge organically and simultaneously.

By the same token, the deep transformation of socioeconomic systems, and especially the revival of the concept of a community for organizing activities, poses the question of the relationship between the community's governance and the *ba* (Bounfour, 2006). On the whole, there arise questions such as "Does a community emerge from a specific deployment of *ba*?" or "Does a community create its own *ba*?" In each case it is crucial to determine the sequence, to differentiate between the physical, mental, and virtual *ba* that eventuate in the final equilibrium of a system in which knowledge transfer could become endogenous.

From the Community-Order Perspective to the *Hau* Theory

Introducing the unavoidable issue of interacting individuals leads to the question of governance and social identity, which is related to the desire to understand why people from communities and inside the *ba* exchange their knowledge. This curiosity is directly linked to the second side of the model, the *hau* theory, derived by the French anthropologist who introduced the notion of the social exchange (Mauss, 1950).

The *hau* theory refers to the triple obligation in primitive societies to use and circulate exchanged objects or symbols, and to give in return. This tacit rule works as a way to transcend competition, war, or conflict. The Maussian gift describes a dynamic of mutual recognition, or acknowledgement, by which the recipients are required to give a gift in return, leaving them with no other choice than to give back accordingly. This powerful notion of return is called the *hau,* the spirit of the gift, the strength of the circulating thing. The economic value or time frame is unimportant in the social exchange where individuals are both free and obliged to give something in return. What is at stake in this rite is closer to recognition than to power. Such a rite can be translated to the organizational context where the goal is to achieve the ability to promote or institute spontaneous knowledge-sharing in occupational communities. It becomes particularly interesting to understand when companies seek to embed the knowledge exchange practices into innovation processes.

Discussing the gift model as a way to explain knowledge exchange is not new in the literature (Alter, 2006; Balkin & Richebé, 2007; Ferrary, 2003). Fayard implicitly associated the spirit of the exchange with the space of knowledge transfer when he noted that "*ba* is fundamentally subjective and relational and one becomes involved in it because it is ruled by common interest and because there are no conflicts within human relationships" (p. 26). From that standpoint, the *hau* provides the rule that is strong enough to erase conflicts, eliminate domination, and facilitate engagement. This contribution establishes the first connection between the *hau* and the *ba*. But above all, we theorize that the set of Maussian exchange rules is inherent in the *ba* and thereby makes both knowledge transfer and acknowledgement between members possible (Bounfour, 2000). These members, then, are part of "quasi-organic communities" (Bounfour, 2005, 2006) governed by the recognition principle (Honneth, 1996).

Lastly, application of the *hau* rule underpins "the equity feeling" (Adams, 1963; Wilkins & Ouchi, 1983) and, in a more basic sense, respect for the tacit psychological contract with the organization itself. This dual scope draws attention to a another kind of social exchange, one that takes place at a macrolevel between employees and managers and that encompasses the exchange of knowledge happening inside occupational communities. The existence of this macrolevel exchange raises the final question: What can function as the initial gift triggering the macro- and meso-processes of organizational exchange processes?

The *Hau* and the *Ba* Together

The Question of Sequences

One cannot link the *hau* and the *ba* without asking other path-dependent questions (Bounfour, 2006; Bounfour & Grefe, 2009). The first one probes the nature of the relationship between the *hau* and the *ba*, requiring precise determination of the gift model's building blocks. The second question relates to the sequence of the *hau* phenomenon and the *ba* transformations. Third, which of the dimensions (physical, mental, and virtual) appear first among and within the *ba* phases (which we also refer to as periods and stages), and why? Lastly, we must determine the whole three-step cycle of giving that exists in an individual phase of *ba* (e.g., the originating *ba* or the interaction *ba*). We have already suggested that every phase of the SECI matrix should correspond to a dedicated cycle of exchange, for giving and receiving are both associated with a single transfer. As for giving a gift in return, we propose that the act must occur within a space that has something in common with the *ba* of the initial transfer. In other words, we suggest having the *ba* include the space in which a return gift is given in order to erase the debt of the initial gift properly and unambiguously.

On this basis we argue that the space of interaction becomes a *ba* after the action that engenders the *hau*. If some potential *ba* pre-exists the *hau* by hosting individuals who have a common will, it is the *hau* phenomenon that reveals the *ba*. Indeed, the metamorphosis of the space into a *ba* comes about once the transformation between the given, the received, and the returned knowledge[2] is observed.

Finding out where the return gift is given helps determine the exact perimeter of the *ba*, which is deemed an extended space. We theorize that if the instances of giving and the receiving happen in the same *ba*, then the giving of a gift in return is part of this same place. We see the reciprocation as the key to the transfer because it makes the transfer sustainable by maintaining recognition as a social link between exchangers. Reciprocation removes the debt and keeps people from feeling contempt. This pacification imbues the reciprocation with legitimacy not only in the transfer but also in the definition of the *ba*. To summarize, a *ba* without an embedded *hau* is inconceivable.

At this juncture, it is necessary to consider several scenarios in which the *hau* enters one or more *ba*. Six different types of sequences can gradually form over time before becoming a stable system in which the *hau-ba* sustains the endogenous flow and creation of knowledge within a quasi-organic community.

Sequence 1: physical ba → mental ba → virtual ba[3]. Traditional human activities based on interaction in physical space have been created because they allow real contact and recognition of others as similar. Workshops as a physical *ba* afford the opportunity to test, exchange, and build respect and confidence. Initial gifts can often be offered there. Depending on the type of activities, different kinds of physical *ba* may be mobilized: shops, offices, cafeteria, meeting or conference rooms, or transportation. In most activities, the physical *ba* is a proven way of creating a mental *ba* based on the "history" shared in it. The subsequent introduction of the virtual *ba* does not pose a problem, but one may legitimately ask whether the virtual *ba* can completely substitute for the two previous kinds of *ba*.

---

[2] When receivers do not possess enough knowledge to reciprocate with knowledge without upsetting the initial giver, then the reciprocation consists of symbols.

[3] The presentation of sequences and some of the subsequent developments build on our previous analysis in Bounfour, Grefe (2009: 88–89).

Sequence 2: physical ba → virtual ba → mental ba. This sequence can be understood in different ways. It is still the dominant, and often the only, way of hiring new workers in many manufacturing enterprises and other organizations seeking to create a community based on the physical experience. The physical *ba* is the way to start, but a shift to the virtual *ba* does not work in this context. Sequence 2 is observed more frequently in "value-added services" such as IT, consulting, and all activities dominated by free-lancing and nomadic behavior.

Sequence 3: virtual ba → physical ba → mental ba. This sequence refers to a context in which the actors build business relationships initially in virtual spaces, as with one-off transactions and permanent or semipermanent transactions or relationships. The shift toward the physical *ba* might be induced by a need the actors might feel to socialize more deeply than they have before any other kind of cooperation is considered. This scenario might develop, for instance, in residential seminars organized with the goal of reinforcing social links among an ad hoc community (e.g., marketing teams or researchers).

Sequence 4: virtual ba → mental ba → physical ba. This sequence certainly pertains to the new generations, for whom the virtual *ba* is the reality of the world. The virtual *ba* (e.g., social networking sites such as Facebook) might be the preparatory phase of the mental *ba*, which is then followed by the physical *ba*.

Sequence 5: mental ba → physical ba → virtual ba. This eventuality is theoretical only. Can a mental *ba* be a prerequisite to the physical or virtual *ba*? One can imagine a potential mental *ba* that precedes the physical one (regarding the level of social proximity of future members of the exchange), but it is basically impossible to conceive of an active mental *ba* starting a set of sequences.

Sequence 6: mental ba → virtual ba → physical ba. In this sequence, too, positing that a mental *ba* precedes the virtual *ba* implies that some mental order spontaneously comes into being without any social interaction (in virtual or in physical spaces). The sequence should be thought of as more theoretical than observable in concrete settings.

In short, the objective is to discover which of the physical, mental, or virtual *ba* come into play first and whether their role is temporary or permanent. The underlying idea is that some *ba* are educational (e.g., training spaces for applying the exchange rules and implementing the *hau-ba* system), whereas others are fundamental, occasional, or continuous. We expect to identify exactly what the physical *ba* does and what kind of physical *ba* (e.g., a workshop or a meeting room) is needed to reinforce the social links necessary to sustain the knowledge transformations described in the SECI matrix. We also seek to determine when it is possible to substitute a virtual *ba* for a physical one, and we aim to understand where the initial gift can be offered. Such insights within an organization can facilitate the design of knowledge-exchange systems that could modify the kind of communities it is prepared to host.

The Central Question of the Mental *ba*

Theoretically, the *hau* can be tied to the *ba* and vice versa. The *ba* concept states that it is important to allocate a particulate place to the mental space in organizations. One can intuitively understand how fundamental this dimension is in the transformation of collective knowledge. Cognitive connections acquired through collective memory are essential to perform these transformations. Yet although it is easy to emphasize how critical the mental dimension and its difficulties are, nothing indicates how to achieve them. Only an empirical approach can shed light on this question.

With regard to the *hau-ba*, the *ba* concept suggests both a particular deployment of the mental space and, to a certain extent, the idea that that space enters an advanced stage of development when the *hau* becomes part of it. Until then, the *hau* is nothing but the rite of a quasi-organic community whose identity is composed of the mature mental *ba*. The *hau-ba* can then be defined as a singular mode of articulating the gift exchange within the spaces serving knowledge transfer. This proposal ties the *hau-ba* to the recognition principle referred to above (Honneth, 1996). The *hau-ba* corresponds to a mode of collective action in which mutual recognition is the fundamental principle.

Lastly, the contingency elements related to the community order have to be assessed, especially when it is deployed within the transactional order that characterizes how organizations work. By transactional order, we mean the economic order that rules markets and societies on the basis of rationality and interest (Bounfour, 2005, 2006). Its inherent logic of power stands in contrast to the struggle for recognition (Honneth, 1996; Ricœur, 2005) mainly achieved within the "communautalism" regime (Bounfour, 2005, 2006).

The *Hau-Ba* Model in Practice

A longitudinal empirical study based on participant observation in an aluminum foundry and on in-depth immersion in its processes and dynamics enabled us to explore the *hau-ba* like ethnographers.

The Focus of Research

The enterprise we studied was experiencing a critical loss of organizational memory when our observations began. The departure of many workers over the years, combined with various restructuring plans and the baby-boomer phenomena, had deprived the company's shop floor of many skills and much experience. Simultaneously, recruiting people and, above all, retaining them had become an ever greater challenge for managers because blue-collar positions no longer attract many members of the young generations. Furthermore, a foundry and its workers, much like mining companies and their miners, are characterized by pride in the industry. New employees who do not feel pride when they join the organization, or, even worse, who do not sufficiently respect the occupation, find that acceptance in the community is difficult, if not impossible, to achieve.

The need to transfer occupational memory became urgent when the headquarters decided to revive the foundry after the closure of another plant, whose activity had to be taken over. This new project brought the prospect of development, but it also presented the organization with a new challenge. It not only had to recruit workers but also transfer the knowledge from senior employees to twenty newcomers as quickly as possible.

Research Questions

Knowledge transfer between two generations of workers raises two primary sets of questions. The first set in our study dealt with defining the knowledge involved in the exchange—"occupational memory" in our study. This initial step is essential to understanding what kind of knowledge the exchange entails. For example,

1. Is it critical? Intensive? Superficial? Tacit? Explicit? Personal? Collective? Official?

   The second set of questions focused on the *hau* cycle and the discovery of the gift as a social rite:

2. Is the knowledge identified as part of the transferred (given) memory?
3. Is this knowledge well received (e.g., effectively used by new employees)?
4. Is any knowledge given in return (new knowledge creation)?
5. Is anything else reciprocated (e.g., symbols or things)?
6. What is the content of the initial gift and who is responsible for it?

   A third cluster of questions centered on characterizing the spaces of knowledge transfer *and* exchange. We therefore asked about the kinds of *ba* that are mobilized in different phases of the exchange:

7. Are any physical, mental, or virtual spaces identifiable? What are their sequences?
8. Do those spaces host any kind of transfer characterized by the SECI matrix? (What is their nature: Originating? Interacting? Cyber? Exercising?)
9. Does gift reciprocation take place within the *ba*?

   Yet another cluster of questions turned attention to the analysis of the exchange's underlying logics of action and governance:

10. What is the exchange paradigm shared by the actors? (What are the motivations behind the scene of the exchange cycle? How do the actors build the common principle for exchanging?)
11. To which organizational modes do they belong? (Is the concept of "community order" the right one?)

    Lastly, we repeatedly posed an overarching question related to the field's specific contingencies, of which two major ones emerged from the initial phases of the research:

12. What are the contingencies affecting the research?
    12.1. Can the survival feeling that exists in endangered industries alter the exchange?
    12.2. Can the concept of occupation (especially employee skill levels, which were high in the organization we studied) have an impact on the exchange?

To answer all these questions fully, we compared this case with a second one embedded in the same organization but related to another occupation (aluminum hard extrusion), which consisted of engineers and researchers. For lack of space, however, that work is not discussed in this chapter (see Grefe, 2010).

Method

An Ethnographic Exploration

In order to build our model of the *hau-ba*, we chose to proceed from the gift to the *ba* and from the *ba* to the return gift. That is, we started by identifying the knowledge transfers (the most obvious observable facts) that also defined the typical *ba*. It thereby became possible to search for return gifts that maintained these *ba* as spaces for positive social interactions. We also opted to examine the *hau-ba* dimensions via a qualitative approach based on coding. This protocol enabled us to identify the *hau* by the fact that the three instances of gifting (giving, receiving, and reciprocating [or giving in return]) have the same symbolic meaning (see Table 3.1). The assets involved in the three instances were identified for particular *ba* at each stage of the transfer. We regarded the metameaning of the exchange—the spirit of the gift (the *hau*)—as the atmosphere of these *ba*. In other words, understanding a *ba* (knowing why it exudes such an atmosphere in relation to identified emotions, motivations, or shared meanings) helps one figure out the *hau*.

To gather the data, we spent 18 months in the foundry, witnessing daily production and observing the different stages of the integration process experienced by 12 newcomers. We adapted Poitou's (1997) "3A" methodology by interviewing eight experienced workers for 3 days each. They described and explained each step of the process in the foundry. This initial collection of material shaping the occupational memory aided our effort to list the knowledge needed in order to practice the occupation as a professional. These lists also allowed us to track which pieces of memory are actually transferred effectively, to whom, when, and where. We considered the transfer to be confirmed when the apprentice put the knowledge to use. Whenever necessary, we interviewed the people engaged in the transfer. In all, 51 individuals participated in the investigation.

While conducting this research, we documented all the significant events that occurred in the foundry during our immersion in the organization. By significant events, we mean not only every observed, relevant interaction between the new and old workers but also innovations or collective decisions. Our analysis of the innovations and collective decisions and of the spaces where they came about allowed us to identify what would work as a return gift. The final step was to combine a gift, a reception, and a return gift into what we called a "triad."

For each triad the return gift worked as another side of the transfer. By displaying symbolic or concrete "acknowledgement of knowledge transfer," it ensured the sustainability of the equity feeling and thereby enabled the transfer from the givers to continue. When the givers felt appropriately recognized, they were willing to pursue the gift.

Table 3.1 The architecture of an empirical study on knowledge exchange in a foundry

Exploration of the *hau-ba* with a grounded theory (Strauss & Corbin, 1990) and an ethnographic approach

Contingencies of case 1: Survival feeling, operator status, historical trade (Osty, 2003, 2005; Osty & Dahan-Seltzer, 2006)

Step 1: What is the knowledge potentially involved in the exchange?	Step 2: Do giving and receiving knowledge work as an effective transfer?	Step 3: What are the *ba* that contain this effective transfer?	Step 4: Do any gifts reciprocated in the *ba* have the same "paradigm" of exchange?
Analysis of the occupational memory	Analysis of the motivations for giving and receiving: Do they share a meta meaning? (paradigm of exchange) Analysis of the use of the transferred knowledge: false or real usage? Conclusion: The first two instances of the gift come with an effective knowledge transfer	Analysis of the spaces where the gift and the receipt (use) happen. Can the transformations be done only into a physical *ba*? Is there a mental *ba* behind that can justify complex cognitive transformation? Conclusion: A mental *ba* made of collective memory develops itself on the basis of the practical physical *ba*.	Record all the significant events that happen during the transfer (18 months). Analysis of potential returns (What kind? Where? Why?) Conclusion: The reciprocation of the gift functions as another side of the transfer.

(continued)

Table 3.1 (continued)

Exploration of the *hau-ba* with a grounded theory (Strauss & Corbin, 1990) and an ethnographic approach

Contingencies of case 1: Survival feeling, operator status, historical trade (Osty, 2003, 2005; Osty & Dahan-Seltzer, 2006)

Step 1: What is the knowledge potentially involved in the exchange?	Step 2: Do giving and receiving knowledge work as an effective transfer?	Step 3: What are the *ba* that contain this effective transfer?	Step 4: Do any gifts reciprocated in the *ba* have the same "paradigm" of exchange?
Prerequisite: Knowledge-mapping (Ermine, 2000) based on archive and expertise owned by the seniors. Adaptation of the "3A method" (Poitou, 1997)	Is the transfer effective and efficient? Is the knowledge used by the new comers? → Analysis of the causes for departures from the job → Analysis of the motivations for staying at the job With the ones who stay, is there any new transfer that starts? → Analysis of the questions, ideas, and new routines developed; identification of other SECI steps.	Analysis of their dimension (physical, mental, virtual?) → Analysis of their nature: What transformation happened in each *ba* regarding to the SECI matrix? → What do they need to happen? (as a way to deduce the hollow presence of the mental *ba*)	Condition: Potential returns must occur in the same *ba* as the initial gift and receiving instances. Then, we must assess and compare the motivation between giving, receiving, and returning such assets. → Does a common "meta" motivation appear to characterize the paradigm of the gift exchange?
Coding (Miles & Huberman, 2003) of the identified experts knowledge (Girod-Séville, 1995)	Coding of the "received" knowledge (newcomers); of the new given knowledge from both tutors and newcomers (happening after the gift of memory)	Coding of the physical and mental *ba* holding the transfer or transforming the knowledge	Interviews with the actors, coding of their answers. Coding of the assets confirmed as returns.

From the articulation of the *hau-ba* system (P0) through the completion of an *initial* SECI matrix (P4)

Notes: Ermine (2000), Girod-Séville (1995), Miles and Huberman (2003), Osty (2003, 2005), Osty and Dahan-Seltzer (2006), Poitou (1997), Strauss and Corbin (1990)

A Process Analysis

We identified the triads by using a synthetic chronological matrix whose columns matched up given, received, or reciprocated gifts coded in each *ba* for every SECI phase through the 18 months of our study. Six periods emerged, beginning with the offer of the initial gift (P0), extending through the initial four SECI periods (P1–P4), and ending with the stabilization of the *hau-ba* system when fully deployed after P5. We conclude that the *hau-ba* needs not only time for initialization (P0) but also an entire SECI spiral to become a community system in which—

1. all the individuals are givers who recognize each other as community members while exchanging;
2. the acts of giving and reciprocating are completely merged; and
3. both the asset given and the asset given in return are knowledge.

The Difficulty of Mental *ba*

The protocol eventually helped determine part of the mental *ba* from the gift-exchange paradigm (Caillé, 2007, p. 9; Caillé et al., 1996, p. 12). The gift-exchange paradigm could be thought of as the mental space that gathers the common motivators for exchange between givers and receivers. It was also associated with the metameaning that the instances of gifting symbolize to the exchange partners. The secondary side of the mental *ba* was slowly defined through the newly created collective memory that emerged from the phases of the SECI matrix. In the end the definitive and cumulative mental *ba* was manifested as an occupational identity (made up of a status, a culture, and expertise linked to a memory) that suffused itself into successive physical *ba*.

Lastly, the research process as the interpretation of the *hau* mechanisms worked through one mental *ba* creation from multiple physical *ba* activities. Our interim conclusion is that four emerging phenomena were a function of the *hau-ba* connection and the creation of the mental *ba*:

1. A relay between two generations of workers
2. The reinforcement of the psychological contracts that link the exchange partners with their organization
3. The rejuvenation of the occupational memory mainly composed of tacit knowledge
4. The rebirth of a community defined by one rite (the *hau*) and a new occupational identity

A Specific Model Derived from the *Hau-Ba* Theory Preliminary Actions in the Field

The implementation of a tutorial system. According to our early survey results, the newcomers believed that employees were not involved in their training on-the-job. The experts did not feel any recognition for their transmission of memory from the organization. If they viewed knowledge transfer as a duty, they wanted it be officially recognized as such. Taking note of this request, middle management built a tutorial system and nominated tutors.

The return to a practice known in the foundry's "glory years" was one way to reconcile "survivors" with their past. It also reminded them that they all belong to a historic, prestigious company. With revived pride, the seniors regained a sense of the value that their jobs have in the French industrial context. All these aspects built strong job identity shared by a "community." First, the foundry workers could truly be called a "community of blood" (Tönnies, 1887/1977, p. 56), for most of the foundry's old generation of workers came from the same village for many years; they had the same roots. (That background applied less to the newcomers.) Second, the foundry could be regarded as a "community of space" (p. 56), for all the workers shared the same shop floor and faced the dangers together working the furnaces. They used a common space in order to work in close coordination. Lastly, the workers represented a "community of spirit" (p. 56) through their development of a common social identity. Belonging to the same historic organization or industry, engaging in union activities, and having similar jobs with specific occupational characteristics (danger, nobility) all contributed to a strong sense of belonging and a powerful social identity. We can therefore declare the foundry workers a community.

But could the name still apply to a community whose identity had been threatened and weakened after years of lay-offs (Boisseroles de Saint-Julien, 2005; Sainsaulieu, 1985)? The open question was whether this community could be reborn, whether it could integrate new members who did not have the same characteristics. In short, the issue was whether a group with a historical identity had the capacity to develop new organic links between members through specific socialization and knowledge exchange (Alter, 2006, pp. 209–225; Blau, 1964; Ferrary, 2003). For both old and new foundry workers, who were henceforth all peers, this interaction generated a new identity as an effect of mutual recognition.

The trigger of the* hau-ba *system: The original gift. The first result of the tutorial system was the positive restoration of the psychological contract tacitly established within the organization (Delobbe, Herrbach, Lacaze, & Mignonac, 2005). Once nominated as "tutors," the senior employees participating in the training process felt that equity was respected again. To them, it was a duty to help the new generation take over trade secrets, which may be passed on only to those who deserve them. Members of the old generation who had the title of "tutor" felt they had an opportunity to leave a legacy, but without disappearing or "being erased" by their own gift. To them, becoming a tutor seemed the right way to formalize the value of a career that represented nearly a lifetime of work. After 25–30 years spent in the same plant, passing on their experience was considered a way to legitimate their whole commitment. As formulated in interviews, it was interpreted as a necessary gift to newcomers who understand that the trade is respectable. The tutors would not risk offering their gift if neither the organization nor the apprentices recognized it.

The organization thus had to show explicit signs that this potential gift *was* recognized. Everyone, from management to the trade representatives, could see this recognition as the "original gift" that triggered another exchange between workers. The tutors felt the obligation to give (transfer) their knowledge in return for this managerial recognition. The apprentices had to quickly show some signs of gratitude—at least intermediary symbolic signs of appreciation, as Mauss accepted

Table 3.2 The first phase of knowledge exchange in the foundry: primary socialization through interaction of tutors and trainees

Gift modality	Gift content	Space
Given	Explicit and tacit noncritical knowledge	Primary original *ba* consisting
Received	Professional application of the knowledge	of physical practical *ba* (cold area)
Reciprocated	Signs of respect and humility	
Two groups: senior employees and junior trainees (intergroup exchange)		

in his early theory—or leave the factory. (Giving knowledge in return was not possible for the apprentices at the outset, for the gap between their expertise and that of more senior workers was too great.)

We note that the original gift concerned both tutors and newcomers. In their eyes, the initial gift (which turned the newcomers into receivers) was the promise of a long-term job[4] after successful training. Ultimately, both trainers and trainees embraced the same paradigm: the "occupational desire" (Osty, 2003), the expression of the need to develop a social identity (or redevelop a previously diminished one).

The *hau-ba* in Action

The start of the **hau-ba** *system: The initiatory gifts of phase 1*. First, "poor" gifts from the tutors were noticeable. Functioning like a test, the early gift dealt with declarative and procedural knowledge (Girod-Séville, 1995, 1996), a kind of "easy-to-hold" memory. No tacit or personal knowledge was at stake. This knowledge transfer occurred in the "cold area" of the foundry, which is separate from the real life of foundry workers' community.

The main life of the community played out in the "hot area," which during casting phases is close to the molten metal, near the furnaces. In the cold area, a tutor with vast experience spent 3 months with the newcomers, passing on the key knowledge about safety and molten metal. The initial 3 months were absolutely critical in the integration process, and most of the newcomers' departures happened during that phase. Departures occurred in one of two ways: (a) The apprentice could initiate the departure. Perhaps the individual had realized the hazards of the work, had come to understand the conditions attached to being part of the community (facing danger and controlling fear), and/or simply could not adjust to the job. (b) The tutor could initiate the departure. After testing the ability of the newcomers to receive and properly use the gift of basic knowledge, the tutors decided whether they could be trusted. Before passing on the trade secrets in the hot area (the "critical knowledge"), tutors rejected the trainees who did not use the already imparted knowledge well and those who do not give in return the signs or confirmation that they respected the exchange (see Table 3.2).

---

[4] In France the law permits short-term work contracts (CDDs) as opposed to contracts of undefined duration (CDIs). CDDs are not temporary missions, for the employer remains the company where the work must be accomplished.

In this primary, original *ba*, there was no risk of knowledge waste, for the training was started in the most basic kind of knowledge. The tutors may sacrifice some "trivial" knowledge to test the ability of the recipient to be a "receiver." We cannot speak of a full Maussian gift model in this phase of the knowledge exchange. The newcomers were not asked to give in return, except to show respect for both the trade and the initial knowledge passed to them. That gesture manifests the readiness to be endowed with the community's trust. The implication was that the recipients acknowledged the *hau* by following the tacit rule of gift exchange, which is that they deserved the gift because they honored it with the proper codes.

Humility, respect, and the desire to do well were summed up in the mind-set of the persons poised to succeed at becoming future members of the community. The process of cultivating those attributes included integration into the hot area of the foundry, a step toward final acceptance into the group of experienced casting workers. It was in the hot area that the experienced workers transferred the ultimate knowledge, which is both richer in its tacit and personal dimensions than basic knowledge is (Polanyi, 1983; Winter, 1987) and untransferable without intense social interaction.

***The total* hau-ba *system: SECI completion and microcycles of gifting*.** At the outset, the newcomers only observed the casting process. They learned how to alleviate their fear and to interpret the codes that workers use with each other to synchronize their work, often in conditions where no words are spoken. This close interaction took place in the space composed of the furnaces, space that can be associated with a second physical *ba*. We observe that sharing it promoted secondary socialization (phase 1 in the SECI matrix by Nonaka & Takeuchi, 1995, pp. 71–72, 89). Note that this physical *ba* would work only temporarily if a second one did not exist to support the following phases of the knowledge transfer and creation.

In fact, another *ba* had to be developed, this time a mental one in order to sustain the transformation of the subsequent SECI phases. It was a mental *ba* made of "collective memory," thanks to the interactions in the physical *ba*. By sharing a charged emotional climate, the individuals who were engaged in exchange experienced a common emotion, a pivotal characteristic of the emerging community's identity. Danger was omnipresent in the hot area. Lethal injuries due to explosions and burns were always possible. Workers had to stay absolutely vigilant and able to control their own fear. Between acceptance and denial, the casting workers mastered their fear and never even alluded to it. To preserve the team's psychological balance, which was essential for the collective safety of the members, exhibiting fear was tacitly forbidden.

The newcomers receiving the trade secrets about the hot area unambiguously proved their membership by agreeing to assist the furnace pilots during the casting operation. Newcomers not ready to express a form of self-confidence by this time were unable to share this mental *ba*, could no longer be part of the knowledge exchanges, and ultimately left the foundry (see Table 3.3).

In addition, other types of interactions were noticed within other spaces. During breaks and social time in the cafeteria, the newcomers used the opportunity to have

Table 3.3 The second phase of knowledge exchange in the foundry: secondary socialization of trainees

Gift mode	Gift content	Space
Given	Tacit highly critical knowledge	Secondary original *ba*, which combines—
Received	Application of the knowledge, denial of the danger	• The physical practical *ba*: the hot area • The mental *ba* (arousing): collective
Reciprocated	Acceptance of the offer of long-term employment (CDI) after the temporary contract	memory (emotional climate shared)
Emerging occupational community		

Table 3.4 The third phase of knowledge exchange in the foundry: externalization

Gift mode	Gift content	Space
Given	Answers (explicit knowledge)	Interacting *ba*, which combines—
Received	Questions (explicit knowledge)	• The physical *ba*: social places (refectory, outside of the factor: places apart the workshop)
Reciprocated	Symbols of honor	• The mental *ba* (active): collective memory (transforms received knowledge and increases itself)
Confirmed occupational community		

tutors talk about what they could not exchange during the operations (the protective gear prevented anyone from speaking in the hot area). Tacit knowledge was transformed into explicit knowledge by questions and comments. In this phase of knowledge exchange, reception preceded the gift, for asking a question can be thought of as a way to receive expected, but not yet transferred, knowledge.

The physical *ba* was not enough to transform tacit knowledge into explicit knowledge. The location of interaction was disconnected from the reality of the trade; cooperation was no longer possible. At that point individuals relied on the mental *ba* to understand each other and transform tacit knowledge. This *ba* consisted of collective memory, which sustained the cognitive process of knowledge transformation and creation. While active, the mental *ba* became self-perpetuating, continuously building new collective memory.

Social time was also rich in "returns." By sharing in social events, such as a sports competition, a strike, or a retirement celebration, the younger generation gave something back socially. They honored the seniors and restored pride in the trade (e.g., by winning a sports competition in the name of the foundry, building miniature casting tools as gifts for tutors who retire, or cooking pastries to celebrate the arrival of the "Three Kings" on Epiphany). That is, they responded with symbols to honor the givers, and both tutors and newcomers experienced the pleasure of conviviality. By virtue of the strong social links already forged in the foundry, the emergence of a community was well confirmed by this stage (see Table 3.4).

Table 3.5 The fourth phase of knowledge exchange in the foundry: conversion

Gift mode	Gift content	Space
Given	Innovation	Cybernetic *ba* consisting of:
Received	Approval and official agreement; routines changed	• Physical *ba*: workshop (not during production)
Reciprocated	Exclusion of the "black sheep": protection of the new community of peers	• Mental Ba (active): collective memory (stronger with parity feeling added)
Mature occupational community (made of peers)		

Almost 18 months after primary socialization, there began a new phase centered on workplace innovations. This change came about when the young foundry workers had learned enough to earn the status of the giver. They developed ideas on ergonomics and safety. If their first gifts seemed modest, then they did not violate the hierarchy of expertise or defy the old experts. The young workers thereby maintained the alliance and organic exchange that had started when they had first come to the foundry, but they also established themselves as peers of their tutors, bringing about a new community in which there was no differentiation among members. The experts acknowledged this "new deal" by receiving the gifts of the young workers. They unambiguously recognized the innovations by drawing attention to them in official meetings with managers or during theoretical courses. Moreover, experts decided to attend the training sessions organized for the young workers, symbolically using this opportunity to show respect for the new input and—through willingness to learn from it—to express the attitude that junior and senior workers are equally valuable.

At this point new peers exchanged knowledge during the combination phase (third phase of the SECI matrix) inside specific spaces (see Table 3.5). These spaces in the workshop were determined by a specific time as well. They were active in "off" times, when the workers were not engaged in casting. At those times (maintenance, cleaning, and training), individuals were still inspired by its physical manifestation but could also think and communicate. We refer to a "subliminal" presence of the trade.

It is important to note that when parity was at issue, the older generation chose to reject the "black sheep," those who did not accept the new consensus. For instance, two older workers known for passive resistance were laid off with the tacit approval of the unions. This rare development was strong proof of cohesion. Implicitly, the older workers supported the future of the foundry and helped the younger generation cope with the transfer of activity from the closed factory to their own plant.

A final phase in the SECI spiral of knowledge exchange, internalization, commenced with the development of new collective competencies. All the knowledge that had been transferred in prior phases was turned into tacit memory and became intrinsic. Knowledge transfer was endogenous to the community, with constant giving and reciprocating among the workers during their cooperation and coordination. By adjusting to each other, they integrated the gift and replied by producing the right skill: efficient, solid competence (see Table 3.6).

Table 3.6 The final phase of knowledge exchange in the foundry: internalization

Gift mode	Gift content	Space
Given	Know-how (competence)	Exercising *ba* that combines—
Received	Integration of other's actions	• Physical *ba*: workshop (during production)
Reciprocated	Adjustment: coordinated know-how (competence)	• Mental *ba* (active): collective memory (saved and enriched) and social (trade) identity.
Occupational community defined as a quasi-organic community		

The *hau* had become fully integrated in the mental *ba* as a cultural rite defining the community identity. Knowledge exchanges were utterly invisible. Giving was endogenous to the community embedded in the organization, with which another social exchange was performed. This context gives rise to the main threat to the *hau-ba* system: How can such a network (Callon & Latour, 1991) last when it is highly dependent on the ways in which the organization and society "recognize the recognizers" (Osty & Dahan-Seltzer, 2006, p. 99)?

A *Hau-Ba*: The Sequence from Physical *Ba* to Mental *Ba* Along an Initial SECI Spiral

Through completion of the SECI matrix and the development of the four *ba* described by Nonaka and Konno (1998), the case of the aluminum foundry presented in this chapter illustrates an example of knowledge exchange governed by the *hau*. It also demonstrates that the articulation of the *hau* within the *ba* achieves the rebirth of a quasi-organic community, that is, a community governed by principles of recognition (Bounfour, 2006). The *hau* works as the social link (Godbout, 2007) that enables individuals to view each other as subjects (rather than objects). Applied to a "prestigious good" such as knowledge, the *hau* definitively conveys some of the spirit of the giver and likens the exchange to what Mauss was describing. Enforcing its metarule among the individuals involved in the dynamic of the reciprocity, the gift subordinates (without erasing) the logic of dominance to the logic of recognition.

This case also shows that a Maussian gift is not only possible in organizations but also embedded in a wider intraorganizational social exchange that appears to be responsible for the offer the initial gift. But our analysis of these two aspects also reveal a weakness of the exchange system: What ensures that organizations know how to receive the reciprocated gift and respond with new recognition accordingly? Stated differently, once the community becomes competent, its reciprocations of gifts take the shape of new gifts to the organization. At that point, the question of how to give the metarecognition to community members becomes unavoidable and does not necessarily have easy answers in practice for organizations.

The *hau-ba* is able to retain the occupational cognitive inheritance of the foundry, and it can also develop a new form of collective memory through the mental *ba* that arises from the physical *ba*. Once the mental *ba* is developed, it becomes a major place for knowledge transformations. This mental *ba* development is facilitated by a strong, but specific, physical *ba*: the hot area, where the trade is in action and proximate danger requiring tacit cooperation. In this case the role of the practical physical *ba* is definitely exaggerated. Although a practical *ba* seems closest to the concept of *basho*, where Nishida's (1921/1990) pure experience is possible, one must keep in mind that occupations and activities are not necessarily embedded in such strong spaces. Nevertheless, providing practical places or anything that can reproduce their specific atmosphere (Maffesoli, 2005) seems to be key when it comes to promoting organic relationships and the transfer of tacit knowledge, for the one does not work without the other.

Upon completing the first SECI spiral, the group is a community (all the members are givers and peers) that is capable of producing competent actions. In other words improvisation, a crucial capacity in an incident, is now possible (Erden, von Krogh, & Nonaka, 2008). It is also what an organization needs from its employees in order to build its competitive advantage.

Once the mental *ba* has fully developed into the completely deployed physical *ba*, the community is mature enough to produce an endogenous gift: Giving and returning the gift are invisible, each constantly prompting the other. At this stage the *hau* is part of the mental *ba* as an adopted rite. One can speak of a superior mental *ba* that is the fundamental dimension of the *hau-ba* system. In fact, when the *hau*, as an element of this mental *ba*, is what produces the "cognition" and "recognition" exchange, it contributes to the development of this mental *ba* after each gifting cycle. Once the *hau-ba* is connected and acknowledged by members of a community, the system achieves autopoiesis: It is able to reproduce itself.

Returning to the question of sequence from a narrower but concrete perspective, we conclude that the physical *ba* acts as a communicational *ba* necessary for initiating the gift and exchanging its subsequent assets. Above all, the physical *ba* is confirmed as the essential place for socializing. As for the mental *ba*, its involvement in the transformation process of knowledge is critical. The mental *ba* also ensures the sustainability of that transformation. Despite the failure of an experimental attempt to show that virtual *ba* figures in the case of the foundry discussed in this chapter, we suggest pursuing such research on occupational backgrounds other than those of manual workers, where the physical *ba*, after its initialization, could be replaced by a virtual one. Hence, information systems can definitely play a major role in relocating the interactions of a physical *ba* in a virtual environment, allowing remote and thus potentially wider and easier exchange than what has been theorized in our field of study thus far.

References

Adams, J. S. (1963). Toward an understanding of inequity. *Journal of Abnormal and Social Psychology, 67*, 267–300.

Alter, N. (2006). *Sociologie du monde du travail* [Sociology of the world of work]. Paris: Presse Universitaire de France.

Balkin, D. B., & Richebé, N. (2007). A gift exchange perspective on organizational training. *Human Resource Management Review, 17*, 52–62.

Berthon, B. (2003). *Pour une approche globale du transfert de connaissance: une illustration empirique à l'intra-organisationnel* [A global approach to knowledge transfer: An empirical intraorganizational case]. Actes de Congrès de la XIIème Conférence de l'A.I.M.S., 3–6 June, Les Côtes de Carthage.

Blau, P. M. (1964). *Exchange and power in social life.* New York: Wiley.

Bounfour, A. (2000). Gestion de la connaissance et systèmes d'incitation: entre théorie du Hau et théorie du Ba [Knowledge management and incentive systems: Between the *hau* theory and the *ba* theory]. *Systèmes d'Information et Management, 5*(2), 12–40.

Bounfour, A. (2005). Modeling intangibles: Transaction regime versus community regime. In A. Bounfour & L. Edvinsson (Eds.), *Intellectual capital for communities: Nations, regions and cities* (pp. 3–18). Burlington, MA: Elsevier Butterworth-Heinemann.

Bounfour, A. (2006). Connaissance, reconnaissance et "communautalisme" [Knowledge, recognition and "communautalism"]. In A. Bounfour (Ed.), *Capital immatériel, connaissance et performance* (pp. 167–194). Paris: L'Harmattan.

Bounfour, A., & Grefe, G. (2009). Designing sequences for knowledge exchange: The *hau-ba* model. In A. Bounfour (Ed.), *Organisational capital: Modelling, measuring, contextualising* (pp. 76–108). London: Routledge.

Caillé, A. (2007). *La quête de reconnaissance, nouveau phénomène social total* [The search for recognition, a new total social phenomenon]. Paris: Editions La Découverte.

Caillé, A., Tarot, C., Dewitte, J., Rospabe, P., Larcebeau, J., Godbout, J., et al. (1996). L'obligation de donner, la découverte sociologique capitale de Marcel Mauss [The obligation to give, the fundamental sociological discovery of Marcel Mauss]. *La revue du M.A.U.S.S., 8*(2), 12–59.

Callon, M., & Latour, B. (1991). *La science telle qu'elle se fait: anthologie de la sociologie des sciences de langue anglaise* [Science as a dynamic process: An anthology of the sociology of sciences of the English language]. Paris: Editions La Découverte.

Boisserolles de Saint Julien, D. (2005). *Les survivants, vers une gestion différenciée des ressources humaines* [The survivors: Toward differentiated human resource management]. Paris: L'Harmattan.

Delobbe, N., Herrbach, O., Lacaze, D., & Mignonac, K. (2005). *Comportement organisationnel: Vol. 1. Contrat psychologique, émotions au travail et socialisation organisationnelle* [Organizational behavior: Vol. 1. Psychological contract, emotion at the workplace, and organizational socialization]. Brussels, Belgium: De Boeck.

Erden, Z., von Krogh, G., & Nonaka, I. (2008). The quality of group tacit knowledge. *The Journal of Strategic Information Systems, 17*, 4–18.

Ermine, J. L. (2000). *Les systèmes de connaissances* [Information systems]. Paris: Hermès Sciences.

Fayard, P. M. (2003). Strategic communities for knowledge creation: A Western proposal for the Japanese concept of *ba. Journal of Knowledge Management, 7*(5), 25–31.

Ferrary, M. (2003). The gift exchange in the social networks of Silicon Valley. *California Management Review, 45*(4), 120–138.

Girod-Séville, M. (1995). *Mémoire et organisation* [Memory and organization]. Unpublished doctoral dissertation, Université Paris-Dauphine, Paris.

Girod-Séville M. (1996). *La mémoire des organisations* [The memory of organizations]. Paris, Éditions L'Harmattan, collection Logiques de gestion.

Godbout, J. T. (2007). *Ce qui circule entre nous* [What circulates between us]. Paris: Seuil.

Grefe, G. (2010). *Les systèmes d'incitation à l'échange de connaissances au sein de communautés métiers de l'aluminium: essai d'explication d'un modèle* [Incentive systems for knowledge-sharing in communities of metalworking: Attempt to explain a model]. Unpublished doctoral dissertation, Université Paris-Sud 11, Paris.

Habib, J. (2008). *Les processus de connaissance et d'apprentissage dans les projets d'innovation: une approche par les systèmes adaptatifs complexes* [Processes of knowledge and learning in innovation projects: A complex adaptive systems approach]. Unpublished doctoral dissertation, Université d'Aix en Provence, France: Marseille.

Honneth, A. (1996). *The struggle for recognition: The moral grammar of social conflict.* (J. Anderson, Trans.). Cambridge, MA: MIT Press.

Maffesoli, M. (2005). Les mémoires des tribus et le réanchantement du monde [The memories of the tribes and the re-enchantment of the world]. In F. Casalegno (Ed.), *Mémoire quotidienne, communautés et communication à l'ère des réseaux* (pp. 129–146). Laval, Canada: Presses Universitaires de Laval.

Mauss, M. (1950). *Sociologie et Anthropologie* [Sociology and anthropology]. Paris: Presses Universitaires de France.

Miles, M., & Huberman, M. (2003). *Analyses des données qualitatives* [Qualitative data analysis] (2nd ed.). Paris: De Boeck

Monnier-Sénicourt, L. (2005). *Utilisation d'un système de gestion des connaissances et capitalisation; l'influence des caractéristiques professionnelles dans les métiers du conseil* [Use of a system for managing and capitalizing on knowledge: The influence of professional characteristics in consulting]. Unpublished doctoral dissertation, Université de Nantes, Nantes, France.

Nishida, K. (1990). *An inquiry into the good* (M. Abe & C. Ives, Trans.). New Haven, CT: Yale University Press. (Original work published 1921)

Nonaka, I. (1994). A dynamic theory of organizational knowledge creation. *Organization Science, 5*, 14–37.

Nonaka, I., & Konno, N. (1998). The concept of *ba*: Building a foundation for knowledge creation. *California Management Review, 40*(3), 40–54.

Nonaka, I., & Takeuchi, H. (1995). *The knowledge-creating company: How Japanese companies create the dynamics of innovation.* New York: Oxford University Press.

Osty, F. (2003). *Le désir de métier, engagement, identité et reconnaissance au travail* [Occupational desire, commitment, identity and recognition at the workplace]. Rennes, France: Sociétés, Presses Universitaires de Rennes.

Osty, F. (2005). Identités au travail et accès à la reconnaissance [Labor identity and access to recognition]. In G. Minguet & C. Thuderoz (Eds.), *Travail, entreprise et ingénierie.* Paris: Presses Universitaires de France.

Osty, F., & Dahan-Seltzer, G. (2006). Le pari du métier face à l'anomie [The power of occupational activities against anomy]. *Nouvelle revue de Psychologie, 2*, 91–106.

Poitou, J. P. (1997). *La gestion collective des connaissances et la mémoire individuelle [Collective knowledge management and individual memory].* Paris: CREPCO-CNRS.

Polanyi, M. (1983). *The tacit dimension.* Gloucester, MA: Peter Smith.

Ricœur, P. (2005). *Parcours de la reconnaissance* [The course of recognition]. Paris: Folio, Essais.

Sainsaulieu, R. (1985). *L'identité au travail: Les effets culturels de l'organisation* [Identity at work: The cultural effects of the organization] (rev. & exp. 2nd ed.). Paris: Presses de la FNSP.

Strauss, A., & Corbin, J. (1990). *Basics of qualitative research: Grounded theory procedures and techniques.* London: Sage.

Tönnies, F. (1977). *Communauté et Société, Catégories fondamentales de la sociologie pure: Introduction et traduction de J. LEIF* [Community and Society: Fundamental concepts in pure sociology (J. Leif, Trans.)]. Paris: Retz-C.E.P.L. (Original German work, *Gemeinschaft und Gesellschaft*, published 1887)

Wilkins, A. L., & Ouchi, W. G. (1983). Efficient cultures: Exploring the relationship between culture and organizational performance. *Administrative Science Quarterly, 28*, 468–481.

Winter, S. G. (1987). Knowledge and competence as strategic assets. In D. Teece (Ed.), *The competitive challenge: Strategies for industrial innovation and renewal* (pp. 159–184). Cambridge, MA: Ballinger.

Command or Conviction? Informal Networks and the Diffusion of Controversial Innovations

Johannes Glückler and Robert Panitz

An innovation is the result of a successful introduction and diffusion of a novelty within a social group (Akrich, Callon, Latour, & Monaghan, 2002; Fagerberg, 2005; OECD, 2005). Such accomplishment, however, can be surprisingly elusive. The famous failure of Sony's Beta video to win out over the VHS cassette as a standard for the producers of video recorders (Cusumano, Mylonadis, & Rosenbloom, 1992) demonstrates that novel technologies, products, and standards do not necessarily do well even though they enjoy a first-mover advantage. At least one reason for that kind of unforeseen outcome is that novel solutions and practices run the risk of being resisted because of misperception, underestimation, lack of attention or understanding, or other controversies (Glückler, 2010; Johnson-Cramer, Parise, & Cross, 2007; Mohrman, Tenkasi, & Mohrman, 2003).

In this chapter we advance the idea that organizational innovations are often controversial because they go hand in hand with a change in procedures and behavior in some or all organizational units of a firm, requiring the employees to learn procedures and processes unfamiliar to them or altogether new. Like every change in regular behavior, these adaptations may create a stressful situation for the employees, who can respond by resisting the innovations (Agócs, 1997). We therefore ask how organizational innovations are evaluated and through which mechanisms they are ultimately negotiated and adopted within an organization. It is especially when an innovation is controversial among the organizational members that its adoption and diffusion critically depends on the quality and structure of communication within a social group (Krackhardt, 1997). How does a controversial innovation spread through an organization? To answer this question both conceptually and empirically, we take a relational perspective to conceptualize management-induced organizational change as situations of controversial innovation and analyze patterns in the diffusion of organizational restructuring.

J. Glückler (✉) • R. Panitz
Department of Geography, Heidelberg University, Berliner Strasse 48,
D-69120 Heidelberg, Germany
e-mail: glueckler@uni-hd.de; panitz@uni-hd.de

A. Berthoin Antal et al. (eds.), *Learning Organizations: Extending the Field*,
Knowledge and Space 6, DOI 10.1007/978-94-007-7220-5_4,
© Springer Science+Business Media Dordrecht 2014

We begin by discussing the concept of controversial innovation and exploring potential sources of resistance as well as mechanisms involved in the diffusion of these innovations. In particular, we distinguish bottom-up from top-down innovation and infer from our conceptual discussion a set of hypotheses about hierarchical versus contagious diffusion. The chapter then continues with a description of our methodology. We first introduce the case of a medium-sized ophthalmological engineering firm that has started to redirect its organization from technology to a market orientation and has been enduring controversy as it diffuses new organizational practices within itself. After explaining our methodological approach to data collection, we turn to the studied firm's organizational location and internal distribution of market orientation, identifying situations of structural controversy and heterogeneity with respect to a market orientation. We then report the results of a social network analysis and tests of our hypotheses about the social diffusion of market orientation, which contrast hierarchical and contagious diffusion as well as formal and informal communication.

Our analysis yields evidence of contagious diffusion of organizational change through informal relations of knowledge exchange rather than down the corporate hierarchy. Although the innovation in question is a management-induced organizational change, formal relations of lateral unit membership and vertical subordination have no effect in the multivariate model we construct. Although valid only in the context of the firm we studied, these findings suggest that, in contexts of top-down organizational innovations, the diffusion and the legitimate adoption of an innovation depend on personal conviction rather than hierarchical demand. We conclude that informal relations of social interaction and knowledge exchange are crucial in organizational change.

Controversial Innovation

Organizational innovations transform, or even replace, an existing organizational action framework, such as routines, rules, authorities, and actions. The diffusion of organizational innovation may therefore encounter a range of opinions and even controversy among the members of an organization. The concept of controversial innovation has been pioneered by Krackhardt (1997). Asking to what extent an innovation may improve a given status quo, Krackhardt distinguishes three types of innovation: rationally superior, rationally inferior, and controversial. Rationally superior innovations are likely to be adopted when members are confronted with them. Because rationally inferior innovations are clearly less suitable than the status quo, they have almost no chance of being adopted no matter how much they are promoted. With controversial innovation, however, it is not evident whether adoption would bring additional benefit or improvement. What matters is how and in which context the members of an organization come to be acquainted with such innovation.

In many ways controversies over organizational change seem justified and may be important. The approach of organizational ecology, for instance, suggests that structural inertia and resistance to change may be necessary in order to retain an organization's competitive advantage of accountability and transparency (Hannan & Freeman, 1984). Hannan, Baron, Hsu, and Koçak (2006) demonstrate empirically that a change in practices relating to the organizational identity may actually harm the performance of a firm. Organizational change therefore means a risk to the organization as a whole and to its individual members. Among the many studies on the problems of organizational change, remarkably little work has addressed opposition to organizational change from the perspective of specific communicational relations and structures of social networks within an organization (Mohrman et al., 2003). In this chapter we concentrate on the sources of innovation within an organization, the sources of controversy, and potential mechanisms that diffuse controversial innovations.

Source of Innovation: Top–Down Versus Bottom–Up Innovation

New organizational practice always originates within the organization. The location of the source depends on which organizational member first demonstrates the practice or makes the proposal to do so. We distinguish between two sources of innovation in formal hierarchies: subordinate loci (bottom-up innovation) and superordinate loci (top-down innovation).

The empirical research on controversial innovation consists predominantly of case studies on bottom-up innovations that were resisted or even rejected by senior management. Famous examples are the innovation of post-it® notes (Brand, 1998), Viagra (Chesbrough, 2003), and IBM personal computers (Krackhardt, 1997). Initially, these technological innovations were either classified as failures or dismissed by management. They became successful innovations after being channeled through lateral and peripheral networks in the organization. Further evidence from a study on a multinational chemical corporation suggests that both technological and organizational innovations, such as new business models, can be invented in lower organizational units (e.g., peripheral market regions) and can run into stiff resistance from senior corporate management (Glückler, 2010).

It is no surprise that many bottom-up innovations, given their subordinate locus, fail when management uses its authoritative and allocative power (Giddens, 1984) to reject controversial and undesirable ones. But not all bottom-up innovations are inferior—indeed, some of them may be advantageous to an organization—so scholars have started to theorize about the conditions and mechanisms that may have a bearing on the success of bottom-up processes of controversial innovation (Agócs, 1997; Becker, 1970; Granovetter, 1973; Weimann, 1982). The notion of peripheral dominance suggests that actors on the fringes of social networks are conducive to controversial innovations because the periphery is more difficult to monitor, more prone to deviation, and less likely to meet the same level of resistance than central regions of a network are (Berthoin Antal, Krebsbach-Gnath, & Dierkes, 2004; Glückler, 2010; Krackhardt, 1997; McGrath & Krackhardt, 2003).

Unlike bottom-up innovations, top-down organizational innovations are usually introduced by senior management. Daft (1978), drawing on his empirical analysis of innovation proposals in U.S. high school districts, derived a dual-core model according to which technical innovations are proposed at operational levels and administrative innovations are promoted by the organization's administrative core. The latter locus is usually represented by the management in the sense that the adoption of the innovation often ensues as top-down diffusion—the direction, according to Daft, in which hierarchical structures can best support this process. However, trying to achieve organizational change through downward promotion of an innovation can be very frustrating for a company's management, for members of organizations tend to resist changes in the established procedures and processes. Because organizational change often entails a change in corporate culture, the lack of experience with new practices, combined with the inertia inherent in existing practices, may often lead to resistance to change (Narver, Slater, & Tietje, 1998). Despite the authority that management wields over subordinate units, top-down innovation often implies a degree of institutional resistance, the "pattern of organizational behavior that decision-makers in organizations employ to actively deny, reject, refuse to implement, repress or even dismantle change proposals and initiatives" (Agócs, 1997, p. 918). This resistance may stem from institutional hysteresis (Glückler, 2007; Martin & Sunley, 2006; Setterfield, 1993) arising from habituation, switching costs, or the fear of losing privileges or comfort.

Controversy in Downward Innovation Diffusion

Several related factors that may eventuate in controversy over management-promoted organizational innovations have emerged from research. One is that reformers in management often do not know where and why resistance forms in an organization (Johnson-Cramer et al., 2007, p. 85). Senior managers tend to be part of a closed and isolated subculture (Mohrman et al., 2003, p. 308). In their role as rule-makers, they have developed perspectives that often diverge from those who have to comply with these rules (Agócs, 1997). Another potential font of controversy over organizational innovations spearheaded by senior management is the authoritative divide, which largely prevents managers from building what Johnson-Cramer et al. call "energizing relationships" (p. 101), that is, those in which "contact with another person adds to one's own enthusiasm and energy level" (p. 101). Without these ties, managers feel it difficult to embrace subordinates and win them over for a top-down process of change. A hierarchical division of labor and its inherent power asymmetries often escalate the resistance against superordinate reformers in cases of controversy. The closed culture leaves managers having to grapple with the problem of misperception and misjudgment about opinions, concerns, and the atmosphere in other areas of the organization. For example, Johnson-Cramer et al. found that all the senior managers in the company they studied believed that consensus and harmony existed with regard to the firm's philosophy and culture, whereas the majority of the staff held the opposite view. This misjudgment was partly due to the strong tendency of the senior managers to communicate among each other rather than with their subordinates. The senior managers were part of a rather isolated group within the company and had created their own version of the state of the firm's philosophy and culture. A third factor in controversy over top-down organizational innovation is that reformers need time to inform, educate, and convince others, and time is an especially scarce resource in senior management (Mohrman et al.).

Downward Diffusion of Controversial Innovations: Hypotheses

Research on management-promoted innovation suggests that the apparent advantage that authoritative power has to promote an innovation down the hierarchy may be neutralized by a social divide between management and subordinate parts of an organization when it comes to perception, communication, and understanding. Given the gap between hierarchical authority to command and the social accessibility to convince, we explore the mechanisms by which controversial innovations are diffused. There are two generic strategies for using knowledge about the structure of informal networks to support an organizational change: (a) educate central actors of the network about the innovation, and (b) identify and convince resisting actors in separate actions (Johnson-Cramer et al., 2007). Stevenson and Greenberg (2000) build on this work in a study on how political actors might gain a majority when two contrary political movements are involved. They propose three strategies. In the first one the actors directly contact political actors from other movements to solicit their secret support. The second strategy is based on structural hole theory (Burt, 1992, 1997) in that promoters try to identify opinion leaders and to prevail upon them to exert their influence to convince followers. The third strategy is to convince the central actors and executives of the merits of the desired political system. Only the secrecy strategy was found to yield a successful political majority when political conditions were unfavorable. When there is controversy, social proximity, personal interaction, and a strategy of convincing through dialogue seem to be more promising than open campaigns. This evidence gives us reason to doubt that hierarchical channels of formal communication within an organization are sufficient or even helpful in promoting the diffusion of a new organizational culture. A tendency to think exclusively in formal, hierarchical, and functional structures can lead to failures in the implementation of an organizational change (Mohrman et al., 2003). In situations of controversy, we therefore expect formal organizational relations of authority to be unrelated to the diffusion of a management-induced innovation. These considerations bring us to our first hypothesis:

> Hypothesis 1: Members of an organization adopt a controversial organizational innovation independently of their social proximity to an innovation promoter in a formal network of authority.

Instead, an organizational innovation such as shifting the corporate orientation from technology to the market implies a profound change in approach, attitude, communication, and individual initiative at all organizational units. That kind of change in corporate culture is possible only if employees are convinced to pursue it rather than told to do so. If one accepts that "debate, criticism, or disagreement do not contribute to resistance" and that individual conviction may deepen through "rigorous critique intended to produce better understanding and solutions" (Agócs, 1997, p. 918), then interaction and discussion are key factors in diffusing organizational change. Interactions of this sort are the foundation for informal information and influence networks. Hence, our second hypothesis:

> Hypothesis 2: The more closely members of an organization are connected to an innovation promoter in a network of informal and interpersonal relations of knowledge exchange rather than in a formal network, the more likely those members are to adopt a controversial organizational innovation.

One of the many different sources of controversy or resistance to an innovation is the set of tasks and practices that a given group of organizational members actually performs. The adoption of an innovation will at least partly depend on those actors who will be most affected by the change that it implies. An innovation that requires comparatively little behavioral change from some organizational members may reduce innovation-related controversy among them and may foster it among those who face greater levels of such adaptation. We therefore expect the level of controversy and adoption of an innovation to fluctuate from one unit of an organization to the next:

> Hypothesis 3: Members of an organization are more likely to adopt a controversial innovation if their organizational tasks and practices are similar rather than dissimilar to the new ones called for by the proposed innovation.

Method

Case Study: An Ophthalmological Engineering Firm

To test our hypotheses, we use the case of Katalux,[1] a medium-sized, owner-managed, ophthalmological engineering firm sited in southern Germany. It specializes in the production of instruments and systems for surgical ophthalmology and distributes three kinds of products: surgical instruments; devices for surgical interventions in eyes; and, through a sister company, liquids and tamponades. From 1996 through 2009, Katalux had grown yearly by around 12 % (measured as the *compound annual growth rate of the turnover*). Compared to the market average, this figure far exceeded that for the German ophthalmologic market as a whole, which had posted an annual rate of less than 3 % from 1996 through 2004 (Hornschild & Weiss, 2005, p. 687). Katalux had enhanced its competitiveness by capturing market share from competitors and had grown mainly by expanding its international sales. Nevertheless, the German home market still accounted for half of the company's sales.

---

[1] Katalux is a pseudonym.

When the company agreed to take part in our study in 2009, it was coping with three challenges. First, it had to reorganize its internal organizational structure in order to adapt to major growth in its workforce over the preceding 13 years. The number of the firm's employees had risen from 80 in 1996 to 214 by the end of 2009, making it necessary to introduce new levels of corporate hierarchy and form new departments with special functions in order to coordinate production. Second, Katalux had to adapt its products and corporate philosophy to the requirements of customers outside Germany, for quality-price ratios and preferences vary widely across international markets. Third, Katalux had to sharpen its competitiveness even in its home market because market reforms and deregulation in Germany had facilitated foreign competition's access to it.

Analytic Strategy: Mixed-Method Research Design and Data

Our research design incorporated situated organizational network analysis (SONA) (Glückler & Hammer, 2012), an approach that uses the strength of mixed-method approaches (Miles & Huberman, 1994; Sieber, 1973). It captures the contextuality and quality of a corporate situation by means of repeated interviews at different levels of the organization and permits structured and stylized analysis of a specific phenomenon through network analysis. SONA involves between-method triangulation (Jick, 1979) and a degree of action research (Susman & Evered, 1978) to validate analytical and interpretive findings in interaction with the participants from the organization.

In this project we applied SONA in six research steps. First, we conducted two exploratory group interviews in executive meetings with members of the board of directors and the owner-manager of the company. Second, we carried out individual semi-structured interviews with all five members of the executive board and with the company's external strategy consultant. We also interviewed selected persons at other levels of management and operations, namely, the head of the department of research and development (R&D), a head of a production department, and a trainee from Production. These interviews permitted us to identify key challenges and controversies in the organization.

In the third step we designed a questionnaire for a network survey with which to analyze the individual strategy orientations of the employees and to identify the formal and informal relationships between the employees within the organization. From December 1 through 23, 2009, all Katalux employees were invited to complete an electronic survey asking them to name every contact who, to them, currently was or at some point had been a source of successful knowledge transfer to improve their work. A total of 171 (80 %) of all 214 employees provided valid responses (see Table 4.1). These 171 respondents named 207 employees. Only seven employees were left completely isolated from the network; they did not respond or were not named by any of the other respondents. All but one division manager answered the questionnaire. The response rate declined with the employment level in the corporate hierarchy. Employees without management responsibilities had the lowest, but still remarkable response rate of 77 %.

Table 4.1 Response rates for the network survey on employees' strategy orientations and formal and informal relationships within the company

Employment level in the company hierarchy	Total	No. of responses	Response rate (%)
CEO	1	1	100
Division managers	5	5	100
Department managers	24	23	96
Unit managers & employees	184	142	77
Total	214	171	80

Fourth, we used methods of social network analysis to analyze intraorganizational relations of knowledge exchange and interpersonal influence on decision-making. This approach reveals relations between the members of an organization and the social structure that emanates from these relations. It rests on the idea that the structure of a social network affects not only the opportunities and constraints of individual actors in the network but also the behavior of the whole network (Mitchell, 1969). Our analyses have been computed with the software package UCINET (Borgatti, Everett, & Freeman, 2002). Fifth, after analyzing our quantitative and qualitative data, we invited all employees to a presentation of our results. We also organized a 3-h group discussion with five senior managers from the main functions to validate our conclusions from the research. In the final step of the research, we met with the management board to develop suggestions for management intervention.

Controversial Organizational Innovation: From Technology to Market Orientation

Our empirical analysis centered on Katalux's redirection of organizational orientation from technology to the market. That change process can be interpreted as a management-induced organizational innovation for thinking about organizational practices in a new way. To explain its radicalism, we briefly review both orientations and draw on a series of qualitative interviews with managers and employees in the firm to illustrate the perceived reluctance, even resistance, associated with implementing this kind of change.

Katalux had long been keen on technology leadership and had invested heavily in new technologies. The paradigm of technology orientation means the use of technological advantages to compete for and retain quality-oriented customers. It stems from the assumption that customers prefer products and services rooted in superior technologies (Zheng Zhou, Yim, & Tse, 2005). A technology-oriented firm can therefore be defined as "a firm with the ability and the will to acquire a substantial technology background and use it in the development of new products" (Gatignon & Xuereb, 1997, p. 78). Because this perspective makes it an internal priority to adopt and create new technologies, the company runs the risk of failing to detect changes in customer preferences. Technology-biased firms may sometimes put even higher priority on technology than on the satisfaction of customers and may eventually fail to understand their needs. Regulated and stabile markets are receptive to that sort of strategy, but volatile, dynamic, and emergent markets require responsiveness to changing customer needs. With Katalux operating in an increasingly competitive international market environment, the traditional procedures and processes were no longer found appropriate:

> The company used to be very successful in a supply market. The issue never came up at all. We just produced fantastic things, and they sold like hot cakes. And now we're being thrown into a market dominated by customers and competitors. ... The company used to be highly successful. I'm analyzing it now and sizing it up to be highly production oriented. (Strategy consultant, 2009)

By contrast, a company with a market orientation seeks to understand "customers' expressed and latent needs [and to] develop superior solutions to those needs" (Slater & Narver, 1999, p. 1165). Jaworski and Kohli (1993) list three sets of activities to measure a firm's market orientation: "(i) organization-wide generation of market intelligence pertaining to current and future customer needs, (ii) dissemination of the intelligence across departments, and (iii) an organization-wide responsiveness to it" (p. 54). Research on market orientation has thus far distinguished between a behavioral and a cultural perspective. Whereas the behavioral perspective has turned attention to organizational activities related to the generation and dissemination of market intelligence (Kohli & Jaworski, 1990), the cultural perspective has helped researchers analyze organizational norms and values that encourage these behaviors (Deshpandé, Farley, & Webster, 1993; Narver & Slater, 1990). By contrast, we are interested in individual attitudes and judgments about the value that market orientation has for the corporation, for market-orientated companies are driven by customer and market needs rather than by the dictates of technology (Atuahene-Gima & Ko, 2001).

The organizational shift from a traditional technology focus to more of a market orientation can be understood as an organizational innovation that touches deeply on established routines, communication, and cooperative practices of the entire workforce. Such a change elicits reluctance and often resistance, responses observable in Katalux as well. The idea of emphasizing a market orientation forces long-standing employees to change their thinking and behavior. In other words, they have to free themselves from established mental models: "A personal mind-set that's been taking shape for years, for decades, now has to be reconciled with the new way of thinking" (Manager, finance division, 2009). Top management has chosen to promote this cultural change throughout the firm. But because market orientation may require a modus operandi different from that of the established technology orientation, employees and even top managers were having trouble adapting. The interviews revealed that it was necessary to introduce mutual coaching and translate management theory into daily life in order to advance the market orientation. The top managers began by starting to coach each other to keep themselves from falling back into traditional routines:

> But we two [extant managers] and both new colleagues are utterly convinced that this is the right way, and we help each other by pointing out "backsliding." We say, "Hey, watch out, that's doing it the old way again. Let's move forward by thinking new." So you see, we monitor each other. (Manager, finance division, 2009)

Table 4.2 *Strategy Orientations of the Employees at Katalux: Responses to the Question* "In my opinion it is more beneficial for Katalux to …"

Response number	Responses as semantic differentials	
	Technology-oriented strategies	Market-oriented strategies
1.	… offer products that are technologically up to date.	… discern new requirements of the market.
2.	… use ambitious technology in the production department.	… satisfy the customer.
3.	… generate technological advantages through patents.	… establish a solid reputation in the market.
4.	… score with products and services of superior technology and quality.	… identify new markets and match the product portfolio to them.

The fast growth of the workforce led us to expect the newer and younger management generation, too, to resist the company's veteran professionals. With a new and controversial organizational orientation having been adopted early by senior managers at Katalux, the company agreed to participate in a network survey of its entire workforce to study the diffusion of this change.

Measures

The dependent variable in our analysis is market orientation. Because technology orientation was the original and dominant philosophy, we choose it as an antipode to the market orientation of each respondent. We measured every respondent's market orientation by means of four questions formulated as semantic differentials (Table 4.2). Each of the four variables contrasts a market-oriented and a technology-oriented statement. The items are taken from previous research either directly or in modified form. The technology-oriented statements 1, 2, and 4 are based on the items used by Zheng Zhou et al. (2005) to measure technology orientation and on Gatignon and Xuereb's (1997) measures, which center on the importance of sophisticated and state-of-the-art technology as indicators of technology orientation. The third statement is taken from Kohli, Jaworski, and Kumar (1993), who also constructed pairs of opposing technology- and market-oriented statements in their item, which read: "Our business plans are driven more by technological advances than by market research" (p. 476). We adapted the market-oriented statements mainly from Kohli et al. and partly also from Zheng Zhou et al.. The fourth market-oriented item acknowledges the results reported by Zheng Zhou et al., which showed that a traditional measurement of market orientation concentrates on the current customer and, hence, on present market structures rather than on new markets. However, our understanding of market orientation included the knowledge about and the response to new markets, so we added this item to our measuring instrument. Every respondent was instructed to choose the statement that best expressed his or her stance as given on a nine-point scale ranging from -4 (*agree with least*) to +4 (*agree with most*). We thereby measured the level of individual market orientation

Table 4.3 The variables in the network survey on employees' strategy orientations and formal and informal relationships within the company

Label	Description
Dependent variable (166 observations)	
Market orientation	Employee's response to the question of how important a market-orientation is as opposed to a technology orientation for the company on a scale from −4 (*strongest agreement with a technology-oriented corporate philosophy*) to +4 (*strongest agreement with a market-oriented philosophy*)
Independent variables	
Distance to the source of market orientation (in formal network)	The shortest geodesic distance from each employee to the promoters of market orientation in the symmetrical formal network (hierarchical relations of subordination and unit affiliation), max method
Distance to the source of market orientation (in informal network)	The shortest geodesic distance from each employee to the promoters of market orientation in the symmetrical knowledge network (max method)
Measures of task similarity	
Corporate functions	Dummy variable, where 0 equals internal functions such as production, R&D, finance, and controlling, and where 1 indicates corporate functions whose tasks involve communications and contacts outside the firm (e.g., customer service, marketing and sales)
External relations	The number of contacts that an employee maintains outside the firm in order to source work-related knowledge
Control variables	
Rank in the corporate hierarchy	Ordinal scale with five levels of hierarchy: CEO, division manager, department manager, unit manager, employee
Age	Year of birth
Length of service	Year of appointment with the Katalux company

as a continuum rather than a dichotomy. For each respondent we averaged the score on these four variables to arrive at an aggregate value for market orientation.

To test the hypotheses about hierarchy and informal communication, we constructed three sets of measures as independent variables (see Table 4.3). The first was distance to sources of market orientation. With our research hypotheses we examined the role of hierarchical versus informal relations of communication, expecting informal relations, not a formal chain of command, to be vital channels of interpersonal conviction. The measures required us (a) to construct a social network of formal and informal relations between all employees in the firm, (b) to identify promoters of market orientation as sources, and (c) to assess the topological distance separating a potential adopter in the informal network from these promoters in the formal network.

Addressing requirement (a), we derived the formal network of relations from the company's organizational chart, including the vertical relations of subordination and the horizontal relations of affiliation with an organizational unit. This picture depicted every employee as being connected to the members of his or her unit and to particular superiors. In addition, we constructed an informal network of relations which portrayed the knowledge exchange between the employees. The conceptualization was derived from responses to a survey item designed to identify bilateral links between employees: "In the past, who among your professional contacts, both inside and outside the company, has helped you solve work-related problems thanks to their experience and expertise?" Because knowledge exchange can be interpreted as a gift that endures only on the basis of reciprocity (Ferrary, 2003), we ignored the direction of knowledge flow in the exchanges.

To meet requirement (b), we identified seven employees whose responses reflected the maximum level of market orientation. Triangulating these views with input from our interviews, we confirmed that these seven employees were promoters of organizational innovation. For requirement (c) we measured the distance between any employee and the seven promoters of market orientation as the shortest geodesic distance in each of the two networks, formal and informal. This operationalization yielded two variables for each employee: the distance from innovation promoters in the formal hierarchical network of authority and unit membership, and the distance from innovation promoters in the informal knowledge network.

Second, and apart from distance to innovation promoters in each of the two networks, we used two measures—corporate functions and external relations—to represent task similarity with the innovation of market orientation. In terms of corporate function, hypothesis 3 suggests that employees will be more likely to adopt than to resist the innovation of market orientation if they work in market-oriented functions. We therefore defined a dummy variable where market-oriented departments (e.g., Marketing and Customer Service) equaled one and where internally oriented departments (e.g., Finance, Production, and R&D) equaled zero. External relations, the second variable used to capture task similarity with the innovation, were tallied as the number of knowledge relations an employee had outside Katalux. The more an employee drew knowledge from outside the organization, the more we expected that person to follow a market orientation.

Third, we included three control variables: rank in the corporate hierarchy, age, and length of service. The logic behind choosing the first of these variables was that our analysis had to do with the diffusion of top-down innovation promoted by senior management, so we expected the level that an employee had in the company hierarchy to affect that person's market orientation positively. This variable was constructed as a five-point scale of hierarchical position ranging from CEO (value 5) to employees without authority (value 1). The variable for the age of each employee and the one for each employee's length of service were intended to account for differences in adoption that were attributable to experience, habituation, and imprinted practices.

Location and Distribution of Market Orientation

The descriptive analysis of the survey responses conveys that the overall distribution of individual orientations across the entire firm (mean = .53; median = .00) proves to be balanced between the two extremes of technology and market orientation.

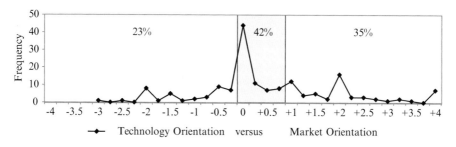

Fig. 4.1 Distribution of ratings indicating the employees' strategy orientation on a scale ranging from −4 (*Total Technology Orientation*) to +4 (*Total Market Orientation*)

Table 4.4 Distribution of market orientation, by organizational unit

Unit	Mean	Median	n	SD
Customer service	0.65	0.50	22	1.21
Production and R&D	0.36	0.00	80	1.49
Marketing and sales	0.75	0.25	27	1.34
Finance and controlling	0.33	0.00	25	1.04
Strategy and corporate development	3.50	3.50	2	0.71
Quality management	1.17	1.37	6	1.09
CEO	1.00	1.00	4	2.58
Total	0.55	0.25	166	1.41

Figure 4.1 presents the distribution of responses across the four semantic differentials from which the general value was aggregated. The distribution suggests a division into three groups of employees. Each of the four distributions has at least three modes in which the highest frequencies of responses tend toward either a technology orientation or balanced attitudes or toward market orientation. About 42 % of the employees reported balanced attitudes, that is, no clear preferences between technology and market orientation. This group in Fig. 4.1 is represented in the center, between the values 0 and 1. The second group (23 % of the employees) is moderately (−.25) to strongly (−3) technology oriented, and the third group (35 %) is clearly market oriented (+1 to +4).

Analysis of the distribution supports the plausible expectation that individual orientations are somewhat affected by functional requirements within the organizational units of the firm. Katalux is divided into six organizational divisions totaling 22 departments. Ten departments constitute part of the Production and R&D divisions. The Marketing and Sales division comprises five departments; Controlling, another five. The Customer Service division contains two departments. The remaining divisions operate without additional subunits. In most of Katalux's divisions, the departments are the lowest organizational entity. Only the largest division (Production) has a department with third-level organizational units, which are called groups.

Table 4.4 shows the number of responses from each division and lists the average scores pertaining to market orientation among the members in those divisions.

Table 4.5 Distribution of market orientation, by organizational hierarchy

Hierarchy	Mean	Median	*n*	*SD*
CEO	0.00	0.00	1	
Division managers	3.30	3.25	5	0.54
Department managers	0.91	0.25	16	1.87
Unit managers	−0.21	0.00	7	0.85
Employees	0.45	0.00	137	1.29
Total	0.54	0.25	166	1.41

The Strategy and Corporate Development division was a key promoter of a new model of market orientation and reported the most definite orientation to the market. The CEO and the members of the Executive Board likewise approved of this new perspective, albeit more moderately. The divisions for Quality Management, Marketing and Sales, and Customer Service exhibited moderate average market orientation, a response that seems plausible given the primarily functional emphasis that these parts of the organization place on existing and potentially new customers. The divisions most characterized by an internal preoccupation with production and operations yielded the lowest scores on market orientation. Although this outcome, too, seems plausible on aggregate, the large difference in the number of responses and the difference in standard deviations from the mean indicate that individual attitudes in general may have diverged considerably from affiliation with an organizational unit.

Because the process of changing the company's orientation from technology to the market was induced by the company's Strategy and Corporate Development division and approved and promoted by senior management, it is instructive to explore the degree to which the distribution reflects the workforce's ranking in the corporate hierarchy (Table 4.5). Whereas the manager-owner (CEO) of the company reports a balanced view on market orientation, the analysis confirms that market orientation is more pronounced among members of Katalux's top management than at any other level in the company. However, of the seven promoters who reported the greatest degree of market orientation, four were division or department managers; the other three promoters were regular employees without personnel responsibility. This discovery indicates that the strength of individual market orientation need not be fully determined solely by hierarchy and that the diffusion of organizational innovation need not be hierarchical in nature.

Diffusion of Market Orientation: Command or Conviction?

The analysis of the distribution of market orientation across the organization illustrates that the company's change to focusing on the market instead of technology had started with senior management and that most promoters of that shift belonged to that circle of persons. Knowing that this innovation was located in that part of the hierarchy, we used a set of regression models (see Table 4.6) to test our hypotheses about the diffusion of market orientation. These analyses

Table 4.6 Multivariate regression analysis of individuals' market orientation as a dependent variable

Variables	Model 1	Model 2	Model 3	Model 4	Model 5
Intercept	17.698***	18.401***	18.801***	−1.948***	17.687***
Distance to promoters (formal network)	−0.209**				−0.138
Distance to promoters (informal network)		−0.903***			−0.661**
Task similarity					
Corporate functions			0.483*		−0.411
External contacts				0.134**	0.079
Control variables					
Hierarchy	0.383**	0.203	0.392**	0.246	0.139
Age	−0.008	−0.008	0.000	−0.000	−0.010
Service length	−0.001	−0.000	0.002	0.004	0.002
R^2	0.099	0.185	0.083	0.105	0.232
(Adjusted R^2)	(0.071)	(0.162)	(0.055)	(0.077)	(0.194)
p	0.006	0.000	0.013	0.008	0.001

$*p<.05. **p<.01. ***p<.001$. 10,000 permutations, 166 cases

help discern and assess the mechanisms governing adoption of a controversial organizational innovation.

Models 1–4 display the regressions of the individual independent variables, including the control variables on the dependent variable called market orientation. In the following paragraphs we examine the individual effects of these variables before discussing the results from model 5, which is a combined multivariate version that integrates the individual effects.

Models 1 and 2 refer to the core arguments about the diffusion of market orientation. Based on the conceptual discussion in the second section of this chapter, our first hypothesis was that an organizational innovation such as market orientation addresses the modus operandi of an entire organization and therefore requires an evolutionary process of interpersonal conviction through informal communicational relations rather than a hierarchical process of downward command and upward compliance.

In hypothesis 1 we posited that the social proximity of the employees and an organizational innovation's promoters in the formal network of authority relations was unrelated to adoption. In model 1, however, formal relations of vertical authority and horizontal affiliation are weakly correlated with market orientation. Model 2 reveals a negative and highly significant association between the distances that adopters in the informal knowledge network have to the promoters of the innovation. The individual associations of these diffusion networks hold even when differences in age, length of service, and hierarchical status are taken into account. The implication is that age and length of service are not intra-corporate barriers to adopting a market orientation. Model 2 confirms hypothesis 2, which posits that the likelihood of corporate members' adoption of an organizational innovation increases with the social proximity those members have to innovation promoters in informal relations of knowledge exchange. Although model 1 seems to contradict our hypothesis, the combined multivariate model (5) demonstrates that the formal network of authority relations, when controlled for all other variables, no longer has significant impact on adoption.

Models 3 and 4 bear out hypothesis 3 and illustrate that employees who are relatively exposed to the market side of the business are more likely to adopt a market orientation than their less-exposed fellow employees are. Model 3 shows that employees working in business functions related to marketing, sales, and customers adopted a stronger market orientation than did those employees working in rather internally focused functions, such as Production, R&D, and Finance and Controlling. Model 4 further substantiates the association between business tasks and market orientation: Employees with a host of external contacts are more conducive to a market-oriented perspective than employees without such contacts are. This association appears evident because the search for work-related knowledge outside the organization is an indicator of an external orientation that fosters an employee's responsiveness to the market.

Note, however, that hypothesis 3 is challenged by model 5. This multivariate model shows that most of the individual effects on market orientation—including corporate functions (model 3) and external contacts (model 4), which corroborate hypothesis 3—become insignificant when combined. There remains just one significant predictor: distance to promoters in the knowledge network. Distance to promoters of organizational innovation leverages the combined model to account for 19 % of the variations in individual market orientation. Moreover, the association between the formal network and adoption of organizational innovation no longer exists. In other words, model 5 confirms that organizational change in Katalux depended on conversation and conviction rather than on command, and on informal and voluntary rather than on formal and mandatory social relations. Each of the 7 innovation promoters was identified by an average of 22 employees as important knowledge sources. This high figure, compared to the overall average of 7 contacts, demonstrates the prestige that innovation promoters enjoyed as knowledge sources and confirms our argument that organizational innovation is diffused by informal contact rather than by hierarchical fiat. Katalux employees were more likely to adopt than to resist a market-oriented perspective on their work if they were close to an innovation promoter through informal knowledge exchange—irrespective of their distance to that promoter in the formal corporate network and no matter what their cooperate function, number of external contacts, hierarchical status, age, and length of service was.

Discussion and Conclusion

This chapter has offered a new way of viewing change in corporate culture, namely, as the diffusion of controversial organizational innovations. We have analyzed the early stages of diffusion of a top-down organizational change in a medium-sized ophthalmological engineering company in southern Germany. Using the mixed methodology of situational organizational network analysis (Glückler & Hammer, 2012), we conducted interviews with managers and employees and ran a network survey of the firm's entire workforce. Because our analysis rested on a survey with "one time point" (Valente, 2005, p. 106), we were not able to observe the diffusion of market orientation as a longitudinal process. Instead, we observed the profiles of individual attitudes as degrees of convergence toward market orientation and interpreted this convergence as the actual pattern of diffusion. The empirical data are valid and reliable because our survey covers 80 % of the entire organization and because our questionnaire was triangulated with qualitative interviews with employees and managers.

Our empirical social network analysis of formal and informal relations between the employees of the firm suggests that direct informal contact rather than formal hierarchical command structures are conducive to the diffusion of a controversial organizational innovation. Whereas prior work has emphasized the importance of hierarchy to promote and follow through on management decisions in organizations, we have argued that such change brought about by hierarchal command may be insufficient when it is controversial and when change is so profound as to concern individual routines, orientations, and conventions of communication and cooperation. As our case study illustrates, such changes can be regarded as a process of implementing an organizational innovation. We identified a shift toward a new corporate practice (market orientation). Although it was imposed top-down by the management, we were able to demonstrate that hierarchical and formal channels had almost no effect on the *diffusion* of such an innovation. Instead, the convergence toward market orientation increased with the social proximity of employees to the strongest promoters of change in the informal knowledge network. This finding contradicts Daft's (1978) assertion that hierarchical structures are the ones best suited to supporting the diffusion of administrative innovations, even when those innovations are imposed by senior management. Our results are consistent with others from research on market orientation and cast doubt on the effectiveness of formal instruments to push market orientation throughout an organization (e.g., Jaworski & Kohli, 1993; Johnson-Cramer et al., 2007; Mohrman et al., 2003).

Our study also has implications for management. Formal authority may not be sufficient to promote profound change in an organization. Whenever the intended change of mental models, new organizational practices, or organizational cultures encounters reluctance, resistance, and controversy, the promotion of such change will depend crucially on dialogue and conviction rather than authority and command. Managers should understand and respect the realities of informal intraorganizational communication and social relations, which often operate as a short cut in corporate communication and bridge between divisions and departments. Because organizational change diffuses through dialogue and contagion rather than through hierarchical command, a great deal of time, attention, and empathy are needed to inform and convince people of the merits of new innovations and to exchange knowledge about them. Our study demonstrates just how useful informal networks of knowledge exchange are for performing various services within an organization. Not only do these networks mobilize knowledge and shape solutions to work-related problems, they also serve as channels for the diffusion of corporate culture.

References

Agócs, C. (1997). Institutionalized resistance to organizational change: Denial, inaction and repression. *Journal of Business Ethics, 16*, 917–931.

Akrich, M., Callon, M., Latour, B., & Monaghan, A. (2002). The key to success in innovation, part I: The art of interessement. *International Journal of Innovation Management, 6*, 187–206.

Atuahene-Gima, K., & Ko, A. (2001). An empirical investigation of the effect of market orientation and entrepreneurship orientation: Alignment on product innovation. *Organization Science, 12*, 54–74.

Becker, M. H. (1970). Sociometric location and innovativeness: Reformulation and extension of the diffusion model. *American Sociological Review, 35*, 267–282.

Berthoin Antal, A., Krebsbach-Gnath, C., & Dierkes, M. (2004). Hoechst challenges received wisdom on organizational learning. *Journal of Learning and Intellectual Capital, 1*(1), 37–60.

Borgatti, S. P., Everett, M. G., & Freeman, L. (2002). *Ucinet 6 for Windows*. Harvard, MA: Analytic Technologies.

Brand, A. (1998). Knowledge management and innovation at 3M. *Journal of Knowledge Management, 2*(1), 17–22.

Burt, R. S. (1992). *Structural holes: The social structure of competition*. Cambridge, MA: Harvard University Press.

Burt, R. S. (1997). A note on social capital and network content. *Social Networks, 19*, 355–373.

Chesbrough, H. (2003). Managing your false negatives. *Harvard Management Update, 8*(8), 3–4.

Cusumano, M. A., Mylonadis, Y., & Rosenbloom, R. S. (1992). Strategic maneuvering and mass-market dynamics: The triumph of VHS over Beta. *The Business History Review, 66*, 51–94.

Daft, R. L. (1978). A dual-core model of organizational innovation. *The Academy of Management Journal, 21*, 193–210.

Deshpandé, R., Farley, J. U., & Webster, F. E., Jr. (1993). Corporate culture, customer orientation, and innovativeness in Japanese firms: A quadrad analysis. *Journal of Marketing, 57*(1), 23–37.

Fagerberg, J. (2005). Innovation: A guide to the literature. In J. Fagerberg, D. Mowery, & R. R. Nelson (Eds.), *The Oxford handbook of innovation* (pp. 1–26). Oxford, UK: Oxford University Press.

Ferrary, M. (2003). The gift exchange in the social networks of Silicon Valley. *California Management Review, 45*(4), 120–138.

Gatignon, H., & Xuereb, J.-M. (1997). Strategic orientation of the firm and new product performance. *Journal of Marketing Research, 34*, 77–90.

Giddens, A. (1984). *The constitution of society: Outline of the theory of structuration*. Cambridge, UK: Polity Press.

Glückler, J. (2007). Economic geography and the evolution of networks. *Journal of Economic Geography, 7*, 619–634.

Glückler, J. (2010). The creation and diffusion of controversial innovations in the organizational periphery. *SPACES online* (Vol. 8, Issue 2008–06). Retrieved from http://www.spaces-online.uni-hd.de/include/SPACES%202010-06%20Glueckler.pdf

Glückler, J., & Hammer, I. (2012). Situative Organisatorische Netzwerkanalyse [Situational organizational network analysis]. In J. Glückler, W. Dehning, M. Janneck, & T. Armbrüster (Eds.), *Unternehmensnetzwerke: Architekturen, Strukturen und Strategien* (pp. 73–93). Heidelberg, Germany: Springer Gabler.

Granovetter, M. (1973). The strength of weak ties. *The American Journal of Sociology, 78*, 1360–1380.

Hannan, M. T., Baron, J. N., Hsu, G., & Koçak, Ö. (2006). Organizational identities and the hazard of change. *Industrial and Corporate Change, 15*, 755–784.

Hannan, M. T., & Freeman, J. (1984). Structural inertia and organizational change. *American Sociological Review, 49*, 165–182.

Hornschild, K., & Weiss, J.-P. (2005). Medizintechnik in Deutschland: Auch in Zukunft dynamisches Wachstum? [Medical technology in Germany: Dynamic growth in the future, too?] *Wochenbericht: Wirtschaft Politik Wissenschaft, 72*, 683–697. Retrieved from http://www.diw.de/documents/publikationen/73/diw_01.c.43818.de/05-46-1.pdf

Jaworski, B. J., & Kohli, A. K. (1993). Market orientation: Antecedents and consequences. *Journal of Marketing, 57*(3), 53–70.
Jick, T. D. (1979). Mixing qualitative and quantitative methods: Triangulation in action. *Administrative Science Quarterly, 24,* 602–611.
Johnson-Cramer, M., Parise, S., & Cross, R. (2007). Managing change through networks and values: How a relational view of culture can facilitate large scale change. *California Management Review, 49*(3), 85–109.
Kohli, A. K., & Jaworski, B. J. (1990). Market orientation: The construct, research propositions, and managerial implications. *Journal of Marketing, 54*(2), 1–18.
Kohli, A. K., Jaworski, B. J., & Kumar, A. (1993). MARKOR: A measure of market orientation. *Journal of Marketing Research, 30,* 467–477.
Krackhardt, D. (1997). Organizational viscosity and diffusion of controversial innovations. *Journal of Mathematical Sociology, 22,* 177–199.
Martin, R., & Sunley, P. (2006). Path dependence and regional economic evolution. *Journal of Economic Geography, 6,* 395–437. doi:10.1093/jeg/lbl012.
McGrath, C., & Krackhardt, D. (2003). Network conditions for organizational change. *The Journal of Applied Behavioral Science, 39,* 324–336.
Miles, M. B., & Huberman, A. M. (1994). *Qualitative data analysis: A source book of new methods.* Beverly Hills, CA: Sage.
Mitchell, J. C. (1969). The concept and use of social networks. In J. C. Mitchell (Ed.), *Social networks in urban situations. Analyses of personal relationships in Central African towns* (pp. 1–50). Manchester, UK: Manchester University Press.
Mohrman, S. A., Tenkasi, R. V., & Mohrman, A. M., Jr. (2003). The role of networks in fundamental organizational change: A grounded analysis. *Journal of Applied Behavioral Science, 39,* 301–323.
Narver, J. C., & Slater, S. F. (1990). The effect of a market orientation on business profitability. *Journal of Marketing, 54*(4), 20–35.
Narver, J. C., Slater, S. F., & Tietje, B. (1998). Creating a market orientation. *Journal of Market-Focused Management, 2,* 241–255.
OECD. (2005). *Oslo Manual: Guidelines for collecting and interpreting innovation data in statistical office of the European Communities* (3rd ed.). Paris: OECD.
Setterfield, M. (1993). A model of institutional hysteresis. *Journal of Economic Issues, 27,* 755–774.
Sieber, S. D. (1973). The integration of fieldwork and survey methods. *The American Journal of Sociology, 78,* 1335–1359.
Slater, S. F., & Narver, J. C. (1999). Market-oriented is more than being customer-led. *Strategic Management Journal, 20,* 1165–1168.
Stevenson, W. B., & Greenberg, D. (2000). Agency and social networks: Strategies of action in a social structure of position, opposition, and opportunity. *Administrative Science Quarterly, 45,* 651–678.
Susman, G. I., & Evered, R. D. (1978). An assessment of the scientific merits of action research. *Administrative Science Quarterly, 23,* 582–603.
Valente, T. W. (2005). Network models and methods for studying the diffusion of innovations. In P. J. Carrington, J. Scott, & S. Wasserman (Eds.), *Models and methods in social network analysis* (pp. 98–116). New York: Cambridge University Press.
Weimann, G. (1982). On the importance of marginality: One more step into the two-step flow of communication. *American Sociological Review, 47,* 764–773.
Zheng Zhou, K., Yim, C. K., & Tse, D. K. (2005). The effects of strategic orientations on technology- and market-based breakthrough innovations. *Journal of Marketing, 69*(2), 42–60.

Collaboration and Knowledge Gains in Organizations

5

Wolfgang Scholl

With the transformation of modern western societies from industrial economies into knowledge economies since the mid-twentieth century, it stands to reason in the twenty-first century that knowledge gains will assume more importance than ever in the handling of political, economic, and private issues of every kind. Indeed, the amount of new knowledge produced is presently doubling every few years, expanding the growth of knowledge exponentially. However, this explosion in the range and types of available knowledge also poses challenges. For one thing, the historical development from primary to secondary and tertiary education and its extension to life-long learning has not kept pace with the ever-widening gap between individual and collective knowledge. That disparity is only partly bridge-able by collaborative knowledge work on confined tasks. For another thing, such collaborative work needs to be organized into increasingly complex tasks if they are to be effective. Scientific and technical developments occur primarily in organizations such as research and university institutes with their workgroups and networks or in enterprises that connect R&D groups with production, controlling, finance, marketing, and sales departments as well as with partners in other firms and in universities. Their efforts are paralleled by those of public and nongovernmental organizations busy coping with the consequences of the resulting changes in life circumstances and trying to improve their understanding of these processes by conceptualizing them in ways that can reasonably guide the production of new structures, regulations, and assistance for the affected groups of people. In other words, acquiring and applying knowledge is predominantly an organized collaborative endeavor in which individual information-processing is constantly intertwined with interpersonal, organizational, and medial communication.

W. Scholl (✉)
Sozial- und Organisationspsychologie & Ingenieurpsychologie,
Humboldt-Universität zu Berlin, Wolfgang Köhler–Haus,
Rudower Chaussee 18, D-12489, Berlin, Germany
e-mail: schollwo@cms.hu-berlin.de

A. Berthoin Antal et al. (eds.), *Learning Organizations: Extending the Field*,
Knowledge and Space 6, DOI 10.1007/978-94-007-7220-5_5,
© Springer Science+Business Media Dordrecht 2014

This sketch of a worldwide historical development calls for analyses that can shed additional light on basic problematic facets of collaborative knowledge acquisition and help people deal with these problems more adequately than without such analyses. I take a general view in this chapter by exploring the negative side of knowledge acquisition, namely, recognizable errors and failures. The multiplicity of information, shaded by differing opinions, interests, and belief systems, breeds "intelligence failures" or "information pathologies" (Wilensky, 1967), which may entail unwelcome outcomes. From this perspective one can consider information pathologies to be an inverse concept of the social production and application of valid knowledge. In an attempt to assess information pathologies and their consequences for the success of innovations, my research team and I conducted the following study, probably the first systematic study in this field.

Conceptual and Theoretical Assumptions

Wilensky (1967) used the term *information pathologies* synonymously with the term *intelligence failures* in order to comprise the various deficiencies and inadequacies of organizational information-processing. High-quality information, he asserted, should be clear, timely, reliable, valid, adequate, and wide-ranging. To Wilensky, an information pathology or intelligence failure therefore meant "the inability to muster the intelligence needed for successful pursuit of organizational goals" (pp. viii–ix). Yet Wilensky's general approach of trying to detect *all* forms of avoidable intelligence failures was not followed up. Instead, various rather specific phenomena became attractive as domains of scientific inquiry, including information overload (e.g., Driver & Streufert, 1969), politically motivated communication bias (Pettigrew, 1973), biases in upward communication (e.g., Jablin, 1979), groupthink (e.g., Janis, 1982), self-serving information-processing (e.g., Brockner et al., 1986), noncommunication of unshared information (Stasser & Titus, 1987), and productivity losses in groups (e.g., Diehl & Stroebe, 1991). By contrast, taking a bird's-eye view like Wilensky's, looking at the different forms of information pathologies together, should lead to more general insights into the processes and impacts of gaining knowledge.

Wilensky (1967) did not formally define information pathologies; instead, he described them with examples.

> Sources of failure are legion: even if the initial message is accurate, clear, timely, and relevant, it may be translated, condensed, or completely blocked by personnel standing between the sender and the intended receiver; it may get through in distorted form. If the receiver is in a position to use the message, he may screen it out because it does not fit his preconceptions, because it has come through a suspicious or poorly-regarded channel, because it is embedded in piles of inaccurate or useless messages (excessive noise in the channel), or, simply, because too many messages are transmitted to him (information overload). (p. 41)

But how does one determine what is and is not an information pathology? What are the measurable criteria? Because the information-processing capacity of individuals and organizations and, therefore, human rationality itself is bounded (Sen, 1977; Simon, 1957; Tversky & Kahneman, 1990), the utopian ideal of perfect rationality—as understood in economic science—should not be taken as a yardstick for the assessment of information pathologies. For instance, if not all alternatives are explored, or if not all available information is acted on, these omissions do not necessarily constitute information pathologies. Instead, I propose that

> information pathologies [be] defined as avoidable failures of distributed information processing, that is, decision-relevant information that is *producible* is not produced, or that is *procurable* is not procured, or that is *transmissible* is not (accurately) transmitted, or that is *applicable* is not (accurately) applied in the decision-making process. (Scholl, 1999, p. 103)

This definition leads to measurable comparisons with other actors (see the next section), and it is more reasonable than the concept of economic rationality, by which measurements would have the problem of ascertaining any instance without biases and errors.

The basic hypothesis states that information pathologies are detrimental to the success of any action—meaning, in this study, innovation processes (hypothesis 1)—because valid knowledge is a precondition of successful action and because information pathologies can be seen as an inverse concept of gaining valid knowledge.

What are the conceptual assumptions about the likely causes of information pathologies? Wilensky (1967, pp. 42–74) saw the roots of failure in (a) steep hierarchy, (b) overspecialization and rivalry, (c) strong centralization, and (d) erroneous doctrines of intelligence. The first three of these factors are organizational properties that seem to be conducive to such failures, but they do not seem to be the causes themselves. The roots of information pathologies probably lie deeper in basic aspects of the relationship between the involved actors and in characteristics of the participants. Relationships are characterized by two primary dimensions: Affiliation (friendliness–hostility) and power (dominance–submissiveness) (Foa, 1961; Kiesler, 1983; Scholl, 2013; Wish, Deutsch, & Kaplan, 1976). The second root of failure as identified by Wilensky, overspecialization and rivalry (see b, above), seems to be based on problems with the affiliation aspect. Because communication, mutual understanding, and consensus formation are important prerequisites for gaining knowledge, any kind of affiliation problem is likely to have negative effects, that is, to breed information pathologies. The first and third roots of failure as identified by Wilensky, a steep hierarchy and strong centralization, depict problems with power relationships. Power, a potential, may be exercised in line with the interests of less powerful people, a use called *promotive control* (as exemplified by the giving of advice or practical support), or against the interests of the other(s), a use called *restrictive control* (as exemplified by physical or mental violation or by ruthless command) (Scholl, 1999; for similar distinctions see Etzioni, 1968, and Hollander, 1985). Regarding these two quite different "faces" of exerting power, information pathologies can be expected primarily from the resort to restrictive control, for attention is diverted from task-oriented effort to calculations about how to best prevail over the other(s) or at least to protect oneself. This hypothesis coincides with failures resulting from a steep hierarchy and from strong centralization, because relatively large power differences tend to foster misuse, meaning the use of power as restrictive control (Kipnis, 1976; Mitchell, Hopper, Daniels, Falvy, & Ferris, 1998). In other words, these two hypotheses about the causes of information pathologies are formulated at a level lower than that of organizational phenomena and are thus applicable beyond that realm. Negative affiliation (hypothesis 2) and restrictive control (hypothesis 3) are likely to breed information pathologies. To put it differently, they hinder appropriate gains in knowledge.

Wilensky (1967), because of his structural perspective on organizations, did not investigate individual properties in detail. Yet any collaboration for gaining knowledge includes not only relationships but also the characteristics of the involved individuals. Especially interesting are the individual motives for acquiring knowledge. On the one hand, they include the tendency to look for the best available knowledge, especially when one's actions are expected to have important consequences (Kruglanski, 1989). This motive is sometimes called "striving for mastery" (Smith & Mackie, 2007, p. 17). On the other hand, people have also a built-in cognitive "conservatism" (Smith & Mackie, p. 18). They do not use new information openly but rather look for cognitive consistency (Abelson et al., 1968). Nor do they use new information impartially; they especially prefer information that enhances, or at least protects, their identity and self-esteem (Dauenheimer, Stahlberg, Frey, & Petersen, 2002), including their social identity and, hence, their social group. This proclivity tends to result in "valuing me and mine" (Smith & Mackie, p. 17) more than is justified. One can therefore expect cognitive conservatism and consistency needs (hypothesis 4) as well as identity-oriented reasoning (hypothesis 5) to lead to specific information pathologies.

The fourth root of failure as identified by Wilensky (1967), erroneous doctrines of intelligence, is neither a relationship nor an individual property but an ideological one depending on how large groups or whole cultures think about knowledge. Referring to a naive philosophy that equates correct information with knowledge, Wilensky saw a prominent erroneous doctrine in "all the facts" (p. 62), pointing out that information always needs interpretation in order to become an appropriate understanding of the situation. More generally, any doctrine is misleading if it ignores the fact that all knowledge is socially constructed and is imprinted with the circumstances and interests of the construction process (Berger & Luckmann, 1966; Kuhn, 1970; Smith & Mackie, 2007). Thus, it is likely that information pathologies also result from improper ideas about "knowledge" and the process by which it is constructed (hypothesis 6).

Method

The six hypotheses presented above have been investigated in a field study on innovation and information from 1990 to 1991 (Scholl, 1999, 2004).[1] Innovations are especially well suited for this purpose because information and knowledge acquisition clearly play a visible role, and the success of the innovation (the effectiveness of the process) can be determined better than that of many other complex problems.

Sample

In 16 firms, my team and I conducted a detailed study of 21 successful and 21 unsuccessful cases of innovation. In each firm we chose, together with executives, one or two successful and one or two unsuccessful product and/or process innovations whose difference in success could not be attributed to differing characteristics of the organization or industry but rather to the innovation process itself.

Procedure

The 3–10 most important participants, 5 on average, were intensively interviewed by two researchers so that they could ascertain the innovation process and detect any blind spots in the report of one interviewee by cross-checking the statements of the others as well as the understandings of the interviewers. Each case was written up from these interviews, with special attention to reported and inferable information pathologies. After the interview each participant received a questionnaire measuring the relevant variables in a standardized format. We received 81 % of the questionnaires back, a high response rate. A preliminary version of the questionnaire was administered in the first four cases and then completely revised. In all, the quantitative analysis rests on 142 responses relating to 38 innovations.

Measurement

For the qualitative analysis, the existence and kind of information pathologies were first discussed immediately after the interviews by the two research team members who had conducted them. After the field work the cases were comparatively rated

[1] I owe many thanks to my collaborators Lutz Hoffmann and Hans-Christof Gierschner, who did most of the fieldwork. They were financed by a research grant I received from the German Research Council, support for which I am also very grateful. The theory and calculations in this article are mine. The same data were reported in Scholl (1999, 2004), and some formulations in this chapter are, of course, very similar or even identical to those in Scholl (1999). The theoretical perspective for the interpretation of the data is different, however. In the 1999 article, the focus is on restrictive versus promotive control, whereas this contribution focuses on knowledge gains, measured inversely as information pathologies.

by one team member (Gierschner) and independently by me, the principle investigator. The correlation between our estimates of the number of information pathologies was .76. The ratings were then compared, and the most plausible estimate and labeling was determined. A classification of the information pathologies according to their apparent causes was developed and carried out in keeping with a preliminary theoretical analysis encompassing the hypotheses described above (Scholl, 1990).

In the questionnaire only the interaction variables discussed in the above theory section were rated. On the basis of the following more or less reliable rating blocks, information pathologies were measured as an inverse of knowledge gain:

The more severe the information pathologies are, the more often it is that—

1. information is received incorrectly, incompletely, in biased form, in a roundabout way, belatedly, or not at all (6 items, α [Cronbach's alpha, an index of reliability] = .84).
2. it is difficult to voice deviant opinions to superiors, colleagues, subordinates, or people from other departments (4 items, α = .55).
3. important information is too abstract or too difficult to comprehend (2 items, α = .59).
4. important information is uncertain, rumored, doubtful, or unofficial (4 items, α = .72).
5. an idea is accepted if the risk is played down (1 item).

Combining these five blocks into a total score of information pathologies per respondent yielded a reliability of α = .72. Subsequently, the scores of all respondents per case were averaged, a calculation that yielded a reliability estimate of α = .91 according to the Spearman-Brown formula for quadrupling the test length.

Sympathy, the most immediate affiliation aspect, was measured with 4 items in a semantic differential format (α = .90, rising to .97 according to Spearman-Brown):

In which way did the innovation partner[2] act toward you during the innovation process?

likable 3---2---1---0---1---2---3 *dislikable*
cordial 3---2---1---0---1---2---3 *cold-hearted*
pleasant 3---2---1---0---1---2---3 *unpleasant*
sympathetic 3---2---1---0---1---2---3 *unsympathetic*

Restrictive control was operationalized in the context of conflict management as contending; promotive control was operationalized as problem-solving + yielding (Pruitt & Rubin, 1986). These two variables were introduced as follows:

Innovation processes often give rise to differences of opinion. Please answer the following questions about the process of discussion and decision-making concerning the innovation:

---

[2] Partners were either colleagues, superiors/subordinates, or employees from other departments. The three most important innovation partners were chosen and rated by each respondent. In order to improve the estimate for the innovation project as a whole, the ratings were first averaged across the three partners and then over all respondents from a case.

When differences of opinion occurred, the process of discussion and decision-making was characterized by—

1. commands from superiors.	*not at all*	0	1	2	3	4	5	6	*very often*
2. pressure from "above."	*not at all*	0	1	2	3	4	5	6	*very often*
3. attention to all opinions.	*not at all*	0	1	2	3	4	5	6	*very often*
4. controversial, intense discussion.	*not at all*	0	1	2	3	4	5	6	*very often*
5. mutual convergence.	*not at all*	0	1	2	3	4	5	6	*very often*
6. harmonization of opposite opinions.	*not at all*	0	1	2	3	4	5	6	*very often*

The first two items for restrictive control (contending) focus on hierarchical restriction where the interests of the subordinates are apparently not taken into account ($\alpha = .82$, rising to .95 according to Spearman-Brown). The last four items for promotive control focus on mutuality in discussion and opinion change and are somewhat more heterogeneous ($\alpha = .62$) than the first two items because the problem-solving items (3 and 4) and the yielding items (5 and 6) made up one factor instead of two. Because these two styles both take the interest of the others into account, the combination of the styles suffices for the measurement of promotive control. The implied mutuality ensures that the opinions of all sides and the interests behind them are respected. With the Spearman-Brown formula, the reliability estimate rises to a good value of .87.

Innovation success was determined in a fourfold manner because there is always some ambiguity in the judgments, especially for intermediate innovations. (a) Successful and unsuccessful innovations were chosen by management at the beginning of the investigation in each firm. (b) Economic data were collected for the product innovations, and the interviews were scanned for the status of the process innovations. With one exception these sources corroborated the dichotomous judgment arrived at in the preceding choice. (c) The questionnaire's respondents rated, with high reliability ($\alpha = .90$), several dimensions of success on a seven-point scale:

Drawing conclusions from what you know about the total development, do you ultimately regard the innovation as rather successful or rather unsuccesful? *Please indicate your current overall assessment on the first of the following seven-point scales and then your assessment pertaining to the aspects addressed by the four subsequent scales.*

• Overall, I regard the innovation as…

a total failure	-3	-2	-1	0	+1	+2	+3	*a total success*
	o	o	o	o	o	o	o	

• Measured in terms of economic performance,

a total failure	-3	-2	-1	0	+1	+2	+3	*a total success*
	o	o	o	o	o	o	o	

• Measured in terms of the experience gained,

a total failure	-3	-2	-1	0	+1	+2	+3	*a total success*
	o	o	o	o	o	o	o	

• Measured in terms of the final solution, I think the innovation is…

a total failure	-3	-2	-1	0	+1	+2	+3	*a total success*
	o	o	o	o	o	o	o	

• With regard to the prior expectancies, I think the innovation is…

a total failure	-3	-2	-1	0	+1	+2	+3	*a total success*
	o	o	o	o	o	o	o	

Reliability of the subjective index of success: $\alpha = +.90$

The average of these scales per respondent was taken and averaged again across all respondents per case, yielding a reliability estimate of .97 (Spearman-Brown). Perfect agreement was reached on management judgment, except in three cases, two of which were excluded from the analysis because of ambiguity. The third judgment was reversed because clear economic data (see b, in the preceding paragraph) supported the questionnaire ratings. (d) Separate ratings of complexity, innovativeness, and phase in the life cycle showed no significant differences between successful and unsuccessful innovations. This monitoring guaranteed that these two groups of innovations were comparable; the failures could be attributed neither to higher complexity of the subject compared with the successes, nor to outstanding innovativeness, nor to an earlier phase in the life cycle in which success may not yet have been visible.

Lastly, coordination capability was introduced as another important determinant of innovation success alongside knowledge gains/information pathologies. Coordination capability describes the ability to accomplish complete decision and implementation cycles. It was measured on a seven-point scale with the following two questions, the first pertaining to the decision-making process, the second to the implementation process. The responses to the two questions constituted a reliable index ($\alpha = .73$, yielding an estimate of .92 based on the Spearman-Brown formula).

• How often did the innovation process come to a standstill and run the danger of deadlock without result?	*seldom*	0	1	2	3	4	5	6	*often*
		o	o	o	o	o	o	o	
• Have the decisions taken during the innovation process always been acted on?	*seldom*	0	1	2	3	4	5	6	*often*
		o	o	o	o	o	o	o	

Results

Qualitative Analyses: The Reconstructed Cases

In the qualitative analysis of the innovation case reports, 135 instances of information pathologies were ascertained. Guided by the preceding definition of information pathologies, we classified them as follows:

- 25 instances of producible information that was not produced (e.g., because of interference by others or a lack of basic knowledge)
- 22 instances of procurable information that was not procured (e.g., by foreclosing participation or by failure to seek the experience of others)
- 40 instances of transmissible information that was not at all or not correctly transmitted (e.g., because of insufficient understanding, overly long communication chains, departmental egoism, or manipulative intentions)
- 48 instances of applicable information that was not at all or not correctly processed and applied (e.g., because of interest-bound bias, pressures to conform, or the well-known "not-invented-here" syndrome)

Table 5.1 Main inferred causes of information pathologies

| | Success of innovation | | Percentage of |
Inferred causes	Yes	No	unsuccessful cases
Lack of problem awareness	9	17	65
Wishful thinking	9	15	63
Problems in consensus formation	5	23	82
Exercise of restrictive control	18	32	64
Inadequate assumptions about knowledge	2	5	71
Total	43	92	68

A test of hypothesis 1 gave an average of 2.2 information pathologies for the 20 successful innovations and 4.74 for the 19 innovation failures.[3] These figures reveal not only a statistically significant difference ($t_{(37)}=6.48$; $p<.001$) but also a very strong effect (effect size $d=1.5$).[4] As expected, the more information pathologies occur in an innovation process—that is, the more the processes of gaining knowledge are undermined—the more likely failure becomes. This result underscores the usefulness of looking at the whole range of information pathologies.

The information pathologies showing up in the case reports were embedded in process characteristics that suggested a causal interpretation. In one report, for example, two project managers had to devise and implement a new computerized system for materials' administration but had enormous problems with the resistance and even sabotage by their former superiors. Only when their superiors retired and the two managers themselves were promoted to these positions they could go ahead with the project. They then decided not to involve the operators of the old and the new system in the change process because they again feared insurmountable interference. When the new system was ready for operation, chaos erupted; the system did not function at all. Only as the operators were included in the correction and the debugging process and permitted to contribute their practical day-to-day experiential knowledge did the system gradually function as intended. We concluded from this narrative that (a) the phase of operators' nonparticipation should be classified as an instance of procurable information that was not procured and (b) that the likely cause of that phase could be classified as an example of hierarchical restrictive control because the project managers deliberately used their newly acquired power to plan and implement the system in a nonparticipatory manner. We proceeded in this way to look for the likely causes of all the ascertained information pathologies and condensed the inferred causes into a fivefold classification inspired by Scholl (1990) (see Table 5.1).

The initial two categories of the general classification presented in Table 5.1 refer to information pathologies centered in the individual. (The numerals in the following parentheses give the number of successful and unsuccessful innovations, respectively.)

[3] Of the 42 original cases, 2 had to be excluded because of success ambiguity (see the method section). For one case the interviews were so sparse that no case report was written.
[4] Conventionally, an effect size of >.20 is seen as small; >.50, as medium; and >.80, as large. In the present case the effect size is almost the double of "large."

The first of these inferred causes of information pathologies—lack of problem awareness (9/17)—contained the following subcategories: lack of information search (5/8), insufficient basic knowledge (1/5), blindness from long-term experience (2/2), and three single instances (1/2). The first category seems to have largely been an outcome of cognitive conservatism, a finding consistent with hypothesis 4.

Table 5.1's second category, wishful thinking (9/15), consisted of biased information selection (4/8), devaluation of the knowledge of others (2/4), and overestimations of one's own knowledge that lead to undervaluation of the problems and the knowledge of others (3/3). This category seems to be an outcome of identity-oriented reasoning and is in line with hypothesis 5.

The third and fourth categories of inferred causes of information pathologies as listed in Table 5.1 focus on characteristics of interactions. Problems in forming proper consensus (5/23), which stem from difficulties with affiliation, included departmental egoism (1/7); deficient efforts to understand (2/3); personal antipathy (0/4); an organizational split between information-processing and decision-making (1/3); overly long information chains (0/3); harmonization instead of critical discussion, a groupthink facet (0/2); and two single instances (1/1). These problems of consensus formation reside partly in personal relationships and partly in organizational structures. They substantiate hypothesis 2. Yet the two cases of harmonization point to the fact that positive affiliation may subvert critical discussion; sympathy should allow at least some dissent before the final consensus is arrived at (Scholl, 2005; Schulz-Hardt, Brodbeck, Mojzisch, Kerschreiter, & Frey, 2006). The affiliation problems are conspicuous in Table 5.1 for having the highest percentage of unsuccessful cases (82 %).

The fourth category of inferred causes in Table 5.1, restrictive control (18/32), was the largest. It includes withholding of information in order to favor one's own intentions (8/3 [!]), refusal to allow subordinates to participate (3/7), obstruction of information acquisition (3/6), camouflaging of bad news to superiors (in anticipation of restrictive control from above) (1/5), concealment of goals in order to push nonlegitimated interests (2/4), disregard of differing opinions because of a superior power position (0/3), manipulation of information (0/2), pressures to conform—another facet of groupthink—(0/2), and a nonlegitimated intervention (1/0). These instances are clearly in line with hypothesis 3. Interestingly, one subcategory—withholding of information in order to favor one's own intentions—was found more often in successful innovations (8) than in failing ones (3). This unexpected result is largely due to "conspiratorial" or "bootlegging" innovations pushed by employees to counter the power of top management.

The final category of information pathology's inferred causes presented in Table 5.1 refers to the idea of knowledge itself and to inadequate assumptions about the nature of knowledge (2/5), which included instances in which practical knowledge acquired through experience was played off against theoretical knowledge acquired through university training and vice versa (1/3), the illusion of objectivity despite the interest-bound nature of relevant information in particular (0/2), and a climate of error avoidance that impedes learning by trial and error (1/0). These cases are interesting specifications of hypothesis 6.

Table 5.2 Solidification of information pathologies and its effects on the success of innovations

	Solidification		
Success	Yes	Partial	No
Yes	0	7	13
No	17	1	1

From *Innovation und Information: Wie in Unternehmen neues Wissen produziert wird* [Innovation and information: How new knowledge is produced in enterprises] (p. 43), by W. Scholl, 2004, Göttingen, Germany: Hogrefe. Copyright 2004 by Hogrefe. Adapted with permission

The qualitative analysis allows additional probing insights into the problem of information pathologies. The sheer number of such pathologies is not always the reason that an innovation fails; a few successful innovations exhibit more information pathologies than some of the abortive ones do. As the pathology metaphor suggests, there may sometimes be sufficient immune reactions by which a pathology is offset by a healing process. The example of the two project managers earlier in this section is such a case. Although they underestimated the value of experience and exercised restrictive control to push their intentions, a course that led to chaos when the system went into operation, they learned to appreciate the advantages of participative decision-making and were thus able to correct their primary information pathologies.

If a piece of information is not transmitted by one person, it may be passed on by another. That act may be the simplest illustration of an organizational immune reaction against an information pathology. In other instances, however, the pathologies solidify instead of dissolve. In the innovation cases examined for this study, we found two main categories of solidification. The first was a cessation of information exchange (14 instances) because of an organizational split between information-processing and decision-making, because of insufficient participation by the organization's better informed people, or because people were not dealing with a tacit conflict and avoided discussion of the problem at hand. The second category of solidification of information pathologies was indicated by exchanges of information that remain fruitless (9 instances). This kind of solidification typically results from departmental egoism or conflict displacement. It often drags discussions away from the task and into personalized conflict, with the persons involved never returning to a task-oriented exchange. Some cases of innovation even manifested both categories of solidification. Table 5.2 shows the distribution of innovation cases with and without solidification as well as with partial solidification that was eliminated later in the process, as in the example above. The result of our examination is unequivocal: With solidification of information pathologies, there is no chance that an innovation will succeed; without solidification, there is a high probability of its success. The good news is that dissolving emergent solidification does not greatly diminish the prospects for the innovation's success.

Quantitative Analyses: The Questionnaire

Having ensured high reliability and at least good face validity of all the variables in question, as shown above, I tested the hypotheses by using Spearman rank correlations, which are distribution free and are insensitive to outlier values. Of course, correlations cannot substantiate the supposed causal ordering, but correlations that are insignificant or of the opposite sign can falsify the theoretical assumptions.

The first hypothesis states that the extent of knowledge gains, measured in inverse terms as the amount of information pathologies, influences the effectiveness of collaboration, which in our study is defined as innovation success ($0=failure$, $1=success$). The empirical correlation between the two variables came to $r_s=.43$ ($p<.01$, $n=36$), which is consistent with both this hypothesis and the qualitative analysis. The effect is not as strong as in the qualitative analysis, probably because the general questionnaire items could not register the special instances of information pathologies in the same way as the inspection of the case descriptions did.

The second hypothesis implies that antipathy as a core aspect of negative affiliation fosters information pathologies, that is, antipathy hampers mutual understanding and this interference leads to less gain in knowledge. The empirical correlation of $r_s=-.24$ ($p<.05$, $n=36$) is in line with this hypothesis. It also corroborates the qualitative analysis but is apparently a weaker effect, probably because the structural organizational causes of information pathologies are not fully captured by personal sympathy and personal antipathy.

The third hypothesis, which states that restrictive control fosters information pathologies, is corroborated by the correlation $r_s=.42$ ($p<.01$, $n=36$). Promotive control, by contrast, has a negative correlation with information pathologies—$r_s=-.39$ ($p<.01$, $n=36$). If a comparatively low number of information pathologies constitutes a good proxy measure for knowledge gains, then the calculations clearly confirm the very general and, in practical terms, important hypotheses that socially produced knowledge is impeded by restrictive control and stimulated by promotive control. In other words, what is decisive is not power per se but rather the manner of exercising it (for field studies see Scholl, 2007; for experimental results see Scholl & Riedel, 2010). As with the first and second hypothesis, the quantitative result reinforced the qualitative one.

Using one's power against the interests of the other(s) involved, wielding it as restrictive control, is often claimed to be justified by the need for the ability to coordinate. We therefore included that variable in our questionnaire. As assumed in that justification, the ability to coordinate is important for effectiveness; it correlates positively with innovation success ($r_s=.45$; $p<.01$, $n=36$). But the objective of this justification is not achieved, for the correlation of restrictive control with coordination capability is not significant ($r_s=-.07$). By contrast, the correlation between promotive control and the ability to coordinate is significant and substantial ($r_s=.45$; $p<.01$, $n=36$).

To check the assumed causal order of the investigated variables, I ran a path analysis, inverting the measure of information pathologies so as to express the growth of knowledge positively. The results confirmed the causal model with a higher than

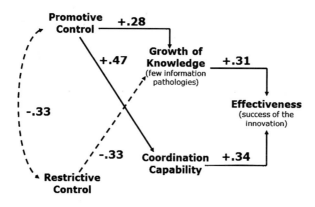

Fig. 5.1 Statistical causal model explaining innovation success at the project level. Path model: $n=36$, $chi^2=5.24$, $df=4$, $p=.26$, $GFI=.94$; →Causal path with path coefficient, Curved, double-headed, arrow denotes a correlation; dotted lines denote negative values

chance probability ($chi^2=5.24$, $df=4$, $p=.26$) and an acceptable goodness of fit ($GFI=.94$). All assumed causal paths were significant (see Fig. 5.1).

The statistical causal analysis confirms in differentiated and profound fashion the qualitative result that restrictive control is the most important cause of information pathologies. One reason for this importance is that restrictive control also has negative side effects on affiliation. The people affected develop antipathy and become less likely to cooperate. The statistical analysis clearly demonstrates that using power promotively instead of restrictively is a superior approach to gaining knowledge, managing the problems of coordination, and being effective.

Discussion and Conclusion

A first critical look at the presented study brings two points to mind: Correlations are open to diverging causal interpretations, and qualitative analyses often induce one to draw definite conclusions from fuzzy material. In particular, it is arguable that the causal ordering of the interaction variables and innovation success might better be changed. It does seem possible that antipathy escalates and restrictive control is exerted when a possible failure is imminent, whereas sympathy and promotive control may prevail if success is more likely than failure. It was at this juncture of uncertainty that the qualitative case histories proved helpful. Sympathy often declined not because of task difficulties but rather because of insufficient cooperativeness (cooperativeness being highly correlated with sympathy). Unsuccessful innovations were largely characterized by political maneuvers in which one party made biased attempts to solve task problems at the expense of the interests of the others concerned and consequently did not integrate the knowledge and experience of those others. By contrast, successful innovations were largely characterized by adaptive problem-solving processes in which the technical aspects of the nascent problems were successively worked through and the diverging interests of the people concerned were considered respectfully and often participatively (see the cases in Scholl, 2004). The path analysis, too, confirmed the assumed causal ordering.

The support for the general theoretical reasoning and the derived hypotheses is therefore strong in our study on innovations, which offers salient examples of how to gain knowledge and ensure effectiveness through collaboration. Empirical examination of a broad spectrum of avoidable errors and failures in the knowledge-gaining process has proven to be a useful scientific strategy. Whereas it seems impossible to track the many instances of small knowledge gains from many diverse innovations or other complex problematic situations, the much rarer cases of apparent information pathologies are much easier to detect, describe, and analyze. Moreover, quantifying the probability of information pathologies by rating typical weaknesses known from literature is probably more differentiated and less biased than asking people how well they communicate and collaborate.

Methodologically, one of this study's strengths is that it combines qualitative and quantitative methods that address the researched phenomena from quite different angles yet come to the same conclusion. Empirically, it is the first systematic study of information pathologies not only to have found plausible examples such as the one by Wilensky (1967), who introduced the concept, but also to have systematically measured and related them to potential causes and consequences.

In the practical sense, information pathologies give distinct guidance on how to improve organized knowledge work. These positive results enabled Hopf (2009), one of my doctoral students, to develop a new, enlarged, and psychometrically better tested questionnaire of information pathologies as a practicable knowledge management tool. It will be especially helpful in large, multinational companies, which are organized as multilevel hierarchies and are therefore prone to excessive use of restrictive control, sometimes even to a degree approaching dictatorship or imperial battles. These enterprises are spatially distributed and thus also highly likely to exhibit several affiliation problems of knowledge production, such as departmental egoism, overly long information chains, and an organizational split between information-processing and decision-making. Lastly, distance diminishes the chance for information deficits to be corrected accidentally as a kind of immune reaction. Studies of these structural aspects should be intensified to continue Wilensky's seminal work.

References

Abelson, R. P., Aronson, E., McGuire, W. J., Newcomb, T. M., Rosenberg, M. J., & Tannenbaum, P. H. (Eds.). (1968). *Theories of cognitive consistency: A sourcebook*. Chicago: Rand McNally.

Berger, P. L., & Luckmann, T. (1966). *The social construction of reality*. Garden City, NY: Doubleday.

Brockner, J., Houser, R., Birnbach, G., Lloyd, K., Deitcher, J., Nathanson, S., et al. (1986). Escalation of commitment to an ineffective course of action: The effect of feedback having negative implications for self-identity. *Administrative Science Quarterly, 31*, 109–126.

Dauenheimer, D., Stahlberg, D., Frey, D., & Petersen, L.-E. (2002). Die Theorie des Selbstwertschutzes und der Selbstwerterhöhung [The theory of self-protection and self-enhancement]. In D. Frey & M. Irle (Eds.), *Theorien der Sozialpsychologie, Band III: Motivations- und Informationsverarbeitungstheorien* (pp. 159–190). Bern, Switzerland: Huber.

Diehl, M., & Stroebe, W. (1991). Productivity loss in idea-generating groups: Tracking down the blocking effect. *Journal of Personality and Social Psychology, 61,* 392–403.

Driver, M. J., & Streufert, S. (1969). Integrative complexity: An approach to individuals and groups as information-processing systems. *Administrative Science Quarterly, 14,* 272–285.

Etzioni, A. (1968). *The active society: A theory of societal and political processes.* New York: The Free Press.

Foa, U. G. (1961). Convergences in the analysis of the structure of interpersonal behavior. *Psychological Review, 68,* 341–353.

Hollander, E. P. (1985). Leadership and power. In G. Lindzey & E. Aronson (Eds.), *Handbook of social psychology* (3rd ed., pp. 485–537). New York: Random House.

Hopf, S. (2009). *Fragebogen zur Identifikation von Wissensbarrieren in Organisationen (WiBa)* [Questionnaire for identifying knowledge barriers in organizations]. Unpublished doctoral dissertation, Humboldt University, Berlin, Germany.

Jablin, F. M. (1979). Superior–subordinate communication: The state of the art. *Psychological Bulletin, 86,* 1201–1222.

Janis, I. L. (1982). *Victims of groupthink: A psychological study of foreign policy decisions and fiascoes* (2nd ed.). Boston: Houghton-Mifflin.

Kiesler, D. J. (1983). The 1982 interpersonal circle: Taxonomy for reciprocity in human transactions. *Psychological Review, 90,* 185–214.

Kipnis, D. (1976). *The powerholders.* Chicago: The University of Chicago Press.

Kruglanski, A. W. (1989). *Lay epistemics and human knowledge: Cognitive and motivational bases.* New York: Plenum.

Kuhn, T. S. (1970). *The structure of scientific revolutions* (2nd ed., with postscript). Chicago: University of Chicago Press.

Mitchell, T. R., Hopper, H., Daniels, D., Falvy, J. G., & Ferris, G. R. (1998). Power, accountability, and inappropriate actions. *Applied Psychology: An International Review, 47,* 497–517.

Pettigrew, A. M. (1973). *The politics of organizational decision-making.* London: Tavistock.

Pruitt, D. G., & Rubin, J. Z. (1986). *Social conflict: Escalation, stalemate, and settlement.* New York: Random House.

Scholl, W. (1990). Die Produktion von Wissen zur Bewältigung komplexer organisatorischer Situationen [The production of knowledge for the management of complex organizational situations]. In R. Fisch & M. Boos (Eds.), *Vom Umgang mit Komplexität in Organisationen* (pp. 107–128). Konstanz, Germany: Universitätsverlag.

Scholl, W. (1999). Restrictive control and information pathologies in organizations. *Journal of Social Issues, 55,* 101–118. doi:10.1111/0022-4537.00107.

Scholl, W. (2005). Grundprobleme der Teamarbeit und ihre Bewältigung: Ein Kausalmodell. [Basic problems of team work and their solution: A causal model]. In M. Högl & H. G. Gemünden (Eds.), *Management von Teams: Theoretische Konzepte und empirische Befunde* (3rd ed., pp. 33–66). Wiesbaden, Germany: Gabler.

Scholl, W. (2007). Das Janus-Gesicht der Macht: Persönliche und gesellschaftliche Konsequenzen Rücksicht nehmender versus rücksichtsloser Einwirkung auf andere [The Janus face of power: Personal and societal consequences of restrictive versus promotive control of others]. In B. Simon (Ed.), *Macht: Zwischen aktiver Gestaltung und Missbrauch* (pp. 27–46). Göttingen, Germany: Hogrefe Verlag.

Scholl, W. (2013). The socio-emotional basis of human interaction and communication: How we construct our social world. *Social Science Information, 52,* 3–33.

Scholl, W. (with Hoffmann, L., & Gierschner, H.-C.). (2004). *Innovation und Information: Wie in Unternehmen neues Wissen produziert wird* [Innovation and information: How new knowledge is produced in enterprises]. Göttingen, Germany: Hogrefe Verlag.

Scholl, W., & Riedel, E. (2010). Using high or low power as promotive or restrictive control— Differential effects on learning and performance. *Social Influence, 5,* 40–58.

Schulz-Hardt, S., Brodbeck, F. C., Mojzisch, A., Kerschreiter, R., & Frey, D. (2006). Group decision making in hidden profile situations: Dissent as a facilitator for decision quality. *Journal of Personality and Social Psychology, 91*, 1080–1093.

Sen, A. K. (1977). Rational fools: A critique of the behavioural foundations of economic theory. *Philosophy and Public Affairs, 6*, 317–344.

Simon, H. A. (1957). *Models of man*. New York: Wiley.

Smith, E. R., & Mackie, D. M. (2007). *Social psychology* (3rd ed.). Philadelphia PA: Psychology Press.

Stasser, G., & Titus, W. (1987). Effects of information load and percentage of shared information on the dissemination of unshared information during group discussion. *Journal of Personality and Social Psychology, 53*, 81–92.

Tversky, A., & Kahneman, D. (Eds.). (1990). *Judgement under uncertainty: Heuristics and biases*. Cambridge, UK: Cambridge University Press.

Wilensky, H. L. (1967). *Organizational intelligence: Knowledge and policy in government and industry*. New York: Basic Books.

Wish, M., Deutsch, M., & Kaplan, S. J. (1976). Perceived dimensions of interpersonal relations. *Journal of Personality and Social Psychology, 33*, 409–420.

Organizing Relational Distance: Innovation as the Management of Sociocultural and Time-Spatial Tensions

6

Oliver Ibert

Innovation is about combining formerly disconnected practices (Stark, 2009) and exploiting cognitive distances (Hautala, 2011; Nooteboom, 2000). Organization scientists and economic geographers, however, have been relatively silent when it comes to theorizing about the spatial consequences of this aspect of innovation. Whereas organization scientists have shown appreciation for spatial issues over the past decade (Kornberger & Clegg, 2003, 2004; Sydow, 2002; Wilson, O'Leary, Metiu, & Quintus, 2008), economic geographers, who, of course, have still greater interest in spatial issues, have so far inquired mainly into the role of physical and relational proximity in innovation (e.g., building trust and institutional safeguards, reducing uncertainty, and establishing a common language). Instances of tension, conflict, and diversity have remained relatively undervalued in geographic accounts of innovation. This chapter straddles the boundary between economic geography and organization science in that the following discussion addresses the extent to which the notion of relational distance can improve the understanding that scholars in these two academic disciplines have of the spatiality of innovation processes.

I start with a review of what is already known about relational distance and posit an operational definition. The relational/physical distinction refers to different qualities of dissimilarity. Physical distance signifies the degree to which coexisting entities come to occupy dissimilar positions in relation to other places, sites, or territories in space (Boschma, 2005). Relational distance contrasts units of analysis in terms of their dissimilar places within systems of cultural norms. Relational distance, in other words, means strangeness in a cultural sense (Schutz, 1964/1976). In this chapter I use the notion of *culture* in a broad sense as a system of shared collective

O. Ibert (✉)
Forschungsabteilung 1 Dynamiken von Wirtschaftsräumen,
Leibniz-Institut für Regionalentwicklung und Strukturplanung e.V. (IRS),
Flakenstraße 28-31, D-15537 Erkner, Germany

Institut für Geographische Wissenschaften [Institute for Geographical Sciences],
Freie Universität Berlin, Malteserstr 74-100, D-12249 Berlin, Germany
e-mail: ibert@irs.net.de

A. Berthoin Antal et al. (eds.), *Learning Organizations: Extending the Field*,
Knowledge and Space 6, DOI 10.1007/978-94-007-7220-5_6,
© Springer Science+Business Media Dordrecht 2014

rules, norms, and conventions that guide the behavior within a group of people (Schoenberger, 1997). The understanding of culture thereby is not restricted to a set of abstract rules; it includes the idea that these rules are incorporated in practical action, contextualized in concrete local situations, and inscribed into material artifacts (Gertler, 1995; Knorr-Cetina, 1999). Relational distance refers to the degree to which people interacting according to dissimilar subsets of cultural rules experience interference from each other's systems of norms and shared beliefs. In this chapter the notion is regarded as fundamental to understanding the generative powers of sociocultural dissonances (Stark, 2009) and to comprehending the unavoidability of conflict in innovation processes.

The following section situates relational distance within current discourses and elaborates an operational definition that highlights both the notion's primarily heuristic function and the aspects of instantiation in social interaction and situatedness in practice. This understanding is then illustrated empirically with an exploratory ethnographic case study on the developmental biography of a scientific device for the marker-free detection of biological molecules (for detailed accounts see Ibert, 2006, 2010). In this case knowledge practices revolve around the relational distance between science and business. The chapter elucidates interactions through which this tension is instantiated and explains the respective knowledge practices in order to show that relational distance is simultaneously tension between divergent norms, rules, and worldviews *and* between divergent practices that evolve differently in physical space. In short, relational distance induces sociocultural and time-spatial tensions. The chapter concludes by pointing out general conceptual implications that such an understanding has for economic geography and organization science.

What Is Relational Distance?

The economic geographic discourse on knowledge creation combines two pivotal dichotomies—relational versus physical and distance versus proximity. Strangely, three of the resulting combinations (physical proximity, distance, and relational proximity) have been probed quite deeply, whereas one (relational distance) has attracted far less notice.

The discourse on localized learning (Malmberg & Maskell, 2002, 2006) scrutinizes the impact of physical proximity on interactive learning. Proximity in space affords interactive learning in the sense that it reduces transaction costs (Scott, 1988). That is, proximity in space makes it easier to initiate and sustain trustful relationships (Morgan, 2004) and to fulfill the functional preconditions for an intensified exchange of tacit knowledge (Maskell & Malmberg, 1999). In a way, physical proximity coproduces relational proximity that is needed for innovation. By contrast, relational distance is examined only in an indirect manner and mainly as a problem for innovation that needs to be reduced or circumvented.

A second line of reasoning about the effects of proximity and distance on knowledge creation focuses on learning across physical distance. Successful knowledge clusters rely on "buzz environments" (Storper & Venables, 2004, p. 365), a term that captures the informal, though intense, local interaction that happens rather in passing among individual professionals within a cluster of colocated firms and organizations (Bathelt & Glückler, 2011, pp. 132–133). However, the most successful clusters are particularly those that also purposefully build up additional "global pipelines" (Bathelt, Malmberg, & Maskell, 2004), a term that denotes selective, highly strategic contacts to the world's leading external partners. These pipelines require constant institutional support, prolonged heavy investment in business travel, and, frequently, continual technical mediation (Bathelt & Glückler, p. 132). Pipelines are examples of relational proximity facilitating collaboration even across physical distance (Amin & Cohendet, 2004). In this strand of thought, relational distance is of subordinate relevance. Within the local buzz, though, fortunate encounters between strangers might turn relational distance into an asset for innovation.

Other scholars diagnose that buzzlike phenomena can also be spatially dispersed (Asheim, Coenen, & Vang, 2007). Asheim et al. (2007) continue to argue that face-to-face interaction is still critical for interactive learning. Such communication need not depend on permanent colocation, however; intermittent co-presence can suffice. Buzzlike phenomena can even be observed in communities that interact primarily in virtual environments (Amin & Roberts, 2008; Wilson et al., 2008). Relational proximity is also seen as the main ingredient of social coherence within spatially dispersed knowledge communities (Grabher, Ibert, & Flohr, 2008). Increased professional mobility (Saxenian, 2006) and cyclically recurring events, such as trade fairs or conferences, give occasion to organize situations of temporary physical proximity. Even though permanent colocation is no longer considered indispensible, physical proximity—realized through temporary co-presence—is still thought to be essential for learning (Bathelt, Maskell, & Malmberg, 2006; Bathelt & Schuldt, 2008; Power & Jansson, 2008). Relational distance is not discussed prominently in these debates.

Another context in which relational distance surfaces as a topic is the internationalization of research and development (R&D) by multinational corporations (Kuemmerle, 1997; Zander, 1999). Multinationals often locate their R&D units next to external sources of knowledge they want to tap into (Florida, 1997). The literature distinguishes two alternative models of how to deal with relational distance in global innovation networks. The "hub model" (Lam, 2003, p. 697) is a centralized approach in which control remains in headquarters and expatriate managers are sent abroad to monitor the local laboratories' work. The "integrated R&D network" (p. 697) model leaves more autonomy to decentralized local research units, which, in turn, become more capable of tapping into local knowledge pools, (e.g., through local recruitment) than is likely with the hub model. Implicitly, the logic underlying the hub model is similar to that developed in the discourse on learning across distance: Relational proximity—in these accounts a coherent internal organizational culture—bridges physical distance. The integrated network model, by contrast, reiterates the logic of the localized learning discourse, according to which the affordances of physical proximity reduce relational distance (meaning, in this chapter, the cultural differences between the multinational corporation's home institutional setting and the local contexts of decentralized R&D units).

Lastly, the contributions of what is known as the French Proximity School (Blanc & Sierra, 1999; Rallet & Torre, 1999; Torre & Gilly, 2000; Torre & Rallet, 2005) cut across the above mentioned discourses. They disentangle the topic of proximity by subdividing it into several dimensions, such as organizational, institutional, social, and cognitive proximity (see Boschma, 2005). This differentiation testifies to the existence of relational distance, albeit again only indirectly. Moreover, these works introduce a problematic differentiation because they use "geographic proximity" (Boschma, p. 69)—the mere metric distance in the physical space—as an analytically distinct dimension. They thereby imply that physical distances have no cultural meaning at all and that cultural differences are completely independent from the physical space.

All in all, these discourses treat relational distance only as a subordinate topic. If anything, relational distance is misrepresented as the mirror image of relational proximity. With relational proximity increasingly being deemed critical for inter-active learning, its opposite, relational distance, gets cast primarily as something that obstructs innovation. This characterization needs reconsideration. First, I propose to see relational distance as a multidimensional notion (Boschma, 2005). Cultural differences can be radically different phenomena. They can, for instance, occur between the world of the arts and that of business (see Chap. 1 by Berthoin Antal, in this volume) or between organizations, such as Microsoft and Apple. I hold that the multidimensionality of relational distance can be conceptually most fruitful for innovation theories when it is used heuristically to delve into the manifold facets of cultural differences. It centers on cultural tensions but permits investigation of these tensions without predefining them. Second, relational distance is a social, interpersonal effect. Relational distance—between the arts and business, for instance—is not consequential per se. It is instantiated only when artists and business people interact. Third, relational distance is enacted in practice. Cultural norms and beliefs are not only abstract rules that guide practical behavior. Culture is always produced and reproduced by practices. It is implicated in what people do (Schoenberger, 1997). Practices are inextricably intertwined with the physical space. They appropriate and create material workarounds (Kirsh, 1996) and are situated at actual sites (Livingstone, 2003).

The last two specifications link the relational with the physical space. Relational distance as enacted in practice means that cultural differences always become manifest in the physical space. However, relational distance as an interactional effect cannot be static in spatial terms because people move through space in order to interact and thereby produce a dynamic spatiality. Accordingly, relational distance is expressed as both a sociocultural and a time-spatial tension (for further discussion see Ibert, 2011).

Method

When relational distance is an effect that occurs in practical interaction, the research design must take this circumstance into account. In this study I examined practices of knowledge creation directly in one concrete case, the innovation biography of a

Table 6.1 An overview of the sample

Interviews			
Format	Settings	Duration	Number
By appointment	Interviewee's office or conference room	45–120 min per interview	8 (8)[a]
During participant observation	Interviewee's workaround, often related to actually ongoing practices	20–40 min per interview	16 (12)
Complete sample	Multisite ethnography encompassing different workarounds at a research institution, a partner's firm and a fair trade	About 16 h of interview material	24 (15)[b]

[a]The number of interviewees is given in parentheses
[b]The sample consisted of 15 interviewees, 5 of whom were interviewed in both formats (by appointment and during participant observation) and are thus counted twice in the respective columns above

sensor system for the detection of biological molecules in small quantities. Because practices are so self-evident to the person using them, it is difficult to inquire about them directly, so I chose an ethnographic method with which to approach this subject (for additional details see Ibert, 2010). As a "professional stranger" (Agar, 1980), the ethnographer is forced to build explicit knowledge about the rules insiders implicitly apply.

First, I conducted daily, full-time participant observation (Spradley, 1980) of the development work on the biosensor system for 2 weeks in September and October 2006. My status as an intern in a publicly funded research organization located in Bonn, Germany, offered me access to diverse practical activities, such as experimental work in the laboratory, formal and informal project meetings, telephone calls with clients and external cooperation partners, in-house training, preparations of meetings with clients, conferences, and marketing travel. Participation also included coffee breaks, lunch hours, debut celebrations, and other occasions of informal gossiping. Participation was usually confined to passive observation. At times, however, I engaged in work routines more intensely, performing simple laboratory routines and attending an in-house training seminar. Occasional observations, such as those at a trade fair in November 2006, expand these daily data. Second, between January 2006 and March 2007 I interviewed 15 persons who either were or had been involved in the biosensor's development (see Table 6.1). I conducted a total of 24 ethnographic interviews (Spradley, 1979), 16 of which took place spontaneously during participant observation and lasted an average of approximately 30 min. These data were supplemented by eight interviews by appointment with key personnel (lasting an average of 1 h).[1]

Interview data were an important source of information during direct observation. They provided the main access to the historical dimension of the work on the biosensor. All in all, the documentation of this device's development history

---

[1] The translations of the following quotations from interviews and field notes are my own.

covered a span of 7 years (from about 2000 to 2006). The story began with the emergence of the initial idea and continued until the termination of the empirical fieldwork for this study. During that time, the idea was always located in the same organization but took shape under different institutional regimes. It sprang from a doctoral project and subsequently unfolded in an externally funded project of applied science. In the final stage, during which the participant observation took place, the idea developed further in an internally funded spin-off project.

According to Spradley (1979), ethnographic interviews are usually asymmetric constellations in which the informant acts as a teacher and the ethnographer as a learner. Spradley adds that ethnographic interviews usually involve a series of conversations during which practically relevant topics can be successively explored in depth. Five members of the development team proved willing to act as informants, and I conducted three to four interviews with each of them.

Divergent Practices, Dynamic Interaction, and Overlapping Spatialities

The concept of relational distance did not serve as a preset category to be tested in subsequent empirical work. It arose instead during the fieldwork and stemmed from the interaction between conceptualization and empirical work. I observed various aspects of relational distance during the participant observations, and the informants explicitly pointed out other ones during the interviews. The idea of relational distance thereby surfaced because of a crucial dissonance frequently commented on by the informants: the contradictory requirements of science and business practices (see also Lam, 2007; Shane, 2004). This dissonance intensified throughout the development history of the device for marker-free detection of biological molecules. Although the innovation's development history commenced in scientific research as a doctoral project and was thus clearly situated in basic research, subsequent funding increasingly accentuated the business orientation, first through an applied-science program and ultimately through internal project support for market entry and the founding of a spin-off.

The argument pertaining to relational distance as elaborated in this chapter starts from this dissonance between science and business. I structure the analysis of the data with the following research questions in mind: (a) How does the relational distance between science and business become manifest in actual practice? (b) To what extent is relational distance enacted in space? To address these questions, I first closely consider different dimensions in which sociocultural tensions between science and business become manifest (object relation, organizational roles; see the next section). In the section on time-spatial tensions, I then elucidate the associated practices (experimental work, knowledge-oriented interaction) and analyze them for ways in which cultural dissonance is expressed in divergent work practices and the conflicting overlaps, uses, and utilizations of the attendant dynamic spaces.

Sociocultural Tensions: Science Versus Business

The divergent requirements of science and business greatly stressed the researchers in the sample. All the participants had a vested interest in the focal device, the biosensor system, but attached different expectations and motivations to it. From a scientist's point of view, it was desirable that the development of the device resembled a process of continuous "unfolding" (Knorr-Cetina, 2001, p. 182). The researchers conducting the biosensor project initially concentrated on developing a microelectronic sensor chip. Later, it became necessary to integrate a fluidic system to convey solute compounds across the sensor chip. The development also required biochemical expertise for studying how biological molecules bind on the sensor chip's reactive area. This problem-driven dynamic of unfolding is much in line with scientists' focus on establishing new knowledge claims and building a scientific reputation.

Business-oriented practices, by contrast, pushed development toward maturation. The primal version of the biosensor was little more than a manually soldered circuit board. The second step of development consolidated the device into a prototype, which served mainly as a vehicle for trying out different applications. The casing was easy to open, and components were easy to plug in and unplug. Eventually, the prototype was replaced by a beta version, which could be handed over to customers. Components in this model were miniaturized and hidden within a casing. From the business point of view, knowledge work was valuable when it helped transform a high-end technology into a marketable commodity (see also Kopytoff, 1986).

All observed researchers and interviewed informants could legitimately refer to two competing role models: either "scientist," representing the scientific logic, or "developer," representing the business logic (field notes; similarly, Schoenberger, 1997). Formally, both roles referred to similar occupations in the organization, and the employees who filled them were classified as "scientific staff" (field notes) as opposed to employees classified as "technical" or "administrative staff." Both the scientist and developer roles required academic qualification (doctoral degree in natural sciences), and both entailed fixed-term contracts. However, scientist and developer differed in how they valued knowledge work. According to the informants, scientists were positively and negatively associated with the curiosity and restless aspiration for newness that are characteristic of scientific creativity. The scientists "always find something new" and were said to be "unwilling to make final development decisions" (field notes). Developers, by contrast, saw knowledge work as valuable as long as it enhanced the usability and marketability of the technology. Instead of inquiring into ever new problems, they reportedly favored "coming to terms" or "bringing things to an end" (field notes). Among developers, knowledge work was oriented to eradicating all technical and other pragmatic obstacles, no matter how trivial they may have appeared to be from a scientific point of view. Despite this personalization (scientist vs. developer), the relational distance between the two roles was not primarily one of interpersonal tension. Almost all respondents regarded both identities as legitimate, though these individuals differed in where they put the emphasis. In practice, the polarity between the roles remained unresolved, and relational distance was partly internalized as loyalty conflict (Grabher & Ibert, 2006).

Time-Spatial Tensions: Divergent Practices and Their Geographies

In practice, the tensions between a scientist's and a developer's identities did not stay abstract. The informants reported that they felt unable to reconcile the divergent requirements, that they were forced to conform to both logics at the same time. However, they were gradually able to shift between them when making decisions or reacting to opportunities. For example, members of the development team were engaged in activities clearly beholden to scientific logic, such as peer-reviewing for scientific journals or preparing presentations for scientific conferences. Simultaneously, the same people also had to deal with customer complaints in lengthy telephone calls and had to attend training courses to prepare to found a firm.

The idea proposed in this chapter about knowledge practices is that their two underlying logics—that of the scientist and that of the developer—interfere not only with the content of work but also with the ways in which researchers use and appropriate space. This section therefore presents an analysis of the time-spatial tensions inherent in relational distance. I first depict experimental practices, inter-action patterns of knowledge work, and their spatiality from the perspective of the scientist, then inspect the developer's practices along the same lines. Lastly, I identify time-spatial conflicts that arise from overlapping geographies of divergent knowledge practices.

Practices in Accordance with the Scientist's Role Model

Test Measurements and Nesting Parallel to Experimental Work That Is in Progress

Test measurements are a type of experimental work in which scientists look into the consequences of modifying a device. During my participant observation, a new chip material, lithium tantalite, was introduced and tested to improve the performance of the device. However, the systemic effects of that alteration were difficult, if not impossible, to predict, for too many variables intervened. To mitigate this problem, scientists set up a stable test environment within which they could experiment with the characteristics of the new material. First, they relied on verified knowledge. For instance, the scientists took measurements during a test routine predetermined by a checklist and used "analytes"—substances to be detected by the sensor system (field notes)—whose properties had already been well documented. Second, the scientists verified additional facts about the new sensor-chip material. One researcher was assigned the task of "characterizing" (field notes) the flow-through properties of every chip of the new generation, a step that sorted out improperly lithographed chips that could later be sources of error. Test measurements on the rest of the chips supplied rich data, including those on the profile of transmission resistance, a scatter band that could be used later to interpret unexpected test results generated by the respective sensor chips. In short, the laboratory was transformed into a context of fixed and controlled variables within which the desired effect of the new material could be isolated and repeatedly observed during performance.

Researchers usually worked on several experiments of that kind, which were called "construction sites" in the jargon of the organization (field notes). Whenever work at one construction site was interrupted, which frequently happened, as when an experimental set-up needed time to stabilize, scientists would hasten to shift their attention to some other construction site in a different lab across the corridor. In other words, parallel experimental workflows that were in progress were nested in one another. Informants explained these patterns with two interrelated scientific rationales, cross-subsidization and scientific reputation.

The sensor system consisted of several sophisticated components: a fluidic system, microelectronics, and a biochemically manipulated chip surface. Each component required specific expertise, but project budgets were seldom generous enough to finance the whole spectrum of expertise for the duration of the work. Nested workflows made project cross-subsidization possible and thereby maintained a more diverse spectrum of expertise within the same research department and overall budget than would otherwise have been the case. For the individual scientists the mutual nesting of experimental workflows gave access to more than one unfolding object, increasing their opportunities to foster their scientific reputations. The number of construction sites a colleague was working on served as a proxy for scientific reputation and responsibility in the lab ("I do not have that many construction sites," "he has many more construction sites"; field notes).

Researcher–Researcher Interaction: Negotiating Technical Interdependencies and Resource Allocation

Interaction within and across the project team was seldom planned long in advance (see also Vinck, 2003). Except for weekly project meetings, there were no fixed and mandatory occasions for communication. Interaction took place in numerous short-term and ad hoc meetings in subgroups instead. Informants explained the rationales of these patterns in terms of technical interdependencies, saying, for instance, that development of the technical components could advance only with the help of dedicated experts and that the whole system would work only if those components meshed well. These interviewees noted that modifications of one component have manifold side-effects on other components within the system. As the originators of the modification cannot oversee all such consequences from their limited point of view, the ramifying effects and side effects of component-modifications have to be disclosed and negotiated collaboratively (Motoyama 2012). The informants believed that spontaneous encounters and short-term appointments were critical to maintaining this interaction pattern. Moreover, these interaction patterns made for highly flexible resource allocation.

As the test measurements illustrated, experiments can be conducted successfully only if they receive the necessary heterogeneous resources. Most resources (the biosensor, computers with the required software installed on them) were shared, and their availability needed to be coordinated. Others, like sensor chips and fluidic cells, were obtained from local infrastructures (clean rooms and fine mechanic workshop). Essential spare parts were ordered from external suppliers. Either way, the corresponding delivery dates had to be taken into account. Furthermore, experiments often required highly qualified preparatory work. For instance, a test measurement could not take place without characterized chips. Time frames had to be considered, and colleagues had to be briefed in a timely manner. This complex resource allocation needed frequent and spontaneous coordination:

> Measurement series and experiments have to be planned long in advance. You have to be sure that the resources will be on hand. That means [seeing to it] that the proper people have enough time and that the required devices are disposable. That's why we always need to come together spontaneously and adjust our time frames in different constellations. (Interviewee, field notes)

Spatiality: Monocentrism

The scientific practices observed in this organization were inherently monocentric. They clearly revolved around its laboratory-office complex. During tentative exploration, researchers stabilized local parameters by connecting specific objects with reliable data. They exploited these local resources to isolate the effects of modifications. Within this center colocalized workplaces yielded the observed interaction patterns among researchers who depended heavily on opportunities for spontaneous meetings. The mutual nesting of workflows that belonged to several construction sites also benefited from colocated workplaces and relied on the local accessibility of parallel experimental work in progress.

These arguments do not suggest that scientific practices have to be local. However, the informants underlined the point that a multilocal environment would cause severe pragmatic problems with coordinating workflows and laboratory resources and with negotiating technical interdependencies on short notice. Nor do these arguments mean that scientific practices are immobile. On the contrary, the local patterns depended on infrastructures (e.g., library, clean rooms, and a precision-engineering workshop) that supplied external documents and the proper equipment locally. Lastly, the local patterns of scientific practice called for personal mobility. Interviewees valued scientific conferences as their main external source of object-related ideas.

Practices in Accordance with the Developer

Application Measurements and Debugging

Application measurements represent a rather different form of experimental work that corresponds rather closely to the developer's identity. The prime aim of application measurements is not to further improve a technology but to demonstrate its practical applicability in a new field. In the observed organization these experiments probed possibilities for detecting new kinds of biological molecules. They were designed to find a way to sensitize the chip's surface to the desired molecules and to demonstrate that the biosensor system produces a signal strong enough (three times more so than the unavoidable noise) to detect these molecules. Like test measurements, application measurements also depend on stability. In this study, however, it was the biosensor that was held constant, whereas analytes and measuring procedures were varied.

Debugging becomes necessary when malfunctions occur in usage. For instance, 2 weeks after receiving the device, a customer complained that the fluidic system had leaked and that emergent fluids had damaged microelectronic parts. The device was returned to the laboratory, where a previously underestimated technical inconsistency became evident. The tubes of the fluidic system have to be resistant against reactive compounds. That resistance, though, also decreases the tubes' adherence to the fluidic cell. To alleviate the problem, researchers conducted a series of tests in which several glues were applied to attach two alternative sorts of tubes to the fluidic cell. After the glues had hardened, their resilience under tension and bending stress was tested.

Researcher–User Interaction: Enrolling Customers and Adapting the Technology to the User's Need

From the developer's point of view, feedback from potential customers and users is vital to making the device marketable as soon as possible. Although the responsible researchers continued their interaction with local researchers, they became more and more involved in direct and repeated customer contact.

According to the informants, the relationship to users is intensified through several successive steps. At trade fairs or during promotion trips to scientific conferences developers have transient contact with numerous potential users, some of whom might show a comparatively deep interest. Responsive users are contacted again to specify their demand. These rather focused interactions usually do not take place face to face. Instead, they entail extensive telephone-calling, the virtual exchange of documents (application notes being the most important), and personal experience with the product. If the potential user shows sustained interest, then developers are invited to visit that site and give a demonstration of the biosensor, usually with a well-established application. Still interested potential users are then invited into the developmental context to conduct their own application measurements. Alternatively, they might send in analytes by mail and have developers report the results back to them. If the customer remains interested, the biosensor system is ultimately transferred to the customer's site. This step often includes personal instruction and training for local workers, usually at the customer's site (Gertler, 1995).

The knowledge practice of debugging is usually triggered by customer complaints and requires constant interaction with the customer. Commonly, a customer complaint results in myriad telephone calls during which the technical experts try to locate the error and figure out how the customer might solve the problem on his or her own. This interaction works best if the developers have experience with the reported error. If the error cannot be identified from a distance, technical staff must be sent to the customer's site to solve the matter. This step usually succeeds if the error derives from improper handling by the customer (von Hippel & Tyre, 1995). More funda-mental problems with the device itself, such as a leaky fluidic system, require addi-tional development work, making it necessary to return the device to the laboratory.

Spatiality: Polycentrism

The developmental knowledge practices described in this chapter rely on informa-tion, expertise, and objects that were not all physically present in a laboratory context. Unlike the monocentric pattern of the scientific practices in the observed organization, the developmental practices there gave rise to a polycentric pattern. First, polycentrism was enacted though blended interaction, whereby developers stayed at their workplaces but connected places via interaction mediated by infor-mation and communications technologies (ICT). However, only a limited share of knowledge that sticks at distant locations could be made accessible by this mode. ICT-mediated interaction was critical primarily for arranging meetings, allocating resources, identifying situated bodies of knowledge, and clarifying problems in general. Second, developers and potential customers traveled in order to meet face to face. For instance, transactions were usually initiated in a series of ever-more intensive face-to-face meetings at different localities.

Polycentrism is not only about temporary co-presence, it is also about choosing and providing the appropriate contexts for interaction. Developers situate face-to-face interaction in places or contexts that afford the desired outcomes. The infor-mants reported that they usually do not let potential users conduct their own application measurements with the biosensor at their own sites. Rather, they prefer to invite interested potential clients into the R&D context because unknown ana-lytes commonly lead to unexpected incidents with the biosensor system. These kinds of problems can be addressed more effectively in the developmental context, where auxiliary equipment, tools, and experienced people are readily at hand.

When the required resources are spread across several sites, it is not possible to situate interaction in the appropriate context just by choosing a proper location. For instance, informants thought it useful to give a presentation at the customer's site if the customer was still relatively indifferent and if interested members of the customer's organization were not yet known personally. At the same time, it is crucial to ensure that a presentation succeeds. Hence, the researchers must take an array of things (e.g., the device, well-known analytes, and spare parts) and personal expertise into the unknown context to minimize the likelihood of failure. This example illustrates that an appropriate context for interaction might not preexist. One may have to create it by importing or otherwise arranging for a set of fitting objects, tools, and people and then coordinating them in time and space.

Time-Spatial Conflicts: Dislocation, Allocation, and Opportunity Costs

The relational distance between science and business is not only a matter of different mindsets and contradictory motivations. It also concerns the ways researchers perform knowledge work (e.g., test measurements vs. application measurements),

Table 6.2 Relational distance between knowledge practices of scientists and developers

Practices	Scientists	Developers
Experimentation	Test measurements: Known analyte, modification of the device	Application measurements: Unknown analytes, stable version of the device
	Nesting of several ongoing experiments: Several epistemic objects at the same location	Debugging according to customer's complaints: Same epistemic object performing at several locations
Interaction	Researcher–researcher: Spontaneous meetings to allocate shared resources and to negotiate technical interdependencies	Researcher–user: Adapting the devices to the customer's interests and idiosyncratic local contexts
Spatiality	Monocentric: Mobility of people and objects is centered on the laboratory	Polycentric: Mobility of people and objects is distributed across the laboratory and manifold places of knowledge application

the people with whom they primarily interact (with other researchers or with clients and potential users), and the manner in which they move through space or use and appropriate locations (see Table 6.2). These observations make it possible to identify time-spatial conflicts induced by relational distance.

A conflict of dislocation occurs when scientists or developers belong to a location that does not offer (or no longer offers) practical activities considered important. Throughout the process of maturation, for instance, the meaning of local routines of researcher–researcher interaction wanes. Researchers who identify with the business logic become strongly oriented to clients. Though physically still present at the laboratory, they become socially less embedded as they become drawn more and more to external places of knowledge use and application. Dislocation brings about the paradox of being close but feeling far (Wilson et al., 2008).

A conflict of knowledge allocation denotes a situation that confronts researchers with divergent requirements of mobilizing and localizing knowledge. For example, scientists can build their scientific reputations best when they are engaged in a multitude of parallel experimental works (construction sites) that are in progress at one locality. Developers of a commodity, by contrast, focus more on one object than on several but keep in mind all locations that turn out to be critical for maturation (von Hippel, 1994). Monocentric practices characterized by deep local engagement are not easy to square with polycentric practices, which iteratively shift between the lab and various sites of production and application.

Increased professional mobility and accelerated object circulation would expand the number and diversity of accessible local bodies of knowledge and could thus strengthen tolerance for the time-spatial ambiguities described above. Why not compensate for the discomforts of dislocation and the conflicts of knowledge allocation by increasing the degree of travel? However, scientific and business-oriented practices depend critically on locally situated activities, both in the lab and at the customer's site. Increased mobility would incur significant opportunity costs: all those activities that cannot be undertaken while the researcher responsible for them is traveling. Time can be invested only once, either in localized action or in mobility.

Conclusions

In the case study presented in this chapter, relational distance was used as a heuristic concept. It is fruitful for innovation theories because it centers on cultural tensions. Its multidimensionality enables one to examine these tensions without predefining them. Moreover, relational distance was conceived in this context as a social, inter-actional effect. Tension does not stem from the mere existence of different cultural rules, such as those in science and business, but rather from social practices in which actors collaborate in the force field of contradictory normative systems. Lastly, relational distance was regarded as being enacted in practice. Cultural tensions always also imply the ways people act in the physical space and appropriate different places. As a consequence, relational distance induces time-spatial tensions. What are the broader implications of such an understanding?

Economic geography is still fixated on proximity. In that field of scholarly endeavor, physical and relational proximity are key topics, with relational distance being treated only indirectly and seen mainly as a problem for innovation. This chapter's proposed understanding of relational distance can help sensitize geographers to the central role of sociocultural tension for innovation. Conflict is not a problem that has to be reduced or circumvented. It is inherent to innovation. One might even hypothesize that it energizes innovation and thus figures as a factor to be anticipated and managed proactively in innovation processes.

Relational distance as an interactional process produces a dynamic spatiality that economic geographers are on the verge of discovering. The discourse on global buzz has already accentuated the essential role of professional mobility, and tempo-rary co-presence for interactive learning (Asheim et al., 2007). These debates have thus far revolved around purposeful knowledge exchange that takes place on neutral ground at clearly identifiable, cyclical events. In addition to this, the account of interaction between the researcher and the user shows that spatial patterns created by professional mobility are even more fine-grained and elusive. First, mobility is not primarily oriented to big events. Numerous short-term and at first glance unspectacular meetings are much more prevalent than major gatherings. Second, face-to-face meetings often take place not in a neutral conference environment but rather in a specific material context—such as the customer's site, a laboratory, or a production facility—that is conducive to the negotiations on the agenda (Grabher et al., 2008). Third, this case study exemplifies how people participating in knowledge interaction actively invent appropriate sites for it if none are available in the desired form (Kirsh 1996). People are not the only agents to travel for the sake of knowledge work. Sometimes knowledge work depends much less on humans than on objects, documents, and artifacts that migrate through space (Law, 1986).

For organization science, the proposed understanding of relational distance poses some unresolved questions about how to manage sociocultural tensions. Organization scientists have already acknowledged that relational distance promotes innovation best at a medium level of intensity. Nooteboom (2000), for instance, argues that an "optimal cognitive distance" has to be "sufficiently small to allow for understanding but sufficiently large to yield non-redundant, novel knowledge" (p. 72; see also Boschma, 2005). In the case study presented in this chapter, I additionally suggest that the intensity of tension is not the only factor that seems important; so is the multidimensional situation on which relational distance has a bearing. The more the idea that "dissonance contributes to organizational learning" (Stark, 2009, p. 159) becomes accepted, the more it seems important to find organizational forms that engender relational distance and to organize situations that make the corresponding tensions tolerable and productive. It is, however, beyond the scope of this chapter to scrutinize organizational formats that could be promising for purposefully creating and maintaining relational distance.

Relational distance as enacted in practice highlights the importance that mobile and immobile artifacts (Latour, 1987; Law, 1986), the material characteristics of places (Livingstone, 2003), and the corporeal existence of people in physical space (Haraway, 2000) have for knowledge practices. The understanding of relational distance as proposed in this chapter impels a renewed emphasis on time-spatial constraints, materiality, and corporeality for both the economic geography of knowledge creation (Ibert & Thiel, 2009) and organization science. The organizational distribution of R&D labor is always reified as buildings and infrastructures. Knowledge work is afforded or obstructed by the architectural layout of the buildings (Kornberger & Clegg, 2004; see also Chap. 7 by Sailer in this volume) and of concrete workarounds (Kirsh, 2001). For instance, the disposition of offices and laboratories in the complex where my case study was carried out helps researchers shift their attention quickly from one workaround to another. Numerous corridors connect the office and laboratory wings, and various elements of a high-tech service infrastructure (clean rooms, electron microscopes) are easily accessible within the same building to keep walking distances short. Furthermore, the building has small offices and separate conference rooms, a spatial setting that reportedly invites spontaneous meetings in small groups.

Not only is R&D-related labor always distributed among organizational units and subunits, it automatically also produces a distinct pattern of sites in space (Lam, 2003; Sydow, 2002; Zander, 1999). This observation suggests that organization scientists should systematically consider how the spatial patterns of sites interact with organizational boundaries. Among other things, the spatial localization of R&D subunits should be consistent with the design of the organizational interfaces in distributed knowledge work. Lengthening the physical distance between sites might attenuate conflicts between subunits (Schoenberger, 1997) but might also exacerbate time-spatial conflicts in collaborative knowledge production, at least if the members of the subunits frequently require spontaneous encounters, ad hoc meetings, and a fine-tuned coordination of resource allocation. The proposed understanding of relational distance might offer other perspectives as well for the interpretation of interorganizational relations (Blanc & Sierra, 1999; Powell, Koput, Bowie, & Smith-Doerr, 2002). The need to reduce time-spatial tensions in knowledge-related collaboration might explain why firms tap into external knowledge bases by establishing branch offices in clusters of competitors, suppliers, or customers.

References

Agar, M. (1980). *The professional stranger: An informal introduction into ethnography*. Orlando, FL: Academic Press.

Amin, A., & Cohendet, P. (2004). *Architectures of knowledge: Firms, capabilities and communities*. Oxford, UK: Oxford University Press.

Amin, A., & Roberts, J. (2008). Knowing in action: Beyond communities of practice. *Research Policy, 37*, 353–369.

Asheim, B. T., Coenen, L., & Vang, J. (2007). Face-to-face, buzz, and knowledge bases: Sociospatial implications for learning, innovation, and innovation policy. *Environment and Planning C: Government and Policy, 25*, 655–670.

Bathelt, H., & Glückler, J. (2011). *The relational economy: Geographies of knowing and learning*. Oxford, UK: Oxford University Press.

Bathelt, H., Malmberg, A., & Maskell, P. (2004). Clusters and knowledge: Local buzz, global pipelines and the process of knowledge creation. *Progress in Human Geography, 28*, 31–56. doi:10.1191/0309132504ph469oa.

Bathelt, H., Maskell, P., & Malmberg, A. (2006). Building global knowledge pipelines: The role of temporary clusters. *European Planning Studies, 14*, 997–1013.

Bathelt, H., & Schuldt, N. (2008). Between luminaries and meat grinders: International trade fairs as temporary clusters. *Regional Studies, 42*, 853–868. doi:10.1080/00343400701543298.

Blanc, H., & Sierra, C. (1999). The internationalization of R&D by multinationals: A trade-off between external and internal proximity. *Cambridge Journal of Economics, 23*, 187–206.

Boschma, R. (2005). Proximity and innovation: A critical assessment. *Regional Studies, 39*, 61–74.

Florida, R. (1997). The globalization of R&D: Results of a survey of foreign-affiliated R&D laboratories in the USA. *Research Policy, 26*, 85–103.

Gertler, M. S. (1995). Being there: Proximity, organization, and culture in the development and adoption of advanced manufacturing technologies. *Economic Geography, 71*, 1–26.

Grabher, G., & Ibert, O. (2006). Bad company? The ambiguity of personal knowledge networks. *Journal of Economic Geography, 6*, 251–271.

Grabher, G., Ibert, O., & Flohr, S. (2008). The neglected king: The customer in the new knowledge ecology of innovation. *Economic Geography, 84*, 253–280.

Haraway, D. (2000). Morphing in the order: Flexible strategies, feminist science studies, and primate revisions. In S. Strum & L. Fedigan (Eds.), *Primate encounters: Models of science, gender, and society* (pp. 398–420). Chicago: University of Chicago Press.

Hautala, J. (2011). Cognitive proximity in international research groups. *Journal of Knowledge Management, 15*(4), 601–624.

Ibert, O. (2006). Zur Lokalisierung von Wissen durch Praxis: Die Konstitution von Orten des Lernens über Routinen, Objekte und Zirkulation [On the localization of knowledge through practice: The constitution of sites of learning via routines, objects, and circulation]. *Geographische Zeitschrift, 94*, 98–115.

Ibert, O. (2010). Relational distance: Sociocultural and time-spatial tensions in innovation practices. *Environment and Planning A, 42*, 187–204.

Ibert, O. (2011). Dynamische Geographien der Wissensproduktion—Die Bedeutung physischer wie relationaler Distanzen in interaktiven Lernprozessen [Dynamic geographies of knowledge production—The relevance of physical and relational distances in interactive learning]. In O. Ibert & H. J. Kujath (Eds.), *Räume der Wissensarbeit. Zur Funktion von Nähe und Distanz in der Wissensökonomie* (pp. 49–69). Wiesbaden, Germany: VS Verlag. doi:10.1007/978-3-531-93328-3_2.

Ibert, O., & Thiel, J. (2009). Situierte Analyse, dynamische Räumlichkeiten: Ausgangspunkte, Potentiale und Perspektiven einer Zeitgeographie wissensbasierter Ökonomien [Situated analysis, dynamic spatialities: Departure points, potentials, and perspectives of a time geography of the knowledge-based economy]. *Zeitschrift für Wirtschaftsgeographie, 53,* 209–223.

Kirsh, D. (1996). Adapting the environment instead of oneself. *Adaptive Behavior, 4,* 415–452.

Kirsh, D. (2001). The context of work. *Human Computer Interaction, 16,* 305–322.

Knorr-Cetina, K. (1999). *Epistemic cultures: How the sciences make knowledge.* Cambridge, UK: Cambridge University Press.

Knorr-Cetina, K. (2001). Objectual practice. In T. R. Schatzki, K. Knorr-Cetina, & E. von Savigny (Eds.), *The practice turn in contemporary theory* (pp. 175–188). London: Routledge.

Kopytoff, I. (1986). The cultural biography of things: Commoditization as a process. In A. Appadurai (Ed.), *The social life of things: Commodities in cultural perspective* (pp. 64–91). Cambridge, UK: Cambridge University Press.

Kornberger, M., & Clegg, S. R. (2003). The architecture of complexity. *Culture and Organization, 9,* 75–91.

Kornberger, M., & Clegg, S. R. (2004). Bringing space back in: Organizing the generative building. *Organization Studies, 25,* 1095–1114.

Kuemmerle, W. (1997). Building effective R&D capabilities abroad. *Harvard Business Review, 75*(2), 61–70.

Lam, A. (2003). Organizational learning in multinationals: R&D networks of Japanese and US MNEs in the UK. *Journal of Management Studies, 40,* 673–703.

Lam, A. (2007). Knowledge networks and careers: Academic scientists in industry–university links. *Journal of Management Studies, 44,* 993–1016.

Latour, B. (1987). *Science in action: How to follow scientists and engineers through society.* Cambridge, MA: Harvard University Press.

Law, J. (1986). On the methods of long-distance control: Vessels, navigation and the Portuguese route to India. In J. Law (Ed.), *Power, action and belief: A new sociology of knowledge?* (pp. 234–263). London: Routledge & Kegan Paul.

Livingstone, D. N. (2003). *Putting science in its place: Geographies of scientific knowledge.* Chicago: University of Chicago Press.

Malmberg, A., & Maskell, P. (2002). The elusive concept of localization economies: Towards a knowledge-based theory of spatial clustering. *Environment and Planning A, 34,* 429–449.

Malmberg, A., & Maskell, P. (2006). Localized learning revisited. *Growth and Change, 37,* 1–18.

Maskell, P., & Malmberg, A. (1999). The competitiveness of firms and regions: 'Ubiquitification' and the importance of localized learning. *European Urban and Regional Studies, 6,* 9–25.

Morgan, K. (2004). The exaggerated death of geography: Learning, proximity and territorial innovation systems. *Journal of Economic Geography, 4,* 3–21.

Motoyama, Y. (2012). *Global companies, local innovations. Why the engineering aspects of innovation making require co-location.* Farnham, UK/Burlington, VT: Ashgate.

Nooteboom, B. (2000). *Learning and innovation in organizations and economies.* Oxford, UK: Oxford University Press.

Powell, W. W., Koput, K. W., Bowie, J. I., & Smith-Doerr, L. (2002). The spatial clustering of science and capital: Accounting for biotech firm-venture capital relationships. *Regional Studies, 36,* 291–305.

Power, D., & Jansson, J. (2008). Cyclical clusters in global circuits: Overlapping spaces in furniture trade fairs. *Economic Geography, 84,* 423–448.

Rallet, A., & Torre, A. (1999). Is geographical proximity necessary in the innovation networks in the era of global economy? *GeoJournal, 49*, 373–380.

Saxenian, A. (2006). *The new Argonauts: Regional advantage in a global economy*. Cambridge, MA: Harvard University Press.

Schoenberger, E. (1997). *The cultural crisis of the firm*. Cambridge, MA: Blackwell.

Schutz, A. (1976). The stranger: An essay in social psychology. In A. Brodersen (Ed.), *Collected chapters: Vol. II. Studies in social theory* (4th ed., pp. 91–105). The Hague, The Netherlands: Martinus Nijhoff. (Original work published 1964)

Scott, A. (1988). *New industrial spaces*. London: Pion.

Shane, S. (2004). *Academic entrepreneurship: University spin-offs and wealth creation*. Cheltenham, UK: Edward Elgar.

Spradley, J. P. (1979). *The ethnographic interview*. New York: Holt, Rinehart and Winston.

Spradley, J. P. (1980). *Participant observation*. Fort Worth, TX: Harcourt Brace Jovanovich College Publishers.

Stark, D. (2009). *The sense of dissonance: Accounts of worth in economic life*. Princeton, NJ: Princeton University Press.

Storper, M., & Venables, A. J. (2004). Buzz: Face-to-face contact and the urban economy. *Journal of Economic Geography, 4*, 351–370.

Sydow, J. (2002). *Towards a spatial turn in organization science? A long wait*. [SECONS Online Discussion Forum Contribution No. 8]. Retrieved from http://www.wiwiss.fu-berlin.de/institute/management/sydow/media/pdf/Sydow-Towards_a_Spatial_Turn_in_Organization_Science.pdf

Torre, A., & Gilly, J.-P. (2000). On the analytical dimension of proximity dynamics. *Regional Studies, 34*, 169–180.

Torre, A., & Rallet, A. (2005). Proximity and localization. *Regional Studies, 39*, 47–59.

Vinck, D. (2003). Socio-technical complexity: Redesigning a shielding wall. In D. Vinck (Ed.), *Everyday engineering: An ethnography of design and innovation* (pp. 13–27). Cambridge, MA: MIT Press.

von Hippel, E. (1994). Sticky information and the locus of problem-solving: Implications for innovation. *Management Science, 40*, 429–439.

von Hippel, E., & Tyre, M. (1995). How learning by doing is done: Problem identification in novel process equipment. *Research Policy, 24*, 1–12.

Wilson, J. M., O'Leary, M. B., Metiu, A., & Quintus, R. J. (2008). Perceived proximity in virtual work: Explaining the paradox of far-but-close. *Organization Studies, 29*, 979–1002.

Zander, I. (1999). How do you mean 'global'? An empirical investigation of innovation networks in the multinational corporation. *Research Policy, 28*, 195–213.

Organizational Learning and Physical Space—How Office Configurations Inform Organizational Behaviors

7

Kerstin Sailer

Organizational Learning and the Physical Environment

Organizational learning, the way in which an organization as a whole adapts, changes, creates, and shares knowledge and reformulates its strategies in a structured way, has been a major concern of scholars in organization studies since the early 1960s, when Burns and Stalker (1961) and Cyert and March (1963) first brought up the topic. During the 1990s in particular, at the same time as knowledge management became a popular issue in organization studies, an increasingly broad discourse on organizational learning emerged. Proposing a rich variety of definitions and concepts of organizational learning, scholars advanced the idea that learning within organizations or by organizations had multiple drivers. They included, among many others, individual cognition (Hedberg, 1981; March & Olsen, 1976; Starbuck, 1992); group learning (Nonaka & Takeuchi, 1995); information acquisition and processing (Argyris & Schön, 1996; Huber, 1991); knowledge creation and sharing (Argote, 1999; Duncan & Weiss, 1979; Levinthal, 1991; March, 1991; March, Sproull, & Tamuz, 1991); dialogue and communication (Chawla & Renesch, 1995; Isaacs, 1999); overcoming inhibitors or learning from failures (Ackermann, 2005; Argyris & Schön, 1996; Dilworth, 1995; Sitkin, 1996); organizational cultures (Cook & Yanow, 1996; Klein, 1999); interpretations, experiences, and sense-making (Levitt & March, 1996; March & Olsen, 1976; March et al., 1991; Weick, 1995; Weick & Roberts, 1993); and environmental cues (Argote, 1999; Levinthal & March, 1993; Probst & Büchel, 1998; von Hippel, 1988).

The literature on organizational learning soon came to be called voluminous and multifaceted and was criticized for its lack of a cumulative and synthesizing perspective (Huber, 1991). Acknowledging the difficulties in achieving an overarching

K. Sailer (✉)
The Bartlett School of Graduate Studies, University College London (UCL),
14 Upper Woburn Place, London, WC1H 0NN, UK
e-mail: k.sailer@ucl.ac.uk

A. Berthoin Antal et al. (eds.), *Learning Organizations: Extending the Field*,
Knowledge and Space 6, DOI 10.1007/978-94-007-7220-5_7,
© Springer Science+Business Media Dordrecht 2014

theory of organizational learning, authors of more recent contributions have either valued the heterogeneity of approaches as a reflection of the complexity of the concept of organizational learning and its emerging pluralistic expressions (Prange, 1999) or have tried to systematize the underlying mechanisms of organizational learning (Lipshitz, Popper, & Friedman, 2002). Still, organization learning remains a vague and predominantly theoretical concept. One rarely finds approaches for quantitatively measuring or qualitatively investigating and thus empirically validating organizational learning concepts.

A search for such approaches reveals that the mainstream discourse on the subject has widely ignored the physical reality of organizations as they strive to become learning organizations. The gap seems odd, given that space has been deemed crucial to "the social organization of everyday life" (Hillier, 1996, p. 4), a "vector of social interactions" (Fischer, 1997, p. 3), and even the "most powerful tool for inducing culture change, speeding up innovation projects, and enhancing the learning process in far-flung organizations" (Peters, 1992, p. 413). Exceptions exist, of course. Some researchers have enriched the spatial understanding of organizational learning from the perspective of economic geography, for example. Contributions since the late 1990s have recognized local clusters and spatial as well as relational proximity as important conditions for organizational learning (Amin & Cohendet, 2004; Amin & Roberts, 2008; Faulconbridge, 2006; Gertler, 1997, 2003; Malmberg & Maskell, 2002; Maskell & Malmberg, 1999). A further significant clue to the role of physical space is found in the seminal contribution by Argyris and Schön (1996), who defined an organizational learning system as being composed of structures that channel organizational enquiry and shape the behavioral world of organizations. Among those structures is the spatial environment "insofar as it influences patterns of communication" (Argyris & Schön, p. 28). It is on such insights that this chapter builds. By contrast, other attempts to explore workplace environments as stimuli of or obstacles to organizational learning (Granath, Lindahl, & Adler, 1995; Lewis & Moultrie, 2005) have remained vague and have not been pursued further.

It may seem surprising at first that an organization's microlevel physical embeddedness and its relevance for organizational learning have not been researched as vigorously as other aspects of the organizational environment, context, and constitution. This paucity, however, is quite consistent with the rather sparse general discourse on physical settings and organizational behavior, which has been criticized for not providing more than "scattered empirical evidence" (Gieryn, 2002, p. 46) on the relation between architectural layout and social interaction.

Yet physical space can be regarded as an affordance for organizational behavior. In this chapter physical space is seen mostly as a form of spatial configuration (i.e., the layout of floor plans). I make this delimitation for one main reason: Environmental and climatic factors (e.g., temperature, light, climate, comfort) matter most at the level of the individual. The same goes for colors, materials, forms, aesthetics, perception, and workplace satisfaction. John's preference is not Sally's, and what motivates Mary comes across only as a hindrance to Tom.

Because the main interest of this chapter is in collective action and organizational responses, physical space as understood in the following pages is confined to design choices that govern supraindividual behaviors. The delimitation derives from Hillier's (1996) investigation of space and society, in which he states that "the relation between space and social existence does not lie at the level of the individual space, or individual activity. It lies in the relations between configurations of people and configurations of space" (p. 31). This perspective can yield important insights into the nature of the relationship between organizations and their spatial constitution.

Physical Space—An Affordance for Organizational Behavior

Physical space first caught attention as a potential influence on behaviors in workplace environments in studies conducted in the Hawthorne Works in the U.S. city of Cicero, Illinois, between 1927 and 1932. In the "Hawthorne studies," as they subsequently came to be known, factors influencing the work motivation of factory workers were tested, such as changes in lighting. The study dramatically lacked scientific rigor and was later harshly criticized for its shortcomings and unsupported conclusions (Carey, 1967). All the same, it posited with confidence the idea that spatial variables were meaningless in explaining behaviors. This aspect of the studies was widely referred to in the years thereafter and contributed to the rise of the human relations approach, which focuses on social determinants of work rather than on physical features (Sutton & Rafaeli, 1987).

The discourse on space and organizations revived during the 1970s and 1980s, when important empirical contributions were made (Allen & Fustfeld, 1975; Tomlin & Allen, 1977). But scholars also collated an array of studies and other sources from organization studies and environmental psychology (Becker, 1981; Pfeffer, 1982; Steele, 1973; Sundstrom, 1986) to underline the way(s) in which space figures in shaping organizational outcomes. Factors such as proximity, density, visibility, office layout, and furniture arrangement were seen as offering crucial affordances for the way organizations behaved. After nearly a decade of lean years, space regained popularity as a topic when the "spatial turn" came in the humanities and social sciences (Massey, 1999, pp. 9–23; Soja, 1996). The result has been an expanding body of literature on issues as diverse as collaboration (Heerwagen, Kampschroer, Powell, & Loftness, 2004; Wineman, Kabo, & Davis, 2009), interaction and knowledge flow (Becker & Sims, 2001; Fayard & Weeks, 2007; Peponis et al., 2007; Sailer & Penn, 2007), innovation (Penn, Desyllas, & Vaughan, 1999; Toker & Gray, 2008), creativity (Förster, Friedman, Butterbach, & Sassenberg, 2005; Kristensen, 2004; Meusburger, 2009; Werth & Förster, 2002), and performance (Kampschroer & Heerwagen, 2005; Kampschroer, Heerwagen, & Powell, 2007; Kelter, 2006, 2007; Kelter & Kern, 2006; Muschiol, 2006)—all of which consider the relation to spatial context and configuration.

Despite all these efforts, very little is understood about the way physical space interrelates with organizational behavior, as the following quotation from a British policy report on office spaces exemplifies:

> The ways in which office accommodation can create value for a business ... are [still] inadequately understood....
>   ... The collective failure to understand the relationship between the working environment and business purpose puts us in the position of early 19th century physicians, with their limited and erroneous notions about the transmission of disease before the science of epidemiology had been firmly established. (Commission for Architecture and the Built Environment [CABE], 2005, pp. 1–2)

Three reasons account for this persistent lack of understanding. First, most studies on the subject have dealt with outcomes for individuals rather than for groups or the organization as a whole. Therefore, complex issues such as performance, value creation, or innovation are hardly ever conclusively studied in their relation to physical space. Second, research in the field has taken place mostly in segregated research communities[1] with little overlap and collaboration. Third, studies lacked scientific rigor, so they produced contradictory findings. On open-plan environments, for example, some studies reported an increase in communication among staff members (Allen & Gerstberger, 1973; Brookes & Kaplan, 1972; Hundert & Greenfield, 1969; Ives & Ferdinands, 1974), some found that communication decreased (Clearwater, 1980; Hanson, 1978; Oldham & Brass, 1979), and again others showed either ambiguous results or no differences from other types of office accommodation (Boje, 1971; Boyce, 1974; Sundstrom, Herbert, & Brown, 1982). Such equivocality may partially be an effect of an incoherent and oversimplified operationalization of variables (for a more detailed criticism see Sailer, Budgen, Lonsdale, Turner, & Penn, 2008), but it also seems that the nature of the entangled relationship between space and organization was long misconstrued.[2] The growing complexity and range of definitions of organizational constructs only seems to have increasingly obscured the relationship between space and organizations.

In essence, this indistinctness has an important consequence for the further study of the relationship between architectural space and organizational learning. The rich diversity of definitions and concepts of organizational learning may hamper attempts to improve the understanding of the bearing that physical space has on the learning processes of an organization. In order to fully embrace the entangled relationship

---

[1] This lack of interdisciplinary communication has been criticized by Price (2007):

> [Concerning] business performance[, there is] ... little hard evidence for the effect of physical space in office settings; ... Such evidence as could be located, especially in managerial journals, was largely anecdotal. Property economists were adept at considering buildings from an investment perspective and building management research covered the technical issues, but the evidence from a business, or even just an individual occupier's, perspective was missing. The literature has discourses on organizations and workspaces whose proponents largely ignore each other. (p. 104).

[2] Only fairly recent contributions (Amin & Roberts, 2008; Fayard & Weeks, 2007) have started suggesting more complex models of a mutual and embedded relationship between the spatial and social realm.

between physical space and organizational learning without narrowing the inquiry to one kind of learning or a specific definition of organizational learning, researchers need an exploratory approach based on a combination of qualitative and quantitative methods. For 6 weeks in the summer of 2006, I therefore used ethnographic methods as well as observations techniques, interaction surveys, social network analysis (Wasserman & Faust, 1994), and tools for the analysis of space syntax (Hillier, 1996; Hillier & Hanson, 1984) to study a research institute in Germany that hosts theoretical physicists. Results from that research are presented in the following section.

Interaction Patterns, Knowledge Flow, and Organizational Learning in a Research Institute

The studied organization, research institute M, was located south of the university campus in Dresden and was part of one of Germany's major publicly funded research societies. The institute worked in the area of classical and quantum physics and attracted a variety[3] of theoretical physicists. It had 181 members of staff at the time of the study and was structured into three main departments, of which two, including all subgroups and three independent research groups (8 research groups totaling 109 staff members), were studied in depth.

An integral aspect of the institute's mission was that of serving the wider international community of theoretical physics by running a visitor's program at two different levels. First, the institute annually hosted around 200 incoming visitors, who stayed from 4 weeks to 1 year and who could work at the institute temporarily, facilitating collaboration between scientists. Second, the institute acted as a conference center, conducting six to ten workshops and seminars on its premises every year, with each event lasting from 1 to 4 weeks. If the organizers of such an event were external researchers, they would receive a few offices on the grounds of the institute during the workshop. Every year 1,200–1,500 visitors attended the workshops and seminars. Thus the organization was therefore extremely dynamic.

The institute occupied a three-storey comb-shaped and purpose-built complex with three adjacent guest houses constructed in 1997 by hammeskrause architekten and enlarged in 2005 to its current configuration with an additional wing (see Fig. 7.1). Most of the workspaces were single and double offices on the first and second floor of the building. Some scientists had to be accommodated in refurbished apartments of Guest House 3 for lack of space. Figures 7.2, 7.3, and 7.4 illustrate the look and feel of the research institute.

The next three sections explain the emergence of patterns of interaction, collaboration, and knowledge flow emerged at the research institute, the degree to which the patterns were informed by spatial configuration, and the embedding of organizational

---

[3]The main research areas of the institute were quantum physics of condensed matter, nonlinear phenomena and dynamics, and biophysics. The physicists interviewed for this project regarded their institute as very "interdisciplinary," even though they had all studied the same subject. Nonetheless, the focus and methodologies used varied significantly.

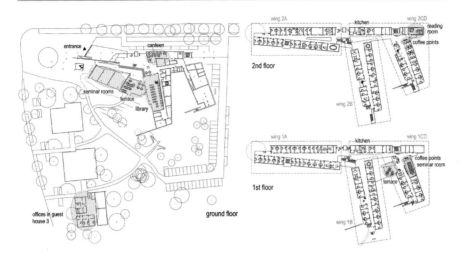

Fig. 7.1 Floor plans of the research institute, with some of the main functions and facilities highlighted (Copyright 2006, design by hammeskrause architekten; annotations by Kerstin Sailer. Adapted with permission)

Fig. 7.2 Exterior view of the research institute (From Sailer 2010, p. 83. Copyright 2010 by K. Sailer)

Fig. 7.3 The bright and open entrance of the research institute (From Sailer 2010, p. 83. Copyright 2010 by K. Sailer)

learning in physical space. First, I contend that the intensity of collaboration in knowledge-intensive workplace environments across a selection of different organizations was driven by the spatial integration of the building that an organization occupies. The case of the research institute is discussed among other cases that served as a benchmark.[4] I assert that space exerts a "generic function" (Hillier, 1996, p. 284). Second, even though the frequency of interaction was affected by spatial parameters such as the distance between the workstations of individuals, I show that this distance-dependency of interactions is far less pronounced in the studied research institute than in similar cases. This finding gives rise to an argument on the specific interplay between forms of "spatial and transpatial solidarity" (Hillier & Hanson, 1984, p. 20) in workplaces. In particular, I outline how both forms of

---

[4]A benchmark of 11 knowledge-intensive organizations from the public sector (universities and research institutions) and the private sector (media businesses) whose members had all studied with a similar methodology and setup was available to me through involvement in a collaborative research project entitled "Effective Workplaces" conducted by University College London and Spacelab Architects, London. (Some of the results are published in Sailer, Budgen, Lonsdale, Turner, & Penn, 2009.) The benchmark consisted of syntactical features of space (visibility, metric integration of the building) and survey data on interaction and collaboration patterns of the organizations (interaction frequency and the intensity of collaboration).

Fig. 7.4 The corridor of the research institute's wing 2B (From Sailer 2010, p. 83. Copyright 2010 by K. Sailer)

solidarity were enacted in the research institute. Third, a software development project undertaken by one of the research groups in the institute is examined in order to understand an organizational learning situation. It becomes evident how spatial configuration aided various steps involved in the collective learning process. This example emphasizes the entangled nature of the relationship between space and an organization.

Collaboration Patterns and Spatial Integration—The Generic Function of Space

Patterns of collaboration between staff members in knowledge-intensive workplace environments arguably depend on a variety of work-related factors, such as task structures, working processes, and organizational cultures. Using empirical studies I conducted on benchmark organizations, however, I will show that collaboration is also informed by the spatial configuration of an office. A 3-point scale was used to identify emergent patterns of collaboration, with staff members being asked which of their colleagues they found useful to getting their own work done. I interpret the resulting level of usefulness in relationships among staff members as evidence

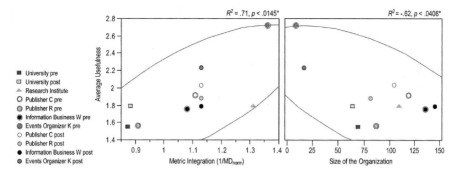

Fig. 7.5   Across a benchmark of 11 organizations, the intensity of emergent patterns of collaboration depends not only on the size of the organizations (*left*) but also on the compactness and metric integration of their workspaces (*right*). Metric integration is calculated as mean depth in metric distance from any line to all other lines and averaged across the whole system. In order to compare between systems of different sizes and configurations, metric mean depth is normalized by the office area ($\sqrt{\text{sqm}}$)

Fig. 7.6   Metric integration showing the spatial configuration of the research institute. *Darker* segments depict more integrated areas; *brighter* segments depict less integrated areas of the office

of emergent collaboration patterns within organizations (as opposed to formal collaboration patterns, which may be thought of as stemming rather from hierarchies, reporting lines, and group affiliation). In the benchmark, the intensity of emergent collaboration ranged from 1.55 (for a medium-sized university department with 69 staff members) to 2.72 (for a small corporate events organizer with 10 staff). The research institute in my study scored 1.79, placing in the lower third of the benchmark. Although size certainly figures in the intensity of emergent collaboration (the two smallest organizations in the benchmark showed the greatest mutual usefulness; see the image on the right in Fig. 7.5), the compactness of the office spaces seemed to be the more important factor, as the multivariate analysis in Fig. 7.5 shows. Compactness of office spaces in this case was modeled as the average metric integration of the whole workspace (i.e., the actual distances along lines of movement measured, in accordance with space syntax methodologies (see Sailer, 2007, for example), from any place in the office to all other places). Figure 7.6 shows the underlying line model of metric integration of the research institute.

Essentially, organizations occupying rather compact office space—those in which walking distances are relatively short and easy—tend toward fairly intense collaborative relationships among staff members. Of course, spatial configuration is not the only factor bearing on collaboration patterns among individuals in workplace environments, a fact that explains the degree of variation shown in the model depicted in Fig. 7.5. This relationship between spatial configuration and emergent organizational behaviors seems to follow a "generic function" of space, as explained by Hillier (1996):

> Generic function refers not to the different activities that people carry out in buildings or the different functional programmes that buildings of different kinds accommodate, but to aspects of human occupancy of buildings that are prior to any of these: that to occupy space means to be aware of the relationships of space to others, that to occupy a building means to move about in it, and to move about in a building depends on being able to retain an intelligible picture of it. Intelligibility and functionality defined as formal properties of spatial complexes are the key 'generic functions', and as such the key structures which restrict the field of combinatorial possibility and give rise to the architecturally real. (p. 282)

In this sense a relatively compact office in which the space is easily walkable and in which all areas are within relatively easy reach for everyone allows for heightened awareness and is thus conducive to the formation of relationships among staff members no matter what functional program a building hosts (for further details see Sailer, 2010).

Interaction Patterns and Proximity—Spatial and Transpatial Forms of Solidarity

In contrast to the previous section's argument that certain functions of space may be of a generic nature, most of the evidence in the literature and in the empirical data underlying this chapter suggests that the effect of spatial configuration is rather ambiguous because similar spatial configurations may lead to distinct organizational responses. This insight is exemplified by the relationship between proximity among actors and their interaction frequency. Figure 7.7 shows characteristic distance curves for the organizations in the benchmark (i.e., the average distance between interaction partners depending on the frequency of their interactions).

Quite clearly, daily interactions took place within 15–22 m (about 50–70 ft) in all organizations (apart from the research institute), yielding a characteristic distance of 18 m (just under 60 ft) for daily interaction. By contrast, weekly interaction ranged much further afield: a characteristic distance of 34 m (about 112 ft). Although most organizations seem to follow spatially induced interaction routines (overall low distances of daily interaction and significantly longer distances for weekly or monthly contact), the research institute is a prime example for transpatial interaction patterns. Daily interactions in this organization occurred at a distance of more than 42 m (about 140 ft) on average, with 22 % of daily interactions spanning more than 80 m (about 260 ft). Interactions between people obviously followed rationales other than, or at least in addition to, physical proximity.

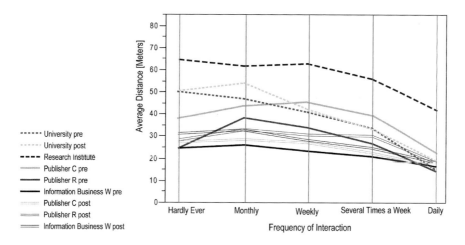

Fig. 7.7 Characteristic distance curves for each organization showing at which distance (on average) different intensities of face-to-face interaction took place; two organizations (events organizer pre and post) were omitted from the benchmark for size reasons; the research institute is shown as *black dashed line* (From Sailer 2010, p. 239. Copyright 2010 by K. Sailer. Adapted with permission of the author)

So how did relationships between people form in the research institute if spatial proximity did not seem to be the major driver? I maintain that collaboration between scientists in the research institute were shaped by the open character of the institute as a local place shared between people in their simultaneous co-presence as well as by the global process of specialized knowledge creation in the field of theoretical physics. Staff members at the research institute commented in a variety of ways on the co-presence of others and how it shaped their collaboration:

> You need the social contact and the exchange of knowledge to know what other people are doing and what can be learned from them in order to avoid reinventing the wheel. It's a way to accelerate research. Gaining insights is quicker in a group of people or in systems that influence each other than it would be for isolated individuals. (Leader of group DY at the research institute)[5]

> Our guest program is something very special because people come and go and you have no chance whatsoever to follow. To have so few people with permanent contracts gives the place a special dynamic. Many people with whom you can discuss your work come here. It so happens that you really do discuss with those around. But imagine if someone else were here; maybe your work would get a very different kick. (Member of group MA at the research institute)[6]

---

[5] "Man braucht schon den sozialen Kontakt, und den Austausch, was andere Leute machen, was man von wem lernen kann bevor man das Rad neu erfindet, ja, so kann man Wege abkürzen. Der Erkenntnisgewinn geht sicher schneller in der Gruppe oder in der Wechselwirkung der Systeme, als wenn die Leute sich isolieren."

[6] "Dieses Gästeprogramm ist schon was Besonderes, dass die Leute hier kommen und gehen, ohne dass man die Chance hat, da mitzukommen. Dass wenig permanente Leute da sind, das verleiht dem Ganzen schon eine besondere Dynamik. Es kommen viele Leute vorbei, mit denen kann man dann diskutieren, und dann diskutiert man halt mit denen und je nachdem wer da wäre, würde die Arbeit vielleicht auch einen ganz anderen Kick bekommen."

In other words, the openness of the institute—inviting scientists to work on site on their research ideas—and the resulting levels of co-presence of people who would normally not share the same space did indeed shape collaboration between people. ("You need the social contact." "You really do discuss with those around.") It also introduced a degree of randomness into the patterns of knowing each other, interacting, and collaborating. ("If someone else were here, maybe your work would get a very different kick.") Thus, co-presence as a result of temporary colocation was the first driver of collaborative relationships between individual staff members.

Team affiliations and special expertise in a field were additional crucial sources of contact for individual researchers:

> In physics you work in very small units, basically your group. (Member of group DY at the research institute)

> In our group we are around 50 people at the moment. All of these people are working in a more or less unique area. In some sense this means that the notions or the literature that you use to express your scientific work is common to all of these people. When you just simply say "The Howard model," all of them will understand what the Howard model is. This is not the case if you talk to other physicists… This makes it easy to contact them and to exchange ideas, to [ask] them, "what do you think about my work?" "What do you think about my ideas?" Or "what are you doing?" More precisely, if you consider the whole group that are more than fifty, you can find at least four or five that are very much experts in the same area you are working in… So five people on exactly the topic you are working on. This is great because you can simply share your ideas. You can even share the details of ideas without needing to explain them for several hours and then discuss them. Just when you say something, they will know [what you are talking about] because they are working on the same thing. This is a very impressive scientific atmosphere. (Member of group EL at the research institute)

As indicated by the four speakers quoted above, work processes seemed to be very specialized ("All of these people are working in a more or less unique area.") and were segregated into areas of expertise that did not involve the organization as a whole. ("In physics you work in very small units." "Gaining insights is quicker in a group of people.") This does not mean that people worked purely for themselves. ("You need the social contact and the exchange of knowledge.") Obviously, working relationships were strongly driven by specialization and the expertise of individuals in a certain field.

The high degree of specialization in the research institute ultimately led to increased selectivity in the choice of collaboration partners, as illustrated by the social networks of emergent collaboration patterns (see Fig. 7.8). Although intense relations emerged within and between groups—every person found an average of 5.6 people who were extremely useful (Fig. 7.8a)—the number of ties in the network shrank significantly if one counts only the reciprocal relationships, that is, the pairs of people who found each other very useful (Fig. 7.8b). Only 0.9 reciprocal relationships per person were found (because many of the surveyed people develop no reciprocal ties at all). The network also shows how selectively people chose their collaboration partners. In some groups, such as group EL (shown as white circles), there evolved no coherent, overarching group structure that would have tied everyone in. Instead small clusters appeared, consisting

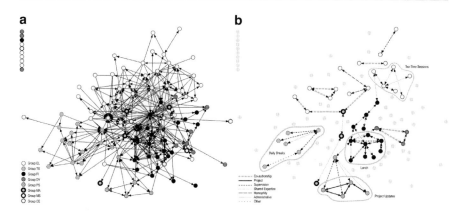

Fig. 7.8 Network of intensive emergent collaboration in the research institute showing all relationships (**a**) and mutual relationships (**b**)

mostly of two or three collaborating scientists. All clusters of more than three people were involved in specific time-space routines. Examples were group TS, which held daily breaks with the whole group; a cluster within group EL that met for daily sessions at tea time; group PS, which was involved in a joint programming project and met for daily progress reports; and group FI, whose members regularly went for lunch together.

The network diagram in Fig. 7.8b also shows different rationales for relationships and types of collaboration. Although most reciprocal ties were substantiated by collaboration anchored in similar expertise and interests (27 %), supervisory relations (24 %) and coauthorship (22 %) were equally important as primary drivers of collaboration. The remaining relationships were administrative in nature (12 %); centered on projects (8 %); rooted in ethnic background, language, or some other homophily between actors (4 %); or derived from other underlying rationales (4 %).

In summary, collaboration arose specifically between people who shared knowledge and expertise (supervision, collaboration, or coauthorship) or who shared certain tasks and work processes (project work or administration and management). The high degree of specialization in the field of theoretical physics and the particular dynamics at the institute, with its strong visitors program, shaped the patterns of collaboration among individual scientists. These patterns were made possible by co-presence enacted within an openly structured and inviting building and articulated by times-space routines and recurring social behaviors such as daily team meetings, tea breaks, or joint lunches.

The message is that predominantly transpatial forms of solidarity (routines, social events, and expertise) provided the necessary "social glue" for the organization and its emerging collaboration patterns. Spatial forms of solidarity, such as proximity among actors, played only a minor role. Differences between the characteristic distance of daily interaction (42 m, or about 140 ft, on average) and weekly interaction (63 m, or about 207 ft, on average) were significant, yet distance did not prevent interactions in which scientists were interested:

> What I would like is to have the overall walking distances reduced for the group. My group leader sits one floor below me, which is not too bad, but when I am walking over to one of the postdocs with whom I collaborate, it's at the end of wing A, which is quite a way… I would like to change the spatial distribution of the groups in order to keep distances within each as short as possible. The distances are really still too long, at least in ours. (Member of group PS, which was spread out over a median distance of 83 m, or just over 270 ft)[7]

> The disadvantage of the wings are, well, [person S] sits 100 m [about 330 ft] in this direction, or maybe 80 [about 260 ft], but you just don't walk that far very often. It simply takes too long, and you're liable to get stuck somewhere on the way because you meet other people. (Leader of group MA, which was spread out over a median distance of 101 m, or about 333 ft.)[8]

Proximity may have facilitated collaboration between researchers in the institute, and distances may have been perceived as a burden, yet a lack of proximity was no major hindrance to collaboration and interactions, for the general co-presence of scientists from all over the world with a shared expertise was appreciated enough that microdistances did not matter that much.

This pattern, an embeddedness of transpatial solidarity within certain spatial configurations, was elaborated by Hillier and Hanson (1984) in their study on the spatiality of societies. They held that relations between individuals could be explained either as a spatial function or as a social function of conceptual closeness, which they call transpatial:

> In their elementary forms, in effect, buildings… can define a relation to others by conceptual analogy, rather than spatial relation. The inhabitant of a house in a village, say, is related to his neighbours spatially, in that he occupies a location in relation to them, but also he relates to them conceptually, in that his interior system of spatialised categories is similar or different from those of his neighbours. He relates, it might be said, transpatially as well as spatially. Now this distinction is very close to that between mechanical and organic solidarity… Durkheim had distinguished between two fundamentally different principles of social solidarity or cohesion: an 'organic' solidarity based on interdependence through differences, such as those resulting from the division of labour; and a 'mechanical' solidarity based on integration through similarities of belief and group structure. This theory was profoundly spatial: organic solidarity required an integrated and dense space, whereas mechanical solidarity preferred a segregated and dispersed space. (pp. 18–20)

In essence, individuals may relate to each other in a dual way, either by means of spatial closeness (spatiality) or of conceptual closeness (transpatiality). Transpatial affinity, however, does not mean that relationships are nonspatial. Given that homogeneity in values often came with the same preferences for spatial ordering, Hillier

---

[7] "Was ich schon gerne hätte, ist dass die Gruppe, also dass die Laufwege im Institut ingesamt geringer wären, also mein Chef sitzt noch eine Etage tiefer, das geht noch, aber wenn ich zu den postdocs gehe, mit denen ich zu tun habe, das ist am Ende des A-Flügels und das ist dann schon ein Stück Weg… Ich würde die Gruppen halt raumtechnisch … verändern, also die Wege innerhalb einer Gruppe möglichst kurz halten, das ist zumindest bei uns in der Gruppe noch zu lang."

[8] "Der Nachteil der Flügel ist, der [S], der sitzt 100 m in diese Richtung oder 80, das ist eine Distanz, da geht man nicht einfach so hin. Weil … es dauert einfach, dann kann man noch irgendwo festhängen, weil man Leute trifft."

and Hanson posited the spatial contextuality of conceptual closeness. My study documents the same spatial contextuality of transpatial solidarity for the research institute, where collaboration was driven by expertise and coauthorship and promoted by specific spatial configurations such as proximity.

Organizational Learning and Its Embeddedness in Physical Space

The two preceding sections have shown how organizational behaviors such as interaction and collaboration were driven partly by physical space and partly by transpatial solidarity enacted within spatial configurations. Likewise, organizational learning can be embedded in physical space, as illustrated by one of the institute's research groups (PS) and a software development project on which the group collaborated in the spring and summer 2006. The group aimed to replace pieces of software that group members had previously written individually. It turned out that the software all the member had used was very similar but tailored to each one's specific research goals. The first objective of the project was to unify the different software solutions so that there would in future be only one standard software into which each individual could plug in his or her own small specific add-ons. The second objective was to implement parallel computing in order to increase calculation speed and thereby allow the researchers to deal with physics problems that they had not been able to analyze before. This innovation was, hence, intended to improve the understanding of research issues confronting each individual and the group.

Group PS contacted one of the IT administrators at the institute for help on a version control system.[9] This person offered profound support in organizing and setting up the project, leading to the involvement of a computer scientist. After 6 months of joint programming, the group finished the software. Four members continued to use and modify the program, and a new person had started familiarizing himself with it. To calculate something new in the field of group PS, only around one hundred lines of code were needed as a result of the new software.

Before the project began, the idea took shape as a common process among the group members:

> In our group at least three people were doing more or less the same thing, so we could have used the same program, but in different ways. Only small bits and pieces would have been needed to extend it for use by each of us. It took a relatively long time until we finally decided to combine it all, and now it works a lot better… The idea came from me, or rather, it came continually [smiles], and I eventually initiated the process. (Member of group PS)[10]

---

[9] Version control systems are commonly used in relatively complex software development projects, specifically for collaborative or joint programming to monitor changes that different people make in the code at different times.

[10] "Also in Bezug auf unsere Arbeitsgruppe, es war ja so, dass zumindest drei Leute quasi das gleiche gemacht haben und wir hätten also das gleiche Programm benutzen können, nur auf verschiedene Art und Weise, da wären nur winzige Dinge drumherum zu schreiben gewesen, die uns betreffen. Und es hat relativ lange gedauert, bis wir uns endlich dazu entschieden haben, das mal zusammenzuwerfen und jetzt funktioniert es auch viel besser… Die Idee kam von mir beziehungsweise sie kam kontinuierlich [schmunzelt] und letztendlich habe ich den Anlass gegeben, das so zu tun."

How exactly the idea emerged cannot be traced, but the process definitely involved various steps: the insight that group members worked on such similar tasks that efforts could be easily joined ("At least three people were doing more or less the same thing."), recognition of certain barriers that had to be overcome first ("It took a relatively long time."), the awareness of its advantages ("It works a lot better."), and then the group decision ("We finally decided to combine it.").

Group PS followed an approach called *extreme programming*. Every morning the members met for 15 min to update each other on the progress they had made, to exchange information, to report on problems, and to adapt objectives if necessary. On a weekly basis, either individuals wrote code for the software or teams of two met to employ methods of *pair-programming*.[11] Pair-programming meant that two people sat in front of a computer, with both of them viewing the screen for a defined period of time (e.g., 2 h). While one of them operated the keyboard and typed code, the other person read the code as it was typed, tried to understand what concepts were applied and what specific constructs were used, asked short and specific questions if things were not clear, or commented whenever it seemed possible to use a better solution. This process is said to enhance the quality of code, advance the learning process of the developers, and lend programming a structure that often comes only by doing. If group PS had chosen a more traditional way to program the code, such as assigning members to program defined parts of it individually on their own, then each of their desks, workstations, and offices would have been sufficient to host the collaboration. Instead, the group chose a creative way with the professional assistance of an in-house expert and thus needed extra spaces where this type of collaborative work could be accommodated. To some degree they were offered by the institute:

> For the project meetings we used the end of the corridor of the A wing… The sunny place was very nice for the status updates, which we gave standing in a circle. After the meetings small teams often formed and immediately began with the detailed planning. These people either disappeared into an office or started discussing details in the corridor on the way back to their offices. (IT administrator and organizer of the project)[12]

The physical design of the building offered these bright and sunny multipurpose areas at the end of the A-wings, and the architects had also built in many other spatial opportunities to meet and collaborate, so the members of group PS actually had a choice of spaces to use. Additionally, the organization was open enough to allow its staff members to use facilities as they wished and needed. For example, group PS utilized the open workstations in wing 1D and the group offices in wing 2D (see Figs. 7.9 and 7.10) for joint programming, although both areas had been equipped for use by short-term visitors attending conferences at the institute and

---

[11] For an introduction to extreme programming and pair-programming, see http://en.wikipedia.org/wiki/Extreme_programming and http://en.wikipedia.org/wiki/Pair_programming (both documents retrieved in 2008).

[12] "Für die Projekttreffen haben wir das Ende des A-Flügels … genutzt. Der sonnige Platz war sehr schön für die Statustreffen, die im Stehen abgehalten werden. Nach den Treffen fanden sich oft kleine Teams, die sofort mit der Detailplanung begannen. Die sind dann im Büro veschwunden oder haben einige Details auf dem Rückweg im Gang geklärt."

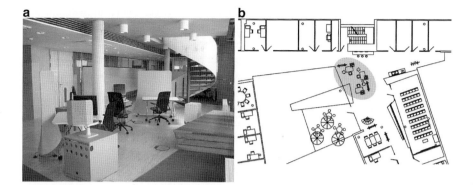

Fig. 7.9 Image (**a**) and floor plans (**b**) of the open areas in wing 1D (Copyright 2010 by K. Sailer)

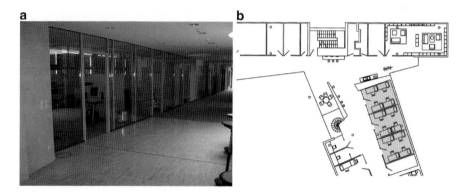

Fig. 7.10 Image (**a**) and floor plans (**b**) of the transparent group offices in wing 2D, which were used by group PS for their joint programming sessions (Copyright 2010 by K. Sailer)

were therefore not exactly suitable for accommodate joint programming sessions. The temporary offices in wing 2D were not bookable, the furniture arrangement of open work stations in wing 1D did not allow intense joint computer work, and ordinary collaboration spaces such as seminar rooms or breakout areas lacked computers (laptops were not available). Nonetheless, the project team was able to appropriate institute spaces for their purposes.

But how did organizational learning happen in this case? Who was mainly driving it—the individual, the group, or the whole organization? And what role did space have in the process? The learning effects for the organization were twofold. First, it learned how to save time and be more efficient through collaboration (potentially across group boundaries, too, by involving an in-house IT expert). Second, the organization enhanced and improved its ability to understand a research field and thereby become more intelligent. The way in which the processes were shaped was innovative and creative and therefore resulted in a better product (good quality code that is easily pluggable and extendable). Moreover, the scope and result of the project included the ability to perform parallel computing, opening up potential new fields for doing physics.

The drivers of the learning effort were found at different levels. Individuals had an important part in kicking things off ("I eventually initiated the process"), but at the same time a good deal of motivation came from the group ("the idea came continually") and the supraindividual need for a better program. Individuals such as the IT administrator had a large hand in shaping the way the collaboration patterns evolved and thereby drove the process, but without a dedicated and committed group the project would not have come to an end. However, the group, because of its slight inertia, also seemed to be the main obstacle to learning ("It took a relatively long time until we decided to combine it all"). The group can thus be seen as both the main driver of learning, especially within a loosely structured organization allowing for broad autonomy, and the element that thwarts change and development. In addition, one can reason that the organization as a whole contributed to making such projects possible in the first place by granting a great deal of autonomy to the groups, supporting the groups and individuals, employing IT staff, affording a variety of physical spaces, and allowing for unconventional usage and appropriation of the spaces. This engagement and supply of resources by the organization was highly appreciated by staff members:

> I think here there is an idea that the environment should be nice, and everything should be done for helping us to work better. I think that here the institution thinks that we are not only brains connected to a computer. If we are expected to produce something that could be some discoveries, this should be combined into an environment that is nice... I think here it is great attention for this. You can see this in the reading room, they put some games, Asterix comics, the coffee machines, all these small things that are not so small. (Member of group MA)

> I like a lot that we only have to do research e have a lot of freedom e have a lot of support from all levels, from your boss, the institute itself helps you a lot in many things and this you won't find in a university and his makes a great difference. (Member of group DY)

The founding director of the institute underlined the importance of this commitment:

> I think the success of our organization lies mainly in the creation of the right climate, where new ideas and developments have the best chance to prosper. I believe new things arise from the creation of an atmosphere. Of course, this is coupled with patterns of behavior. An important issue is generosity, which is crucial, and the delegation of responsibility as early as possible. You have to leave as much latitude as possible for the initiatives of individuals. (Leader of group EL)[13]

In this sense the organization drove the learning efforts and supported individuals or groups in their learning. The contributions of actors at different levels in the research institute I studied underline Nonaka and Takeuchi's (1995) assertion that the core of the learning process lies in the group but that the organization as a whole

---

[13] "Der Erfolg unserer Organisation, den sehe ich hauptsächlich darin, ein Klima zu erzeugen, das richtige Klima zu erzeugen, wo neue Ideen und neue Entwicklungen eine möglichst hohe Chance haben, dass sich neue Dinge entwickeln, über die Erzeugung eines Klimas. Das ist natürlich gekoppelt mit Verhaltensmustern. Ein wichtiger Punkt ist Großzügigkeit. Das ist sehr wichtig. Und möglichst frühzeitige Delegation von Verantwortung, da wo es möglich ist. Man muss den Initiativen der Einzelnen möglichst viel Spielraum lassen."

needs to provide enabling conditions. The evidence from the study discussed in this chapter thus shows that learning was prevalent at all three levels in the observed research institute: the individual, the group, and the organization as a whole.

As outlined above, the learning processes were embedded within physical space. The spaces at the institute gave them enough room to unfold and not only made for a rich variety of meeting opportunities and additional temporary working areas but also created an open atmosphere by means of wide corridors, bright and sunlit spaces, and high visibility within the institute. Conceptually, too, space may have affected organizational learning in two ways. First, co-presence arguably increased the likelihood that people would continue pursuing an innovative project. If a new situation ever called for a collaborative programming project, the previously involved IT administration, who was still on hand, could help apply the lessons learned and could induce a new cycle of organizational learning. Moreover, it was possible that the jointly produced software would lead to new processes of learning and benefit other researchers in the future. Second, the spatial configuration of the institute was likely to continue to shape patterns of interaction and collaboration by forging groups of individuals previously unknown to each other.

> Many more discussions arise now because of the new coffee machines. You simply bump into each other there. (Leader of group MA at the research institute)[14]

> I love the spaciousness. Every morning when I enter the building, I think "wow." The stair-case, the big windows, everything is very bright. It makes you communicate with the people in the wide spaces. You linger on your way somewhere. You see someone coming who you wanted to talk to anyway, and then you stop and start talking. (Member of the research institute's central administration)[15]

Thus, the configuration of physical space in the research institute may pave the way to new opportunities for communication, sharing of knowledge, learning, and change.

Conclusions—Who Is Afraid of Physical Space?

I have contended that the relationship between physical space and organizational behavior is governed by different rationales. On the one hand, spatial configuration may exert a generic function on basic anthropological constituents such as occupancy, movement, and awareness. On the other hand, people regard the relationship between space and organization as being shaped by the interplay between forms of spatial and transpatial solidarity (for a more detailed discussion of both principles, see

---

[14] "Durch die neuen Kaffeemaschinen, da kommen sehr viel mehr Diskussionen zusammen, weil man sich da einfach trifft."

[15] "Ich mag die Großzügigkeit, ich komm hier jeden Morgen in das Haus rein und sage: toll. Die Treppe, die großen Fenster, es ist alles sehr hell. Irgendwie bringt es einen dazu, dass man mit Leuten kommuniziert in den weiten Flächen, dass man auch mal stehen bleibt, sich anlehnt, und sagt, oh, jetzt kommt jemand, den wolltest du mal was fragen oder mit dem hattest du eh was zu besprechen und dann bleibt man stehen."

Sailer & Penn, 2009, and Sailer & Penn, 2010). Patterns of transpatial solidarity may differ from one organization to the next. In the research institute I studied, the main identified drivers of emergent interactions and collaboration were the disciplinary character of theoretical physics, the special expertise required by that field, and the nature of the institute as a temporary and shared place creating co-presence among scientists from all over the world. These patterns were enacted within the particular spatial configurations of the institute—its relative compactness as a building, which allowed easy access to all areas within it; its wide corridors; and its plentiful, flexible, and available informal meeting spaces. This setup was underlined again by the story of the programming project conducted by group PS and how that interaction created a potential for organizational learning embedded in space.

From the perspective of research on human geography, stressing the important role of physical space and specifically acknowledging a generic function of space underplays the fundamental principles of human agency; falls short of understanding the interplay between society, action, and space; and instead follows a path of environmental or geodeterminism. Human geographers have criticized that space has been wrongly reduced to a confined container enclosing physical objects. Instead, they posit "subjective agency as the only source of action and hence of change" (Werlen, 1993, p. 3). As a consequence, space has increasingly come to be considered a result of social relations and the relational ordering of social goods and people (Meusburger, 1999, 2008; Weichhart, 1999; Zierhofer, 1999).

For three main reasons the approach presented in this chapter is anything but geodeterministic. First, it keys on physical space as a driver of organizational behaviors. In this chapter I have not examined space as a fixed container but rather have analyzed an elaborate conceptualization of spatial configuration. Space syntax as a morphological approach is relational in itself, for it takes the perspective of an entire system of spaces into account in the analysis of their consequences for and the potential of the quality of life prevalent at one of the system's locations. My study of physical space therefore does not reduce space to a simple container function. Second, I have not taken physical space to be the sole determinant of human behavior. Various parameters emerged as important, including organizational character, research cultures, and human agency. Third, and most important, aggregate human behaviors have been borne in mind. Space is seen to influence the probability of certain behaviors but not the individual behaviors themselves. In a study of cities in relation to the quality of life they create, Hillier, Burdett, Peponis, and Penn (1987) have suggested that cities as configurational and spatial structures create a potentiality:

> Cities are mechanisms for generating a potential field of probabilistic co-presence and encounter. What happens beyond that is not the direct effect of the city, but an effect of culture. The prevailing culture may, however, itself be an indirect, evolutionary product of the city... The field of probabilistic co-presence and encounter generated by an urban layout has a definite and describable structure, one which varies greatly with the structuring of space; it can be sparse or dense, localised or globalised, predictable from the intelligible structure of space or unpredictable, and mix inhabitants and strangers in different degrees. In other words, the pattern of co-presence has both a describable pattern and a known cause. (p. 248)

The same potentiality and field of probabilistic co-presence and encounter that Hillier et al. (1987) ascribe to cities can likewise be seen in office spaces. For example, the study of characteristic distance curves has shown that intense interactions have a higher probability of taking place if actors are located in proximity to each other. Of course, individual pairs of people may choose to interact at any intensity they wish, no matter how far away they are located from each other, but a distance relationship emerges more or less clearly for each organization when one takes the collective interaction patterns into account statistically.

In conclusion, physical space informs organizational behaviors collectively even though the physicality of a workplace environment is only one factor in an intricate tangle of spatial and transpatial forms of solidarity operating within any organization. I have shown how organizational learning may be embedded in a specific spatial configuration, yet much remains to be learned about its constitution and what part physical space may have in its occurrence.

References

Ackermann, M. (2005). *Systemisches Lernen: Individuelle und organizationale Lernprozesse in Kommunikationsarchitekturen* [Systemic learning: Individual and organizational learning processes in communication architectures]. Frankfurt am Main, Germany: Peter Lang Verlag.

Allen, T. J., & Fustfeld, A. R. (1975). Research laboratory architecture and the structuring of communications. *R&D Management, 5*, 153–164.

Allen, T. J., & Gerstberger, P. G. (1973). A field experiment to improve communications in a product engineering department: The non-territorial office. *Human Factors, 15*, 487–498.

Amin, A., & Cohendet, P. (2004). *Architectures of knowledge: Firms, capabilities, and communities.* Oxford, UK: Oxford University Press.

Amin, A., & Roberts, J. (2008). Knowing in action: Beyond communities of practice. *Research Policy, 37*, 353–369.

Argote, L. (1999). *Organizational learning: Creating, retaining and transferring knowledge.* Boston: Kluwer Academic Publishers.

Argyris, C., & Schön, D. A. (1996). *Organizational learning II: Theory, method, and practice.* Reading, MA: Addison-Wesley.

Becker, F. (1981). *Work space: Creating environments in organizations.* New York: Praeger Publishers Inc.

Becker, F., & Sims, W. (2001, October). *Offices that work: Balancing communication, flexibility and cost* [Electronic Version]. Ithaca, NY: International Workplace Studies Program, Cornell University. Retrieved from http://iwsp.human.cornell.edu/file_uploads/offices1_1238256905. pdf. Also available at: http://media.miamiherald.com/smedia/2008/07/27/10/IWS_0002.source. prod_affiliate.56.pdf

Boje, A. (1971). *Open plan offices.* London: Business Books.

Boyce, P. R. (1974). Users' assessment of a landscaped office. *Journal of Architectural Research, 3*(3), 44–62.

Brookes, M. J., & Kaplan, A. (1972). The office environment: Space planning and effective behavior. *Human Factors, 14*, 373–391.

Burns, T., & Stalker, G. M. (1961). *The management of innovation.* London: Tavistock Publications.

CABE (Commission for Architecture and the Built Environment). (2005). *The impact of office design on business performance.* London: The Commission for Architecture and the Built Environment.

Carey, A. (1967). The Hawthorne studies: A radical criticism. *American Sociological Review, 32*, 403–416.

Chawla, S., & Renesch, J. (Eds.). (1995). *Learning organizations: Developing cultures for tomorrow's workplace*. Portland, OR: Productivity Press.

Clearwater, Y. (1980). *User's assessment of a landscaped office*. Doctoral dissertation, University of California, Davis, CA.

Cook, S. D. N., & Yanow, D. (1996). Culture and organizational learning. In M. D. Cohen & L. S. Sproull (Eds.), *Organizational learning* (pp. 430–459). Thousand Oaks, CA: Sage.

Cyert, R. M., & March, J. G. (1963). *A behavioral theory of the firm*. Englewood Cliffs, NJ: Prentice-Hall.

Dilworth, R. (1995). The DNA of the learning organization. In S. Chawla & J. Renesch (Eds.), *Learning organizations: Developing cultures for tomorrow's workplace* (pp. 243–255). Portland, OR: Productivity Press.

Duncan, R., & Weiss, A. (1979). Organizational learning: Implications for organizational design. In B. M. Staw (Ed.), *Research in organizational behavior* (Vol. 1, pp. 75–123). Greenwich, CT: JAI Press.

Faulconbridge, J. R. (2006). Stretching tacit knowledge beyond a local fix? Global spaces of learning in advertising professional service firms. *Journal of Economic Geography, 6*, 517–540.

Fayard, A.-L., & Weeks, J. (2007). Photocopiers and water-coolers: The affordances of informal interaction. *Organization Studies, 28*, 605–634.

Fischer, G. N. (1997). *Individuals and environment: A psychosocial approach to workspace*. Berlin, Germany/New York: De Gruyter.

Förster, J., Friedman, R. S., Butterbach, E. B., & Sassenberg, K. (2005). Automatic effects of deviancy cues on creative cognition. *European Journal of Social Psychology, 35*, 345–359.

Gertler, M. S. (1997). Between the global and the local: The spatial limits to productive capital. In K. Cox (Ed.), *Spaces of globalization: Reasserting the power of the local* (pp. 45–63). New York: The Guilford Press.

Gertler, M. S. (2003). Tacit knowledge and the economic geography of context, or the undefinable tacitness of being (there). *Journal of Economic Geography, 3*, 75–99.

Gieryn, T. F. (2002). What buildings do. *Theory and Society, 31*, 35–74.

Granath, J. A., Lindahl, G. A., & Adler, N. (1995, June). *Organizational learning supported by design of space, technical systems and work organization: A case study from an electronic design department*. Paper presented at the 5th international conference of Flexible Automation and Intelligent Manufacturing (FAIM), Stuttgart, Germany.

Hanson, A. (1978). Effects of a move to an open landscape office. *Dissertation Abstracts International, 39*(6), 3046B.

Hedberg, B. (1981). How organizations learn and unlearn. In P. C. Nystrom & W. H. Starbuck (Eds.), *Handbook on organizational design* (Vol. 1, pp. 3–27). Oxford, UK: Oxford University Press.

Heerwagen, J., Kampschroer, K., Powell, K., & Loftness, V. (2004). Collaborative knowledge work environments. *Building Research and Information, 32*, 510–528.

Hillier, B. (1996). *Space is the machine: A configurational theory of architecture*. Cambridge, UK: Cambridge University Press.

Hillier, B., Burdett, R., Peponis, J., & Penn, A. (1987). Creating life: Or, does architecture determine anything? *Architecture et Comportement/Architecture and Behaviour, 3*, 233–250. Retrieved from http://discovery.ucl.ac.uk/101/. See also http://eprints.ucl.ac.uk/101/1/hillier-etal-1987-creating-life.pdf

Hillier, B., & Hanson, J. (1984). *The social logic of space*. Cambridge, UK: Cambridge University Press.

Huber, G. P. (1991). Organizational learning: The contributing processes and the literatures. *Organization Science, 2*, 88–115.

Hundert, A. T., & Greenfield, N. (1969). Physical space and organizational behavior: A study of an office landscape. *Proceedings of the 77th Annual Convention of the American Psychological Association, 4*, 601–602.

Isaacs, W. (1999). *Dialogue and the art of thinking together*. New York: Random House.

Ives, R. S., & Ferdinands, R. (1974). Working in a landscaped office. *Personnel Practice Bulletin, 30*, 126–141.

Kampschroer, K., & Heerwagen, J. (2005). The strategic workplace: Development and evaluation. *Building Research and Information, 33*, 326–337.

Kampschroer, K., Heerwagen, J., & Powell, K. (2007). Creating and testing workplace strategy. *California Management Review, 49*(2), 119–137.

Kelter, J. (2006). *Office-Excellence-Check: Ergebnisse der Zwischenauswertung zur Orgatec 2006* [Office excellence check: Results of the interim analysis at Orgatec 2006]. Stuttgart, Germany: Fraunhofer Institut Arbeitswirtschaft und Organisation.

Kelter, J. (2007, September). *Office Excellence: Konzepte, Messung, Bewertung* [Office excellence: Concepts, measurement, evaluation]. Paper presented at the A+A Congress, 30th international congress on Occupational Health and Safety, Düsseldorf, Germany.

Kelter, J., & Kern, P. (2006, March). *Office Excellence—Kennzahlen für Büroqualität* [Office excellence—Quality benchmarks for office]. Paper presented at the 52nd Congress of the Gesellschaft für Arbeitswissenschaft, Stuttgart, Germany.

Klein, L. (1999). Lebensfähige Strukturen der lernenden Organisation: Beispiel Human Resource Management [Viable structures of the learning organization as exemplified by human resource management]. In M. Schwaninger (Ed.), *Intelligente Organisationen: Konzepte für turbulente Zeiten auf der Grundlage von Systemtheorie und Kybernetik, Wissenschaftliche Jahrestagung der Gesellschaft für Wirtschafts- und Sozialkybernetik vom 2.–4. Oktober 1997 in St. Gallen, Schweiz* (pp. 177–188). Berlin, Germany: Duncker & Humblot.

Kristensen, T. (2004). The physical context of creativity. *Creativity and Innovation Management, 13*, 89–96.

Levinthal, D. A. (1991). Organizational adaptation and environmental selection-interrelated processes of change. *Organization Science, 2*, 140–145.

Levinthal, D. A., & March, J. G. (1993). The myopia of learning. *Strategic Management Journal, 14*, 95–112.

Levitt, B., & March, J. G. (1996). Organizational learning. In M. D. Cohen & L. S. Sproull (Eds.), *Organizational learning* (pp. 516–540). Thousand Oaks, CA: Sage.

Lewis, M., & Moultrie, J. (2005). The organizational innovation laboratory. *Creativity and Innovation Management, 14*, 73–83.

Lipshitz, R., Popper, M., & Friedman, V. J. (2002). A multifacet model of organizational learning. *The Journal of Applied Behavioral Science, 38*, 78–98.

Malmberg, A., & Maskell, P. (2002). The elusive concept of localization economies: Towards a knowledge-based theory of spatial clustering. *Environment and Planning A, 34*, 429–449.

March, J. G. (1991). Exploration and exploitation in organizational learning. *Organization Science, 2*, 71–87.

March, J. G., & Olsen, J. P. (1976). *Ambiguity and choice in organizations*. Bergen, Norway: Universitetsforlaget.

March, J. G., Sproull, L. S., & Tamuz, M. (1991). Learning from samples of one or fewer. *Organization Science, 2*, 1–13.

Maskell, P., & Malmberg, A. (1999). Localised learning and industrial competitiveness. *Cambridge Journal of Economics, 23*, 167–185.

Massey, D. (1999). *Power-geometries and the politics of space-time*. Hettner-Lecture: Vol. 2. Heidelberg, Germany: Department of Geography, Heidelberg University.

Meusburger, P. (1999). Subjekt–Organisation–Region: Fragen an die subjektzentrierte Handlungstheorie [Subject–organization–region: Questions for subject-centered action theory]. In P. Meusburger (Ed.), *Handlungszentrierte Sozialgeographie: Benno Werlens Entwurf in kritischer Diskussion* (pp. 95–132). Erdkundliches Wissen: Vol. 130. Stuttgart, Germany: Franz Steiner.

Meusburger, P. (2008). The nexus of knowledge and space. In P. Meusburger, M. Welker, & E. Wunder (Eds.), *Clashes of knowledge: Orthodoxies and heterodoxies in science and religion* (pp. 35–90). Knowledge and Space: Vol. 1. Dordrecht, The Netherlands: Springer.

Meusburger, P. (2009). Milieus of creativity: The role of places, environments, and spatial contexts. In P. Meusburger, J. Funke, & E. Wunder (Eds.), *Milieus of creativity: An interdisciplinary approach to spatiality of creativity* (pp. 97–153). Knowledge and Space: Vol. 2. Dordrecht, The Netherlands: Springer.

Muschiol, R. (2006, March). *Begegnungsqualität in Bürogebäuden* [The quality of encounters in office buildings]. Paper presented at the 52nd Kongress der Gesellschaft für Arbeitswissenschaft, Stuttgart, Germany.

Nonaka, I., & Takeuchi, H. (1995). *The knowledge-creating company: How Japanese companies create the dynamics of innovation.* New York/Oxford, UK: Oxford University Press.

Oldham, G. R., & Brass, D. J. (1979). Employee reactions to an open-plan office: A naturally occurring quasi-experiment. *Administrative Science Quarterly, 24,* 267–284.

Penn, A., Desyllas, J., & Vaughan, L. (1999). The space of innovation: Interaction and communication in the work environment. *Environment and Planning B: Planning and Design, 26,* 193–218.

Peponis, J., Bafna, S., Bajaj, R., Bromberg, J., Congdon, C., Rashid, M., et al. (2007). Designing space to support knowledge work. *Environment and Behavior, 39,* 815–840.

Peters, T. (1992). *Liberation management: Necessary disorganization for the nanosecond nineties.* London: Macmillan.

Pfeffer, J. (1982). *Organizations and organization theory.* Cambridge, MA: Ballinger.

Prange, C. (1999). Organizational learning: Desperately seeking theory? In M. Easterby-Smith, L. Araujo, & J. G. Burgoyne (Eds.), *Organizational learning and the learning organization: Developments in theory and practice* (pp. 23–43). London: Sage.

Price, I. (2007). Lean assets: New language for new workplaces. *California Management Review, 49*(2), 102–118.

Probst, G. J. B., & Büchel, B. (1998). *Organisationales Lernen. Wettbewerbsvorteil der Zukunft* [Organizational learning: The competitive advantage of the future] (2nd ed.). Wiesbaden, Germany: Gabler.

Sailer, K. (2007). Movement in workplace environments: Configurational or programmed? In A. S. Kubat, Ö. Ertekin, Y. I. Güney, & E. Eyüboglu (Eds.), *Proceedings of the sixth international space syntax symposium: Vol. 2* (pp. 068-01–068-14). Istanbul, Turkey: ITU Faculty of Architecture.

Sailer, K. (2010). *The space-organisation relationship: On the shape of the relationship between spatial configuration and collective organisational behaviours.* Doctoral dissertation, Technical University Dresden, Dresden. Retrieved from http://www.qucosa.de/fileadmin/data/qucosa/documents/3842/Sailer_PhD_final_print.pdf

Sailer, K., Budgen, A., Lonsdale, N., Turner, A., & Penn, A. (2008, July). *Evidence-based design: Theoretical and practical reflections of an emerging approach in office architecture.* Paper presented at the Design Research Society Conference, Sheffield, UK.

Sailer, K., Budgen, A., Lonsdale, N., Turner, A., & Penn, A. (2009, June). *Comparative studies of offices pre and post: How changing spatial configurations affect organisational behaviours.* Paper presented at the 7th international space syntax symposium, Stockholm.

Sailer, K., & Penn, A. (2007, May). *The performance of space: Exploring social and spatial phenomena of interaction patterns in an organization.* Paper presented at the International Architecture + Phenomenology Conference, Haifa, Israel.

Sailer, K., & Penn, A. (2009, June). *Spatiality and transpatiality in workplace environments.* Paper presented at the 7th international space syntax symposium, Stockholm.

Sailer, K., & Penn, A. (2010, May). *Towards an architectural theory of space and organisations: Cognitive, affective and conative relations in workplaces.* Paper presented at the 2nd workshop on Architecture and Social Architecture, EIASM, Brussels, Belgium.

Sitkin, S. B. (1996). Learning through failure: The strategy of small losses. In M. D. Cohen & L. S. Sproull (Eds.), *Organizational learning* (pp. 541–577). Thousand Oaks, CA: Sage.

Soja, E. W. (1996). *Thirdspace: Journeys to Los Angeles and other real-and-imagined places.* Malden, MA/Oxford, UK: Blackwell Publishing.

Starbuck, W. H. (1992). Learning by knowledge-intensive firms. *Journal of Management Studies, 29*, 713–740.

Steele, F. I. (1973). *Physical settings and organization development.* Reading, MA: Addison-Wesley.

Sundstrom, E. (1986). *Work places: The psychology of the physical environment in offices and factories.* Cambridge, UK: Cambridge University Press.

Sundstrom, E., Herbert, R. K., & Brown, D. W. (1982). Privacy and communication in an open plan office: A case study. *Environment and Behavior, 14*, 379–392.

Sutton, R. I., & Rafaeli, A. (1987). Characteristics of work stations as potential occupational stressors. *The Academy of Management Journal, 30*, 260–276.

Toker, U., & Gray, D. O. (2008). Innovation spaces: Workspace planning and innovation in U.S. university research centers. *Research Policy, 37*, 309–329.

Tomlin, B., & Allen, T. J. (1977, June). *Organizational structure and inter-location communication in an R&D organization* (Working Paper No. 940-77). Cambridge, MA: Alfred P. Sloan School of Management, MIT. Retrieved from http://dspace.mit.edu/bitstream/handle/1721.1/1930/SWP-0940-03581816.pdf?sequence=1

von Hippel, E. (1988). *The sources of innovation.* Oxford, UK/New York: Oxford University Press.

Wasserman, S., & Faust, K. (1994). *Social network analysis: Methods and applications.* Cambridge, UK: Cambridge University Press.

Weichhart, P. (1999). Die Räume zwischen den Welten und die Welt der Räume. Zur Konzeption eines Schlüsselbegriffs der Geographie [The spaces between the worlds and the world of spaces: On the inception of a key concept of geography]. In P. Meusburger (Ed.), *Handlungszentrierte Sozialgeographie: Benno Werlens Entwurf in kritischer Diskussion* (pp. 67–94). Erdkundliches Wissen: Vol. 130. Stuttgart, Germany: Franz Steiner.

Weick, K. E. (1995). *Sensemaking in organizations.* Thousands Oaks, CA: Sage.

Weick, K. E., & Roberts, K. H. (1993). Collective mind in organizations: Heedful interrelating on flight decks. *Administrative Science Quarterly, 38*, 357–381.

Werlen, B. (1993). *Society, action and space: An alternative human geography* (G. Walls, Trans.). London: Routledge.

Werth, L., & Förster, J. (2002). Wie Sie als Führungskraft Kreativität steigern oder blockieren können [How you as an executive can increase or block creativity]. *Wirtschaftspsychologie, 2*, 13–20.

Wineman, J., Kabo, F., & Davis, G. F. (2009). Spatial and social networks in organizational innovation. *Environment and Behavior, 41*, 427–442.

Zierhofer, W. (1999). Die fatale Verwechslung: Zum Selbstverständnis der Geographie [The disastrous mistake: On the self-conception of geography]. In P. Meusburger (Ed.), *Handlungszentrierte Sozialgeographie: Benno Werlens Entwurf in kritischer Diskussion* (pp. 163–186). Erdkundliches Wissen: Vol. 130. Stuttgart, Germany: Franz Steiner.

The Unexpected Neighbor: Learning, Space, and the Unconscious in Organizations

Russ Vince

In this chapter I reflect on spatial relations and unconscious dynamics created in management learning. I explain why it is important to acknowledge the interplay between learning, space, and the unconscious and point out how to use these three concepts in helping managers and students of management understand aspects of the emotional and political context within which their practice is situated. Opportunities to explore spatial and unconscious dynamics together in management learning are unlikely to be found in didactic approaches to managers' teaching and learning. Therefore, I look at two examples in which spatial and unconscious dynamics within the management classroom are linked to experiential group work.

I argue that connecting learning, space, and the unconscious in the management classroom can stimulate creativity in the approaches to educating managers and can deepen the understanding of organizational dynamics. There are explicit benefits to managers in examining spatial disparities of knowledge that emerge around complex organizational concepts. For example, the notion of leadership is primarily defined and taught in terms of individuals' skills, knowledge, and behavior or in terms of leaders' heroic endeavor, charisma, or positive attitudes. However, leaders can use their preferred skills, knowledge, and behavior successfully in one organizational setting and yet fail in another. I suggest that an improved awareness of spatial relations and unconscious dynamics can provide insights into the complexity of relations and actions mobilized by individuals within a leadership role.

From my thoughts on the interplay between learning, space, and the unconscious and on the use of this relationship in the management classroom, I build a provisional conceptual framework for reflection on unconscious dynamics created in the relational space of management and organizational learning. I see this framework as a useful contribution to a growing body of literature that acknowledges learning as

R. Vince (✉)
School of Management, University of Bath, Claverton Down,
Bath, North East Somerset BA2 7AY, UK
e-mail: r.vince@bath.ac.uk

A. Berthoin Antal et al. (eds.), *Learning Organizations: Extending the Field*,
Knowledge and Space 6, DOI 10.1007/978-94-007-7220-5_8,
© Springer Science+Business Media Dordrecht 2014

a profoundly emotional experience and recognizes such experience as inseparable from questions of politics and power (Coopey, 1995; Gherardi, 1999; Vince, 2001). My framework combines the group-analytic concept of relatedness (French & Vince, 1999), with the spatial concept of "throwntogetherness" (Massey, 2005, p. 151) in order to express the way in which conscious and unconscious emotional dynamics connect to political tensions inherent in relational space.

Thoughts on the Concepts of: Learning, Space, and the Unconscious

The attempt to cover three major concepts like learning, space, and the unconscious in one short chapter is not without its challenges. In order to contain these concepts into a sense-making framework, I make very personal choices about their meaning and the literatures associated with them. This venture is necessarily both a partial and a subjective engagement with the literatures.

Learning

Learning is the capacity to doubt those things that seem unquestionable. The ability to learn is a fundamental human quality that allows people to engage with and change their world. Learning implies both an awareness of the limitations of existing knowledge and the ability to transform knowledge through new information or insight. In organizations, learning is understood as improvement in performance and as a continuous process of transformation. Learning is related to improvements in the ways in which a role or task is performed, individually or collectively. It is also a potential outcome of the relationship between reflection and action over time. Organizations need to be good at learning because of the importance of generating, appropriating, and exploiting knowledge for growth and renewal.

There are two particular ways in which the relationship between learning and organizing has been understood. The *learning organization* refers to an ideal type of organization that has the capacity to effectively modify its behavioral tendencies by experience and, therefore, to prosper. Learning organizations have been seen as environments where "people continually expand their capacity to create the results they truly desire, where new and expansive patterns of thinking are nurtured, where collective aspiration is set free, and where people are continually learning to see the whole together" (Senge, 1990, p. 24). *Organizational learning* refers to the study of learning processes of and within organizations in order to understand and critique what is taking place (Easterby-Smith & Lyles, 2003). The term does not mean that an organization is learning, but it does imply that learning and organizing are related. This connection has been instructively captured by Gherardi and Nicolini (2001) when they talk about organizational learning as "learning-in-organizing" (p. 51). They recognize that learning and organizing "are not distinct activities within a practice" (p. 53). Efforts to understand organizational learning have profited in recent years from a general shift away from individuals' learning within organizations and toward social, political, and relational interpretations of learning and organizing.

Learning is likely to remain a particularly useful concept in relation to organizations because it is a lens through which researchers and practitioners can view the many and varied emotional and political dynamics from which seemingly stable and rational organizations are made. One of the most interesting aspects of the relationship between learning and organizing is that learning is both desired and avoided in organizations. For example, leaders want a structure that supports improvements in individual practice and organizational performance yet resist and avoid potential changes that derive from learning if those changes challenge existing power relations and threaten "the way we do things here." Attempts to define what should be learned (in order to perpetuate and to police that standard way of doing things) are double-edged. As soon as organizational members have identified a range of competencies that indicate what should be known within particular roles, the limitations of that combination of competences become apparent. Although it can be useful to prescribe a role's finite set of competencies, skills, and behaviors, it is equally important to realize that any prescriptive combination is as likely to inhibit as to underpin knowledge, innovation, and further learning.

Space

There is an emerging literature concerned with space, organization, and management theory (Brocklehurst, 2006; Clegg & Kornberger, 2006; Dale & Burrell, 2007; Ford & Harding, 2004; Kornberger & Clegg, 2003; Taylor & Spicer, 2007). Whether the focus of these studies is space as materiality (Kornberger & Clegg) or space as social product (Taylor & Spicer), they all call attention to space as an important dynamic in understanding organization and management. Organizations are inspired and impeded by spatial relations and interactions (Meusburger, 2008). Space is categorized, choreographed, configured, and corporatized in the service of governing organizational members and social systems and of supporting identities of compliance and resistance. "Thus, space is inextricably linked to power: it limits and enables, it creates and hinders through precise spatial arrangements" (Kornberger & Clegg, p. 78). Space is a complex web of relations; it is full of "strange juxtapositions" (Massey, 1993, p. 156), accidental separations and unintended consequences, location and dislocation, and "spatial disparities of knowledge" (p. 159). In an essay entitled "Space as a Key Word," Harvey (2005) creates "a general matrix of spatialities" (p. 105) by interconnecting Lefebvre's (1991) tripartite division of space (*material space*, *representation of space*, and *spaces of representation*) with his own understanding of space as absolute, relative, and relational. I have used this structure to construct the matrix shown in Table 8.1. It affords broad scope for playful speculation on spatial matrices that relate to specific fields of knowledge.

Absolute space expresses uniqueness of location. It is a way of describing bounded territories, something that is fixed and, therefore, amenable to measurement. *Relative*

Table 8.1 A matrix of spatialities for management learning in the Bath School of Management

Harvey's (2005) understanding of space	Lefebvre's (1991) division of space		
	Material space	Representation of space	Spaces of representation
Absolute	The flat room, the lecture theater, the professor's tidy office, the MBA students' coffee lounge, long corridors and brown carpet	Configuration or placement of chairs (circle, rows, conference format), positions and juxtapositions, deliberate separations and alliances	Feelings of security or contentment, fear of others, anxiety, spatial assignations or ambivalence, the "dungeon room" that has no windows, the walls crowding in
Relative	Connection or disconnection to ideas and knowledge, differences of perspective on the distances between others, the politics implied by positions in the room	Situated knowing; what students reveal about their existing knowledge; the raising of hands; resolute silences	The anticipation of learning; concern at not getting to class on time; longing to be outside; the delight of new knowledge; feelings of respect, hatred, ambivalence* for the tutor (* delete as appropriate)
Relational	Shifts in proximity and attention with others in the same or different roles, foci of perceptions, connections and disconnections to experience	Knowing more than the tutor, competing for attention, positioning of the self relative to assignments, the discomfort of peer assessment, differences of engagement and attention	Visions, fantasies, desires, dreams, frustrations, the memory of chalk, strange juxtapositions and unwanted emotions, complicated peer relations, a tendency toward fight or flight

Sources: Harvey (2005), Lefebvre (1991)

space expresses multiplicity of location, and comparisons between different perceptions and perspectives can pose differences of political choice, such as the one between executive decision-making based on financial management and executive decision-making informed by social responsibility. Measurement in relative space depends on the observer's frame of reference. In *relational space* it is impossible to disentangle space and time, for processes do not occur "in" space but instead define their own spatial frame. Relational space is therefore "embedded in or internal to process" (Harvey, 2005, p. 95). Material space, or spatial practice (Lefebvre, 1991), is the space of experience; and perception is "open to physical touch and sensation" (Harvey, p. 96) in order to include practices such as walking, occupying, and meeting (Taylor & Spicer, 2007). Representations of space are "the dominant space in any society, which is tied to the relations of production and thus to knowledge, signs, codes, etc." (Ford & Harding, 2004, p. 815). Representations of space reflect spatial planning "architecture, regional and city planning, ergonomics and office landscaping" (Taylor & Spicer, p. 328). Spaces of representation refer to the lived space of sensation, the imagination and emotions that are incorporated into how people live day by day.

The Unconscious

The word *unconscious* has several different uses. It can refer to loss of consciousness, or to lack of consciousness (being unaware of what is happening around you). According to Weinberg (2007), such lack of awareness may arise from something that is not perceived (it is not known), or it may be perceived but not acknowledged (it is denied), or it may be acknowledged but not taken as problematic (it is given). In relation to individuals, the unconscious describes a realm that is beyond awareness and knowing; at the same time, the unconscious "has structure and order and a very tangible role in the generation of behavior" (Carr & Hancock, 2007, p. 6). For example, the Chief Executive Officer's personality and attitudes, both conscious and unconscious, have a profound influence on the feelings and actions within an organization (Gabriel, 1997). The unconscious is often most apparent in the pictorial and visual language everyone uses in combination with words. Expressions such as "Freudian slip" and "free association" and psychoanalytically derived words like "projection," "regression," and "denial" are all commonplace in everyday language. The imagery that connects to people's use of language represents both the conscious and unconscious minds.

Unconscious processes not only apply to individuals but are also integral to collective experiences: within groups, in relation to tasks, within organizations, and in society (Stokes, 1994). "Whenever two or more individuals are together, there is a shared unconscious field to which they belong and of which by definition they are not aware. We can talk about a relational unconscious process co-created by both participants" (Weinberg, 2007, p. 308). Unconscious group and intergroup dynamics influence the state of mind in an organization. Through such unconscious behavior, groups of people co-create common defenses, fantasies, and assumptions that connect to and reinforce structures and designs to form an "establishment" in the mind (Vince, 2002, p. 1192)—an unconscious organizational design that represents and further reinforces "the way we do things here." This design has been referred to as "the organization-in-the-mind" (Bazelgette, Hutton, & Reed, 1997, p. 113). People in organizations have a mental image of how their organization works. These diverse images and ideas about an organization are not consciously negotiated or agreed upon among by its members—but they exist. In other words, all organizations exist in the mind, and it is in interaction with these in-the-mind entities that humans live. There are also material factors, such as other people, profits, buildings, resources, and products. But the meaning of these factors derives from the context established by the organization-in-the-mind. "These mental images are not static; they are the products of dynamic interchanges, chiefly projections and transferences" (Shapiro & Carr, 1993, pp. 69–70).

A Provisional Conceptual Framework

Although Harvey's (2005) matrix of spatialities yields a suitably complex and encompassing conceptual model of space, it is too complex for the purposes of linking learning, space, and the unconscious in the context of management and organizational learning. Such a framework needs to offer a way to think about and connect to the emotions and politics that are mobilized in management and organizational learning. However, I think it is possible to draw on aspects of all three of my interpretations of the meaning of these concepts (learning, space, and the unconscious) in order to create a simple, provisional conceptual framework concerning the interplay between them. In this chapter my interpretations of the words learning, space, and the unconscious are all connected to social relations, and these relations can be understood in both emotional and political terms.

Learning in organizations is both desired and avoided at the same time. Managers *feel* that learning is desirable, possible, or necessary within the organization because they know that change is unlikely to happen without transformations of existing knowledge. At the same time managers may *act* against learning if the potential transformation of knowledge seems to be transgressing aspects of the status quo. The designs and strategies for learning that organizations create can function (deliberately or not) as processes for emotional compliance with an ideal of corporate citizenship and as political control over the velocity and direction of change.

Emotions "are rarely, if ever, located within a purely individual space; like power they are part of the medium within which all social relations occur" (Hoggett & Thompson, 2002, p. 112). Groups of people, when they interact, create an emotional dynamic that makes a group more than the sum of its individual parts. Such underlying dynamics shape and are shaped by the mutual activity of the groups, such as their similarities and differences, their antagonisms and consensus, their incapacity to reflect, or a determination to act. This process in groups has been called *relatedness*, for it is not so much about the relationships between people in the group as about "conscious and unconscious emotional levels of connection that exist between and shape selves and others, people and systems" (French & Vince, 1999, p. 7). It is in these unconscious layers of connection, in the interplay between belonging and becoming, that the organization-in-the-mind is created.

Representational spaces invite distinction between space and place because place implies process as well as materiality. Place is "constructed out of constellations of relations articulated together at a particular locus" (Ford & Harding, 2004, p. 818). If organizations are simultaneously inspired *and* impeded by spatial relations and interactions (Meusburger, 2008), then it is within the particular locus of place that the politics of this tension are worked out. Place

> as an ever-shifting constellation of trajectories poses the question of our *throwntogetherness* [my emphasis] . . . The chance of space may set us down next to the unexpected neighbour. The multiplicity and the chance of space here in the constitution of place provide (an element of) that inevitable contingency which underlies the necessity for the institution of the social and which, at the moment of antagonism, is revealed in particular fractures which pose the question of the political. (Massey, 2005, p. 151).

Therefore, these notions of relatedness (an emotional layer of connection) and throwntogetherness (a political layer of connection) can be combined to interrogate spatial and unconscious dynamics when they are mobilized within the relational space of learning groups. The following assumptions summarize what one might be looking for in such groups:

- Relatedness (emotion/space)

  A learning group is more than the sum of its parts; it is constructed from both conscious and unconscious relations and dynamics. Groups create rituals, expectations, unvoiced assumptions, distinctive language, and complex delusions, all of which then unconsciously support and recreate "the way we do things here."

- Throwntogetherness (politics/place)

  Within learning groups the unexpected neighbor may be the shock of new knowledge, one's own prejudice and bias, old and/or new anxieties, similarities and differences with others, patterns of social connection and exclusion, relations of domination and subordination, and/or of solidarity and cooperation. The political tension inherent in the relational space of a learning group is that learning is both desired and avoided at the same time.

In the following section of this chapter, I cite two examples of management learning that illustrate the interplay between learning, space, and the unconscious. I then use the above framework to analyze these examples and to elaborate an explanation of the interplay between relatedness and throwntogetherness and of how these concepts can promote engagement with management and organizational learning. In the chapter's final section I discuss how spatial and relational dynamics within the management classroom are linked to the unconscious in groups and organizations. I now return briefly to the concept of leadership in order to emphasize the potential importance of the ideas to key organizational roles and relations.

Two Examples from Learning Groups

In this section I offer two examples from management learning in which an attempt was made to use the interplay between space, learning, and the unconscious in order to understand emotional and political dynamics of organizing. The initial example focuses on the behavior-and-structure exercise I developed for the Master of Science (M.Sc.) in Advanced Management Practice (AMP) within the School of Management. In the second example I discuss the unconscious dynamics collectively mobilized by pharmacists in Wales who were part of an action learning group that was addressing leadership.

The AMP Behavior-and-Structure Exercise

The M.Sc. in AMP is designed as a fast-track program for adults in their early twenties who have recently graduated with initial degrees in fields related to business and management. The students are often bright, enthusiastic, and diverse in their backgrounds and experience. The experiential exercise is designed to illustrate the importance of understanding the way in which structure and behavior are inextricably linked in agency. The lesson that I hope students take from the event is on the importance of the generative consequences of behavior, action, and inaction—how working together (and apart) creates explicit and implicit structures that then further

Fig. 8.1 The woman sign, used for the configuration of chairs in the behavior-and-structure exercise conducted in the master's program for advanced management practice at the Bath School of Management

determine how people work together (or do not). In this particular exercise, however, the learning space contains a specific juxtaposition of chairs that is closely linked to interpersonal and social emotions and politics (see Fig. 8.1). The students are aware of entering a room with a configuration of chairs, but they are not aware of the reason the chairs are so arranged.

This pattern is chosen because it has social and political potency for most learning groups. It represents a perpetual emotional and political issue within groups, the desire to avoid interacting with the complex dynamics between the men and the women within the group. In addition, it is designed to mirror behavior in organizations by emphasizing the significance of gendered power relations in terms of organizational practice and performance. I have used this exercise with two AMP groups so far (AMP1: 19 students, encompassing 11 women and 8 men; and AMP2: 27 students, encompassing 16 women and 11 men). The instructions that the students receive at the beginning of this exercise are usually something like the following formulation: "This is an exercise called the Behavior-and-Structure Exercise. What you do during the time allocated for the exercise is for you to decide and to manage. Your only restriction is that you are not allowed to move the chairs." The exercise itself lasts for 1 h. Then there is another hour to discuss what happened and what it implies for an improved understanding of management and organization.

In the AMP1 group three things occurred that I want to draw to attention. First, during the hour-long exercise, the participants did not recognize the "chair structure" they were in. In the review after the exercise, one individual said that he had noticed the structure but had not said anything about it. Second, several participants left their seats and moved around the chair structure, looking at it from the outside, going back into the structure, and sitting in different places. Third, there was one chair on which each man in this group sat at different times. None of the women in the group sat in this chair. It was the one at the very base of the structure. In the AMP2 group (27 students), the structure was recognized right away by a few of the students. While the exercise was beginning I heard a student near to me whisper to her neighbor that "the chairs are in the woman sign." Not once throughout the hour was this statement made to the whole group. Therefore, some people in the group remained unaware of the structure (the behavior, the issue) that others had recognized. In addition, the members of the AMP2 group were not willing to sit in the structure as a whole and very quickly congregated together in the circle (despite the discomfort for some of having to sit on the floor for an hour).

An important point to remember is that the most relevant interpretations of such behavior are the ones made in context. What matters are the interpretations that belong to the individuals in the room during the hour and the discussions that the interpretations stimulate in terms of reflective dialogue and learning. The key question is "what do the interactions between behavior and structure within the AMP group mean?" For example, my interpretation of the behavior in the AMP1 group, both at the time of the experiment and now, is that the fact that one of the chairs had been occupied by each man in the group but by none of the women at some point or another during the hour is a reflection of unconscious, gendered dynamics in the group. To me, the fact that the whispered knowledge of the gendered structure of the classroom was never voiced in the group as a whole is a very realistic unconscious enactment of gendered dynamics within organizations, where such things are talked about in small groups but rarely in the organization as a whole. However, it really does not matter for the purposes of the exercise whether these unconscious dynamics are referred to as a coincidence (which indeed they were by some of the participants). The unconscious in this situation, as in any such exercise, does not necessarily convey the meaning of behavior in the group. However, it invariably stimulates conversation about gendered relations within the group. The unconscious therefore stimulates "public reflection" (Raelin, 2001) about the politics and power relations in the group, and it stimulates reflection on how "the chance of space may set us down next to the unexpected neighbor" (Massey, 2005, p. 151). It also raises an issue that I could refer to as the unwanted neighbor, for the AMP members were not eager to engage with the gendered unconscious dynamics they were producing.

The Group Dynamics of the Pharmacists' Leadership Program

Action learning is an experiential method designed to help managers learn (McGill & Beaty, 2001). The central premise is that managers learn most effectively not by being taught about leadership, for example, but by examining their own leadership practice over time, by reflecting and acting on their own practice in order to transform it. This examination is usually undertaken within a group of peers who are all similarly engaged in attempts to learn and change. An aspect of action learning that makes it an important method for learning about leadership is that it helps individuals improve their understanding of their own leadership in the emotional and political context of the organizations to which they belong (Vince, 2004, 2008; Vince & Martin, 1993). When people come together in groups, they often bring with them a variety of assumptions and ways of working that characterize their profession, represent ways of thinking to which they are particularly attached, or mirror aspects of the wider organization within which their role is situated. One can therefore understand learning groups as being more than the sum of their individual parts, as having a dynamic that is constructed collectively and unconsciously through the interaction of the individuals involved and through people's mental images of how organizations work ("the way we do things here"). These images are made up of diverse ideas and assumptions that are often unconscious, nonstatic, and connected to politics and relations of power.

In the particular action learning group I am talking about here, each meeting included a period set aside in order to consider the "group process" issues that might have an impact on the work the group was attempting to do on that day. This allowed the participants, pharmacists based in Wales, to reflect on a range of dynamics wider than those belonging only to individuals within the group. For example, in the early stages of the group's development, individuals behaved in ways that reflected the uncertainty of being in a group. This uncertainty was expressed through the difficulty of finding a clear role for oneself in the group without falling into habitual or stereotypical roles and relations. For example, one member of the group positioned herself as the inexperienced young person in the group, another as the older woman who is implicitly elected as the group's "Mum." Although individuals put themselves into these roles (through feelings of anxiety, through past habits, or through discomfort in the present moment), it is the group that locks them into the roles. They start to take on such roles unconsciously and *for the group*. The Mum is therefore relied on to be the person who looks after the group, makes them feel better about conflicts, and speaks up during uncomfortable silences. Once locked into such a role, an individual finds it difficult to escape, and it inhibits both individual and group learning.

The example is apt because it concerns the unconscious dynamics that were mobilized for this group by a change in material space. In this session, the group-process reflections were affected by the fact that the group had been moved from its normal (large, relatively comfortable) room to a different (small, relatively uncomfortable) room. The room "we should have been in" was being used for a meeting of senior managers discussing changes that were taking place within the pharmacists' professional association. One of the members started to reflect on changes in his organization. "There is so much going on politically, lots of uncertainty, lots of change. There are rumors of a new Chief Executive; it is unsettling." And "they are going to be moving us because of a problem with space." Group members were "worried about the reorganization, it is all so unknown. There is a rumor that we might merge with other trusts into one big health authority. It's a big change." There were strong feelings in the group: feelings of uncertainty about the working environment for pharmacists, about the learning group, and about "what is going on downstairs; knowing that there are discussions about the future of the profession. What is the impact on us and on our jobs?" One of the group members said: "We haven't got a clue about what is going on downstairs." The physical process of being moved connected to and stimulated emotions and associations about the broader changes and uncertainties that were part of pharmacy going forward. There were unconscious associations between experience "here and now" in the discomfort of a new location (a "dislocation") and the emotional discomforts and dislocations that were integral to being a pharmacist at a time of change and uncertainty within the profession.

These examples from the M.Sc. in AMP and the pharmacists' action learning group illustrate why it might be important for managers and management students to be given opportunities to relate learning, space, and the unconscious. The material space of the classroom connects to the relational space of learning, affording opportunities to view the ways in which conscious and unconscious organizational dynamics are enacted in the classroom. The material space of the classroom and the relational space of learning combine to provide a temporary container within which to view emotional and political processes that are difficult to address within organizations. In addition, there are opportunities to examine and transform the organization-in-the-mind, both individual and collective. Struggles with learning often mirror broader struggles with organizing: to let go of defenses; to engage emotionally; to give voice to social and political dynamics; and to encourage interpretations of behavior, action, and inaction. In the final section of this chapter, I develop these ideas further, link them to leadership, and present some thoughts on the future development of this area.

Discussion and Conclusion

In this final section I discuss spatial and relational dynamics within the management classroom and the ways they are linked to the unconscious in groups. I have used my provisional conceptual framework to analyze the two examples above. Through this analysis, I was looking for a more detailed explanation of the interplay between relatedness and throwntogetherness, in order to elaborate these concepts and assert their importance in developing an understanding of management and organizational learning. The examples provide insights into ways that management learning can be designed with an awareness of the interaction between learning and space. Such awareness is likely to include spatial relations (juxtapositions of power in material space), relational space (process dynamics, concerning, for example, questions of proximity, perception, positioning, fantasy, and projection), and political relatedness (the intersection between power and process).

   The outcome of a spatial perspective on management learning is an understanding of the predictability of organizational behavior and its complexity. The chair structure produces behavior that represents space (representation of space). Such behavior is tied to existing knowledge, implicit codes, and underlying assumptions that constitute the "architecture of the invisible" (Isaacs, 1999, p. 99). Behavior in the chair structure mirrors behavior in organizations. For example, gendered power relations in the chair structure were whispered about in little groups of two or three AMP2 members but were never engaged with in the overall AMP2 learning group. In organizations, gendered power relations are often spoken about in subsystems but rarely engaged with in terms of the system as a whole. The danger implicit in systemic engagement with power relations is that the organization may have to change. The chair structure also produces complexity. It produces strange juxtapositions, antagonisms, and fractures as well as unwanted emotions, senses, and desires (spaces of representation). In other words, the chair structure reveals the politics of place. Unconsciously, the learning group refuses to recognize the chair structure even though parts of the group know its meaning. Whereas the conscious knowledge of the structure has an impact on the few, unconscious social defenses protect the group (or organization) as a whole against the anxiety produced by relations of power.

In the action learning group of pharmacists, individuals get themselves stuck in a role—the inexperienced person, the group mum, the individual who can facilitate the group. This role pattern is not only an expression of the feelings that individuals have about being in the group or a reflection of their habitual individual behavior within groups. It is also an unconscious process of limiting the learning potential within the group. Such potential for learning arises from being able to share roles, from discarding habitual ways of thinking and working, and from challenging the stuckness that the group creates in order to limit learning. Once again, these responses can be seen as a mirror of organizational dynamics, in which organizations find sophisticated unconscious mechanisms to defend against change. Despite evident desires to make change happen, organizations are always at the same time concerned with defending the status quo.

The constant tension in organizations, and in the experience of organizational members, about simultaneously making and resisting change creates unconscious ambivalence about management and organizational learning. When a member of the action learning group declares (on behalf of all group members) that, as a result of changes in material space, "we haven't got a clue about what is going on downstairs," this dislocation connects what is happening now, what is occurring in the organization (they are "worried about the reorganization"), and the broader uncertainties with the pharmacists' profession ("so much going on politically, lots of uncertainty, lots of change"). Dislocation and antagonism (much more than consensus) grant individuals and organizations opportunities for learning and change. However, organizational members often struggle to avoid the emotions generated within such conflicts and thereby create and mobilize unconscious organizational designs that limit members' contact with and understanding of the emotional and political dynamics that surround them. These reflections on space, learning, and the unconscious imply a shift in the way that emotion and power are connected in organizations. This change poses a complex question for further research: "not what kind of affects should we allow—but what kind of affects should be allowed to dominate and through what expressive forms?" (Hoggett & Thompson, 2002, p. 114).

The interplay between learning and space is expressed unconsciously and consciously in organizations. Through patterns of relatedness, through the emotional and political dynamics of relational space, organizations manufacture and reinforce "the way we do things here." However, there are ambiguities of throwntogetherness that can *place* people alongside the unexpected neighbor, and thereby offer opportunities to be surprised or confused, to notice the unexpected, and to engage with the implications that arise for learning within and from relational space. In the introduction to this chapter, I cited the example of leadership in organizations. Leadership is most often thought of and related to individuals, and I suggested that an improved awareness of spatial relations and unconscious dynamics might underpin insights into a broadened understanding of leadership within organizations. Noticing the unexpected neighbor, in whatever emotional and political form it takes, connects to a different model of leadership, one that offers both an individual and a collective perspective on leadership in organizations. This emerging model constructs leadership on the basis of the individual and collective ability to "notice what you are noticing" (James & Ladkin, 2008, p. 19) and to see leadership less in relation to what an individual knows and more in terms of interpreting, connecting, and intervening in spaces of learning and change.

References

Bazelgette, J., Hutton, J., & Reed, B. (1997). The organization-in-the-mind. In J. E. Neumann, K. Kellner, & A. Dawson-Shepherd (Eds.), *Developing organizational consultancy* (pp. 113–126). London: Routledge.

Brocklehurst, M. (2006). Space, organization and management. In S. Clegg & M. Kornberger (Eds.), *Space, organization and management theory* (pp. 101–126). Copenhagen, Denmark: Copenhagen Business School.

Carr, A., & Hancock, P. (2007). Paris, art, aesthetics, work and the unconscious. *Tamara, 6*, 5–11.

Clegg, S., & Kornberger, M. (2006). *Space, organization and management theory*. Copenhagen, Denmark: Copenhagen Business School.

Coopey, J. (1995). The learning organization: Power, politics and ideology. *Management Learning, 26*, 193–213.

Dale, K., & Burrell, G. (2007). *Spaces of organization and the organization of space: Power, identity and materiality at work*. Basingstoke, UK: Palgrave Macmillan.

Easterby-Smith, M., & Lyles, M. (2003). Introduction: Watersheds of organizational learning and knowledge management. In M. Easterby-Smith & M. Lyles (Eds.), *The handbook of organizational learning and knowledge management* (pp. 1–16). Oxford, UK: Blackwell.

Ford, J., & Harding, N. (2004). We went looking for an organization but could only find the metaphysics of its presence. *Sociology, 38*, 815–830.

French, R., & Vince, R. (1999). *Group relations, management and organization*. Oxford, UK: Oxford University Press.

Gabriel, Y. (1997). Meeting god: When organization members come face to face with the supreme leader. *Human Relations, 50*, 315–342.

Gherardi, S. (1999). Learning as problem-driven or learning in the face of mystery? *Organization Studies, 20*, 101–124.

Gherardi, S., & Nicolini, D. (2001). The sociological foundations of organizational learning. In M. Dierkes, A. Berthoin Antal, J. Child, & I. Nonaka (Eds.), *The handbook of organizational learning and knowledge* (pp. 35–60). Oxford, UK: Oxford University Press.

Harvey, D. (2005). *Spaces of neoliberalization: Towards a theory of uneven geographical development*. Hettner-Lecture: Vol. 8. Stuttgart, Germany: Franz Steiner.

Hoggett, P., & Thompson, S. (2002). Towards a democracy of the emotions. *Constellations, 9*, 106–126.

Isaacs, W. (1999). *Dialogue and the art of thinking together*. New York: Random House.

James, K., & Ladkin, D. (2008). Meeting the challenge of leading in the 21st century: Beyond the 'deficit model' of leadership development. In K. James & J. Collins (Eds.), *Leadership learning: Knowledge into action* (pp. 13–34). London: Palgrave Macmillan.

Kornberger, M., & Clegg, S. (2003). The architecture of complexity. *Culture and Organization, 9*, 75–91.

Lefebvre, H. (1991). *The production of space* (D. Nicholson-Smith, Trans.). Oxford, UK: Blackwell.

Massey, D. (1993). Politics and space/time. In M. Keith & S. Pile (Eds.), *Place and the politics of identity* (pp. 141–161). London: Routledge.

Massey, D. (2005). *For space*. London: Sage.

McGill, I., & Beaty, L. (2001). *Action learning* (2nd ed.). London: Kogan Page.

Meusburger, P. (2008). The nexus of knowledge and space. In P. Meusburger, M. Welker, & E. Wunder (Eds.), *Clashes of knowledge: Orthodoxies and heterodoxies in science and religion* (pp. 35–90). Knowledge and Space: Vol. 1. Dordrecht, The Netherlands: Springer.

Raelin, J. A. (2001). Public reflection as the basis of learning. *Management Learning, 32*, 11–30.

Senge, P. (1990). *The fifth discipline: The art and practice of the learning organization.* New York: Doubleday.

Shapiro, E., & Carr, A. W. (1993). *Lost in familiar places.* New Haven, CN: Yale University Press.

Stokes, J. (1994). The unconscious at work in groups and teams: Contributions from the work of Winfred Bion. In A. Obholzer & V. Z. Roberts (Eds.), *The unconscious at work: Individual and organizational stress in the human services* (pp. 19–27). London: Routledge.

Taylor, S., & Spicer, A. (2007). Time for space: A narrative review of research on organizational spaces. *International Journal of Management Reviews, 9*, 325–346.

Vince, R. (2001). Power and emotion in organizational learning. *Human Relations, 54*, 1325–1351.

Vince, R. (2002). The politics of imagined stability: A psychodynamic understanding of change at Hyder plc. *Human Relations, 55*, 1189–1208.

Vince, R. (2004). *Rethinking strategic learning.* London: Routledge.

Vince, R. (2008). 'Learning-in-action' and 'learning inaction': Advancing the theory and practice of critical action learning. *Action Learning: Research and Practice, 5*, 93–104.

Vince, R., & Martin, L. (1993). Inside action learning: The psychology and the politics of the action learning model. *Management Education and Development, 24*, 205–215.

Weinberg, H. (2007). So, what is this social unconscious anyway? *Group Analysis, 40*, 307–322.

Can Social Space Provide a Deep Structure for the Theory and Practice of Organizational Learning?

9

Victor J. Friedman and Israel J. Sykes

In opening the sixth symposium on knowledge and space, entitled *Knowledge and Learning in Organizations*, Peter Meusburger raised the rhetorical question of whether "environment" is a social or a spatial phenomenon. The either–or framing of this question implies that the social and the spatial are discrete phenomena. In this chapter we challenge the either–or framing, arguing that the social world *is* a spatial phenomenon, that is, that all social phenomena can be understood as configurations of and changes in social space.

According to the perspective we set forth, social space has a reality of its own and is distinct from physical space, though the two are related and influence each other. Both social science and popular discourse are deeply infused with the idea of social space; they constantly refer to "a space for ...." or to different kinds of "spaces." These usages of the term *space* are largely metaphorical, rarely referring to physical space. However, the meaning of space in these contexts is rarely defined in a rigorous way.

Two of the greatest pioneering and influential social scientists of the twentieth century, the psychologist Kurt Lewin (e.g., 1948, 1951) and the sociologist Pierre Bourdieu (e.g., 1985, 1989, 1998), both viewed the social world as a spatial phenomenon. Lewin and Bourdieu are seldom associated with one another, but they both used social space as the basic construct in building their respective *field* theories, which constituted the foundation for all their work. Nevertheless, the underlying concept of social space has largely been ignored in subsequent theory and research.

V.J. Friedman (✉)
Department of Sociology and Anthropology/Department of Behavioral Sciences,
Max Stern Yezreel Valley College, Jezreel Valley 19300, Israel
e-mail: victorf@yvc.ac.il

I.J. Sykes
Independent Consultant, Levy 10, Jerusalem 93628, Israel
e-mail: Israels@jdc.org.il

A. Berthoin Antal et al. (eds.), *Learning Organizations: Extending the Field*,
Knowledge and Space 6, DOI 10.1007/978-94-007-7220-5_9,
© Springer Science+Business Media Dordrecht 2014

In this chapter we revisit social space, picking up the trails blazed by Lewin and Bourdieu, in order to clarify the meaning of this construct and then explore its potential for building theory and guiding practice in organizational learning. This initial exploration of social space addresses the following questions: Why are social scientists interested in space? What is social space and how does it affect behavior and experience? What does "organizational learning" mean as a spatial phenomenon? What, if anything, does the idea of social space add to what people can see, think, feel, or do?

The Experience of Social Space

Our exploration of social space began with personal experiences that we had had long before we met.

Victor: It was my first job as a high school teacher in the late 1970s. Because I had had no formal training as a teacher and no experience in schools, I had to learn how to teach on the job and discovered that I was able help kids learn more than they thought possible. My first year of teaching was challenging, enjoyable, and rewarding. Despite many complaints I heard from other teachers—especially about the principal—I loved the work, the students, and the school. During the second year, however, I became aware of limits to what I could accomplish with the students in my classroom. I felt it had something to do with what was happening in the rest of school, and I could see quite a few things that needed to be changed. Rather than complain, I came up with an idea for change and the principal gave his approval, but my efforts failed. Later, I found out that the change project had been undermined by the principal and others in the school. I became extremely angry and was easily swept up in the stream of gossip and criticism against the principal, which only made things worse. It was like hitting a wall. When I tried to push this wall back, it pushed back at me. The harder I pushed the wall, the harder it pushed back, until it felt like the walls were closing in on all sides. I still loved teaching and my students, but my perception of the school completely changed. I felt trapped in a closed, dark, and suffocating space and left the school at the end of my second year.

Israel: While taking a course in psychopathology as part of a master's degree in family therapy, I was exposed to the diagnosis of bipolar disorder and recognized that much of what I had undergone in the previous 10 years matched the symptoms described in the diagnosis. A year later I decided that my reflections on my own experience with the illness could be used as a basis for a thesis. In the attempt to convey my encounter with the manic and depressive phases of the illness, I recognized that the universally accepted imagery of ups and downs captured my experience much less well than did the three-dimensional imagery of an oscillating expansion and contraction of my experience of myself and my place in the world. I discovered Lewin's concept of the life space and found that it gave me a construct with which I could analyze what I had been living through. I found that conceptualizing hypomania as an expansion of the life space and depression as a contraction of it helped me make sense of many experiences—not only those of the bipolar individual but also those of the healthy spouse with whom he or she lives—that the common two-dimensional imagery failed to capture.

The common denominator between these two very different cases is space. In both, and quite independently, Lewin's concept of the life space spoke to our experienced psychosocial realities. *Physical* space played little role in either of them, but their spatial nature was quite real, not just metaphorical.

According to Lewin (1937), an individual's life space encompasses all the dimensions of existence of which that person is aware: self/environment, individual/group, physical/psychological, fantasy/reality, and past-present-future time (see Gold, 1999, p. 68). Within this framework, it is possible to understand human experience by identifying the structure of one's life space and by tracking the effects that changes in that structure have on experience. Thus, Victor's perception that the walls were "closing in" within the school context reflected a shift from an open to a highly restricted life space. Similarly, Israel's shift from hypomania to depression reflected a transition from a relatively boundless life space of immense possibility to a highly restrictive narrowing of the life space. In both cases, limits to our "space of free movement" created a high state of tension and even pathology (Lewin, 1948, p. 150). Victor was able to relieve the tension by leaving the organization and, thus, changing the life space. For Israel, medication was required to help neutralize the alternating expansion and contraction.

Our shared interest in life space led us into an in-depth exploration of Lewin's work (Gold, 1999; Lewin, 1948, 1951) and a search for more conceptualizations and applications of social space. We found numerous references to the word "space" but were surprised to discover few systematic, theoretical treatments of *social* space. The exception was the work of Pierre Bourdieu, who built his entire sociology on a theory of fields that, though different than Lewin's, shared the same fundamental assumptions about the social world. In the following sections we draw on both Lewin and Bourdieu to define social space and present a set of constructs that might enable us to use this concept as a tool for understanding and engaging social phenomena such as organizational learning.

Social Space as an Invisible Relational Reality

In presenting the concept of social space, Bourdieu (1998) drew a contrast between a "substantialist" and a "relational" understanding of the social world:

> Why does it seem necessary and legitimate for me to introduce the notions of social space and field of power into the lexicon of sociology? In the first place, to break with the tendency to think of the social world in a substantialist manner. The notion of *space* contains, in itself, the principle of *relational* understanding of the social world.... Apparently, directly visible beings, whether individuals or groups, exist and subsist in and through *difference*; that is, they occupy *relative positions* in a space of relations which, although invisible and always difficult to show empirically, is the most reality ... (p. 30, italics in the original).

Substantialist thinking is manifest whenever a theory explains behavior in terms of properties or attributes of any entity, such as personality or cultural traits. It focuses on observable properties of entities and reflects common-sense thinking, one of the reasons for its strong hold over both lay thinking and social science.

The relational approach to understanding the social world accords primacy to relations among agents. In other words, reality is best understood not as consisting *in* people or things but as the relationships *between* people and things. Relations are invisible and can be inferred but not directly observed. However, these hidden relationships are what cause, or explain, surface behavior. As Bourdieu (1989) put it, "the visible, immediately given, hides the invisible which determines it" (p. 16). Lewin (1951) shared this relational understanding of the social world and the belief about the "reality" of social space: "The popular prejudice that the physical space is the only empirical space has made sociologists regard their spatial concepts as merely an analogy…. [T]he social field is actually an empirical space, which is as "real" as a physical one" (p. 151). Both Bourdieu and Lewin argued that one needs to look beyond what is substantive and examine relationships and principles of action that are not directly observable but constitutive of social reality.[1] The irony and counterintuitive facet in these lines of reasoning is the idea that what is most real cannot be seen. There can be no substantive, physical representation of social space. Social space represents the "architecture of the invisible" (Isaacs, 1999, p. 239, as quoted by Russ Vince during the symposium). It can only be thought or experienced—though Lewin, in particular, went to great lengths in trying to represent social spaces graphically.

The Structure of Social Fields

Both Lewin (1948) and Bourdieu (1998) employed the concept of field as the basis for conceptualizing social space, but they focused on different aspects of the field and used different terminology to do so. For Bourdieu, fields consist of individuals who occupy points in social space and become linked in particular configurations (e.g., groups) that themselves become linked in particular ways. As a sociologist, he was concerned with how fields are constructed in social space, how position[2] within a field influences not only behavior and the formation of groups but also the formation and maintenance of dominance relationships, and how fields can be transformed.

Lewin (1951), as a psychologist, sought to understand and influence human behavior, which he conceived to be the product of changes in position in the life space over time (p. 248). "Field theory" represented his endeavor to make these changes accessible to empirical study. He stated that "behavior has to be derived from a totality of coexisting facts" and that "these coexisting facts have the character of a 'dynamic field' in so far as the state of any part of this field depends on every other part of the field" (pp. 24–25). He studied how changes in the life space led to changes in experience, and how such changes affected human development and behavior at individual, group, organizational, and societal-cultural levels.

Both Bourdieu and Lewin pointed to the simultaneous existence of a multitude of dynamic fields, often overlapping or intersecting, within a given society. Bourdieu

---

[1] At this point in our inquiry, our intention is not to enter the hotly debated question of what constitutes social reality but rather to communicate our understanding of the position taken by Lewin and Bourdieu.

[2] Bourdieu commonly used the word *position* in referring to what, strictly speaking, is a point occupied by a particular agent in a field.

(1998) indeed saw society as a complex web of fields. An individual's existence may be defined by a single field, but most people exist simultaneously in a variety of fields—as points where these fields intersect. One of the authors of this chapter, for instance, is a male, a husband, a father, an organizational psychologist, an associate professor, an action researcher, a Jew, an Israeli, an American, a liberal, and so forth. Each of these aspects of self connects him with a field to which he is potentially related. His position vis-à-vis these fields determines both the perspective from which he views the social world around him and the forces that shape his actions.

The social world is dynamic and continually evolving through processes in which fields differentiate themselves from existing sets of relationships and take on structures and identities of their own. This process of differentiation leads to the emergence of fields that link people in different ways and guide behavior according to different logics. Fields have a historical existence, having differentiated themselves during a specific period of time, under a specific set of circumstances, and as the result of specific actions.

This idea of differentiation is critical to understanding not only the relations between fields but also the relational structure within any given field. Bourdieu (1998) describes each field as having its own "structure of difference" (p. 32)—a unique logic and pattern (hierarchy) of relations. He describes a social field as a multidimensional space of positions that makes it possible for every agent (person or group) within that particular field to be defined in terms of a specific set of coordinates pertinent to it.

For Lewin, the fundamental elements of a life space are differentiated regions and the boundaries that define them. The life space of an individual or a group can be composed of any number of regions, each representing a psychologically important element. The structure of the life space is the number and position of each region relative to every other region in the life space.

Forces Promoting the Stability of Social Fields

For Lewin (1951), an individual's orientation to his or her life space derives from "valences" (p. 80), a general construct for representing the effect of needs, motives, ideals, or any psychological state that orients an individual or group toward, or away from, a particular region in the life space (e.g., a goal). Positive valence means that a region is attractive; negative valence means that the person or group is repelled by that region (pp. 256–257). The forces toward a positive, or away from a negative, valence can be called *driving forces*, and barriers to driving forces are *restraining forces* (p. 259).

Lewin (1997) attributed the constancy of fields to self-regulatory processes acting on a constellation of counteracting forces, keeping group life at the same level despite disturbances (p. 286). When a life space is in a state of equilibrium, the sum of the counteracting forces is zero. Equilibrium does not mean that fields are static. On the contrary, Lewin (1948) saw fields as "quasi-stationary equilibria" (p. 46) or as equilibria in movement. A culture is not a static affair but a live process like a river which moves but still keeps a recognizable form. Food habits of a group, as well as such phenomena as the speed of production in a factory, are the result of a multitude of forces. Some forces support each other, some oppose each other. Some are driving forces, others restraining forces. Like the velocity of a river, the actual conduct of a group depends on the level at which these conflicting forces reach equilibrium. (Lewin, 1951, p. 172).

Bourdieu (1998) explained the relative stability of social fields by pointing to the mutually reinforcing properties of social structures and individual consciousness. On the one hand, a social field consists of objective structures independent of the consciousness and will of agents, which are capable of guiding and constraining their practices or their representations. On the other hand, it is also distinguished by *habitus*, a durable, cognitive structure that represents the internalization of the external, objective set of relations determined by location in the field of power. The habitus is "a kind of practical sense for what is to be done in a given situation—what in sport is called a 'feel' for the game" (p. 25). Habitus functions at a preconscious level. Social agents employ relatively fixed and predictable "strategies" of which they are unaware. This feature of habitus explains why people and groups in dominated positions within a given field act in ways that implicitly accept the rules of the game and reinforce their own domination.[3]

Habitus not only shapes the thinking and action of people but also the social field itself. People's perceiving, thinking, feeling, and behaving are shaped by the social spaces in which they exist. At the same time, however, fields (social spaces in which people exist) are shaped by people's perceiving, thinking feeling, and behaving. When people act on the basis of habitus, they reconstruct the social world, which then reimposes itself on people, reinforcing or reshaping the habitus.

The force that holds a field together, gives it shape, and lends power to the rules implicit in the habitus, are the meanings that people in the field share with one another. Lewin's (1948) studies of conflict in marriage and industry illustrated that the meanings people attach to a particular situation or goal play a central role in keeping the field together. At the Knowledge and Space symposium Charles Savage called it *Sinnergie*, or the "energizing power of meaning." *Fields* exist as independent entities only as long as the system of shared meanings among agents lends sense and coherence to their relationships and the rules governing their behavior. When meaning breaks down, the forces that hold the field together weaken, setting the stage for change or even dissolution of the field.

---

[3] There is a striking resemblance between the idea of habitus and the idea of theory-in-action developed by Argyris and Schön (1974, 1978). Both represent mental models that guide perception, thinking, and behavior in a wide variety of situations. Both are shaped by external structures (e.g., organizational theories of action) and then, through action, shape these structures. Both function almost automatically and outside conscious awareness. Bourdieu, like Argyris and Schön, stresses that behavior cannot be understood through the explanations given by people (i.e., espoused theory) but only through observation and study of the habitus (theory-in-use). All three authors use these concepts to explain how people act in ways that are self-defeating (ineffectiveness) or reinforce their own dominance without being aware of their own agency or causal responsibility.

Processes of Learning, Change, and Transformation in Social Fields

To Lewin (1951), learning, as a "change in cognitive structure" (p. 66) meant going from a less to a more differentiated life space. Differentiation represented the cognitive structuring of a situation, and learning entailed a cognitive restructuring of the life space. He saw the differentiation of the life space into clearly defined regions as characteristic of both normal human development and learning in general. Lewin considered changes in valences and values as a form of learning that went beyond differentiation. Essentially, it involved changing the meanings—the likes and dislikes—applied to the particular regions.

On the one hand, fields tend to be highly conservative and self-reinforcing. Bourdieu and Lewin questioned illusionary notions of freedom by illustrating how deeply embedded human behavior is in fields that are generally beyond people's awareness. However, they also argued that awareness and understanding of fields held the key to human freedom of choice. Bourdieu (1998) believed that his approach to social science "offers some of the most efficacious means of attaining the freedom from social determinisms which is possible only through knowledge of those very determinisms" (p. ix).

Change is possible because the social world (i.e., fields) always contains a certain degree of ambiguity. The objects of the social world can be perceived and expressed in a variety of ways. This objective element of ambiguity provides a basis for the multiplicity of visions of the world that is linked to the plurality of positions in social space. Thus, any given structure is not immutable; people are capable of literally thinking outside the box.

Change processes in social fields can be seen as "symbolic struggles over the power to produce and to impose the legitimate vision of the world" (Bourdieu, 1989, p. 19). Change may be introduced by acts of naming or representation that make hidden realities visible or that transform the categories of perception, appreciation, and evaluation through which the social world is constructed (Bourdieu, 1998). Social conflicts and struggles are waged to promote the dominance of alternative possible meanings—the very words and names that would be used to construct and express social reality.

Organizational Learning as Patterns of Change in Social Space

Over the past 20 years, organizational learning has emerged as a critical concern for managers (Arthur & Aiman-Smith, 2001, p. 738; Senge, 1990). It has been called an "essential core competency" for managers, consultants, and researchers (Sugarman, 2001, p. 62). Today, it would be hard to find any organization that does not aspire to be a "learning organization" (Gherardi, 1999, p. 103). Nevertheless, organizational learning remains an elusive concept to managers and researchers alike (Arthur & Aiman-Smith, 2001; Crossan & Guatto, 1996; Crossan, Lane, & Roderick, 1999; Easterby-Smith, 1997; Garvin, 2000). Despite the explosive growth in the literature, the field still lacks theoretical integration or convergence on what is meant by the term (Crossan et al., 1999; Friedman, Lipshitz, & Popper, 2005; Garvin, 2000; Snell, 2001). Operationally defining and measuring organizational learning has proven to be "excruciatingly hard to do" (Arthur & Aiman-Smith, 2001, p. 739), so there is still a lack of cumulative, empirical research (Lant, 2000).

Lipshitz, Friedman, and Popper (2007) have attributed this state of affairs to the "mystification" of organizational learning. One of the causes of mystification has been the tendency of different scientific disciplines to generate their own terminologies, assumptions, concepts, and research methods. Early in the history of this concept, Argyris and Schön (1978) concluded that the challenge was to "invent a productive synthesis of fragmentary approaches" (p. 331), but synthesis has been difficult to come by. Another cause of mystification has been anthropomorphism—extrapolation from individual, human learning processes to a nonhuman entity, such as an organization (Doving, 1996), a practice that obscures the critical question of how the learning of individual organizational members becomes "organizational." To overcome mystification, Lipshitz et al. (2007) called for concepts that avoid the pitfalls of multiple parochial disciplines and anthropomorphism, that can guide the study and practice of organizational learning in a wide variety of organizational contexts and at all levels of management, that provide a terminology clearly connectable to observable phenomena, and that are neither overly visionary nor overly skeptical.

We suggest that social-space field theory, by providing a new (though old) set of constructs by which organizational learning can be reconceptualized, has the potential to bridge and integrate the different disciplinary approaches to organizational learning—and can provide a surprising remedy for the issue of anthropomorphism. Both Lewin and Bourdieu regarded social space and field theory as a way of unifying the social sciences by representing psychological, social, cultural, and economic phenomena through a single set of constructs. In other words, learning can be understood as particular patterns of changes within the structure of a field (e.g., differentiation or restructuring) or the rules governing its behavior (e.g., habitus). These changes can occur at various levels: within an individual, among individuals, between the individual and the organization, between groups and the organization, and between the organization and its environment. However, the *pattern* of change is the same regardless of the level. This approach stands the problem of anthropomorphism on its head. Rather than positing organizational learning as an extension of individual learning, it suggests that both individual and organizational learning can be understood in terms of a set of constructs that are neither specifically human nor organizational.

Using the field constructs described earlier, we suggest that organizational learning be understood as processes of maintaining, reforming, deconstructing, and/or reconstructing patterns of connection through which different regions in a field interrelate. Learning entails changing the structure of the field by redefining (i.e., differentiating) boundaries and by discovering new regions. It may also encompass reshaping the symbolic structure of the field in ways that reorder position in the hierarchy, change the meaning of existing structures, or create entirely new meanings.

Given this overall approach, we have identified at least five patterns of change in social space that we call "learning": knowing your place, migration, emigration, reformation, and transformation. In the rest of this section, we describe these patterns and illustrate them with findings of action research aimed at helping secondary schools better serve "socially excluded" student populations in Israel (Friedman, Razer, & Sykes, 2004).

Pattern 1: Knowing Your Place

This pattern of learning relates to both an acceptance of a position within a particular field and an alignment between the organization's representation of itself (habitus) with the principles of differentiation and rules of the game that govern the field. Knowing your place represents a form of adaptation or socialization and internalization—acceptance of an externally designed structure and set of expectations. Strictly speaking, one might say that "knowing your place" is not learning at all. This criticism is probably valid when an organization's strategy and structure are perfectly aligned with the worldviews and rules that govern the field. In practice, however, there are gaps to which the organization must respond. And since fields are dynamic, knowing one's place does not necessarily imply passivity or lack of movement. There is always the danger of falling, or being pushed, out of one's place, so maintaining one's current position requires learning.

The schools and classrooms we worked with serve students who have the potential to succeed but who become caught up in a cycle of failure and disruptive behavior, a spiral that leads to their concentration in special frameworks marked by disorder, severe behavioral problems, little academic achievement, violence, and alienation.[4] Most teachers are untrained for work with these students and experience chronic failure, helplessness, shame, and fear, displaying high levels of absenteeism, low motivation, and verbal aggressiveness toward students, parents, and peers. School administrators feel that they are blamed for failures not of their making and that their school is used as "dumping grounds" for students (and teachers) on whom the system has given up. The administrators often react by blaming the teachers, who feel increasingly unsupported, abandoned, marginalized, and alienated from the system.

In this case the field can be defined as the school system as a whole, in which certain regions (schools and classrooms) have been differentiated as frameworks for students regarded by the system as low achievers and behavior problems that cannot be managed in the regular classrooms. Despite the special characteristics of the school's students, these frameworks operate, and are evaluated, in reference to performance norms applied to the larger field. Administrators and faculty tend to internalize these standards and to accept the system's view of the students as being chronic failures and deviants, who are at the lowest level of the hierarchy.

---

[4]These students generally come from comparatively low socioeconomic levels, new immigrant groups, ethnic minorities, and/or family situations characterized by breakdown and neglect.

The "learning" at the level of the school has to do with developing strategies (blame, withdrawal, rigidity, and apathy) for survival within an intolerable and unchangeable situation that generates feelings such as helplessness, guilt, and fear. There is little or no learning at the level of the region, for the governing habitus is unchallenged and the connections between regions in the social field remain stable.

Pattern 2: Migration

Migration as a pattern of learning is a moving from one place to another, usually a more advantageous one, within a field. Migration reflects an acceptance of the structure and rules of the field, including the values implicit in the relations of hierarchy or dominance among positions. Learning means a jockeying for position in which agents attempt to raise their status relative to perceived competitors. It is about developing strategies through which agents change their positions or perceptions of their position. Such migration leaves the overall structure of the space unchanged, but as some agents migrate "up," they may create vacuums that need to be filled, exerting pressure on other organizations to migrate "down" or on the field as a whole to redefine what constitutes position.

Many of the schools that serve excluded students try to migrate out of the position in which they have been placed in the field. Implicit within this strategy is an acceptance of the norms and standards of the field but a refusal to be reconciled with the position imposed on educational institutions in that field. The most straightforward strategy for migration is to improve student performance on standardized tests significantly, but these schools generally lack the capacity do so.

Alternatively, schools seek to portray themselves to the outside as "normal" and to deny or minimize the existence of a problematic student population, continually trying to attract "better students" through a heavy investment in "marketing." The latter strategy requires significant learning and, like the strategy of improving performance, is rarely successful. The difficulty these schools face in changing their position seems to indicate that maintenance of their position is particularly functional for the rest of the field: It helps other schools function relatively unhindered, at least in the short term.

When a school does succeed in migrating to a more advantageous position by attracting better students, it leaves the structure of the field unchanged but creates a tension in the field that must be addressed. One way of dealing with this tension is for another school to migrate down. Another way is for the system to simply readjust the norms and standards for moving up in the hierarchy, recourse that manifests itself in "grade inflation" or the erosion of a particular academic degree's value so that a higher degree is essential for upward mobility.

Pattern 3: Emigration

The pattern of learning we call emigration means leaving one field and moving to another. Emigration relates to a rejection of the principles of differentiation, values, and rules of one field and the acceptance of those of another. It is similar to a process of conversion because it entails taking on a new habitus. Emigration may be a matter of choice or it may be imposed on an organization. Either way, it requires significant learning in terms of differentiating and reshaping the meaning structure of an existing field in order to fit into a new field. Examples of emigration include nonprofit organizations turning themselves into for-profits (or vice versa), a production organization becoming a marketing organization (or vice versa), public or cooperative firms undergoing privatization, and private firms undergoing nationalization. In terms of the schools we studied, emigration rarely occurs, for most of the schools do not have the necessary freedom of choice to switch fields. However, it sometimes takes place when a school leaves one school system and enters another. An example might be the decision to leave a secular system to join a parallel religious educational system, or vice versa. Similarly, a school might decide to leave the official state-supervised educational system and establish an unrecognized school in which it is free to operate according to alternate values.

Pattern 4: Reformation

This pattern of learning involves reshaping or constructing spaces within an existing field. It may mean creating a new space among existing agents or filling an existing space with new meaning. Reformation often leads to the creation of "alternative" spaces within a field, that is, spaces with rules different than those dictated by the field as a whole. It encompasses the exercise of conscious choice, either by management or by individuals or groups within the organization, to create alternative spaces that challenge the structure of the larger field.

Creating alternative spaces and keeping them open requires considerable symbolic work and generates a degree of tension within the system. In the long run, the fate of these spaces depends on the field's response to the tension that their existence creates. There seem to be three alternative paths that reformation takes over time:

1. A new equilibrium that accommodates the larger field's ongoing tension caused by the existence of an alternative space
2. A closing down of the alternative space or a change of the alternative nature of that space so that it becomes governed by the values of the larger field (a change that might eventually prompt occupants of that space to emigrate from the field)
3. A transformation of the larger field as it adopts the values developed and maintained in the subspace

In terms of the schools, reformation is illustrated by the intervention program aimed at changing relations among the main agents—teachers, administrators, students, and, to some extent, parents—and at changing the meaning structure that the field imposes on the schools. The reformation process in these schools is based on a conscious *choice* by school faculty to work with this population. It is not a matter of blaming or passing these intractable problems on to others. This choice means accepting an extremely complex and difficult, but not impossible, task that depends on developing a level of professionalism and specialized skills not required of teachers in mainstream settings. By learning to see students as whole and complex individuals and becoming acquainted with their lives outside of schools, the faculty creates a much more differentiated map of the student region than teachers elsewhere generally do. At the same time, the school's faculty and administrators create an ever more differentiated map of their regions by deepening their awareness of their own resources as individuals and as a team. This differentiation vastly increases the variety of options for matching needs to resources.

Pattern 5: Transformation

Transformation as a pattern of learning has to do with a complete reorganization of the field, a change in the principles of differentiation and the rules of the game. Transformation may be a relatively rapid process that requires one to let go of the meanings that hold a field together so as to allow for complete reconstruction. This letting go is what Lewin (1951) referred to as the process of "unfreezing" (p. 231) that needs to take place for change to occur (Friedman & Lipshitz, 1992). We can think of two examples of transformation, both of which relate to fields that are much larger than organizations. One is the transformation that Germany underwent after Hitler came to power in 1933. Within an amazingly short time, both the relational and meaning structure of German society completely shifted. A similar transformation occurred with the fall of the Berlin Wall in 1989 and the collapse of the Soviet Union in 1992. In both cases, the transformation was preceded by a period of chaos in which the structures and meaning systems that held the field together became progressively ineffectual.

Transformation may involve conscious choice. Friedman and Lipshitz (1992) called this process "shifting cognitive gears"—a process that entails accepting a temporary loss of control for the purpose of learning. It can be the product of the deterioration or destruction of a previous field, but it can also result—with or without a precipitating crisis—from intentional work by organizational leaders who recognize the need or desirability of transformation and navigate the transition of the field to a new phase in which it is governed by new values and relationships. Such a process is inevitably fraught with tension, extreme existential anxieties, and pressures toward regression.

Conclusion

The goal of this chapter has been to take a first step in exploring the concept of social space and its utility as a deep structure for understanding organizational learning. The idea of a deep structure reflects a relational, rather than substantialist approach to understanding the social world. It implies that a true understanding of social phenomena requires constructs that are not directly observable but capable of explaining a wide variety of phenomena at different levels of analysis based on the same set of constructs. In our exploration we have revisited the work of Kurt Lewin and Pierre Bourdieu, pioneering social scientists who based their innovative theoretical and methodological approaches on the concept of social space and field theory. We have tried to clarify what these concepts meant to these theorists and to distill a number of basic constructs and principles.

If the concept of social space captures social reality, it should lead to a significant redefinition of what we mean by knowledge and learning. For the purposes of this chapter, we have applied these constructs to organizational learning, suggesting this phenomenon can be understood as five patterns of change in social fields: knowing your place, migration, emigration, reformation, and transformation. Each of these patterns reflects a different way in which organizations learn and the degree of choice that people in organizations exercise in the learning process.

As a deep structure, social space offers a potential unifying framework that can clarify the conceptual confusion created by multiple parochial disciplines. In addition, the treatment of learning as a spatial phenomenon addresses the problem of anthropomorphism because one uses constructs that do not mimic the function of the human nervous system and can apply them at both the individual and organizational level. The exploration in this chapter has been only a first step toward developing a conceptual framework based on social space. Although we have sought to identify useful concepts from both Lewin and Bourdieu, it remains to be seen how they can be integrated into a single framework and studied empirically.

In this chapter we have argued that social space and physical space are different aspects of reality. Physical space appears to be a boundary condition that impinges on and conditions social space. However, it is far from clear how this relationship works and whether it is a one-way or two-way relationship. Another important relationship is that between the concept of social space and other approaches to identifying deep structures, such as system dynamics or systems thinking (Senge, 1990). The latter, for example, explains a wide range of phenomena in terms of causal loops, levels, flows, and time delays. Are these two ways of understanding the social world related or do they instead represent two different and irreconcilable paradigms?

According to the values of the authors of this chapter, these concepts will prove worthy if they enhance the ability to see the social world differently, to explain social phenomena, to make conscious choices, and to act effectively to shape one's world. We began with an intuition that these concepts are indeed of great value, and in this chapter we have attempted to clarify them and demonstrate their usefulness by applying them to the field of organizational learning. If we have been successful, our description of social space and field theory will have at least resonated with the intuitive experience of interested readers, aroused a sense that there is something to these concepts, and piqued curiosity to explore them further and connect additional dots.

References

Argyris, C., & Schön, D. A. (1974). *Theory in practice: Increasing professional effectiveness*. San Francisco: Jossey-Bass.

Argyris, C., & Schön, D. A. (1978). *Organizational learning: A theory of action perspective*. Reading, MA: Addison-Wesley.

Arthur, J. B., & Aiman-Smith, L. (2001). Gainsharing and organizational learning: An analysis of employee suggestions over time. *Academy of Management Journal, 44*, 737–754.

Bourdieu, P. (1985). Social space and the genesis of groups. *Theory and Society, 14*, 723–744.

Bourdieu, P. (1989). Social space and symbolic power. *Sociological Theory, 7*, 14–25.

Bourdieu, P. (1998). *Practical reason: On the theory of action* (R. Johnson, Trans.). Stanford, CA: Stanford University Press.

Crossan, M. M., & Guatto, T. (1996). Organizational learning research profile. *Journal of Organizational Change Management, 9*, 107–112.

Crossan, M. M., Lane, H. W., & Roderick, E. W. (1999). An organizational learning framework: From intuition to institution. *Academy of Management Review, 24*, 522–537.

Doving, E. (1996). In the image of man: Organizational action, competence, and learning. In D. Grant & C. Oswick (Eds.), *Metaphor and organizations* (pp. 185–199). London: Sage.

Easterby-Smith, M. (1997). Disciplines of the learning organization: Contributions and critiques. *Human Relations, 50*, 1085–1113.

Friedman, V., & Lipshitz, R. (1992). Teaching people to shift cognitive gears: Overcoming resistance on the road to model II. *The Journal of Applied Behavioral Science, 28*, 118–137.

Friedman, V., Lipshitz, R., & Popper, M. (2005). The mystification of organizational learning. *Journal of Management Inquiry, 14*, 19–30. doi:10.1177/1056492604273758.

Friedman, V., Razer, M., & Sykes, I. (2004). Towards a theory of inclusive practice: An action science approach. *Action Research, 2*, 167–189. doi:10.1177/1476750304043729.

Garvin, D. A. (2000). *Learning in action: A guide to putting the learning organization to work.* Boston: Harvard Business School Press.

Gherardi, S. (1999). Learning as problem-driven or learning in the face of mystery? *Organization Studies, 20*, 101–124.

Gold, M. (Ed.). (1999). *The complete social scientist: A Kurt Lewin reader.* Washington, DC: American Psychological Association.

Isaacs, W. (1999). *Dialogue and the art of thinking together.* New York: Random House.

Lant, T. (2000). Book review [of *Organizational learning: Creating, retaining, and transferring knowledge,* by L. Argote]. *Administrative Science Quarterly, 45*, 622–624.

Lewin, K. (1937). Psychoanalysis and typological psychology. *Bulletin of the Menninger Clinic, 1*, 202–211.

Lewin, K. (1948). *Resolving social conflicts.* New York: Harper & Row.

Lewin, K. (1951). In D. Cartwright (Ed.), *Field theory in social science: Selected theoretical papers.* New York: Harper & Row.

Lewin, K. (1997). *Resolving social conflicts & field theory in social science.* Washington, DC: American Psychological Association. (Original work published 1948)

Lipshitz, R., Friedman, V., & Popper, M. (2007). *Demystifying organizational learning.* Thousand Oaks, CA: Sage.

Senge, P. (1990). *The fifth discipline: The art and practice of the learning organization.* New York: Doubleday.

Snell, R. S. (2001). Moral foundations of the learning organization. *Human Relations, 54*, 319–342.

Sugarman, B. (2001). A learning based approach to organizational change: Some results and guidelines. *Organizational Dynamics, 30*, 62–76.

Learning in Temporary Organizations: The Case of UN Global Conferences

Kathrin Böhling

At the largest gathering of heads of state and government in world history, the former Secretary-General of the United Nations, Kofi Annan, aimed to establish a vision of global solidarity and collective security. This event was the Millennium Summit. It was held at the UN headquarters in New York, September 6–8, 2000, and came to be known for the Millennium Development Goals, which include the eradication of extreme poverty, the reduction of child mortality, and the achievement of environmental sustainability. Kofi Annan wanted to use the opportunity of a summit to gain support for various international legal documents and multilateral treaties among the 189 heads of government and state who attended (Schechter, 2005). Beyond that goal, he called for "better governance" by which to manage successful globalization, meaning increased involvement coupled with accountability. The United Nations must be

> opened up further to the participation of the many actors whose contributions are essential to manage the path of globalization. Depending on the issues at hand, this may include civil society organizations, the private sector, parliamentarians, local authorities, scientific associations, educational institutions and many others. (Annan, 2000, p. 13)

It is no coincidence that Kofi Annan picked the Millennium Summit to make this plea. UN global conferences and summits reflect a "can-do mentality": the understanding that complex social and economic processes are manageable and must not be met with passive resignation (Taylor, 1989, p. 11). These assemblies offer a framework other than the existing organizations of the United Nation's system—with its Security Council, General Assembly, Economic and Social Council, and numerous specialized agencies and programs—and their dominant function is to give new impetus to policy-making on global problems through declarations and

K. Böhling (✉)
TUM School of Management, Chair of Forest and Environmental Policy,
Hans-Carl-v.-Carlowitz-Platz 2, 85354 Freising, Germany
e-mail: boehling@tum.de

A. Berthoin Antal et al. (eds.), *Learning Organizations: Extending the Field*,
Knowledge and Space 6, DOI 10.1007/978-94-007-7220-5_10,
© Springer Science+Business Media Dordrecht 2014

action programs (Rittberger, 1983). In other words, UN global conferences are temporary organizations in global politics. Action rather than decision-making lies at the heart of temporary organizations (Lundin & Söderholm, 1995). Temporary organizations are restricted in time and space, with the termination of the purposes for which they are conceived being fixed from the outset (Ibert, 2004). If successful, temporary organizations benefit from the multiple social contexts in which they are embedded and provide fertile soil for creativity and innovation. If unsuccessful, ventures come to an end at low cost and little disturbance to the context of the permanent organizations involved (Schneider, 1997; Sydow, Lindquist, & DeFillippi, 2004).

Temporary organizations are usually associated with construction projects, movie sets, and the organization of sporting events (see Bakker, Cambré, & Provan, 2009, and Gkeredakis, 2008, for example), but they also exist as special task forces, program committees, and action groups (Lundin & Söderholm, 1995). In this chapter I look at learning in the temporary organization called the World Summit on the Information Society (WSIS), a two-part summit held in Geneva in 2003 and Tunis in 2005. It was set up to address the global disparity in access to information and communication technologies, an imbalance also referred to as the "digital divide," which parallels other global inequities such as those in the areas of education, health, and income. It is pertinent to examine the topic of learning at the WSIS because that summit has been a locus of experimentation with an institutional innovation, the "multistakeholder approach" to global governance. The expectation is that endorsement of this approach implies organizational learning (Böhling, Busch, Berthoin Antal, & Hofmann, 2006; Messner, 2001).

The General Assembly's call for creation of the WSIS in 2002 (Res. 56/183, p. 2) marked the first time that nonstate actors were officially invited "to contribute to, and actively participate in, the intergovernmental preparatory process of the Summit and the Summit itself."[1] The WSIS symbol, a flower with four petals around a dot, represents governments, international organizations, the private-sector, and civil society, reflecting the commitment to the multistakeholder approach. The summit raised the hope that the multistakeholder approach to global governance would take hold in the UN to improve overall problem-solving capacity with societal participation and control.

The gap between rhetoric and reality, however, was significant. Civil society actors in particular were disappointed with their limited impact on the policy process (Dany, 2006). The WSIS was seen as just another event of global politics in which the wheel of participation had to be reinvented (Selian, 2004). Actors from the nonstate sphere were challenged to maintain and extend their rights to participate in UN global conferences (Willets, 1989) within the limits set by state sovereignty (Clark, Friedman, & Hochstetler, 1998). In addition to coping with such lessons from the past, the WSIS continued experimenting with the multistakeholder approach to global governance and eventually lent legitimacy to the policy output

[1] Retrieved from http://www.itu.int/wsis/docs/background/resolutions/56_183_unga_2002.pdf

(Dany, 2008). The event put the matter of information and communication firmly on the global agenda and afforded space in which new ways of dealing with global issues were explored (Raboy, 2004).

The fact that civil society's participation in the WSIS elicited limited responsiveness of the intergovernmental policy process (Dany, 2008) but nonetheless exemplified a "meaningful exercise in global governance" (Mueller, Kuerbis, & Pagé, 2007, p. 293) raises the question of its legacy for future conferences. The WSIS experience with the multistakeholder approach to global governance fits somewhat uneasily with the constitutive principles and practices of international cooperation in UN summitry, which is primarily an intergovernmental process that underscores the supremacy of the nation-state and relegates nonstate actors to the fringes (Hofmann, 2007). It is unclear whether the multistakeholder experiences of WSIS have found an appropriate channel and become embedded in the "template" for the organization of UN conferences: the "establishment of a temporary secretariat headed by a secretary-general, often from outside the UN system; a series of preparatory committees; participation of NGOs; standard outcomes (final declarations and programs of action); and, increasingly in the 1990s, follow-up and monitoring institutions" (Emmerij, Jolly, & Weiss, 2001, pp. 80–81). Does the WSIS' experimentation with the multistakeholder approach generate a legacy? To help answer that question, the next section presents a framework for the analysis of learning in summits as temporary organizations.

Understanding Learning in Temporary Organizations

Research on project-based learning indicates that temporary organizations tend to be "forgetful" but that they are strong in "reflective learning" (Ibert, 2004). The ephemeral, task-oriented, and interpersonal intensity of temporary organizations fosters new ideas and innovative strategies, as does embeddedness in multiple contexts (Bathelt & Schuldt, 2008; Gkeredakis, 2008). To put it differently, guiding principles are reviewed and knowledge is created, whereas little of use for subsequent projects is retained. Researchers in this area argue that temporary organizations lack the qualities of organizational memory, implying that little scope exists for routinized learning and that there is a danger of reinventing the wheel (Sydow et al., 2004; see also Bakker et al., 2009; Prencipe & Tell, 2001).

Without memory, knowledge cannot be identified as relevant, and the mechanisms for disseminating and making sense of that knowledge are lacking (Huber, 1991). An organization's memory consists of mental and structural templates that have an impact on interpretation and action (Walsh & Ungson, 1991). This "repository of organized knowledge" (Walsh, 1995, p. 286) takes the form of data banks and files, routines, structures, and frames of reference; it also includes stories passed from one generation to another (Berthoin Antal, 2000). These different manifestations of organizational memory make for continuity of organizational activity; they

"preserve certain behaviors, mental maps, norms, and values over time" irrespective
of personnel turnover or changes in leadership (Hedberg, 1981, p. 6). There is evidence
that memory has an impact if the knowledge that is acquired serves established
beliefs and practices (Weick & Ashford, 2001) or if the existence of a "Not-Invented-
Here-Syndrome" stifles communication among the various units in an organization
(Berthoin Antal, Lenhardt, & Rosenbrock, 2001).

Attention to the role of memory in organizational learning stems from the behavioral approach to organizations. From this perspective, much of what organizations
do is accomplished through routines (Cyert & March, 1963; March & Simon, 1958).
Organizations are seen as learning by encoding inferences from history into routines that guide behavior. "Unless the implications of experience can be transferred
from those who experienced it to those who did not, the lessons of history are likely
to be lost" (Levitt & March, 1988, p. 328).

The generic term *routines* includes the rules, procedures, forms, rituals, and
beliefs around which organizations are constructed and through which they operate.
Seen from this angle, organizations, and permanent organizations in particular, are
essentially a collection of learning-based routines. They run the risk of "myopia"
and are locked into the task of refining existing practices and beliefs, as exemplified
by competency traps and superstitious learning (Levinthal & March, 1993).
Temporary organizations, rather than the permanent ones that most theories of organizational learning are concerned with, are thus a means for achieving change
(Lundin & Söderholm, 1995).

Memory in organizational learning is crucial to advancing the understanding of
learning in temporary organizations (Böhling, 2007). To move beyond the assertion
that temporary organizations are strong in reflective learning, it is helpful to ask
about the ways in which this kind of learning is transferred from those who experience it to those who do not. If no project is an island (Engwall, 2003), then, arguably, no temporary organization is either. Certain structures and procedures that are
adopted in temporary organizations "have to be understood in relation to previous
and simultaneous courses of activity, to future plans, and to standard operating procedures, traditions and the norms of its surroundings" (p. 789). That is, temporary
organizations are nested (Sydow et al., 2004). Even if they are unique undertakings,
they need to include organizational forms that transcend organizational levels of
analysis. Like permanent organizations, temporary ones are based on institutions
that their participants set up in situations of uncertainty (Beckert, 2006), such as a
period when the relevant framing is being reconstructed and manipulated (Ibert,
2004). The institutions on which temporary organizations rest can be described as
an "overarching normalizing process that shapes [temporary organizations] through
'templates' of values, beliefs, norms, and structures" (Coopey & Burgoyne, 2000,
p. 873). How and how much these templates matter for learning in temporary
organizations are empirical questions.

One way to inquire into the templates of a temporary organization and
the manner in which they affect its tendency to engage in reflective learning is
the framework adopted by Crossan, Lane, and White (1999), which puts the

relationship between feedforward and feedback processes at the center of organizational learning: "Organizational learning is a dynamic process. Not only does learning occur over time and across levels, it also creates a tension between assimilating new learning (feedforward) and exploiting or using what has already been learned (feedback)" (p. 532). Crossan et al. draw on March's (1991) distinction between exploration and exploitation to define feedforward and feedback learning and combine it with the view that learning takes shape at multiple levels. To Crossan et al. these levels are linked by social and psychological processes. In the conception of these three researchers, feedforward learning is exploration and includes activities such as search, experimentation, and discovery. It starts at the individual level, where innovative ideas are discerned and comprehended through intuition, and is followed by sharing and sense-making at the group level through interpretation, then by the learning that becomes embedded and integrated with the organizational memory in order to institutionalize new structures, strategies, and procedures. Conversely, Crossan et al. see feedback learning as exploitation, a process that operates within a context of embedded routines through which subsequent events and experiences are interpreted at the group level and perceived among individuals.

Sense-making can be conceptualized as a key part of feedforward and feedback learning in temporary organizations (Prencipe & Tell, 2001). Uncertainty and ambiguity diminish through this learning (Maitlis, 2005), and it becomes possible to make reasonable guesses about whether different kinds of knowledge are brought together and used to create more or less coherent understandings of dynamism and turbulence in the given context. In feedforward learning, sense-making involves communities of individuals who create representations that they can use to interpret and elaborate on experiences they have. In feedback learning, ways of seeing and doing things that have worked in the past are enacted to make sense of what is feasible in equivocal situations. Language, the intricacies of practice, and stories told by community members are important in both processes because they affect what can be learned and preserve what has been learned. This context of embedded learning reflects the interests of powerful actors and coalitions and is therefore supported by them (Brown & Kenney, 2006).

A revised version of Crossan's et al. (1999) framework (Fig. 10.1) serves as a heuristic for the empirical part of this chapter on learning from the adoption of the multistakeholder approach at the WSIS. The broken lines in Fig. 10.1 between "Interpreting," "Integrating with Organizational Memory," and "Legacy for Future Temporary Organizations" point out the decisive issues for the analysis of learning in temporary organizations: (a) how the new learning in the feedforward process builds momentum as the organizational memory of a temporary organization and (b) how this process is related to feedback learning in which the context of embedded routines affects the sense-making of the new ideas and strategies. From this framework it follows that the dynamic relationship between the two types of processes determines the legacy of learning in temporary organizations for corresponding future events.

Fig. 10.1 A framework for an analysis of learning in temporary organizations (TO)

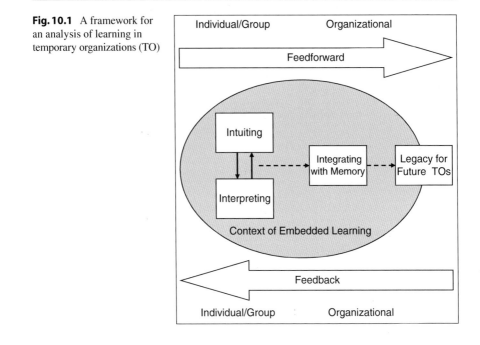

The Multistakeholder Approach in the WSIS: A Legacy for Future Conferences?

The WSIS is part of the UN's history of convening global conferences on global issues. With its secretariat, rules and procedures, preparatory process, and follow-up, the WSIS is certainly not an island. To analyze the legacy resulting from the adoption of the multistakeholder approach, I therefore set out by extending the time frame of the summit and relating it to the institutionalized norms and values of the surrounding context. Since the early 1970s, nonstate actors have been an integral part of UN conferences. Their presence in "global conference diplomacy" (Rittberger, 1983), where they have sought to affect international deliberations and interest accommodations, has changed the character of UN conferences from predominantly functional events of multilateral policy-making into more public-oriented events of global norm-setting (Brühl & Rosert, 2008) and into platforms for "peaceful challenges to the monopolization of global affairs by states" (Friedman, Hochstetler, & Clark, 2005, p. 4). The 1992 UN World Summit on Environment and Development in Rio de Janeiro ranks as a milestone in this process of moving from the merely consultative role of NGOs to participatory arrangements for their involvement in decision-making on global problems (Caldwell, 1996; Selian, 2004). The official accreditation of NGOs for the first time at the Earth Summit did much to shape the climate for interstate dialogue and interest accommodation (Kreibich, 1998). Their presence has challenged the rigid rituals of international diplomacy and made them a subject of public scrutiny (Martens, 1998).

Embedded Routines in UN Global Conferences

UN conferences are convened to change priorities of the global agenda by developing common understandings about issues of general concern, such as climate change, human rights, and the digital divide and to forge consensus on practical solutions. These gatherings expand institutional capacity—such as the UN Environment Programme, the UN High Commissioner for Human Rights, and the UN Internet Governance Forum—to tackle global problems and have become a means to legitimate global governance by making it more inclusive, transparent, and responsive. Although the conferences do not produce treaties, international public law, or any other binding rules, they do create norms on which actor expectations converge, as was illustrated at the Earth Summit by the agreement on the "sustainable development" concept, its acceptance as a desirable policy objective, and its translation into policies and measures.

Once a conference is initiated by a government or an international organization and authorized by a resolution of the UN General Assembly, it typically proceeds through three stages: preparation, decision-making, and implementation (Rittberger, 1983; Willets, 1989). An executive secretariat is created in one of the UN's specialized agencies to make all necessary administrative arrangements for the proceedings. The secretary-general of the UN agency in charge is usually also appointed as secretary-general of the corresponding conference and entrusted with the task of exercising political leadership in agenda-setting and seeking potential areas for consensus.

During conference preparation, a series of regional and global meetings takes place to develop a framework for negotiation, draw up a draft agenda, approve the rules of procedure, and, often, prepare first drafts of the final conference documents. This stage is vital to the success or failure of global conference diplomacy, and it represents a major arena for nonstate actor involvement. Decision-making, by contrast, has traditionally been the exclusive province of governments. In recent decades, however, nonstate actors have developed their repertoires for lobbying national delegations or have gained access even to formally closed working groups, albeit with no right to vote (Clark et al., 1998; Friedman et al., 2005). The main formal element of conference decision-making is the plenary, where governments lay out their views and negotiating positions and where nonstate actors make suggestions and comments.

> The summit meeting itself is the last stage of a prolonged period of negotiation, and is primarily an opportunity for heads of state and government to make public statements and commit their countries to a formal declaration. The real work takes place in complex discussions over the previous year or two, in a series of regional meetings and preparatory committees (PrepComs). These are where what will become the final texts are hammered out and disputes addressed. (Souter, 2007, p. 11)

Action on conference documents is more a formal target than a practical reality because UN conferences lack the authority and the resources to prescribe policies and measures. The increased presence of nonstate actors at conferences, however, may have set in motion a process by which governments are held accountable for promises made at these events (Brühl & Rosert, 2008). A relatively new way to live up to the promises made at conferences is through "Type II" partnerships—those consisting of public, civil society, and business actors—which have proliferated since the Johannesburg Summit in 2002. But Type II partnerships are regarded with suspicion among civil society actors, who criticize them as "marketing ploys" or attempts to "greenwash" corporate activities (Seyfang, 2003). Evidence shows that corporate activity is slight and that very little money for implementing activities has come from sources other than governments (Hale & Mauzerall, 2004).

Feedforward Learning at the WSIS

Feedforward learning is essentially about seeking out and discovering new experiences and integrating them by developing shared understandings and undertaking coordinated action at the group and organizational level. The significance that this process has for understanding the WSIS lies in the lack of a common view about how to implement the multistakeholder approach at this summit. The vague wording in the UN General Assembly resolution that invited nonstate actors to participate actively in the intergovernmental preparatory process of the summit and in the summit itself resulted in heated discussions of its practical meaning (Kleinwächter, 2005). Procedures had to be worked out and rules defined so that nonstate actors had chances to formulate their own positions and negotiable language for drafting official documents. These exigencies confronted national delegations with substantial intervention from participants with observer status. Such prospects had not been envisaged when the International Telecommunications Union (ITU), the UN organization in charge of coordinating the WSIS, launched the summit in Resolution 73 in 1998. The ITU had no experience with organizing such events and made no mention of an explicit role of civil society in the summit process (Raboy, 2004). Instead, the organization put itself at center stage, arguing that it was "best able to seek appropriate ways to provide for development of the telecommunication sector geared to economic, social and cultural development."[2]

Creating a Bottom-Up Structure for Coordinated Action

However, civil society actors at the WSIS developed their ability to articulate their own positions and have them recognized in the policy process pertaining to summit commitments. Kleinwächter (2005), for instance, observed that civil society actors found ways to develop consensual positions, take decisions despite great heterogeneity of the participants, and articulate their positions vis-à-vis governments. The creation of mechanisms and forums operating at different levels and for different functional purposes reconciled feedforward learning with the heterogeneity of the different groups that constitute civil society in the WSIS. This type of learning afforded possibilities for

---

[2] Retrieved from http://www.itu.int/wsis/docs/background/resolutions/73.html

mobilization and self-organization to contribute meaningfully to the preparation of summit documents. Civil society coordinated its activities from the bottom up mainly by means of two organs: the "Civil Society Plenary" and the "Content and Themes Group." The Plenary was open to all civil society participants at the WSIS and was the ultimate civil society authority in the process as a whole. It oversaw the deliberations of some 20 thematic working groups and caucuses, such as the patent, copyright, and trademark working group; the Internet governance working group; the community media caucus; the gender caucus; and the human rights caucus. These working groups and caucuses emerged because the actors of civil society were uncomfortable with the top-down civil society structure recognized by the UN bureaucracy, which set up a Civil Society Bureau with 21 "families" of NGOs (Mueller et al., 2007). These families did not make sense to most civil society participants and were perceived as rather arbitrarily chosen to make procedural and logistical matters work.

Above the thematic working groups and caucuses of civil society came the Content and Themes group as the second layer of debate and interaction. It reported to the Civil Society Plenary, was closely linked to the official summit process, and worked to meet the official deadlines with joint positions that could inform the intergovernmental negotiations. Civil society's ability to coordinate itself challenged the narrow definition of the Information Society that was postulated by the ITU (Siochrú, 2004). Coordinated action of civil society at the WSIS co-evolved with the Campaign for Communication Rights in the Information Society (CRIS) and the entrepreneurial efforts its proponents undertook to form transnational advocacy networks (Mueller et al., 2007). Members of this campaign broadened the picture of the Information Society by asking who owns and controls information and who can use it most effectively for goal achievement. The ITU's definition, by contrast, was essentially about the spread and infrastructure of information and communication technologies pursued through a global process of liberalization and privatization in which governments create a suitable political and regulatory environment. What Siochrú (p. 207) has called the "second conceptual strand" of the Information Society at the WSIS stressed the importance of communication for the Information Society, which includes matters as diverse as Internet surveillance, concentration of media ownership, commercial censorship, and intellectual property rights. Attention to these topics grew among civil society actors who saw the WSIS "as an opportunity they had been waiting for, a forum in which a diverse set of civil society actors could converge and interact, to learn from each other and from others, and to begin to mobilize transnationally around these issues" (p. 210).

The bottom-up structure that enabled civil society to participate meaningfully in the summit's official process also led it to withdraw at the end of the first part, just before the Geneva meeting in November 2003. At that stage civil society announced that it would stop giving input to the intergovernmental documents, the aim being to emphasize its dissatisfaction with the endorsement of the lowest common denominator among governments. Stated differently, civil society learned how to contribute collectively to the official process and refrained from it when governments' responsiveness to its argumentations waned toward the end of negotiations (Dany, 2008).

The narrow definition of the Information Society prevailed in the official Summit Declaration when it was approved in Geneva by the participating heads of state and government (Siochrú, 2004). Civil society, however, found an alternative channel to leverage the result of its joint exploration. It issued its own declaration on the "Information and Communication Societies," which accentuated the commitment to human rights, social justice, and an inclusive and sustainable Information Society.[3]

Institutionalizing the Multistakeholder Approach to Internet Governance

As widely perceived, the WSIS achieved little of substance but much in terms of structures and processes that now lend meaning to the innovative multistakeholder approach in UN summitry (Dany, 2008; Mueller et al., 2007; Raboy, 2004). In the second part of the summit—the meeting in Tunis in November 2005—the debate shifted to the initial intent to conceive of finance mechanisms that could bridge the digital divide and the reorganization of Internet governance. Yet it was only in the discussion on Internet governance, not finance mechanisms, that governments used the multistakeholder approach to resolve the conflicts between their entrenched, diametrically opposed positions on national control over the network infrastructure (Hofmann, 2007).

> In short, the USA and the EU favored regulation of the Internet, meaning the existing sys-
> tem with a reformed Internet Corporation for Assigned Names and Numbers (ICANN) as
> the main regulatory body; China and other developing countries, such as South Africa and
> Brazil, would have liked to see the International Telecommunication Union in charge, thus
> favoring multilateral governmental leadership; business actors opposed any governmental
> influence on the Internet and argued for self-regulation; civil society, for its part, promoted
> the decentralization of responsibility. (Dany, 2008, p. 62)

The Working Group on Internet Governance (WGIG) was formed because governments agreed to disagree. Its mandate was to develop a working definition of Internet governance, that is to identify the kind of public policy issues that are relevant according to that definition and the distinct responsibilities of the stakeholder groups involved (Hofmann, 2007).[4] "Civil society participated as a peer in [this group] and dominated its substantive output" (Mueller et al., 2007, p. 292). As in

---

[3] See "Civil Society Summit Declaration: Shaping Information Societies for Human Needs," WSIS Civil Society Plenary, Geneva, December 12, 2003. Retrieved from http://www.itu.int/wsis/docs/geneva/civil-society-declaration.pdf

See also http://www.worldsummit2003.org, especially the section entitled "Creating a bottom-up structure," p. 3.

[4] Hofmann (2007) notes that Internet governance, in its future form, will probably be embedded in rather comprehensive regulatory contexts that have a direct or indirect impact on the Internet. Examples of such contexts may be international agreements on trade and competition, guidelines on copyright production, data privacy protection, and cyber crime, and national measures on consumer protection and the regulation of telecommunications. Meanwhile, the prevention of state interference—once the leitmotif of debates on Internet governance—has been quietly pushed to the side.

the Commission on Sustainable Development, which was created in the aftermath of the Earth Summit in 1993 (Dodds, 2002), the WGIG created a space in which experimentation with the multistakeholder approach continued. It also "paved the way for a new UN process, the Internet Governance Forum, which has in turn institutionalized MuSH [MultiStakeholder] Governance and kept alive many of the caucuses and thematic groups of WSIS civil society" (Mueller et al., p. 292). The ongoing Internet Governance Forum facilitates the emergence of "dynamic coalitions" (Currie, 2007, p. 21) on privacy, open standards, spam, and an Internet bill of rights. Representatives from governments, international organizations, business, and civil society interact on equal footing in this forum to make recommendations on the future regulation of the Internet. That the forum cannot decide may be an important reason why the experiment with shifting boundaries between state and nonstate actors has been able to continue in international negotiations. However, the fact that such fluidity is feasible with Internet governance but not with the digital solidarity fund (Souter, 2007) simultaneously presses the point that the interests of governments and the dominant discourse framing policy issues set the boundaries for the ways in which the multistakeholder approach generates a legacy for global governance in the UN.

Feedback Learning at the WSIS

Looking at learning in temporary organizations merely in terms of feedforward processes does not sufficiently explain how new learning creates a legacy to affect ways of doing and seeing aspects of analogous events in the future. For new learning to be integrated into memory, it must be related to previously embedded learning. To arrive at conclusions about the relationship between feedforward and feedback learning in the WSIS case, I now examine how emergent multistakeholder practices are nested. This section sheds light on the ways in which established routines or structures affect the emergence of these practices. One way to address the nestedness of multistakeholder practices is to analyze their relationship with WSIS rules of procedure.

When the heads of state and government adopt the rules of procedure in the first plenary session of each world summit or global conference, they also decide on the modalities of consultation and participation of nonstate actors in the policy process. The regulatory frameworks of previous UN summits and conferences thus serve as an important template for the formulation of procedural rules for a given summit or conference. Examples of such templates are the definition of criteria and principles for creating relationships with nonstate actors, the establishment of an accreditation process as a prerogative of member states, and the granting of opportunities for nonstate actors to speak.[5]

---

[5] See Office of the President of the Millennium Assembly (2001).

Dynamism in Written and Unwritten Rules at the WSIS

These templates initially applied to the WSIS as well. With the advent of the multistakeholder approach, national delegations were challenged to rethink their role and the status of nonstate actors in global conference diplomacy. To gain agreement on procedural rules for the WSIS, delegates at the first preparatory conference for the Geneva Summit (PrepCom 1, July 2002) dealt primarily with the question of what was actually entailed by the UN General Assembly's WSIS resolution inviting nonstate actors to participate actively in the summit (Kleinwächter, 2005). In the face of significant differences between the states in their views and perspectives on the role and involvement of nonstate actors (Papenfuß, 2003), a UN standard was eventually settled on. Drawing on the established rules of the World Summit on Sustainable Development in Johannesburg (2002) and the Financing for Development Conference in Monterrey (2002), the WSIS rules of procedure codified the categories of observers from international governmental organizations, civil society organizations, and private sector entities that had consultative status with the UN Economic and Social Council. Formally, these participants had the right to observe public meetings. They were also permitted to comment on matters within their areas of special competence when invited to do so by the presiding chairperson or officer of the body concerned.

PrepCom 1 "set the tone for a summit which would be overfocused on process at the expense of content" (Raboy, 2004, p. 230). Once decided upon, the rules of procedure enacted during the WSIS were a vehicle for negotiating the status of the different actors in the overall process (Hofmann, 2006).

> Efforts by some Governments, to keep non-governmental observers out of the conference room, produced turmoil before the closed doors. During the "InterSessional" (July 2003), the chair of "Working Group 2" used its "right to invite" and opened the door to observers with limited speaking rights in negotiation groups. The idea was that governments if they start negotiations on a certain paragraph, interrupt formally the negotiations and invite observers to make a statement to the point. Such "stop-and-go-negotiations" would *de jure* not change the character of inter-governmental negotiations, but could bring de facto innovative input and transparency to the process. (Kleinwächter, 2005, p. 111)

Opening up the preparatory process and the summit meeting itself to representatives from civil society generated its own dynamics and crystallized into "unwritten rules," also referred to as "WSIS practice."[6] It existed alongside the formalized rules without contradicting them and allowed the actors from civil society to make written contributions to the drafting of summit text, to speak during the PrepComs, and to attend working groups and informal open-ended meetings. The WSIS thereby went beyond the approach of previous summits and conferences. The generality of these rules of procedure for participation gave rise to both restrictive and inventive use of WSIS practice. Restrictive use was evident when states responded to the upheavals of the multistakeholder approach by ceding as little of their sovereignty as possible

---

[6] See "The multi-stakeholder participation in WSIS and its written and unwritten rules." See section B at http://www.itu.int/wsis/basic/multistakeholder.html

(Coglianese, 2000) or by resorting to procedural motions (Sabel, 1997). The WSIS's internal substantive conflict over Internet governance, for instance, was bypassed by procedural means (Hofmann, 2007).

Inventive use of WSIS practice was demonstrated by the German, Canadian, and Danish national delegations, which assigned some of their civil society actors to working groups that were hammering out summit text (Cammaerts & Carpentier, 2005). Similarly, a chair of the plenary session, a subcommittee, or a working group used his discretionary latitude to open up the intergovernmental negotiations within working groups. The introduction of the 5-min-to-8 rule at the summit is an instructive example of WSIS practice (Hofmann, 2003). Discontent among actors of civil society and the private sector about being excluded from negotiations met with sympathy among a number of national delegations that had favored allowing nonstate actors to comment and make suggestions in working groups, too. Although that degree of participation was not provided for in the official rules of procedure, a compromise was found to allow contributions from nonstate actors slightly before the working groups formally convened, after which point the nonstate actors did have to leave the room (Dany, 2008).[7] The compromise was respected in some working groups but ignored in others, depending on the person presiding.

Discussion

An important point of departure for feedforward learning in the WSIS was ability of the civil society actors involved to intuit and make sense of the vague intent to have the summit organized as a multistakeholder process. Among them, a collective understanding of what multistakeholderism meant in practical terms evolved along with the actions taken to participate actively in summit preparation and the summit itself. Specifically, these actions entailed setting up the Civil Society Plenary, a broad range of thematic working groups, and the Content and Themes Group. At the same time, rules for arriving at common positions were emerging, as were routines for using the Plenary as the ultimate authority of civil society represented at the WSIS. The new learning among the civil society actors gained momentum through the creation of repositories of organized knowledge. These repositories promoted coordinated action among the heterogeneous civil society actors and enabled them to tie into the intergovernmental process.

Further evidence for an emergent memory among civil society actors at the WSIS was the collective decision to announce their withdrawal from the intergovernmental negotiations at the end of the summit's Geneva phase. This step did not lead to a breakdown of civil society activities at the WSIS. Working on the joint Civil Society Declaration and its finalizing statement indicates the emergence of a

---

[7]Yet not all of the nonstate actors left the room after the 5 min. Some of them stayed because of their membership in national delegations. When they started to report directly out of the room via the Internet, however, they were again excluded from the working groups (Dany, 2008).

collective identity.[8] Such continuous processes of sense-making and building of coherence among civil society actors were also instrumental in their use of the opportunity that governments afforded to resolve the issue of Internet governance procedurally. The WGIG reflects the constant struggle for suitable forms of Internet governance when visions of transnational democracy clash with the rights of sovereign, territorially defined nation-states (Hofmann, 2007). The WGIG and its sequel—the UN-based Internet Governance Forum (IGF)—institutionalized some of the multistakeholder practices that have emerged in the WSIS. In the preparatory process to Rio+20—the United Nations Conference on Sustainable Development held in Rio de Janeiro, Brazil, June 20–22, 2012—Nitin Desai, former IGF chair and a member of the Brundtland Commission,[9] among others, asked whether reform of the Commission on Sustainable Development could produce such a multistakeholder meeting. Could it become "a political space designed for listening rather than talking, for dialogue rather than confrontational negotiations" (Desai, 2011, p. 6)?

Previously embedded learning is related to this feedforward process. Rules of procedure of previous summits and conferences embodied the context of embedded routines at the WSIS. Among national delegations and the ITU they framed the effort to make sense of the initially nebulous multistakeholder approach in the temporary organization of the WSIS. Sticking to the associated conventions and standards did not work when the tried and tested procedures of UN summitry became subject to public scrutiny. Alongside the written rules, unwritten rules proliferated in the WSIS. At some point the formal side of things lost its axiomatic character. There emerged a political space in which the boundaries between governments and nonstate actors were shifting, canonical practices were challenged, and consolidated patterns of relationships were suspended, most notably in the WGIG and its successor institution, the IGF. Emergence of these spaces seems crucial for the institutionalization of principles such as inclusiveness, transparency, and responsiveness in the UN system. The fact that these stakeholding principles were operant mainly in the field of Internet governance, however, reflects that feedback processes are ultimately the outcome of underlying power relations. Interests and the use of rules among powerful stakeholders—particular national delegations and perhaps also the summit secretariat—determined the scope of learning within embedded routines. They may be suspended in alternative spaces for deliberation among multiple actors but cannot be transformed through learning in the WSIS as a temporary organization of WSIS.

---

[8] See http://www.worldsummit2003.de/download_en/WSIS-CS-summit-statement-18-12-2005-en.pdf for the final statement of civil society on WSIS. Civil society is presented therein as a corporate actor that has contributed positively to the WSIS process despite rather limited resources. This contribution could have been greater "had the opportunity been made available for an ever more comprehensive participation on our part" (p. 3).

[9] Named after former Norwegian Prime Minister Gro Harlem Brundtland, appointed its first chairperson in 1983, this body has the mission of bringing preservation of the environment and economic prosperity in both the developed and less developed world together.

Conclusion

Temporary organizations may serve as a seedbed for creativity and innovation (Schneider, 1997; Sydow et al., 2004). This assumption from research on project-based organizing and learning is supported by this chapter's findings on learning from the multistakeholder approach at the WSIS. Experimentation with the idea of having this summit organized as a multistakeholder event triggered feedforward learning as described by Crossan et al. (1999). It generated a range of inventive activities among civil society actors and challenged the established way of going about UN summitry. Civil society actors gathered momentum at the WSIS because they created repositories of organized knowledge: structures, procedures, and norms. Not only did these actors link up with the intergovernmental process and win recognition of their positions, their joint declaration and finalizing statement turned heterogeneity into a collective identity. Even after the WSIS came to an end in Tunis in late 2005, traces of civil society activity continued.

Interestingly, however, the evidence of experimentation with the multistakeholder approach at the WSIS is likely to survive in only one substantial area of debate—Internet governance—not in others such as funding mechanisms. The latter discussion lies much closer to the WSIS's official intention of overcoming the digital divide between countries from the North and countries from the South and seems to offer occasion for diffusion of the Johannesburg Summit's Type II partnerships. Whereas multistakeholderism did not become an option for decisions on funding efforts to overcome the digital divide, the WSIS's multistakeholder experiences may change governance of the Internet infrastructure. The fact that multistakeholderism is used in the WSIS's successor to resolve the conflicting views on Internet governance fits the ITU's rather technical definition of the Information Society, which prevailed during the overall summit and which gives participating governments the chance to make the summit outcomes look successful.

Rio+20 showed that involvement of diverse stakeholders in the preparatory process and in the conference itself has become a foregone conclusion at such events.[10] It further indicated that giving stakeholders access to what used to be the relatively closed interstate diplomacy of UN global conferences generated pressure on states to deliver on promises they made and perhaps catalyzed the normative appeal of alternative ways to pursue stated goals. Given the disappointing record of action by states, great hopes are now attached to multistakeholder strategies for scaling-up and mainstreaming sustainable development by means of partnerships and governance networks (Beisheim, 2012). The suggestion of modeling the Conference on Sustainable Development on the IGF is part of this development. But is such an idea indeed evidence that temporary organizations are a means to achieve change in the more enduring context in which they are embedded (Lundin & Söderholm, 1995)?

---

[10] See General Assembly Resolution A RES 64/236 on "Implementation of Agenda 21, the Programme for the Further Implementation of Agenda 21 and the Outcomes of the World Summit on Sustainable Development," March 31, 2010, §21–22. Retrieved from http://www.un-documents.net/ares64-236.pdf

The question calls for further research into the conditions under which the dynamism of feedforward and feedback processes generates momentum.

Basically, the new learning of feedforward processes in temporary organizations is nested. It takes previously embedded learning as a starting point. But the repositories of organized knowledge that are created in this *dis*embedding process may develop a life of their own, as illustrated by the history of arrangements with multiple stakeholders in UN global conferences. Achieving change requires their *re-embedding* in the permanent context, which, in the case discussed in this chapter, is the UN bureaucracy and interstate diplomacy. The relationship between feedforward and feedback processes in the learning by temporary organizations is therefore not necessarily dynamic in the sense of mutually reinforcing, as suggested by Crossan et al. (1999). Learning in temporary organizations can suspend some of the framework conditions on which it rests, but it cannot transform them, at least not within its restrictions in time and space. Powerful stakeholders of the permanent organizations involved must try to link both processes and strive to maintain and modify established ways of doing and seeing things. In order for the new learning to become a legacy and achieve change, it must become part of the permanent context in which it is nested. This re-embedding is partly an outcome of power relations and partly the result of changes in what people expect of that context.

References

Annan, K. (2000). *We the peoples: The role of the United Nations in the 21st century*. New York: United Nations.

Bakker, R. M., Cambré, B., & Provan, K. G. (2009). The resource dilemma of temporary organizations: A dynamic perspective on temporal embeddedness and resource discretion. In P. N. Kenis, M. K. Janowicz-Panjaitan, & B. Cambré (Eds.), *Temporary organizations: Prevalence, logic and effectiveness* (pp. 201–219). Cheltenham, UK: Edward Elgar.

Bathelt, H., & Schuldt, N. (2008). Between luminaires and meat grinders: International trade fairs as temporary clusters. *Regional Studies, 42*, 853–868. doi:10.1080/00343400701543298.

Beckert, J. (2006). The social organization of interpretation. *Journal of Institutional and Theoretical Economics, 162*, 194–198.

Beisheim, M. (2012, February). *Partnerships and sustainable development: Why and how Rio+20 must improve the framework for multi-stakeholder partnerships* (English Express, e.K., Trans.) (SWP Research Paper 20/2011). Berlin, Germany: Stiftung Wissenschaft und Politik.

Berthoin Antal, A. (2000). Types of knowledge gained by expatriates. *Journal of General Management, 26*, 32–51.

Berthoin Antal, A., Lenhardt, U., & Rosenbrock, R. (2001). Barriers to organizational learning. In M. Dierkes, A. Berthoin Antal, J. Child, & I. Nonaka (Eds.), *Handbook of organizational learning and knowledge* (pp. 865–885). Oxford, UK: Oxford University Press.

Böhling, K. (2007). *Opening up the black box: Organizational learning in the European Commission*. Frankfurt am Main, Germany: Peter Lang.

Böhling, K., Busch, T., Berthoin Antal, A., & Hofmann, J. (2006). *Lernprozesse im Kontext von UN-Weltgipfeln: Die Vergesellschaftung internationalen Regierens* [Learning processes in context of UN summits: The societal appropriation of international governance] (WZB Discussion Paper SP III 2006-102). Berlin Social Research Centre (WZB). Retrieved from http://bibliothek.wzb.eu/pdf/2006/iii06-102.pdf. Last Accessed on 9 Aug 2013.

Brown, M. L., & Kenney, M. (2006). Organizational learning: Theoretical and methodological considerations. In M. L. Brown, M. Kenney, & M. Zarkin (Eds.), *Organizational learning in the global context* (pp. 1–17). Aldershot, UK: Ashgate.

Brühl, T., & Rosert, E. (2008). Another quiet revolution? New governance forms in the United Nations system. In Global Policy Forum & Foundation for Environment and Development North-Rhine-Westphalia (Eds.), *The future of civil society participation at the United Nations: Documentation of a workshop held at the ACUNS annual meeting, June 6, 2008* (pp. 5–20). Bonn, Germany: Foundation for Environment and Development North-Rhine Westphalia.

Caldwell, L. K. (1996). *International environmental policy* (3rd ed.). Durham, NC/London: Duke University Press.

Cammaerts, B., & Carpentier, N. (2005). The unbearable lightness of full participation in a global context: WSIS and the civil society participation. In N. Servaes & N. Carpentier (Eds.), *Towards a sustainable Information Society: Deconstructing WSIS* (pp. 17–55). Bristol, UK/Portland, OR: Intellect.

Clark, A. M., Friedman, E. J., & Hochstetler, K. (1998). The sovereign limits of global civil society: A comparison of NGO participation in UN World conferences on the environment, human rights, and women. *World Politics, 51*, 1–35.

Coglianese, C. (2000). Globalization and the design of international institutions. In J. S. Nye & J. D. Donahue (Eds.), *Governance in a globalizing world* (pp. 297–318). Washington, DC: Brookings Institution Press.

Coopey, J., & Burgoyne, J. (2000). Politics and organizational learning. *Journal of Management Studies, 37*, 869–885.

Crossan, M. M., Lane, H. W., & White, R. E. (1999). An organizational learning framework: From intuition to institution. *Academy of Management Review, 24*, 522–537.

Currie, W. (2007). Post-WSIS spaces for building a global Information Society. In K. Banks, R. Bissio, W. Currie, A. Esterhuysen, C. G. Ramilo, & M. Sigillito (Eds.), *Global Information Society Watch, 2007* (pp. 16–23). n.p.: APC and ITeM. Retrieved from http://www.giswatch.org/sites/default/files/gisw_2007.pdf

Cyert, R. M., & March, J. G. (1963). *A behavioral theory of the firm*. Englewood Cliffs, NJ: Prentice-Hall.

Dany, C. (2006). *The impact of participation: How civil society organisations contribute to the democratic quality of the UN World Summit on the Information Society* (Paper of SFB 597: Staatlichkeit im Wandel, Project B5). Bremen: University of Bremen.

Dany, C. (2008). Civil society participation under most favourable conditions: Assessing the deliberative quality of the WSIS. In J. Steffek, C. Kissling, & P. Nanz (Eds.), *Civil society participation in European and global governance: A cure for the democratic deficit?* (pp. 53–70). Houndmills, UK: Palgrave Macmillan.

Desai, N. (2011, July 19–21). *Global institutions for sustainability*. Address presented to the High Level Dialogue on the Institutional Framework for Sustainable Development held in Solo City, Indonesia. Retrieved from http://www.uncsd2012.org/content/documents/desaisolo.pdf

Dodds, F. (2002). The context: Multi-stakeholder processes and global governance. In M. Hemmati (Ed.), *Multi-stakeholder processes for governance and sustainability: Beyond deadlock and conflict* (pp. 26–38). Abingdon, UK: Earthscan.

Emmerij, L., Jolly, R., & Weiss, T. G. (2001). *Ahead of the curve? UN ideas and global challenges*. Bloomington, IN: Indiana University Press.

Engwall, M. (2003). No project is an island: Linking projects to history and context. *Research Policy, 32*, 789–808.

Friedman, E. J., Hochstetler, K., & Clark, A. M. (2005). *Sovereignty, democracy, and global civil society: State-society relations at UN World conferences*. Albany, NY: State University of New York Press.

Gkeredakis, E. (2008, July). *Coordinating in temporary organizations: New insights from a longitudinal study of a major construction project*. Paper presented at the European Group for Organization Studies (EGOS) Colloquium.

Hale, T. N., & Mauzerall, D. L. (2004). Thinking globally and acting locally: Can the Johannesburg partnerships coordinate action on sustainable development? *Journal of Environment & Development, 13*, 220–239.

Hedberg, B. (1981). How organizations learn and unlearn. In P. Nystrom & W. H. Starbuck (Eds.), *Handbook of organizational design* (Vol. 1, pp. 3–27). New York: Oxford University Press.

Hofmann, J. (2003). Erfahrungsbericht der zivilgesellschaftlichen Vertreterin in der deutschen Regierungsdelegation, Jeanette Hofmann, über die Teilnahme an der dritten Vorbereitungskonferenz zum Weltgipfel über die Informationsgesellschaft (PrepCom 3), vom September 2003 [Field report by a third-sector representative in the German government delegation, Jeanette Hofmann, on participation at the third preparatory conference for the World Summit on the Information Society (PrepCom 3), September 2003]. *Internationale Politik, 58*(12), 103–109.

Hofmann, J. (2006). (Trans-)formation of civil society in global governance contexts–Two case studies on the problem of self-organization. In G. F. Schuppert (Ed.), *Global governance and the role of non-state actors* (pp. 179–202). Baden-Baden, Germany: Nomos.

Hofmann, J. (2007). Internet governance: A regulative idea in flux. In R. K. Jain Bandamutha (Ed.), *Internet governance: An introduction* (pp. 74–108). Hyderabad, India: The Icfai University Press.

Huber, G. P. (1991). Organizational learning: The contributing processes and the literatures. *Organization Science, 2*, 88–115.

Ibert, O. (2004). Projects and firms as discordant complements: Organisational learning in the Munich software ecology. *Research Policy, 33*, 1529–1546.

Kleinwächter, W. (2005). A new diplomacy for the 21st century? Multi-stakeholder approach and bottom-up policy development in the Information Society. In D. Stauffacher & W. Kleinwächter (Eds.), *The World Summit on the Information Society: Moving from the past into the future* (ICT task force series, no. 8, pp. 110–114). New York: United Nations.

Kreibich, R. (1998). Nach den Gipfeln von Rio und Berlin—Was taugen die UN zur Bekämpfung der weltweiten Umweltschädigung? [After the Rio and Berlin summits—What use of the UN to address global degeneration of the environment?]. In U. Albrecht (Ed.), *Die Vereinten Nationen am Scheideweg: Von der Staatenorganisation zur internationalen Gemeinschaftswelt?* (pp. 89–107). Münster, Germany: LIT Verlag.

Levinthal, D. A., & March, J. G. (1993). The myopia of learning. *Strategic Management Journal, 14*, 95–112.

Levitt, B., & March, J. G. (1988). Organizational learning. *Annual Review of Sociology, 14*, 319–340.

Lundin, R. L., & Söderholm, A. (1995). A theory of the temporary organization. *Scandinavian Journal of Management, 11*, 437–455.

Maitlis, S. (2005). The social processes of organizational sensemaking. *The Academy of Management Journal, 48*, 21–49.

March, J. G. (1991). Exploration and exploitation in organizational learning. *Organization Science, 2*, 71–87.

March, J. G., & Simon, H. A. (1958). *Organizations*. New York: Wiley.

Martens, J. (1998). Reformchancen und Reformhindernisse in den Beziehungen zwischen UNO und NGOs [Reform of relationships between the UN and NGOs: Opportunities and obstacles]. In U. Albrecht (Ed.), *Die Vereinten Nationen am Scheideweg* (pp. 123–134). Münster, Germany: LIT Verlag.

Messner, D. (2001). Weltkonferenzen und Global Governance: Anmerkungen zum radikalen Wandel vom Nationalstaatensystem zur Global Governance-Epoche [World conferences and global governance: Notes on the radical change from the nation-state system to the age of global governance]. In T. Fues & B. I. Hamm (Eds.), *Die Weltkonferenzen der 90er Jahre: Baustellen für Global Governance* (pp. 13–43). Bonn, Germany: Dietz.

Mueller, M. L., Kuerbis, B. N., & Pagé, C. (2007). Democratizing global communication? Global civil society and the campaign for communication rights in the Information Society. *International Journal of Communication, 1*, 267–296.

Office of the President of the Millennium Assembly. (2001, August). *Reference document on the participation of civil society in United Nations conferences and special sessions of the General*

Assembly during the 1990s, Version 1. United Nations General Assembly, 55th session. Retrieved from http://www.un.org/ga/president/55/speech/civilsociety1.htm. Last Accessed on 9 Aug 2013.

Papenfuß, A. (2003). Einleitung [Introduction]. *Internationale Politik, 58*(12), 78–79.

Prencipe, A., & Tell, F. (2001). Inter-project learning: Processes and outcomes of knowledge codification in project-based firms. *Research Policy, 30*, 1373–1394.

Raboy, M. (2004). The World Summit on the Information Society and its legacy for global governance. *Gazette: International Communication Gazette, 66*, 225–232. doi:10.1177/0016549204043608.

Rittberger, V. (1983). Global conference diplomacy and international policy-making: The case of UN-sponsored world conferences. *European Journal of Political Research, 11*, 167–182.

Sabel, R. (1997). *Procedure at international conferences.* Cambridge, UK: Cambridge University Press.

Schechter, M. G. (2005). *United Nations global conferences.* London: Routledge.

Schneider, U. (1997). Reengineering und andere Managementmoden: Vorüberlegungen zu einem temporären Ansatz von Organisation [Reengineering and other management fashions: Preliminary considerations about a temporary approach of organization]. In H.-P. Liebmann (Ed.), *Vom Business Process Reengineering zum Change Management: Kritische Bestandsaufnahme, Perspektiven und Erfahrungen* (pp. 181–212). Wiesbaden, Germany: Gabler.

Selian, A. (2004). The World Summit on the Information Society and civil society participation. *The Information Society, 20*, 201–215.

Seyfang, G. (2003). Environmental mega-conferences: From Stockholm to Johannesburg and beyond. *Global Environmental Change, 13*, 223–228.

Siochrú, S. Ó. (2004). Will the real WSIS please stand up? The historic encounter of the 'Information Society' and the 'Communication Society'. *International Communication Gazette, 66*, 203–224. doi:10.1177/0016549204043606.

Souter, D. (2007). The World Summit on the Information Society: The end of an era or the start of something new? In K. Banks, R. Bissio, W. Currie, A. Esterhuysen, C. G. Ramilo, & M. Sigillito (Eds.), *Global Information Society watch, 2007* (pp. 11–15). n.p.: APC and ITeM. Retrieved from http://www.giswatch.org/sites/default/files/gisw_2007.pdf

Sydow, J., Lindquist, L., & DeFillippi, R. (2004). Project-based organizations, embeddedness and repositories of knowledge [Editorial]. *Organization Studies, 25*, 1475–1489.

Taylor, P. (1989). The origins and institutional setting of the UN special conferences. In P. Taylor & A. J. R. Groom (Eds.), *Global issues in the United Nations' framework* (pp. 7–34). Houndmills, UK: Palgrave Macmillan.

Walsh, J. P. (1995). Managerial and organizational cognition: Notes from a trip down memory lane. *Organization Science, 6*, 280–321.

Walsh, J. P., & Ungson, G. R. (1991). Organizational memory. *The Academy of Management Review, 16*, 57–91.

Weick, K. E., & Ashford, S. J. (2001). Communication and organizational learning. In F. M. Jablin & L. Putnam (Eds.), *New handbook of organizational communication* (pp. 704–731). Thousand Oaks, CA: Sage.

Willets, P. (1989). The pattern of conferences. In P. Taylor & A. J. R. Groom (Eds.), *Global issues in the United Nations' framework* (pp. 35–63). Houndmills, UK: Palgrave Macmillan.

When Arts Enter Organizational Spaces: Implications for Organizational Learning

11

Ariane Berthoin Antal

The need for organizations to learn is undisputed: The speed of technological change, the severity of problems in societies and the natural environment, and the pressure from competitors imply that organizations cannot simply continue doing the same things in the same way and expect to flourish in a sustainable system. The challenge is not limited to the private sector; public sector and civil society organizations are experiencing similar pressures to learn, intensified by shrinking budgets. Although the need is evident, how to address it is not. Of course, numerous techniques to stimulate and sustain organizational learning already exist (Dierkes, Berthoin Antal, Child, & Nonaka, 2001), but the size and scope of problems require experimentation with fresh approaches. A new type of experimentation is "artistic interventions," which bring people, products, and practices from the world of the arts into organizations, with a more or less clearly defined learning orientation.

At first glance this entrance of the world of the arts into the world of organizations may appear either very obvious or very surprising. Different logics underpin these two possibilities, which coexist in practice.

1. The "obvious" connection is that creativity generates new ideas. The arts are associated with creativity, so bringing employees into contact with the arts should develop their creativity. This is an attractively simple solution, based on the assumption that once the creativity of employees is stimulated, it will then automatically be at the service of the organization.
2. The idea is surprising because "to multitudes art seems to be an importation into experience from a foreign country" (Dewey, 1934/2005, p. 11). The world of arts has its own codes, behaviors, and values, and these are usually[1] perceived to be

---

[1] Some scholars have noted that "new management" has absorbed many terms from the world of the arts and blurred the boundaries (Boltanski & Chiapello, 1999; Boltanski & Thévenot, 2006; Chiapello, 1998), but overall, people still tend to see these worlds as distinct.

A. Berthoin Antal (✉)
Research Unit "Cultural Sources of Newness," Social Science Research
Center Berlin (WZB), Reichpietschufer 50, 10785 Berlin, Germany
e-mail: ariane.berthoin.antal@wzb.eu

A. Berthoin Antal et al. (eds.), *Learning Organizations: Extending the Field*,
Knowledge and Space 6, DOI 10.1007/978-94-007-7220-5_11,
© Springer Science+Business Media Dordrecht 2014

very different, even diametrically opposed to, those that operate in organizations like companies, hospitals, or municipal authorities. The logic behind the "surprising" idea of bringing the "foreign" world of the arts into organizational spaces is that the discovery of different possible ways of seeing and dealing with the world should permit the organization to learn by expanding its repertoire of potential interpretations and responses (Huber, 1991; Swidler, 1986). New knowledge can emerge from the combination of, or clash between, different bodies and forms of knowledge (Abel, 2008; Nonaka & Takeuchi, 1995; Stark, 2009). Clashes between the presumably very different cultures can reveal and challenge the assumptions and routines engrained in the organizational culture and thereby trigger double-loop learning (Argyris & Schön, 1978).

Both lines of reasoning have potential, and in combination they may even drive artistic interventions into becoming a new management fad. It is therefore important from the outset to recognize that they both also raise questions. Is it really so obvious that bringing the arts into organizations can stimulate individual creativity and thereby trigger organizational learning? Years of research in organizations, specifically with the power of organizational cultures and the barriers to organizational learning, make the last link in the chain particularly questionable (Berthoin Antal, Lenhardt, & Rosenbrock, 2001). The established ways of seeing and doing things are embedded in routines and power relations that make it difficult or even dangerous for employees to express new possibilities that challenge existing procedures, structures, and beliefs (Schein, 1993). Psychologists have shown that individual and collective creativity can indeed be stimulated (e.g., Amabile, 1996; Funke, 2009), and interactions with the arts can play an important part in that process (Barry, 1994; KEA, 2009). But under what conditions does the introduction of the arts into organizations make of that space a milieu of creativity in which cultural change is possible (Meusburger, 2009)? Similarly, the "surprising" logic that artistic interventions can stimulate organizational learning through the clash of cultures is appealing, but how realistic is it? Research on individual learning from exposure to different cultures suggests that the outcome is far from predictable (Adler, 2002; Friedman & Berthoin Antal, 2005). Confrontations between different people with world views may contribute to strengthening rather than dismantling stereotypes, and they may trigger defensiveness rather than encourage engagement. If mechanistic models that imply an instrumentalization of the arts in organizations are misleading, what kinds of models are appropriate?

The literature in this field is growing rapidly enough to generate curiosity about these questions. In the past decade an increasing number of scholars, consultants, and artists have written about ways of bringing ideas and practices from the world of the arts into organizations (e.g., Adler, 2006; Anderson, Reckhenrich, & Kupp, 2011; Barry & Hansen, 2008; Barry & Meisiek, 2004; Biehl-Missal, 2011b; Brellochs & Schrat, 2005; Chodzinski, 2007; Seifter & Buswick, 2005; Taylor & Ladkin, 2009). But too little empirical research has been conducted to provide answers to such questions at this time (Barry & Meisiek, 2010; Berthoin Antal, 2009; Berthoin Antal & Strauß, 2013). The purpose of this chapter is to explore the phenomenon of artistic interventions in organizations from the perspective of organizational learning, knowledge, and space in order to formulate a research agenda. I start by illustrating the multiplicity of ways that arts are being brought into organizational spaces, then present some conceptual maps and models that structure the field, highlighting aspects that are relevant for organizational learning. This review shows the need to expand the theoretical framework in future research on organizational learning because artistic interventions have put issues of space and the diverse human senses, to which little attention has been paid to date, squarely on the agenda.

Artistic Interventions in Organizations: A Multifaceted Phenomenon

Artistic interventions, which I define broadly and neutrally[2] as processes in which people, practices, and/or[3] products from the world of the arts enter into the world of organizations, vary greatly along several dimensions, such as time, purpose, and connection to other organizational processes.[4] Some artistic interventions are long term (several months, even years), use multiple art forms, and are embedded in the organizational culture and strategy; however, most are short, lasting hours or days, and use one art form. Many interventions are launched to develop people or to develop the organization (Berthoin Antal, Taylor & Ladkin, 2013); some are intended to develop new ideas for products and services. Interventions are often brought in by a senior manager (e.g., CEO, director of a business unit, head of HR or marketing) who wants to try a new idea and has heard about or experienced an artistic intervention in another context (e.g., conference, business school). Many artistic interventions also come in projects with consultants who draw on artists and artistic processes to complement their approach. The idea of trying an intervention is often introduced by intermediary organizations, which have recently emerged in several countries to bridge between the world of the arts and the world of organizations in various ways. They help organizations define a need and select an artist, they generate funding and provide guidance during the intervention; some

---

[2] Artistic interventions are not neutral, as my chapter demonstrates in many ways, but the term itself is used neutrally here, drawing on the Latin root, *inter-venire*, to come between, to involve someone or something in a situation so as to alter or hinder an action or development (*American Heritage Dictionary of the English Language*, 2000). I emphasize this reasoning because some British participants at an "artful research" workshop I conducted in 2009 were concerned that the term *intervention* is associated with military activities, and they suggested instead that we refer to artistic collaborations. However, I consider "collaboration" to be problematically loaded with associations (either very negative, as in "collaborating with the enemy," or very positive, as in "working closely and well together").

[3] As will be seen later in this chapter, an intervention sometimes involves just one of these three elements. But it often involves two or even all three, and in these cases the boundaries become somewhat blurred.

[4] I draw on examples from the literature as well as from my own research interviews, which have not been published. In some cases the organizations choose to remain anonymous.

also train artists to enter the workplace (Berthoin Antal, 2011b; Grzelec & Prata, 2013).

There is no complete overview over the past artistic interventions and current ones that are arising around the world. The intention in this chapter is to start by illustrating the wide variety of possibilities that have been tried in three broad categories—products, people, and practices—as suggested in my working definition of artistic interventions and by Barry and Meisiek's (2010) review of the field of "workarts." In the following pages I focus on artistic interventions at the workplace; however, many interesting experiments are underway in schools and communities to address societal issues such as unemployment and peace-building.[5]

Product-Based Artistic Interventions

Art collections are the longest lasting (and probably also the oldest) type of artistic intervention in organizations. They are traditionally associated more with impressing stakeholders than with stimulating learning, although there are important exceptions, such as the collection of American magnate Albert C. Barnes, who wanted to edify his employees through art in the first quarter of the twentieth century.[6] Many organizations' art collections may still just be about "personal aggrandizement, organizational prestige, and long-term investment and the decoration of the work environment," but a number of collectors are coming to view their art collections as a possible resource for learning to see and think differently in the organization (Barry & Meisiek, 2010, p. 1511). Far from simply decorating the workplace in a pleasing manner, some collections (e.g., EA Generali in Austria and Novo Nordisk in Denmark) are intended to provoke and irritate, thereby generating "creative unrest" and signaling to employees that unusual ideas and projects are welcome in the organization (p. 1512).

I consider an art collection to be an intervention in an organization because it brings products from the world of art into the work space. Artworks are either a presence or an absence on the walls, in the air, and on the ground in an organization. Their presence has the potential to break the routine of the use of organizational space, activate the senses (touch, sight, hearing, smell), and stimulate sense-making, for example, by stimulating individual or collective questioning of the purpose, value, and relevance of this art and of art at work in general. When an artwork enters

---

[5] For example, a special issue of the *Action Research* journal (Brydon-Miller, Berthoin Antal, Friedman, & Gayá Wicks, 2011a), which explores the arts and action research, contains articles relating to unemployment, schools, and homelessness. An issue of the online journal *Music and Arts in Action* focused on artistic interventions in conflict transformation (Bergh & Sloboda, 2010).

[6] "Combining his educational concepts and his compassion for the working man with his burgeoning interest in the arts, Barnes initiated educational seminars and hung paintings by William Glackens, Ernest Lawson, and Maurice Prendergast in his Argyrol factory to be studied and discussed by his workers. His first formal classes in art appreciation were held at the factory for the benefit of his employees" (Barnes Foundation, 2010, retrieved from http://www.barnesfoundation.org/h_main.html).

the space, employees may feel it is beautiful, sad, funny, or grotesque, and when objects are replaced or removed, they may feel the space is empty, clear, peaceful, or boring, to name just a few possible responses. In between the arrival and departure of the art, people may welcome it, or they may find it irritating each and every day, and for most the presence may make itself felt entirely subliminally. Employees are most likely to be aware of the art if they engage personally with the collection. For example, Würth, a German company that started its fortunes by making screws and is now a world leader in its field (http://www.wuerth.com), has built a substantial art collection from which employees can choose works to put in their offices. Reinhold Würth and his curator have noticed a development in the way employees select artworks, from having at first wanted pieces from well-known artists to discovering and expressing their own tastes. The implications for organizational learning have yet to be studied.[7]

Artist-led Interventions

Barry and Meisiek (2010) identify a significant shift that occurred in the field "when managers brought artists, rather than artworks, into the workplace to catalyze new perspectives" (p. 1513). This category includes the multitude of activities with musicians, actors, photographers, dancers, and any other potentially interested artists who enter the workplace to interact with employees. The artists draw out the similarities and differences between ways of working and knowing in the world of art and the world of organizations, show employees how to apply artistic skills to their work, or develop their ability to create artworks. Artist-led interventions vary in the degree of employee participation. For example, some theater-based interventions entail actors putting on a play to illustrate issues in the organization and stimulate discussion about them, whereas others involve employees in acting out a play they create together.[8]

Probably the most wide-ranging and frequently cited example of experimenting with artist-led interventions is the Catalyst program that the multinational company Unilever has in the United Kingdom (Darsø, 2004; Schiuma, 2009). Since its launch in 1999, the program has addressed business issues such as reframing the market, developing feedback and coaching, and stimulating entrepreneurship through almost all conceivable arts, including visual arts, poetry, photography, playwriting, circus performance, and jazz. The activities have taken many forms, ranging from lunchtime activities to evening events in London to arts courses (Boyle & Ottensmeyer, 2005; Buswick, Creamer, & Pinard, 2004, p. 4).

Although few, if any, organizations have worked with artistic interventions as extensively as Unilever, there are many other long-term projects in different countries. In Sweden, for example, an intermediary organization (TILLT) has been placing

---

[7] An early, but unfortunately unpublished, study in this direction is Nissley (1999).

[8] Theater-based interventions are perhaps the most frequently documented art form. For critical reviews see especially Clark (2008) and Biehl-Missal (2010).

dancers, actors, writers, and other artists in companies, hospitals, and municipal agencies since 2002 to address organizational issues such as improving cooperation across functions or interpreting and applying core values. Over a period of 10 months the artist comes into the organization on a part-time basis to work with a team of employees interested in addressing the issue at hand (Styhre & Erikson, 2008). In Spain other intermediary organizations (disonancias and connexiones improbables) have run about 30 placements since 2005 in which international artists help small and medium-sized companies as well as larger organizations to explore new business ideas and new business models over 9 months (Berthoin Antal, 2011b; Grzelec & Prata, 2013).

Unlike artist-led interventions in which management defines a relatively clear organizational learning objective, some projects start out with a very open learning brief, namely, "to see what happens" when employees are exposed to artists at work. The earliest example commonly cited is the Artist Placement Group in the UK, which started in 1970 to seek organizations willing to engage in residency projects that would make the organization, its work, and its people the focus of art (Ferro-Thomsen, 2005; Velthuis, 2005). A recent case is Eurogroup Consulting in France, which launched a four-part residency program over two and a half years, during which a conceptual artist or artist collective was invited to spend 4–5 months creating inside the organization. The program was based on an assumption, not a goal: that the interaction between the artists and the employees during the artistic residency would stimulate fresh ways of seeing the organization, its way of working, and the environment surrounding it (Berthoin Antal, 2011a). A French business school, too, has been experimenting with residencies of this kind for several years, and the project leader has noticed that some members of the staff (but not the professors) have started becoming aware of aesthetic aspects in their work setting and have begun changing the criteria for taking some decisions.

Many companies try out an artistic intervention as a one-off activity from which they hope to get ideas or stimulate new behaviors, whereas others embed them in other programs and processes in the organization. For example, Cornelsen, a German publishing house, agreed to, so to speak, pose as a model in the nude for some 16 artists and artist groups, who then presented their works to the company as a kind of organizational analysis. One output of the project is an interesting book from which readers can learn a great deal (Brellochs & Schrat, 2005). But the learning effect in the organization appears to be disappointing to the organizers, artistic as well as corporate, as Strauß (2012) discovered when she conducted interviews for her doctoral thesis several years later. Another example of a one-off intervention with ambiguous learning outcomes is in a medium-sized German company that prides itself on experimenting with diverse forms of management development.[9] The CEO invited a team of artists to help address problems in the leadership style. The team worked with graffiti art to get the managers to express their perception of current leadership issues and their image of a desirable organizational culture on

---

[9] The information provided here is drawn from interviews I conducted with diverse stakeholders in the project in 2009 and 2010.

large panels the height of the former Berlin Wall. The managers were fired up by the experience and returned to work intending to implement changes, but a survey a few months later revealed too little improvement, so the CEO decided to expand the intervention to include all the employees. An external consultant who had worked for several years with the company accompanied the project, but because the visual and oral expressions from the artistic intervention were experienced by some managers as "too critical," the management put the relationship with the consultant on hold, leaving managers and employees to figure out on their own how to take things forward (or not).

In contrast to the many one-off experiments are artistic interventions that are embedded into an overall arts-based program or into an organizational culture with values closely related to the arts. Some organizations, such as Deutsche Bahn AG (the German national railroad corporation), bring different kinds of artists into many training and development programs and corporate conferences in order to develop various skills and to explore and express corporate values. Few organizations are as comprehensive and consistent in integrating the arts into the organization and its processes as the German drugstore chain dm-drogerie markt, which has a corporate culture based on anthroposophical values. In 2000, for example, it introduced a theater module in its apprenticeship program, in keeping with the organizational cultural emphasis on developing the whole person (Weller, 2009). The company, consciously using the concepts of the artist Joseph Beuys, also draws on the arts for management development and in some strategic workshops because the owner considers management to be a "social-artistic process" and an organization to be a "social sculpture" (Chodzinski, 2007, p. 265).

Practice-Based Artistic Interventions

Artistic practices are, of course, part of artist-led interventions, but another form of artistic intervention is emerging, which Barry and Meisiek (2010) call "artistic experimentation" when members of organizations try to "forego formal artworks and artists and foster mindfulness through artistic experimentation in their everyday worklife" (p. 1517).[10] They cite a few examples, such as the Imagination Lab in Switzerland that uses Lego blocks for "serious play" in strategy workshops with clients (Statler, Roos, & Victor, 2009) and a Norwegian aluminum smelting company whose new CEO surprised the employees by spending a large sum to repaint the factory white when the company was facing bankruptcy. Cost-cutting measures were also taken, but the artful intervention created "a deliberate break with the prevailing corporate rationality" that contributed to a rapid turnaround (Barry & Meisiek, 2010, p. 1518). This approach moves away from treating artistic work as

---

[10] Barry and Meisiek (2010) point out quite logically that working without an artist can increase the sense of ownership for ideas generated through artistic experimentation. Artists I have interviewed, however, have often mentioned (with a mix of satisfaction and resentment) that employees quickly take such pride and ownership in a project that they seem to forget the artist's contribution!

"a mysterious property of the privileged few, but is something that can be learned and nurtured within organizational environments" although such practices are not easily or quickly acquired (p. 1517). For organizational learning, this category of artistic intervention differs significantly from the first two because it aims to embed artistic practices in organizations rather than being a "foreign import" from the world of the arts that disrupts routine ways of thinking and doing things.

Mapping Learning from Artistic Interventions

Having introduced these three broad categories to illustrate the wide variety of ways in which the arts have been intervening in organizational spaces, I now offer two kinds of conceptual maps that provide different perspectives on organizational learning dimensions of the phenomenon. The first focuses on one part of the field—interventions by artists in business organizations—and it shows how the mapping process shifted the understanding of the learning processes involved (Darsø, 2004). The second map zooms in to look inside organizations, revealing the differences and connections between individual-, group-, and organizational-level learning in artistic interventions (Berthoin Antal, 2009; Schiuma, 2009).

Learning Trajectories: The Heart of Artistic Interventions. At Learning Lab in Denmark, Darsø (2004) undertook the first review that started defining the field of "arts-in-business" (p. 14). She noted that business uses the arts for decoration and entertainment, it applies them as instruments for team-building, communication training, leadership development, and innovation, and it integrates the arts in strategic processes of transformation (p. 14). There are also other relationships between business and the arts, such as the long-standing tradition of corporate philanthropy, the relatively new marketing-related field of sponsoring, and the collection of art for investment purposes, but she does not include them under the label of arts-in-business.[11] Her focus (and mine) is on the arts-based activities that are embarked upon with the intention of stimulating some form of learning in the organization.

To map the field, Darsø (2004) started with a matrix distinguishing between the artist's degrees of involvement with the organization and degrees of ambiguity associated with the intervention. Over the course of her study, she revised the matrix model in several significant ways. I present both her models here (see Figs. 11.1 and 11.2) because they build on each other and reveal a shift in thinking about organizational learning possibilities through artistic interventions.

---

[11] Philanthropic and sponsoring relations with the arts may be at opposite ends of the spectrum, one being "disinterested, very arm's length" and the other being very instrumental. However, philanthropic and sponsorship relations may be precursors, outgrowths, or complementary or parallel activities to the kind of artistic interventions described in this chapter. The boundaries between these kinds of activities are distinct but permeable. Learning-oriented activities may grow out of an interaction of a different kind, such as when an organization brings into a developmental workshop a musician from an orchestra that it has supported philanthropically.

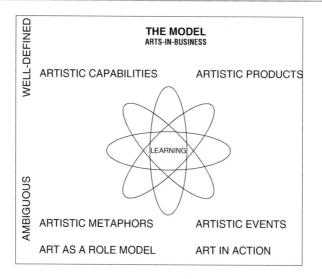

Fig. 11.1 The arts-in-business matrix (From Darsø 2004, p. 41. Copyright 2004 by Lotte Darsø and Samfundslitteratur. Reprinted with permission)

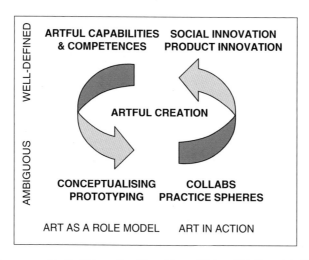

Fig. 11.2 The new model of artful creation (From Darsø 2004, p. 150. Copyright 2004 by Lotte Darsø and Samfundslitteratur. Reprinted with permission)

The original categories (Fig. 11.1) are helpful for distinguishing between types of artistic interventions; the new categories are more useful for exploring how these interventions can contribute to organizational learning. The revised model (Fig. 11.2) replaces the role-modeling function of "metaphors" with "conceptualizing and pro-totyping" to specify the processes that artistic interventions can support in the early stage of learning new ways of seeing and doing things. She amended the category "artistic capabilities" to "artful capabilities and competences" because she discovered that when arts enter organizational spaces, the learning is not only around specific capabilities but also around intangible, elusive qualities, especially "energy" (Darsø, 2004, p. 152). The art-in-action categories of "artistic events" and "artistic products" are replaced by "collabs [collaborative laboratories], practice spheres" and "social innovation, product innovation," respectively. Collaborative and practice spheres are the "socially safe spaces" created to enable people to explore, experiment with, and apply the ideas that arts bring into organizations (p. 153). The fourth field of the new matrix describes possible outcomes of artistic interventions in terms of social innovations and product innovations, which can encompass new services and organizational changes as well.

Possibly the most significant change between the two models is in the heart: The new model revolves around "artful creation." The term highlights that when arts enter organizational spaces it is not just about transferring the ideas from one realm to another, which is what is usually associated with "learning from the arts," but also about an interaction between different forms of knowing, from which new ways of knowing and doing can emerge.

Darsø's groundbreaking work is still valuable today as a way of sorting through the multifaceted field and highlighting features that are relevant for learning and creating knowledge when arts enter organizational spaces. Although her focus was on arts in business, what she discovered is equally relevant to other kinds of organizations. Her map is not about fitting activities into categories but rather tracing processes, and the model explicitly refers to space by recognizing the need for safe spaces in which to try out new ideas, features that are emphasized in the literature on organizational learning (e.g., Friedman, Lipshitz, & Overmeer, 2001; Schein, 1993).

Mapping Learning Flows in Organizations. Having mapped the field of artistic interventions, I now turn to the organizational spaces where their effects make themselves felt. In a report for Arts and Business in the UK, Schiuma (2009) proposed a concentric model of the organization in its environment. At the center he placed effects on individuals, which spill over to the intermediate circle of effects on interactions between people and then to the outer circle of effects on organizational strategy, performance, and culture (p. 9). But this concentric model is flawed because it implies that individuals are completely engulfed by their organizational context. I therefore developed a different model (see Fig. 11.3) that recognizes "the fact that individuals are not just employees encircled by an organization; they are citizens who spend a considerable amount of time at work but who also have activities and relationships in the surrounding socio-economic and natural environment" (Berthoin Antal, 2009, p. 31). Despite the role differentiation that distinguishes work life from other spheres of life, people bring in ideas, expectations, and values from their lives outside the organization, and they take what they get from experiences in the organization back into the society in which they are embedded.

My research confirms the centrality of effects at the individual level and their *potential* outward flow through levels of the organization. Just as individuals are agents of organizational learning (Friedman, 2001; Kim, 1993), so are they the ones

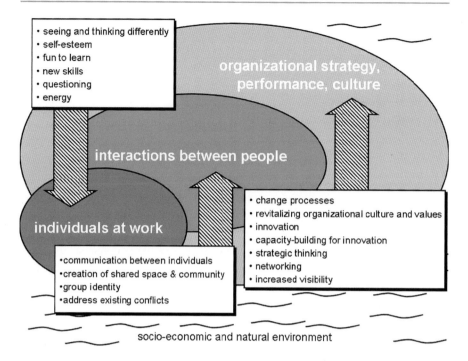

Fig. 11.3 Where to look for the values that artistic interventions can add in organizations (From *Transforming Organizations with the Arts. Research Report*. Berthoin Antal, 2009, p. 45)

who can experience an artistic intervention and learn from it, and they are more likely to engage if they see personal value in doing so than if they see no such value. If people choose not to engage (for example, because of lack of interest in or discomfort with artistic expression in general or at work in particular[12]), the artistic intervention is unlikely to generate much value for the organization. Participants in artistic interventions have reported that the benefits from individual learning have flowed outwards from the individual level to groups in the organization, for example, enabling people to discover how their work relates to others and to develop ideas and activities together. Individual learning shared with others *may* then lead to organizational change by challenging engrained assumptions about how things are done in the organization or by rejecting old routines and developing new approaches, for example (Berthoin Antal, 2011a, 2013a; Berthoin Antal et al., 2013). Such changes *can*, in turn, improve the organization's competitiveness and innovation (Berthoin Antal & Strauß, 2013). The research so far suggests that these effects

---

[12] Little has been written to date about unwillingness to participate, but my interviews with artists show that they often have to start an intervention by getting people to overcome anxieties. My interviews with participants indicate that some of them held back and others regretted having had to reveal more of themselves via artistic expression than they felt was appropriate in the work context.

cannot be targeted directly; they may be more likely to emerge as uncontrolled by-products of individual and collective learning experiences in an artistic intervention than from ever more refined management instruments (Berthoin Antal, 2009, 2011a; Schiuma, 2009).

So How Do Organizations Learn from Artistic Interventions?

This review indicates that far more is currently known about the kinds of learning objectives associated with bringing the arts into organizations than about whether or how those outcomes are achieved. Overall, the expectations are high, diverse, and generally positive (Berthoin Antal, 2009). But actually very little is known about *how* the arts "work"[13] in organizations and how organizations learn from artistic interventions. A mix of reasons is probably responsible for this black-box state of affairs. The relatively new phenomenon first needed to be discovered by researchers as worthy of study, but there is no single discipline into whose purview the topic falls, so there is no body of theory and established methodology that fits the task. Research access to cases has been limited not only by the still small number of cases but also by skepticism about research. In numerous conversations I have found that managers and artists who have experience with artistic interventions have been concerned that the dominant research methods applied to analyzing organizational processes would not be able to do justice to the nature of artistic interventions (Berthoin Antal, 2013a; Berthoin Antal & Strauß, 2013).

The lack of research in the field is problematic because not only do we organizational researchers know little, what we think we know is quite biased toward a positive view of the phenomenon and toward managerial interests. Much of the published material to date has been generated by people close to the project (managers, artists, and consultants), a state of knowledge that is a double-edged sword. They have insider knowledge of processes that external researchers have difficulty obtaining, but they understandably also have a stake in publishing success stories. Divergent and critical views have less of a chance of being expressed and recorded. Researchers, too, have contributed to this problem. The literature they have produced documents primarily the intentions of managers and the hopes of academics who tend to share the aspiration that "the application of artistic and artful processes can move business forward to make better business in two interdependent ways: one towards innovation and profit, the other towards more humane and energetic organizations" (Darsø, 2004, p. 155). Very little has been written from the perspective of employees; unfortunately, their voices are often reduced to providing supportive quotations about positive experiences. Nor has there been much research on the intentions of the

---

[13] Not only do we researchers know little about how the arts "work" in organizations, we know surprisingly little about how the arts work for individuals. Fine-grained research, such as that conducted by DeNora (2000) about music in everyday life, shows that the relationship between people and music is reflexive and contextual. It entails sense-making categories that differ significantly from those used by musicologists in traditional "music appreciation" mode.

artists. Initial work shows that artists engage in artistic interventions for very different reasons. Some see in organizational settings the materials and space needed to create their art, others want to earn a living that will allow them to practice their art, and some seek the opportunity to influence the workplace "for the better" with their skills, energy, and values (Berthoin Antal, 2008, 2013a; Brellochs & Schrat, 2005; Ferro-Thomsen, 2005). No research has yet been conducted on how the different intentions of artists might affect organizational learning.

The implications of these biases are significant. The paucity of articles addressing potential problems that could arise from artistic interventions in organizations may be closely related to the fact that very little has been written from the perspective of the employees. In this sense the field of artistic interventions suffers from a drawback similar to that in the field of organizational learning: a naïve assumption that learning (or art) is good, and more is better. That idea leaves unattended the possibility that people and organizations can learn to do "bad" things (e.g., damaging the natural environment or human beings) and experiencing arts in a work context might have negative consequences for the individuals involved or beyond. Little attention is paid to the potential dangers of making work-related decisions "under the influence of" exciting artistic experiences, when people's enthusiasm may override their critical faculties. Questions of power, too, are rarely raised in the literature on artistic interventions, although the exercise and distribution of power are inherent aspects of relations and processes in organizations. The need for such work is illustrated by Clark and Mangham's (2004) study on the use of Forum Theater[14] in a company in the United Kingdom. Their analysis revealed how the potential of the arts to address underlying issues in an organization can unwittingly be subverted in an intervention, so that the existing problems are masked or even reinforced (see also Berthoin Antal et al., 2013; Gibb, 2004; Hüttler, 2005; Nissley, Taylor, & Houden, 2004; Strauß, 2012; for a broader critique, see Pelzer, 2006).

New Research Opportunities Require New Research Agendas

Bob Dylan's song "The Times They Are a-Changin'" comes to mind because three significant developments are offering additional opportunities to conduct potentially really interesting research on artistic interventions.

1. More interventions: The number of interventions has expanded considerably and is likely to keep expanding in the coming years as a result of several factors. The trend toward including artistic interventions in business school programs and the rising number of publications about these experiences (e.g., *Economist*, 2011; Taylor & Ladkin, 2009) will probably give more managers the confidence to try

---

[14] The importation of the idea of Forum Theater, which Augosto Boal developed in the streets of Brazil to help poor people change their lot in life, into the corporate setting is an interesting phenomenon. It is telling that the name has been changed in the process: "Theater of the oppressed" is not a label that lends itself to adoption in the new setting. The "taming" of this form of theater to a management technique is troubling.

bringing artists into their organizations. Even though decision-makers cannot know precisely what will happen there, the fact that they have seen or heard about arts entering the business school space will probably make them more likely to "trust the process" (McNiff, 1998b) in their own organizational space. The growth of intermediary organizations that are actively seeking to build bridges between the world of the arts and the world of organizations is another factor that will stimulate an increase in the use of artistic interventions (Berthoin Antal, 2011b; Grzelec & Prata, 2013). The concomitant discovery by more artists that such engagements are not only financially but also artistically rewarding and the inclusion of courses in arts schools to prepare artists for such activities will support the trend as well.

2. More demand for research: There is a greater demand for research on artistic interventions than was the case a few years ago. Policy-makers in Europe are calling for evidence of the impacts of artistic interventions to provide a basis for funding decisions and to give a justification for decision-makers in organizations to invest in this type of activity (Berthoin Antal & Strauß, 2013). Artists are expressing curiosity in working with researchers to help them understand what they have been doing. Intermediary organizations, too, are looking for research partners to study their projects and are opening the doors of organizations they have worked with.

3. More researchers: The academic community (at least the Academy of Management) is signaling a need for reorienting research to "reclaim unconventional research contexts and samples in organizational scholarship" (Bamberger & Pratt, 2010, p. 665). Artistic interventions are still "unconventional," as is listening to the voices of employees and artists in organizational learning. The call to conduct more research in this area will also be welcomed because a mounting number of scholars have developed a very personal interest in the arts and its potential connections to their work on and in organizations.[15]

The time is therefore ripe for developing a meaningful research agenda. The agenda will require appropriate research methodologies for understanding the processes and effects of artistic interventions in organizations. My sense, coming from a research background in organizational culture and learning, both of which are multidisciplinary ventures, is that the agenda and the methodologies must draw on multiple disciplines and engage diverse stakeholders in order to overcome the biases and gaps that characterize the field so far. Given this stance on research and learning, an agenda-setting process is obviously subjective. In formulating a research agenda on artistic interventions in organizations, I outline below the topics I believe are worth studying and the questions that puzzle me as an invitation for others to connect with and expand upon.

---

[15] Recent annual conferences of the Academy of Management have included well-attended tango sessions related to leadership, art exhibits by members of the Academy, and jazz sessions connected to team-working. Books and articles by members of the Academy include references to personal experiences with various art forms (e.g., Adler, 2006, 2010; Hatch, 1999; Shrivastava & Cooper, 2008).

Puzzle 1

The artist Robert Irwin and the physicist Ed Wortz conducted an experiment in May 1970 in the National Symposium on Habitability (Wechsler, 1982, pp. 131–133) whose outcome resonates with aspects of research on artistic interventions that puzzle me. They brought together an interdisciplinary mix of experts to explore the topic of habitability, for which they created very unusual meeting spaces. (One of them consisted of a pristine white room without chairs and accessible only through a hole in a brick wall at the end of a dirty alley. On the third day the room opened at one end so that people drifted in from the street. The five breakout rooms were different, too, one being a reverberating room that forced people to move their chairs closer together in order to hear each other.) The organizers observed how the different spaces affected the behavior of the participants, but when the organizers asked these experts at the end what effects they had noticed, the experts said they had not noticed any. One might have expected the topic of the symposium to prime the experts to notice the effects that the extreme differences in spaces had had on their own behavior over 3 days. But it did not. Why?

Several possible explanations come to mind, each pointing to two gaps that research needs to address: lack of attention to bodies in knowing, especially to one's own body, and limited attention to spaces in organizational learning theory.

Bodily knowing. An engagement with the arts entails forms of knowing to which little attention has been paid in the field of organizational learning so far: the bodily senses. Strati (2000) has repeatedly warned that researchers continue making the "cognitive and rational error of ignoring the bodies of the people involved in the decision process and only considering their minds" (p. 20). Organizational learning occurs through the individuals who participate in experiences, and these individuals have bodies: undeniable but overlooked. Throughout the literature on organizational learning, knowing is usually reduced to what takes place in and is retained by the brain. It is as though the rest of the body were not present, with its ability to touch, hear, smell, see, and taste— and its concomitant ability to experience and express affects. Artistic interventions bring these dimensions of the learning experience explicitly into the organizational space and therefore put them onto the research agenda (Hansen, 2005; Chap. 13, McNiff, in this volume; Chap. 12, Pässilä & Oikarinen, in this volume).

Taking the body seriously in studying the effects of artistic interventions will be a challenge because it entails noticing and expressing things of which people may be only subliminally aware or to which they are unaccustomed to attributing an effect. Taylor (2002) has characterized the problem aptly as "aesthetic muteness." The challenge for researchers is a double one because they need to elicit knowledge from others that they are not well-equipped to elicit from themselves. The fact that the experts in the Habitability Symposium did not notice the effects of changing spaces on their behavior is probably also a reflection of how little many scientific experts attend to their bodily experience of the world. The papers the participants had prepared for the symposium contained all the knowledge they believed was worth considering at the event. The limited approaches to knowing that are characteristic of the social sciences contrast sharply with those of artists who take their bodily experience as a source of knowledge. Lehrer (2007) shows that the results of such artists' ways of knowing "what reality *feels* like" predate findings neuroscience is now arriving at (p. viii, italics original). Experiments to partner with artists in research processes could therefore help social scientists develop new methodologies in this area (see, for example, Berthoin Antal, 2013b; Brattström, 2012; McNiff, 1998a).

Theoretical approaches with appropriate terminology to address this issue are also needed. Some of them may well come from the domain of the arts. For example, Biehl-Missal (2011a) has productively applied theater theory to analyze perceptions of management performances "through atmospheric, bodily sensations, which are influenced by the interplay of aesthetic elements, by the whole behavioral, temporal and spatial situation" (p. 622). Another possible theoretical avenue is actor–network theory, with its concept of actants, but it would need to be adapted from its scientific origins to interactions with art and aesthetics in organizations. Göbel's (2012) doctoral research on "atmospheric network theory" is a promising exploration of such an adaptation.

Space matters. Understanding what happens when arts enter organizational spaces also requires better conceptualizations of space than have been generated so far in the literature on organizational learning. Although there has been talk of a "spatial turn" in the social sciences since the 1990s (Kivinen, 2006, p. 4), too little empirical work has been done. There are a few promising elements to work with. Ikujiro Nonaka and his colleagues introduced the idea of different kinds of space for knowledge creation with the Japanese concept of *ba* (Nonaka & Konno, 1998), and Grefe (2010) developed the empirical usefulness of Nonaka's categories by differentiating between "hot" and "cold" *ba* (see also Chap. 3, Bounfour and Grefe, in this volume). The need for safe spaces has been addressed by various scholars of organizational learning (e.g., Friedman et al., 2001, p. 762) and for learning with the arts (Gayá Wicks & Rippin, 2010). Scholars are exploring the relevance of the concept of liminal space for studying the betwixt-and-between of the world of the arts and the world of organizations (e.g., Biehl-Missal, 2011b; see also Chap. 13, McNiff, in this volume). Artistic interventions seem to create temporary "interspaces" in which participants experience possible ways of thinking, doing, and being that they may then want to try to apply in their organizational settings (Berthoin Antal & Strauß, 2013, p. 32). Reflection and active support from management are essential for the learning in the ephemeral interspaces to be sustained as organizational learning (Berthoin Antal & Strauß, 2013, pp. 34–35; see also Chap. 12, Pässila et al., in this volume).

Researchers in other disciplines, such as geography, have attended more to space than have organizational scholars, but it will not be enough just to import their terms and findings. This limited strategy risks misusing those concepts, as geographers have criticized (e.g., May & Thrift, 2001). Furthermore, despite geographers' research on action settings (Weichhart, 1996, 1999, 2003), action theory (Werlen, 1993, 1998), and the role of places, spaces, and milieus (Harvey, 2005; Massey, 1985, 1999, 2005), the field of geography has not yet dealt sufficiently well with bodies in organizational spaces to provide the answers organizational scholars need.[16] Collaborative ventures across disciplinary boundaries will therefore be required to strengthen research in this area.

Puzzle 2

Public policy-makers and decision-makers in organizations who have not tried artistic interventions are asking for "hard evidence" to document the effects of these activities on competitiveness and innovation, for example. When I interview the people who are best placed to provide the answers, namely, their peers in organizations that have experience with artistic interventions, the questions are rebuffed as inappropriate for this topic. These people are accustomed to measuring and accounting for their time and investments. Why not here?

One possibility is that "perhaps this lack of clarity is a form of complicity" between managers and artists, who recognize that "for art to 'work' its results cannot be pinned down in advance" (Barry & Meisiek, 2010, p. 1515). Even when managers and artists agree in advance on "a well-defined task[,] . . . the company will use the time needed to help the artist understand the aim and purpose, but, of course, the artist will still often surprise the company in the solution to the task—and that is, in fact, why they asked an artist to do it" (Darsø, 2004, p. 46). In this logic, measuring effects of past artistic interventions with traditional business measures might interfere with the capacity of future artistic interventions to work. Such a line of thought rings mysterious—and in fact the word "mystery" has cropped up surprisingly often in my interviews with managers about artistic interventions. This concept does not belong to the traditional management vocabulary, but it is used positively in these interviews. Might the very fact of not understanding how the arts work be part of their attraction? A related possibility is that the people I have interviewed might be protecting a last reserve of organizational space against the curse of "accountability overload" that has penetrated almost every facet of organizational activity in societies (Bovens, Schillemans, &'T Hart, 2008, p. 227). Despite the fact that it is tantamount to heresy in the world of organizations to challenge the need for ever more precise measurements to account for the transformation of inputs to outputs to outcomes, research could dare to tread on the path of understanding this puzzling situation.

Such an unorthodox research project will not, however, excuse researchers from participating in the search for useful indicators for the effects of artistic interventions in organizations. Without solid indicators, there is a great risk that policy-makers will base decisions on wishful thinking and superstitious learning (March & Olsen, 1975), possibly leading to the trap of "great expectations" experienced in other policy domains (Pressman & Wildavsky, 1984). The challenges entailed in developing appropriate indicators for social value creation and achieving an

---

[16] Geographers at the Ninth Symposium on Knowledge and Space (Heidelberg, June 2010) commented that their discipline has not yet paid much attention to the body in space, especially organizational space.

appropriate balance between pursuing project goals and responding to evaluation demands are being addressed but have not yet been satisfactorily resolved (e.g., Jennings & Baldwin, 2010; Tuan, 2008; Wood & Leighton, 2010). Artistic interventions are often part of larger planned change processes, so obviously many other things happen in and around organizations during projects. The introduction of people, products, or practices from the world of the arts make it is impossible to isolate effects directly. Rather than specifying single factors, the research should identify constellations of elements associated with constellations of effects in and across cases under study (Bergh & Sloboda, 2010). Among the elements to explore in such constellations are the degree of embeddedness of arts in the organization, the duration of the intervention, the features of the spaces, the nature of the media (for useful suggestions see Taylor & Stattler, 2009), the kind of engagement offered and used by participants, the roles of intermediaries, and the power relations. The indicators are likely to come in multiple and, for management research, unusual shapes and sizes. For example, a striking pattern in my interviews so far is that managers reject my attempts to get them to specify traditional kinds of indicators, but they refer (unprompted) to bodily indicators of changes they notice in their organizations after people have participated in artistic interventions. The managers speak, for example, of "the light in the eye," "standing taller," and "not turning away when managers walk by." These responses bring me back to the first puzzle and the need to attend to bodily ways of knowing in organizations.

Puzzle 3

My last puzzle (for the time being) is rooted in academia. The past few years have seen a flurry of publications in the field of management relating to "beauty," research that has overridden the "'taboo' associated with discussing beauty in contemporary times" (Ladkin, 2008, p. 40). Why? Scholars in management who have delved into aesthetics (e.g., Gagliardi, 2006; Guillet de Monthoux, 2004; Guillet de Monthoux, Gustafsson, & Sjöstrand, 2007; Strati, 1999, 2000) have highlighted that there are numerous aesthetic categories, but their work has not yet been integrated into the general discussion, which tends to equate aesthetics with beauty. This reduction to a single aesthetic category is problematic because the narrow emphasis on beauty suggests that the arts should simply decorate organizations and that artistic interventions should please people. Such a perspective severely curtails learning possibilities and risks instrumentalizing the arts to mask problems in the organization. An understanding of how artistic interventions may trigger, sustain, or block organizational learning would be deepened significantly by applying additional aesthetic categories (Strati, 2000, pp. 21–25) such as the grotesque, the comic, the sublime, the ugly, the sacred, and the agogic (i.e., relating to rhythm). Exploring artistic interventions with multiple aesthetic categories would also help reveal the potential dark sides of artistic interventions, which have received almost no attention. The roles of the important, but misused, category of beauty in organizations would thereby probably also become clearer than they currently are. Such research might also throw light on resistance to efforts at demystifying the way art works by measuring it with profane management indicators noted in my second puzzle.

How should such research be undertaken? First and foremost in my mind, research that seeks to understand what is happening when the arts enter organizational spaces must enable employees and artists to bring in their experiences, perspectives, and interests. Actors who see no value in the research or feel it is confined to satisfying managerial or academic interests are likely to limit their contribution to the process and thereby affect the quality of the data and the analysis. In order to appreciate the different ways of knowing and doing, the different logics and values, and the different expectations and experiences of these stakeholders, appropriate ways of involving them in designing and conducting the research are needed. Participative inquiry, and action research evaluation in particular, offer ways of involving stakeholders in generating and appreciating multiple understandings of how artistic interventions in organizations work by making the underlying espoused theories and the theories in use explicit and testable (Argyris & Schön, 1978; Friedman & Rogers, 2009; Reason & Bradbury, 2008). This research will need to be flanked by other research methods, including more "classical" case studies and surveys[17] (Berthoin Antal, 2009; Berthoin Antal & Strauß, 2013). Experimental forms of research may be designed in future to benefit from the relatively recent emergence of interest in performative social science and from experiments with the use of the arts in qualitative research (Brydon-Miller, Berthoin Antal, Friedman, & Gayá Wicks, 2011b; Knowles & Cole, 2008).

Scholars of organizational learning have been encouraged to move out of their comfort zones in order to improve their understanding of processes in diverse contexts (Berthoin Antal, Dierkes, Child, & Nonaka, 2001, pp. 933–934). The kind of research I advocate in this chapter to generate a sound understanding of what happens when arts intervene in organizational spaces is likely to stretch researchers and managers out of their comfort zone for several reasons. First, it is premised on the view that the knowledge, ways of knowing, and values of the diverse stakeholders are essential, so the research questions and methods cannot be set, as is traditionally the case, just by academics and managers. Second, the research is likely to generate insights about problems associated with arts in organizations—insights that some stakeholders will not welcome, given the currently dominant discourse about the arts bringing beauty and creativity to the workplace to stimulate productivity and competitiveness. These types of discomforts will be manageable because some researchers and managers have experience with such difficulties.

The greatest discomfort, I expect, stems from the unresolvable tension between the emphasis on knowing and controlling that are inherent to management and much mainstream research on the one hand and the unpredictability of artistic

---

[17] My initial experiments in 2012 and 2013 with web-based survey instruments in France and the Basque country to collect the thoughts and feelings of employees, managers, and artists before and after participating in artistic interventions generated rich data. A preliminary analysis that includes the use of a software package for lexical analysis (Alceste) will be presented at EGOS 2013 in Montreal with Gervaise Debucquet.

processes and the "unknowing" that underlies their unfolding on the other. Indeed, it appears that one of the most important qualities that artistic interventions may contribute to organizational learning is the capacity to work with not-knowing (Berthoin Antal, 2013b). In order to discover what artistic interventions can offer in organizations, managers and researchers will need to enter the uncomfortable, but essential, "messy area" (Cook, 2009, p. 285) together, let go of their knowing-stance, and accompany employees through the unaccustomed uncertainty of not being expected to know. And all the stakeholders will have to avoid the temptation to delegate to the artists the responsibility for control and for knowing.

Acknowledgment This contribution was written during a fellowship in 2010 at the Institute for Advanced Study Konstanz, for which I am deeply grateful. I am also grateful to numerous colleagues around the world who commented on earlier drafts of this chapter, especially Arild Bergh, Victor Friedman, Friedrich Lenger, Stefan Meisiek, Peter Meusburger, André Sobczak, Anke Strauß, and Steve Taylor.

References

Abel, G. (2008). Forms of knowledge: Problems, projects, perspectives. In P. Meusburger, M. Welker, & E. Wunder (Eds.), *Clashes of knowledge: Orthodoxies and heterodoxies in science and religion* (pp. 11–33). Knowledge and space: Vol. 1. Dordrecht, The Netherlands: Springer.

Adler, N. J. (2002). *International dimensions of organizational behavior* (4th ed.). Cincinnati, OH: South-Western College Publishing.

Adler, N. J. (2006). The arts and leadership: Now that we can do anything, what will we do? *The Academy of Management Learning and Education, 5*, 486–499.

Adler, N. J. (2010). Going beyond the dehydrated language of management: Leadership insight. *Journal of Business Strategy, 31*(4), 90–99.

Amabile, T. M. (1996). *Creativity in context: Update to the social psychology of creativity.* Boulder, CO: Westview Press.

Anderson, J., Reckhenrich, J., & Kupp, M. (2011). *The fine art of success: How learning great art can create great business.* New York: Wiley.

Argyris, C., & Schön, D. (1978). *Organizational learning—A theory of action perspective.* Reading, MA: Addison-Wesley.

Bamberger, P., & Pratt, M. (2010). From the editors—Moving forward by looking back: Reclaiming unconventional research contexts and samples in organizational scholarship. *Academy of Management Journal, 53*, 665–671.

Barnes Foundation, The. (2010). About Barnes. Retrieved from http://www.barnesfoundation.org/h_main.html

Barry, D. (1994). Making the invisible visible: Using analogically-based methods to surface unconscious processes in organizations. *Organizational Development Journal, 12*(4), 37–48.

Barry, D., & Hansen, H. (Eds.). (2008). *The SAGE handbook of new approaches in management and organization.* London: Sage.

Barry, D., & Meisiek, S. (2004, September 15). *NyX innovation alliances evaluation report.* Retrieved from http://www.dpb.dpu.dk/dokumentarkiv/Publications/20051215151928/Current Version/rapport.pdf

Barry, D., & Meisiek, S. (2010). Sensemaking, mindfulness and the workarts: Seeing more and seeing differently. *Organization Studies, 31*, 1505–1530.

Bergh, A., & Sloboda, J. (2010). Music and art in conflict transformation: A review [Theme issue on music and arts in conflict transformation]. *Music and Arts in Action, 2*(2), 2–18. Retrieved from http://musicandartsinaction.net/index.php/maia

Berthoin Antal, A. (2008). *"Artful conversations" at the WZB*. Retrieved from http://www.wzb.eu/gwd/kneu/veranstaltungen.en.htm

Berthoin Antal, A. (2009). *A research framework for evaluating the effects of artistic interventions in organizations* (p. 45). Gothenburg, Sweden: TILLT Europe.

Berthoin Antal, A. (2011a). Manifeste, corporel et imprévisible: l'apprentissage organisationnel de la Résidence d'artistes [Manifest, corporal, unpredictable: Organizational learning and artists in residence]. In Eurogroup Consulting (Ed.), *La Résidence d'artistes Eurogroup Consulting* (pp. 10–19). Catalogue No. 5. Puteaux, France: Eurogroup Consulting.

Berthoin Antal, A. (with Gómez de la Iglesia, R., & Vives Almandóz, M.). (2011b). *Managing artistic interventions in organisations. A comparative study of programmes in Europe* (2nd updated and expanded ed.). Gothenburg, Sweden: TILLT Europe.

Berthoin Antal, A. (2013a). Seeking values: Artistic interventions in organizations as potential cultural sources of values-added. In D. Baecker & B. P. Priddat (Eds.), *Ökonomie der Werte/Economics of values* (pp. 97–128). Marburg, Germany: Metropolis-Verlag.

Berthoin Antal, A. (2013b). Art-based research for engaging not-knowing in organizations. *Journal of Applied Arts & Health, 4*, 67–76.

Berthoin Antal, A., Dierkes, M., Child, J., & Nonaka, I. (2001). Organizational learning and knowledge: Reflections on the dynamics of the field and challenges for the future. In M. Dierkes, A. Berthoin Antal, J. Child, & I. Nonaka (Eds.), *Handbook of organizational learning and knowledge* (pp. 921–939). Oxford, UK: Oxford University Press.

Berthoin Antal, A., Lenhardt, U., & Rosenbrock, R. (2001). Barriers to organizational learning. In M. Dierkes, A. Berthoin Antal, J. Child, & I. Nonaka (Eds.), *Handbook of organizational learning and knowledge* (pp. 865–885). Oxford, UK: Oxford University Press.

Berthoin Antal, A., & Strauß, A. (2013). *Evaluating artistic interventions in organizations: Finding evidence of values-added*. Berlin, Germany: Wissenschaftszentrum Berlin für Sozialforschung. Retrieved from http://www.wzb.eu/sites/default/files/u30/effects_of_artistic_interventions_final_report.pdf

Berthoin Antal, A., Taylor, S., & Ladkin, D. (2013). Arts-based interventions and organizational development: It's what you don't see. In E. Bell, J. Schroeder, & S. Warren (Eds.), *Routledge companion to visual organization* (pp. 263–274). London: Routledge.

Biehl-Missal, B. (2010). Hero takes a fall: A lesson from theatre for leadership. *Leadership, 6*, 279–294.

Biehl-Missal, B. (2011a). Business is show business: Management presentations as performance. *Journal of Management Studies, 48*, 619–645.

Biehl-Missal, B. (2011b). *Wirtschaftsästhetik. Wie Unternehmen Kunst als Instrument und Inspiration nutzen* [Business aesthetics. How companies use art as an instrument and inspiration]. Wiesbaden, Germany: Gabler.

Boltanski, L., & Chiapello, E. (1999). *Le nouvel esprit du capitalisme* [The new spirit of capitalism]. Paris: Gallimard.

Boltanski, L., & Thévenot, L. (2006). *On justification: Economies of worth* (C. Porter, Trans.). Princeton, NJ: Princeton University Press.

Bovens, M., Schillemans, T., & 'T Hart, P. (2008). Does public accountability work? *Public Administration, 86*, 225–242.

Boyle, M.-E., & Ottensmeyer, E. (2005). Solving business problems through the creative power of the arts: Catalyzing change at Unilever. *Journal of Business Strategy, 26*(5), 14–21.

Brattström, V. (2012, May). *Artistic knowledge and its application in organizational change: Reflections on using my artistic knowledge in the KIA project*. Paper presented at the Cumulus Helsinki 2012 conference, Helsinki, Finland.

Brellochs, M., & Schrat, H. (Eds.). (2005). *Raffinierter Überleben. Strategien in Kunst und Wirtschaft* [Sophisticated survival techniques: Strategies in art and economy]. Berlin, Germany: Kadmos.

Brydon-Miller, M., Berthoin Antal, A., Friedman, V., & Gayá Wicks, P. (Eds.). (2011a). Arts and action research [Special issue]. *Action Research, 9*(1).

Brydon-Miller, M., Berthoin Antal, A., Friedman, V., & Gayá Wicks, P. (2011b). The changing landscape of arts and action research. *Action Research, 9*, 3–11.

Buswick, T., Creamer, A., & Pinard, M. (2004). *(Re)educating for leadership: How the arts can improve business: Arts & business*. Retrieved from http://www.aacorn.net/members_all/buswick_ted/ReEducating_for_Leadership.pdf

Chiapello, E. (1998). *Artistes versus managers. Le management culturel face à la critique artiste* [Artists versus managers: Cultural management and artist critique]. Paris: Editions Métailié.

Chodzinski, A. (2007). *Kunst und Wirtschaft. Peter Behrens, Emil Rathenau und der dm-drogerie markt* [Art and business: Peter Behrens, Emil Rathenau, and the dm-drogerie markt]. Berlin, Germany: Kulturverlag Kadmos.

Clark, T. (2008). Performing the organization: Organization theater and imaginative life as physical presence. In D. Barry & H. Hansen (Eds.), *The SAGE handbook of new approaches in management and organization* (pp. 401–411). Los Angeles: Sage.

Clark, T., & Mangham, I. (2004). Stripping to the undercoat: A review and reflections on a piece of organization theatre. *Organization Studies, 25*, 841–851.

Cook, T. (2009). The purpose of mess in action research: Building rigour though a messy turn. *Educational Action Research, 17*, 277–291.

Darsø, L. (2004). *Artful creation: Learning-tales of arts-in-business*. Frederiksberg, Denmark: Samfundslitteratur.

DeNora, T. (2000). *Music in everyday life*. Cambridge, UK: Cambridge University Press.

Dewey, J. (2005). *Art as experience*. New York: Penguin Group. (Original work published 1934)

Dierkes, M., Berthoin Antal, A., Child, J., & Nonaka, I. (Eds.). (2001). *Handbook of organizational learning and knowledge*. Oxford, UK: Oxford University Press.

Economist. (2011, February 17). Schumpeter: The art of management—Business has much to learn from the arts. Retrieved from http://www.economist.com/node/18175675

Ferro-Thomsen, M. (2005). *Organisational art: A study of art at work in organisations*. Unpublished master's thesis, University of Copenhagen, Copenhagen. Retrieved from http://www.ferro.dk/academic/orgart.htm

Friedman, V. (2001). The individual as agent of organizational learning. In M. Dierkes, A. Berthoin Antal, J. Child, & I. Nonaka (Eds.), *Handbook of organizational learning and knowledge* (pp. 398–414). Oxford, UK: Oxford University Press.

Friedman, V., & Berthoin Antal, A. (2005). Negotiating reality: A theory of action approach to intercultural competence. *Management Learning, 36*, 69–86.

Friedman, V., Lipshitz, R., & Overmeer, W. (2001). Creating conditions for organizational learning. In M. Dierkes, A. Berthoin Antal, J. Child, & I. Nonaka (Eds.), *Handbook of organizational learning and knowledge* (pp. 757–774). Oxford, UK: Oxford University Press.

Friedman, V., & Rogers, T. (2009). There's nothing so theoretical as good action research. *Action Research, 7*, 31–47. doi:10.1177/1476750308099596.

Funke, J. (2009). On the psychology of creativity. In P. Meusburger, J. Funke, & E. Wunder (Eds.), *Milieus of creativity: An interdisciplinary approach to spatiality of creativity* (pp. 11–23). Knowledge and space: Vol. 2. Dordrecht, The Netherlands: Springer.

Gagliardi, P. (2006). Exploring the aesthetic side of organizational life. In S. R. Clegg, C. Hardy, T. B. Lawrence, & W. R. Nord (Eds.), *The SAGE handbook of organization studies* (2nd ed., pp. 701–724). London: Sage.

Gayá Wicks, P., & Rippin, A. (2010). Art as experience: An inquiry into art and leadership using dolls and doll-making. *Leadership, 6*, 259–278.

Gibb, S. (2004). Arts-based training in management development: The use of improvisational theatre. *The Journal of Management Development, 23*, 741–750.

Göbel, H. (2012). *Practicing urban atmospheres: The re-use of ruins in the culturalized city*. Unpublished doctoral thesis, University of Konstanz, Konstanz, Germany.

Grefe, G. (2010). *Les systèmes d'incitation à l'échange de connaissances au sein de communautés métiers de l'aluminium: essai d'explication d'un modèle* [Incentive systems for knowledge sharing in communities of metalworking: Attempt to explain a model]. Unpublished doctoral thesis, Université Paris-Sud 11, Paris.

Grzelec, A., & Prata, T. (2013). *Artists in organizations. Mapping of producers of artistic interventions in Europe. Creative Clash report*. Gothenburg, Sweden: TILLT. http://www.creativeclash.eu/wp-content/uploads/2013/03/Creative_Clash_Mapping

Guillet de Monthoux, P. (2004). *The art firm: Aesthetic management and metaphysical marketing.* Stanford, CA: Stanford University Press.

Guillet de Monthoux, P., Gustafsson, C., & Sjöstrand, S.-E. (2007). *Aesthetic leadership: Managing fields of flow in art and business.* Basingstoke, Hampshire, UK: Palgrave Macmillan.

Hansen, K. (2005). Positionists' productions: The scope of a correlative art practice in contexts of organizing. In M. Brellochs & H. Schrat (Eds.), *Produkt und Vision—Reader—Sophisticated survival techniques—Strategies in art and economy* (pp. 171–181). Berlin, Germany: Kadmos.

Harvey, D. (2005). Space as a key word. In D. Harvey (Ed.), *Spaces of neoliberalization: Towards a theory of uneven geographical development* (pp. 93–115). Hettner-Lecture, Vol. 8. Stuttgart, Germany: Franz Steiner.

Hatch, M. J. (1999). Exploring the empty spaces of organizing: How improvisational jazz helps redescribe organizational structure. *Organization Studies, 20,* 75–100.

Huber, G. P. (1991). Organizational learning: The contributing process and the literature. *Organization Science, 2,* 88–115.

Hüttler, M. (2005). *Unternehmenstheater—vom Theater der Unterdrückten zum Theater der Unternehmer?* [Corporate theater: From the theater of the oppressed to the theater of management?]. Stuttgart, Germany: Ibidem Verlag.

Jennings, M., & Baldwin, A. (2010). Filling out the forms was a nightmare: Project evaluation and the reflective practitioner in community theatre in contemporary Northern Ireland. *Music and Arts in Action, 2*(2), 72–89. Retrieved from http://musicandartsinaction.net/index.php/maia

KEA European Affairs. (2009). *The impact of culture on creativity. A study prepared for the European Commission (Directorate-General for Education and Culture).* Brussels. Retrieved from http://www.keanet.eu/docs/impactculturecreativityfull.pdf

Kim, D. H. (1993). The link between individual and organizational learning. *Sloan Management Review, 35*(1), 37–50.

Kivinen, N. (2006). *Entering organisations: Essays on image, space and difference.* Abo, Finland: Oy Nord Print.

Knowles, J. G., & Cole, A. L. (Eds.). (2008). *Handbook of the arts in qualitative research: Perspectives, methodologies, examples, and issues.* Los Angeles: Sage.

Ladkin, D. (2008). Leading beautifully: How mastery, congruence and purpose create the aesthetic of embodied leadership practice. *The Leadership Quarterly, 19,* 31–41.

Lehrer, J. (2007). *Proust was a neuroscientist.* New York: Houghton-Mifflin.

March, J. G., & Olsen, P. (1975). The uncertainty of the past: Organizational learning under ambiguity. *European Journal of Political Research, 3,* 147–171.

Massey, D. (1985). New directions in space. In D. Gregory & J. Urry (Eds.), *Social relations and spatial structures* (pp. 9–19). New York: St. Martin's Press.

Massey, D. (1999). Philosophy and politics of spatiality: Some considerations. In D. Massey (Ed.), *Power-geometries and the politics of space time* (pp. 27–42). Hettner-Lecture: Vol. 2. Heidelberg, Germany: University Department of Geography.

Massey, D. (2005). *For space.* London: Sage.

May, J., & Thrift, N. (Eds.). (2001). *TimeSpace: Geographies of temporality.* London: Routledge.

McNiff, S. (1998a). *Art-based research.* London: Jessica Kingsley.

McNiff, S. (1998b). *Trust the process: An artist's guide to letting go.* Boston: Shambala.

Meusburger, P. (2009). Milieus of creativity: The role of places, environments, and spatial contexts. In P. Meusburger, J. Funke, & E. Wunder (Eds.), *Milieus of creativity: An interdisciplinary approach to spatiality of creativity* (pp. 97–153). Knowledge and space: Vol. 2. Dordrecht, The Netherlands: Springer.

Nissley, N. (1999). *Viewing corporate art through the paradigmatic lens of organizational symbolism: An exploratory study.* Unpublished doctoral dissertation, The George Washington University, Washington, DC.

Nissley, N., Taylor, S. S., & Houden, L. (2004). The politics of performance in organizational theatre-based training and interventions. *Organization Studies, 25,* 817–839.

Nonaka, I., & Konno, N. (1998). The concept of *ba*: Building a foundation for knowledge creation. *California Management Review, 40*(3), 40–54.

Nonaka, I., & Takeuchi, H. (1995). *The knowledge creating company: How Japanese companies create the dynamics of innovation.* New York: Oxford University Press.

Pelzer, P. (2006). Art for management's sake? A doubt. *Culture and Organization, 12*, 65–77.

Pressman, J., & Wildavsky, A. (1984). *Implementation: How great expectations in Washington are dashed in Oakland* (3rd expanded ed.). Berkeley, CA: University of California Press.

Reason, P., & Bradbury, H. (Eds.). (2008). *The SAGE handbook of action research: Participative inquiry and practice* (2nd ed.). London: Sage.

Schein, E. H. (1993). How can organizations learn faster? The problem of entering the green room. *Sloan Management Review, 34*(2), 85–92.

Schiuma, G. (2009). *The value of arts-based initiatives—Mapping arts-based initiatives: Arts & business*. Retrieved from http://www.artsandbusiness.org.uk/Media%20library/Files/Research/Mapping%20ABIs%20-%20Prof%20SchiumaFINAL.pdf

Seifter, H., & Buswick, T. (Eds.). (2005). Arts-based learning for business [Special issue]. *Journal of Business Strategy, 26*(5).

Shrivastava, P., & Cooper, M. (2008). *Leading with passion: Art of management conference proceedings*. Banff, Alberta, Canada: Banff Center.

Stark, D. (2009). *The sense of dissonance: Accounts of worth in economic life*. Princeton, NJ: Princeton University Press.

Statler, M., Roos, J., & Victor, B. (2009). Ain't misbehavin': Taking play seriously in organizations. *Journal of Change Management, 9*, 87–107.

Strati, A. (1999). *Organization and aesthetics*. London: Sage.

Strati, A. (2000). The aesthetic approach in organization studies. In S. Linstead & H. Höpfl (Eds.), *The aesthetics of organization* (pp. 13–34). London: Sage.

Strauß, A. (2012). *Researchers, models and dancing witches: Tracing dialogue between art and business*. Unpublished doctoral thesis, University of Essex, Colchester, UK.

Styhre, A., & Eriksson, M. (2008). Bring in the arts and get the creativity for free: A study of the artists in residence project. *Creativity and Innovation Management, 17*, 47–57.

Swidler, A. (1986). Culture in action: Symbols and strategies. *American Sociological Review, 51*, 273–286.

Taylor, S. S. (2002). Overcoming aesthetic muteness: Researching organizational members' aesthetic experience. *Human Relations, 55*, 821–840.

Taylor, S. S., & Ladkin, D. (2009). Understanding arts-based methods in managerial development. *The Academy of Management Learning and Education, 8*, 55–69.

Taylor, S. S., & Statler, M. (2009, August). *Material matters: Designing arts-based learning processes in organizations*. Paper presented at the Annual Conference of the Academy of Management, Chicago.

Tuan, M. (2008). *Measuring and/or estimating social value creation*. Paper prepared for the Bill and Melinda Gates Foundation. Seattle, WA. Retrieved from http://www.gatesfoundation.org/learning/documents/wwl-report-measuring-estimating-social-value-creation.pdf

Velthuis, O. (Ed.). (2005). *Imaginary economics: Contemporary artists and the world of big money*. Rotterdam, The Netherlands: NAI Publisher.

Wechsler, L. (1982). *Seeing is forgetting the name of the thing one sees: A life of contemporary artist Robert Irwin*. Berkeley, CA: University of California Press.

Weichhart, P. (1996). Die Region—Chimäre, Artefakt oder Strukturprinzip sozialer Systeme? [The region—Chimera, artifact, or structural principle of social systems]. In G. Brunn (Ed.), *Region und Regionsbildung in Europa: Konzeptionen der Forschung und empirische Befunde: Vol. 1. Schriftenreihe des Instituts für Europäische Regionalforschung* (pp. 25–43). Baden-Baden, Germany: Nomos.

Weichhart, P. (1999). Die Räume zwischen den Welten und die Welt der Räume. Zur Konzeptioneines Schlüsselbegriffs der Geographie [The spaces between the worlds and the world of spaces: On the inception of a key concept of geography]. In P. Meusburger (Ed.), *Handlungszentrierte Sozialgeographie: Benno Werlens Entwurf in kritischer Diskussion* (pp. 67–94). Erkundliches Wissen: Vol. 130. Stuttgart, Germany: Franz Steiner.

Weichhart, P. (2003). Gesellschaftlicher Metabolismus und Action Settings. Die Verknüpfung von Sach- und Sozialstrukturen im alltagsweltlichen Handeln [Social metabolism and action

settings: The link between technical and social structures in everyday action]. In P. Meusburger
& T. Schwan (Eds.), *Humanökologie: Ansätze zur Überwindung der Natur-Kultur-Dichotomie*
(pp. 15–44). Erdkundliches Wissen: Vol. 135. Stuttgart, Germany: Franz Steiner.

Weller, S. (2009). *Kunst als Entwicklungskonzept im New Management. Das Beispiel dm-drogerie
markt* [Art as development concept in new management: The example of dm-drogerie markt].
Unpublished master thesis, Freie Universität Berlin, Berlin.

Werlen, B. (1993). *Society, action and space: An alternative human geography* (G. Walls, Trans.).
London: Routledge.

Werlen, B. (1998). Political regionalism. In L. Embree (Ed.), *Alfred Schutz's theory of social
sciences* (pp. 1–22). Dordrecht, The Netherlands: Kluwer Academic.

Wood, C., & Leighton, D. (2010). *Measuring social value: The gap between policy and practice*.
London: Demos.

Research-based Theater as a Facilitator of Organizational Learning

12

Anne Pässilä and Tuija Oikarinen

Toward Polyphony and Joy

Once upon a time, a humanist, economists, artists, an industrial manager, sales managers, and researchers sat around a table and searched for common ground. As the two researchers, we were members of this group when the following questions cropped up: "Is the present organization management so tied to the traditional orientation of control and command that the humanistic dimension of the organization as a community of individuals has been forgotten? Where is the process of joy and enthusiasm?" The managers thought that it might be obscured by the contemporary focus on efficiency and analytical problem-solving. Everyone present wondered whether the existing situation of complex organization was causing people's holistic perspective to be blocked behind technical rationality. What if there is hidden learning potential?

In that phase of searching for ways to tackle these probing questions, the humanist, economists, artists, industrial manager, and sales managers pointed out the social dimension of every employee's knowledge creation. The research and development process from which this chapter stems therefore started with the experimental hypotheses that the aim of organizational development was to stimulate dialogue within an organization through art-based learning practices and that the aim of the research that would be needed to support that process was to describe a learning process based on art-based methods and action-based learning. With the help of art-based actions, particularly applied theater, my coauthor and I wanted to find out how employees are able to become sense-makers of organizational events. Different voices, human experiences, and worldviews of an organization were treasured. Hence, we ask in this study (a) whether polyphonic learning space can be constructed

A. Pässilä (✉) • T. Oikarinen
LUT Lahti School of Innovation, Lappeenranta University of Technology,
Saimaankatu 11, 15140 Lahti, Finland
e-mail: Anne.Passila@lut.fi; tuija.oikarinen@lut.fi

A. Berthoin Antal et al. (eds.), *Learning Organizations: Extending the Field*,
Knowledge and Space 6, DOI 10.1007/978-94-007-7220-5_12,
© Springer Science+Business Media Dordrecht 2014

by combining theater techniques and applying them to that space and (b) what kind of knowledge creation process might arise from this endeavor. In polyphonic learning spaces a key element of change and organizational events are seen as a continuous, possibly evolving, cumulative, and emergent process (Hargrave & Van de Ven, 2006; Van de Ven & Poole, 1995, 2005; Weick & Quinn, 1999). From this perspective learning is a collective and interpretive action process in which the members of an organization construct meanings together and change itself is a pattern of endless modifications in day-to-day work and social practices (Abma, 2000; Pässilä, Oikarinen, & Kallio, 2013).

We follow the path that Weick (1979, 1995), Schein (1999), and Czarniawska (2001, 2008) have pioneered, that of loosely organized actions, concrete incidents, and the power of narratives. However, we move further along the course of dialogue and suggest that if an organization is able to make sense of events related to a problem and become empowered through art-based action (Abma, 2000; Barry & Hansen, 2008; Barry & Meisiek, 2010; Boal, 1995), then its members will be able to create new relationships that tie them together in a fresh way. Our contribution to the discussion of organizational learning and knowledge creation is to stress the social infrastructure of an organization by asserting that narratives encourage engagement (employees with different perspectives doing things together) and that it is possible to gain knowledge by interpreting personal experiences.

Through a case study we describe an interpretive action approach to learning where employees, managers, researchers, and artists seek and create polyphonic understanding together. (For an explanation of polyphonic organizational learning, from which the concept of polyphonic space is derived, see Oswick, Anthony, Keenoy, Mangham, & Grant, 2000.) Polyphonic space inside an organization is built on a dialogue in which the role of management changes from the setting of goals to the shaping of directions (Lester & Piore, 2004; Oswick et al., 2000; Palmer & Dunford, 2008). In construction of the polyphonic space, our research and development is based on the ideas of the Brazilian theater philosopher and practitioner Augusto Boal, who has applied theater-based techniques to various purposes (Boal, 1995; Nissley, Taylor, & Houden, 2004; Schreyögg & Höpfl, 2004; Taylor, 2003).

In the first three sections of this chapter, we describe the theoretical and methodological framework of the study. In the second and third sections we also discuss learning and theater in an organization. The fourth section deals with research orientation and the application of theater in an organization. We then turn to the description of the case we researched and to our conclusions, in which we suggest that polyphonic space opens temporarily between participants with the help of aesthetic distance and enriches the participants' way of being and relating. The concept of aesthetic distancing means embodied and cognitive engagement in a process wherein participants use their senses, bodies, and experiences to reflect on their experiences of social reality of work and those of others with the help of imaginative thinking. Imaginative thinking is done via various theatrical techniques. Metaphors, for example, create aesthetic distance and enable to people deal with sensitive work-related issues.

Facilitating Learning Within an Organization

Boal (1995) claims that theater is a way to form knowledge, and the artists in our case study readily agreed with him. At a practical level Boalian theater is a learning dialogue where conceptual thinking and awareness are based on everyday experiences. This type of learning dialogue is very sensitive and leaves its speakers vulnerable. Therefore, it should be facilitated with full respect for each individual. Mezirow (2000) and Kolb (1984) point out that individuals construct their own worldviews by grasping experiences and reflecting upon and conceptualizing them in a social context. In an ideal learning situation, learners comprehend their own sense-making and schemas and thus are able to generate a deeper understanding of their own organization and work than in suboptimal contexts. Through sense-making new ideas may occur, and learners may identify problems and interpret them with others in social processes (Abma, 2003; Argyris & Schön, 1978; Boonstra & de Caluwé, 2007; Crossan, Lane, & White, 1999; Kemmis & Wilkinson, 1998). Although even these human issues are well known in organizations (see, for example, Abma, 2003; Brown & Duguid, 1991; March, 1991; Marshak & Grant, 2008; Van de Ven, Rogers, Bechara, & Sun, 2008), mainstream traditional management is concerned with controlling and monitoring business activities. The managers in our case study pointed out that learning is too often impeded by the demands of unanimity, operational effectiveness, analytical problem-solving, and technical rationality. Organizational diversity comes to be seen as a threat, not a possibility.

At this juncture Weick (1979, 1995) might point out that valuing an organization as a collection of multiple, socially constructed, loosely coupled realities with competing interests and conceptions contributes to learning possibilities. Tying into "Weickian tradition," we claim that if an organization wants to provide for dialogic learning, it has to create a safe environment and procedures for nurturing diverse worldviews among its employees (see also Chap. 13, McNiff, in this volume). For this reason we argue that events in an organization and narrative reflection (Czarniawska, 2008) on them offer possibilities for learning (Pässilä, Oikarinen, & Vince, 2012). Stories, narratives, and myths are practical tools for framing new, shared meanings, changing mindsets (Ford & Ford, 1995; Marshak & Grant, 2008), and creating self-understanding in an organization (Abma, 2003; Nissley, 2010; Reissner, 2008). Narratives may be used in various contexts in an organization. Bruner (1996), for example, calls attention to narratives as an expression of the individuals' ways of constructing meanings, and Hänninen (1999) points out the process of inner narratives and socialization. By contrast, Gergen (1994); Gergen, Gergen, & Barrett, 2004) describes a more collective and community view of narratives. Lämsä and Sintonen (2006) argue for structuring the interactions in an organization, Oswick et al. (2000) concentrate on interrelationships, and Rhodes (1996) has an interest in the narrative approach to change.

By this time the economists, humanists, artists, industrial managers, sales managers, and researchers around the table were arguing again. They had various interests, all headed in different directions. As the storm settled, they decided to follow the human-related path, which treats narratives as constructed images of experience that connote real life but are not actually images of reality. The group's members shared Jarnagin and Slocum's (2007) argumentation that narratives more or less channel a logical, intuitive, and emotional understanding when employees interpret internal sociocultural actions in the work community (p. 294). They also ascribed to in Oswick et al.'s (2000) application of narratives to dialogic scripting, a creative process of fictionalizing a real event. The group supposed that narratives enable the learners to disengage themselves from the context-specific elements of the event and to attend to the underlying "intertextual aspects."

Scripting is a way of gaining aesthetic distance and of interpreting one's own organization with the help of narratives. A group selects a key incident and uses it as a springboard to produce a fictionalized narrative (script) through collective interaction. According to Abma (2003) and Reissner (2008), a storyteller as a learner has an active role. The storyteller is able to examine the problem and its possibilities and to produce different points of view on the subject at hand through the script. Bruner (1986, 1990) emphasizes that learning through narratives is a sensitive system of searching, selecting, organizing, and interpretation whereby the learners, building on knowledge drawn from subjective experiences, interpret their social reality together (Gergen, 1994). The dialogue during this interaction to gain aesthetic distance takes place in the act of giving and receiving meanings (Hänninen, 1999).

Theater in an Organization

Theater has attracted increasing attention as an intervention technique, as a resource or technology in organizational change, development, and learning (Chap. 11, Berthoin Antal, in this volume; Boje & Rosile, 2003; Clark, 2008; Darsø, 2004; Josendal & Skarholt, 2006; Meisiek, 2002; Nissley et al., 2004; Schiuma, 2011; Schreyögg & Höpfl, 2004). The practical application of various theater techniques to an organizational setting has increased as well (Berthoin Antal, 2009; Meisiek, 2004; Meisiek & Barry, 2007). Barry (2008) thinks that this mounting interest is related to a new paradigm of artful turn in organization studies. With our study we are taking part in the discussion of application (Mienczakowski, 1995; Mienczakowski & Morgan, 2001; Mienczakowski, Smith, & Sinclair, 1996) that centers on the interpretation of existing situations from different points of view. Standing in this tradition, we offer a way to see organizational events differently with the help of art, especially its distancing effect. From the perspective of art education, dialogic scripting is like a serious playfulness; people interpret their own actions in a context of play (Heikkinen, 2002). Drawing on previous research in a field of applied theater, we propose an approach called *research-based theater* (RBT) as a practical orientation and method to bringing together alternative worldviews distributed throughout the organization.

From the RBT tradition, we understand art-based action in a frame of postmodernism rather than of modernism. Therefore, our theater philosophy and practices related to organizational learning are based on open dramaturgy, which inherits narration from the epic drama of Bertolt Brecht (1964). Brecht was a creator of the distancing effect (*Verfremdungseffekt*, also known as the alienation effect and the estrangement effect), which has interesting potential for organizational learning. Theater offers techniques for both expressing and challenging one's own world-views and for interpreting the worldviews, attitudes, and behavior of others. In this sense theater operates in a field of experiential and transformative learning (Boal, 1992, 1995, 1996). Because communicating the views of different groups is the key to deepening peoples' understanding within an organization, it is important to bridge gaps and facilitate discourse between different work units, to plot the reality together, so to speak.

The theater practices examined by Boal (1992, 1995, 1996), including open dramaturgy, are considered postmodern in that the theater acquires the new role of heightening awareness and plotting reality (Taussig & Schechner, 1994). Unlike conventional modern theater or Aristotelian dramaturgy, in which episodes are constructed through a hero's actions in a linear and causative plot, open dramaturgy is like a puzzle. Likewise, we approach the organization as a puzzle, seeing it as a fragmented and open-ended community; its narratives, as fractured and unfinished stories, even as a multinarration (Schechner, 1988) or, from the perspective of narrative organizational studies, an *ante narrative*, as Boje (2001) suggests.

In the context of diversity, theater is not about finding one solution or truth. In theatrical interactions, the participants explore many different meanings hiding somewhere in the processes of finding solutions and possibilities (Boje, Luhman, & Cunliffe, 2003; Pässilä, 2012). In keeping with Clark and Mangham (2004), we define RBT as a way of telling polyphonic stories inside an organization. Our definition casts theater as a performative narration formed by gesture, text, and interpretation.

The roots of applied theater lie within the community-based orientation of theater. The meaning of theater is more like storytelling than a performing art (Nissley et al., 2004), and its pedagogical core is situated in critical learning (Asikainen, 2003). The process of plotting reality is based on the philosophy of theater that emphasizes significant incompleteness and insufficiency (Heikkinen, 2002; Oddey, 1994); in the context of plotting, reality is more puzzling than explanatory. Theater techniques can help build bridges between analogies and social reality, with the metalanguage of the theater promoting the generation of dialogue (Asikainen, 2003; Heikkinen, 2002), or as Boal (1995) puts it, "making thought visible" (p. 137). We have applied this metalanguage to the process of "making representations and power relationships visible" and to Burke's (1969) idea of a dramatic analysis of reality, an inquiry in which we are interested in "different 'realities'" (Rhodes, 1996, 6th heading: "The sides of the story") among communities within an organization. The function of applied theater is like a transformative agent or mirror. The audience has an active role as a storyteller and sense-maker deeply involved in the situation, in which communication is shaped by the interpretation of different situations that are presented or constructed during drama (Boal, 1995). Theater thereby becomes a communicational space for conversation and interpretation, setting things in motion, raising people's awareness, breaking gridlocks, shaking things up, and unfreezing them (Ford & Ford, 1995; Heikkinen, 2002; Marshak & Grant, 2008; Oswick et al., 2000; Pässilä et al., 2013).

Theater as an Aesthetic Learning Space

In RBT the interactions are based on Boal's Image Theatre approach (Boal, 1995), by which the human body is used as a tool to represent experiences in life: attitudes, feelings, behaviors, ideas, and patterns of power relationships. The interest in practical and research learning lies in dialogue that unfolds in a performance context through an encounter between members of the organization and trained theatre actors. If circumstances are favorable, the learning may emerge in a social space between fiction and fact, between encounters of individuals. The still images (which illustrate events happening in organization) are symbolic depictions of something that has happened or could happen in real life. When people interpret body images, they reconstruct and reflect on their own view of the issue.

Frozen Images as a Learning Initiative in an Aesthetic Learning Space

In our study a Boalian technique called *frozen images* is applied as a data-collection method and as a narrative technique for reflection. The participants (individually or in groups) create and reflect on an image or an impression of a situation. Frozen images offer an opportunity to treat problems in fragmented time. In a frozen image, time and reality are conceptual; linear time is modified and checked as episodes from the past and from the future (Neelands, 1990, p. 4).

Boal explains aesthetic space through the concept of *metaxis*, the idea that symbolic actions in a role-play scene help the participants observe the existing situation ("as is") and a nonexisting possibility ("as if") in order to investigate habits, beliefs, language, feelings, and social relationships. The aesthetic space, formed through imitation in drama, is a specific place of representation (*mimesis*) situated in time and reality. It is a human property that allows people to observe themselves in action with the aid of aesthetic distance. The self-knowledge thereby acquired empowers the person "to be the subject (the one who observes) of another subject (the one who acts)" (Boal, 1995, pp. 13–20).

Understanding in Between, in the Metaxis of Aesthetic Learning Space

Aesthetic space stimulates knowledge creation in a specific manner, enabling transformational learning processes to arise in reflections and in the interpretation between the experience of lived and fictional life situations. Similarly, the pedagogical core of applied theater is situated in reflective and critical learning, but the actual here-and-now moment of subjective understanding is situated between, in the *metaxis* of, interpretations of imitations constructed in the aesthetic space (Boal, 1995). We see vast learning potential and an interesting subject for research in the aesthetic space as a forum for contextual and situated understanding and as a way to share tacit and self-transcending knowledge. As a learning space where sense-making takes place, theater sets up a template allowing for the observation of familiar taken-for-granted reality from an unfamiliar angle, one that uses well-known elements and signs of daily work life in a fictional setting. The character of reality as a social construction may become apparent; the taken-for-granted reality is likely to become contingent, making it evident that it could be different. This duplication process is not straightforward. It does not produce unequivocal, predictable outcomes, so it is unnecessary to guide the process as a linear project (Schreyögg & Höpfl, 2004).

Research Orientation—Acting on the Organization from Within It?

The relationship between studying an organization and acting on it from within and with its members was integral. The research had two levels: (a) problems of a rather conceptual nature that were related to research and (b) practical problems related to the organization's development work. We posed the following research questions:

1. In what way could applied theater be a device for research?
   - In terms of theater as a process of acquiring knowledge, how can personal and unformulated knowledge be shared with others? What kind of a co-construction and creation process of new knowledge does RBT represent?
2. How can an organization construct a polyphonic space for organizational learning?
   - How should learning processes be triggered by art-based techniques? How can ideals and ideas of all the organization's members be shared organizationally?

These questions suggested qualitative research, which involves a participative, subjectivist investigation of a detailed case. The importance of participatory and democratic elements was outlined in both the research and the development process. Figure 12.1 illustrates our combination of research and development work in an organization.

The formulation of the research problem guided us to a phenomenological constructivist view of knowledge. The main idea, both theoretically and practically, was that the learning process in an organization is a social and cultural event, where all the members of the organization (with various competences, backgrounds, needs, skills, experiences, and feelings) should be seen and heard, and that everyone's ideals and experiences are valued. Taking on this view, we started our process of action

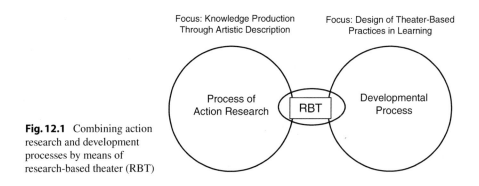

Fig. 12.1 Combining action research and development processes by means of research-based theater (RBT)

research. Instead of taking an analytical problem-solving or linear decision-making approach, we decided to pursue a more interpretive line by which we would study together with the members of the selected company how to create a polyphonic space that would enrich learning and the generation of knowledge among all of them. A second central aspect of the research was theater's relation to embodied tacit knowledge—the actual process and art of doing something in a specific context, not just talking about it.

Our research orientation emphasized social interaction between people and the changing practices of social processes (Kemmis & McTaggart, 2000). We created forums in which people could join each other as co-participants in developing the practices related to their daily work life (Kemmis & Wilkinson, 1998). The aim was to create a process in which people collectively try to understand how they stand in relation to and interact with one another and the world. This approach included sense-making dialogue. According to Barry (2008), the artistic approach stresses problem-finding, and the narrative approach revolves around the artful reframing of problems. By his definition, which we adopted, artistic actions in research are an iterative and emergent perspective on a problem.

As we worked on our case study, we encountered a multilayered process of action research in which various aims existed. We found it crucial to be aware of one's own position, power, and purpose when acting within an organization. One critical phase of action research became evident: The organization's practical orientation to the process accommodated the desire of the members to improve effectiveness through functional social practices. Managers and employees sought concrete outcomes and benefits. However, we researchers had humanistic aspirations for change, desiring to see how the social dimension of the learning process is shaped and shifted by the ways the members of the organization see and understand themselves (Barry, 2008; Kemmis, 2001). The artists, for their part, were also interested in actions and events related to the artistic process and play that increase possibilities for emancipation, empowerment, or both. Various existing interests caused a measure of communicational confusion that signaled a lack of common ground and shared language. RBT seemed to reveal the power relationships among different communities inside the organization. Power issues are exceedingly hard to deal with, and they made it difficult to see and interpret existing situations from different points of view. As a result, researchers and artists were involved in various social processes (roles, rules, needs, interests, feelings, emotions, and power between different groups) during interactions.

Even though there was agreement that the learning process would allow also for an interpretive orientation to the organizational landscape, the needs for actions were quite often framed only from a rational and instrumental perspective. The artists in particular could not understand the worldview of functional rationality. They were amazed at how members of the organization claimed that only rationality drives practices. The artists argued that all human practices also have social elements. By the same token, participatory action research emphasizes the dynamics of social factors related to knowledge creation. Learning and action researcher Kemmis (2001), too, claims that social elements (power, trust, engagement, collaboration, and communication) operate more or less through interpretation.

Case Description

Our intention with this case study on RBT as a vehicle for organizational learning to describe a knowledge creation process derived from art-based methods and action-based learning. The enterprise we worked with was a factory of a multinational forestry company in Finland. This company operated (and still does operate) on a fiercely competitive market in an industry whose entire tradition is shifting in Finland and the rest of Europe. In the course of our study, several downsizings of forestry enterprises occurred in Finland, with the individual factories having to modernize themselves and be innovative in order to survive. The need for change was in the air. Across the production, sales, and product development units of our case company, the situation had culminated in a shower of accusations about who was to blame. This type of tension could hardly be solved in an analytical way or through top-down management, so the starting point of the research in this organization was the need for connections between people inside it.

The first challenge was to bridge different views—regarding art, artists, art education, research, researchers, and development work; the daily operations of the factory, employees, and managers; innovation activities; and learning—to have them converge on a joint, meaningful point of interest. Efforts to connect people were far from harmonious. The process was sometimes chaotic, and participants survived it by discussing with each another and listening to "others' odd" voices. An engineering manager and an applied theater artist worked hard together to build common ground for the participants. At the outset we had both virtual and face-to-face conversations and meetings between theater workers and the researchers, the researchers and the managers, the researchers and the employees, and the employees and the managers. It took many discussions to create a shared, multivoiced vision of what everyone involved was to achieve, and it changed during the journey. Two basic elements of the research vision on which agreement was eventually reached were that everyone involved was interested in the employees' sense-making and that the employees felt that it is important to express their views. From that point onward, we researchers understood theater as an active, participatory place for sense-*making* (as a learning action) as well as sense-*breaking* (as unlearning and critical reflection) in an organization.

In the spring of 2008, about 70 workers of our case company started participating in the learning process, which lasted for 18 months altogether. This chapter probes the first intense 3-month period. In keeping with action research practice, interventions in the organization were recorded on videotape. We realized that it would be difficult to describe the richness of the interactions during the research process adequately, so we captured events and feelings in a 12-min movie that served as a basis for our traditional research report.

A Case Based on Participatory Action Research

Our use of theater for closely, yet sensitively, examining the social interactions and practices of our case organization—how people act, react, think, talk, and feel—had the main goal of helping us understand its *social* infrastructure, for we

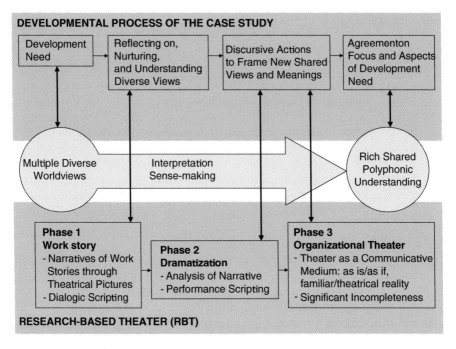

Fig. 12.2 The developmental process of the case study

noticed that the company's *technological* infrastructure had primacy. The production and manufacturing process had been attended to, but human processes had been accorded less importance. Figure 12.2 illustrates our approach to knowledge creation, specifically, the manner in which we linked interpretive process and art-based activities into the case study's development process. Our theoretical assumption was that RBT is a way to form knowledge. At a practical level it is a learning event and a dialogue in which conceptual thinking and awareness is constructed and based on everyday experiences.

Plotting Realities with the Help of Theatrical Pictures (Phase 1)

The interactions began with five separate work-story workshops (9–28 people in each) whose participants were employees and managers from the same department. We researchers wanted to hear what the employees from various units—production, post-production, sales, design—had to say about the situation in the organization. First, the participants recalled individual experiences. They were then divided into smaller groups of 4–7 people. With the help of seven premade theatrical pictures (see Fig. 12.3), the members of each group collectively constructed a story related to significant moments in their daily work. These work-story interventions were an application of a specific Boalian resource, the frozen-image technique from Image

Fig. 12.3 The sets of theatrical pictures used to narrate work stories in the case study

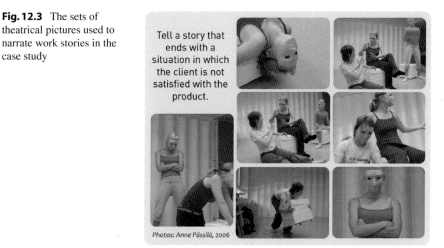

Tell a story that ends with a situation in which the client is not satisfied with the product.

Photos: Anne Pässilä, 2006

Theatre—by which combined elements of mask theater and Johnstone's (1981) technique of low and high status. Participants used the theatrical pictures[1] to trace significant meanings in the lived and experienced social life of the organization. They were instructed to interpret pictures as images of reality: "Imagine that these pictures are a description of what happens in your company." The employees then sequenced the pictures and plotted their story by telling what is done; when and where it is done; and who does it, how, and why. Through storytelling, members of the same work unit shared their ideals and ideas of the organization and their work. The main idea of this phase was dialogic scripting. We asked the employees to tell the story step by step.

Phases of Research-Based Theater

In phase 1 we collected stories about details of the organization's life. People told us how they act in a specific situation, how they see each other, what kind of tensions are related to encounters, what people say to each other, what they think of each other, and how they feel (see Fig. 12.2). The objective of this phase was to shape a space for interaction and discourse inside the different work units. Table 12.1 illustrates the learning focus and potential mode of knowledge creation in this phase.

---

[1]As part of a larger research project, Anne Pässilä has created and produced over 500 such theatrical pictures (photographs of still images) with a graphic designer, photographer, and three actors. Each image, or sequence of images, was constructed on the basis of five elements of drama—act, scene, agent, agency, purpose (Burke, 1969) and from other influences and resources, including Boal's (1995) practices of image theater, mask theater (based on Brecht's alienation effect), and the "statues" technique of improvisation theater (Johnstone, 1981).

Table 12.1 Phase 1 of the case study on constructing polyphonic space: the work story

Technique	Learning focus
Storytelling interventions based on theatrical pictures at five different work units (January 2008)	To reflect on one's own experience
	To construct a shared meaning of the experience
	To provide for experiential knowing

Table 12.2 Phase 2 of the case study on constructing polyphonic space: dramatization of narratives

Technique	Learning focus
Researchers and artists analyze employees' stories and devise a script based on them, then dramatize the script for performance (seven role-play scenes) and rehearse the scenes with the employees (January–March 2008)	To make groups' worldviews visible
	To make power relationships visible from different perspectives
	To design reflective questioning: How to define and share relevancy of knowledge

In the dramatization of these narratives (phase 2, see Fig. 12.2), researchers and artists analyzed the narratives, scripted stories, and translated them into performance—into theatrical scenes (performance scripting). This step resulted in stories illustrating the employees' experiences, revealing concrete events, feelings, fears, hopes, and tensions. Analysis began with evocative reading of the stories through dramaturgical lenses. The researchers and artists traced what employees were doing and why and categorized the stories into themes that pointed in the same direction: the relationships between the groups inside the organization and the power struggles concealed in these relationships. Table 12.2 explains the learning focus in the dramatization phase.

Role-play scenes were the triggers for the action-based learning in the third phase of the intervention, organizational theater (see Fig. 12.2), in which the intent was to reveal barriers and blocks in communication and to uncover the problem through the use of play-acting and an action-based learning assignment. During the theater session, the members of the organization watched theatrical scenes enacted by trained applied theater actors and then interpreted what they saw. Events were situated in the context of daily work and events were performed by three main characters on stage: a customer, a salesperson, and an operator from the production line. After each role-play scene, the participants reflected in groups on what had happened in the scene. Next, the members of each group summarized their conversation and the spectrum of the meanings, shared it with the other groups, and commented on each other's views.

The employees and managers worked together in small groups, each of which had one participant from the five different work units. In this phase, the group members outlined the problems and potential inherent in the events on stage. They analyzed themselves by dialoguing about their own practices, behaviors, and relationships. Employees and managers shared, repeated, amplified, and interpreted the social practices of everyday work and reinterpreted as well as resequenced them. Table 12.3 illustrates the learning focus in this phase.

Table 12.3 Phase 3 of the study on constructing polyphonic space: organizational theater

Technique	Learning focus
Participatory intervention of applied theater and reflective questioning	To discuss different worldviews, uncover problems, question and make assumptions transparent, confront things taken-for-granted, trace potential from one work unit to the next
	To redefine and reconstruct narratives
	To increase employees' creation of knowledge about their worldviews on the basis of their own sense-making

Based on this experience, employees suggested practical actions that concentrated on how to change the existing situation. They shared ideals and ideas about what kinds of social engagements needed to be done, what skills they would need to reach their target, how they would encourage each other, how they would learn from each other and from the customers, and what kind of plan they required to do it. They engaged in problem-shifting and planned their own development targets. The following dialogue illustrates the concept of aesthetic distance manifested by their insights.

Salesman: You see, these two men at stage one from production and one from the sales department don't understand each other.

Operator: This person from production does not know that the information has changed. Nobody has told him.

Salesman: So he is working with the wrong data.

Operator: But is it his fault?

Salesman: He is making a mistake because of someone else.

Operator: Of course, in the end it is always the production unit's fault.

Being very sensitive this type of dialogue is facilitated by aesthetic distance. Even as members of the organization were discussing what was happening on the stage, they were also interpreting their own behavior, communication, and attitudes by gaining distance from it. Without such openness and atmosphere of trust, it becomes difficult to do things together or construct an image of one's own organization. In an ideal situation, members of the organization draw a picture of their own sense-making and schemas and are then able to deepen their understanding of their own organizational actions and how they are related to it. Our claim, based on this case, is that space for creating knowledge is formed among the employees, between them and managers, and between both those groups and the actions on stage. Play and imagination created an atmosphere that was serious yet playful and open to the emergence of polyphony.

The Organization as a Storyteller

Ultimately, the humanist, artists, industrial manager, sales managers, and researchers gathered around the table one last time. This group constituted a metaphor—the organization as a storyteller that illustrates learning as a continuous process and

Table 12.4 Outcomes of the interventions during the case study

Work story intervention	Organizational theater intervention
Learning orientations	
Expressing one's own worldview	Gaining exposure to others' worldviews
Sharing first with one's closest colleagues, whose conceptions probably are in accord with one's own	Conducting dialogue with opposing viewpoints
Reflecting and interpreting experienced reality	Imagining possible worlds and ways to reach them
Practicing critical self-reflection	Prioritizing what should be done
Entering into collaborative discourse	Reflecting what we have done vs. how and why "the others" are doing it
Negotiating and collective sense-making	Engaging in social reinterpretation
Knowledge creation	
Related to emotion, body, and action	Related to the logic of social events, mind, and collective memory

stresses the collective self-understanding of the kinds of plots, scenes, tensions, and roles that are presented within the organization. We researchers and artists claim that experience and nascent knowledge are bound to people's bodies. We thus venture to argue that knowledge creation through art-based processes has a tacit and embodied dimension. When people reflect on organizational events on the stage as a spectator they think by acting. A person's thinking is thus related to physical movements, gestures, and encounters involving another person engaged in the act. Whenever people have to describe thinking by acting, it is a translation process. Then they translate contextual action into conceptual text, so they change communication from one language (embodied) into another (written). These acts are probably a general issue of how to express one's own individual embodied experiences, or how to describe the experiences of the organization's members conceptually. On the theater stage a person may act, but on a research stage one has text only, and sometimes it does not capture the whole spirit. Or perhaps a gesture enables one to catch another, novel view.

We have thus far described how applied theater may serve as a device for research and how an organization may construct a polyphonic space for organizational learning by applying theater techniques and engaging in action-based learning. Our case study has described how learning processes were triggered by art-based techniques and how ideals and ideas of all members of the organization were shared through storytelling and theater techniques at the organizational level. Table 12.4 illustrates the learning orientations of the interventions and the creation of knowledge.

We found collective knowledge creation to be a matter of *metaxis* born in the space of storytelling. Knowledge creation took place simultaneously in two different worlds: the image of reality and the reality of the image during interaction. While interacting, members of the organization shared their personal and unformulated experiences in order to accumulate different pieces of information and to structure those of practical use into a meaningful pattern. We cherish the idea that everyone is involved in knowledge creation. Coordinating this total participation is

POLYPHONIC SPACE FOR ORGANIZATIONAL LEARNING

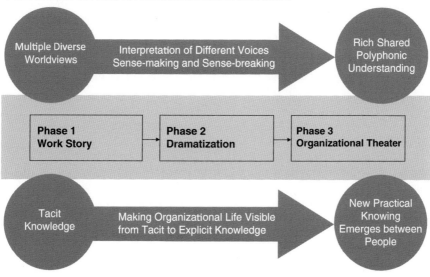

Fig. 12.4   A model of polyphonic space for organizational learning

possible if the organization, at both the social and structural levels, is willing to acknowledge these tensions and is ready to learn from them. Employees and managers empower themselves by sharing identities through roles and by dialoguing their voices through interpretations of the script.

Polyphonic space (see Fig. 12.4) divides reality into two levels: the usual, familiar reality and the theatrical reality as it appears on stage. This approach underlines that learning through theater is a social, cultural, and collective construction, that knowledge creation takes place between people in a suitable setting. It suggests that learning in a context of theater and action-based learning is understood as the sensitive contributions of learners and that different knowledge is generated between them during the interpretations of lifelike narratives.

A Co-construction and Creation Process of New Knowledge in Research-Based Theater

In polyphonic space the learners articulate their own worldviews, conceptions, and experiences. They pay full attention and listen to other, possibly opposing points of view and build a shared polyphonic understanding together. The polyphonic space is constructed from an interrogative and evocative reading of the narratives conceived by the employees and managers themselves. Through the polyphonic space, learners try to trace significant meanings. The perceptions of the organization's members, the ways in which different communities share their interpretations of reality through theatrical signs and role-play scenes, shorten the distance between them. The dynamics of the learning process are often conflicted and chaotic because of the nature of diversity. One participant verbalized the dynamics of the socially constructed space by saying, "Even though we tried to be open to different points of view [and] tried to see things from another's perspective … the conversation drifted to our own perspective. … We took a defensive position." In critical reflection, however, we suggest that an awareness of different positions is the cornerstone of sociocultural renewal.

We claim that it is crucial for an organization to hear different voices; that learning as an element of change is multilayered, highly complex, and conflicted; and that organizational events are understood differently in the various phases of the process and in different roles within the organization. As the story of this case study wound to a close, the last observations around the table were that there is no single specific change related to renewal but rather several different interpretations of change, and that organizations need to cherish diversity, not control it.

References

Abma, T. (2000). Fostering learning-in-organizing through narration: Questioning myths and stimulating multiplicity in two performing art schools. *European Journal of Work and Organizational Psychology, 9*, 211–231.

Abma, T. (2003). Learning by telling storytelling workshops as an organizational learning intervention. *Management Learning, 34*, 221–240.

Argyris, C., & Schön, D. A. (1978). *Organizational learning: A theory of action perspective.* Reading, MA: Addison-Wesley.

Asikainen, S. (2003). *Prosessidraaman kehittäminen museossa [Development of process drama in a museum].* Joensuu, Finland: Joensuun yliopistopaino.

Barry, D. (2008). The art of …. In D. Barry & H. Hansen (Eds.), *The SAGE handbook of new approaches in management and organization* (pp. 31–41). London: Sage.

Barry, D., & Hansen, H. (2008). Introduction: The new and emerging in management and organization: Gatherings, trends, and bets. In D. Barry & H. Hansen (Eds.), *The SAGE handbook of new approaches in management and organization* (pp. 1–10). London: Sage.

Barry, D., & Meisiek, S. (2010). Seeing more and seeing differently: Sensemaking, mindfulness, and the workarts. *Organisation Studies, 31*, 1505–1530.

Berthoin Antal, A. (2009). *Research report: Research framework for evaluating the effects of artistic interventions in organizations.* Göteborg, Sweden: TILLT Europe. Retrieved from http://www.wzb.eu/sites/default/files/u30/researchreport.pdf

Boal, A. (1992). *Games for actors and non-actors* (A. Jackson, Trans.). London: Routledge.

Boal, A. (1995). *The rainbow of desire* (A. Jackson, Trans.). London: Routledge.

Boal, A. (1996). Politics, education and change. In J. O'Toole & K. Donelan (Eds.), *Drama, culture and empowerment* (pp. 47–52). Brisbane, Australia: IDEA Publications.

Boje, D. M. (2001). *Narrative methods for organizational and communication research.* London: Sage.

Boje, D. M., Luhman, J. T., & Cunliffe, A. L. (2003). A dialectic perspective on the organization theatre metaphor. *American Communication Journal, 6*(2), 1–16. Retrieved from http://ac-journal.org/journal/vol6/iss2/articles/boje.htm

Boje, D., & Rosile, G. A. (2003). Theatrics of SEAM. *Journal of Organizational Change Management, 16*, 21–32.

Boonstra, J., & de Caluwé, L. (2007). Looking for meaning in interactions. In J. Boonstra & L. de Caluwé (Eds.), *Intervening and changing – Looking for meaning in interactions* (pp. 3–28). Chichester, UK: Wiley.

Brecht, B. (1964). *Brecht on theatre*. London: Methuen.

Brown, J. S., & Duguid, P. (1991). Organizational learning and communities-of-practice: Toward a unified view of working, learning, and innovation. *Organization Science, 2*, 40–57.

Bruner, J. (1986). *Actual minds, possible worlds*. Cambridge, MA: Harvard University Press.

Bruner, J. (1990). *Acts of meaning*. Cambridge, MA: Harvard University Press.

Bruner, J. (1996). *Culture of education*. Cambridge, MA: Harvard University Press.

Burke, K. (1969). *A grammar of motives*. Berkeley, CA: University of California Press.

Clark, T. (2008). Performing the organization: Organization theatre and imaginative life as physical presence. In D. Barry & H. Hansen (Eds.), *The SAGE handbook of new approaches in management and organization* (pp. 401–411). London: Sage.

Clark, T., & Mangham, I. (2004). Stripping to the undercoat: A review and reflections on a piece of organization theatre. *Organization Studies, 25*, 841–851.

Crossan, M. M., Lane, H. W., & White, R. E. (1999). An organizational learning framework: From intuition to institution. *Academy of Management Review, 24*, 522–537.

Czarniawska, B. (2001). Anthropology and organizational learning. In M. Dierkes, A. Berthoin Antal, J. Child, & I. Nonaka (Eds.), *Handbook of organizational learning and knowledge* (pp. 118–136). Oxford, UK: Oxford University Press.

Czarniawska, B. (2008). *A theory of organizing*. Cheltenham, UK: Edward Elgar.

Darsø, L. (2004). *Artful creation: Learning-tales of arts-in-business*. Frederiksberg, Denmark: Samfundslitteratur.

Ford, J. D., & Ford, L. W. (1995). The role of conversations in producing intentional change in organizations. *Academy of Management Review, 20*, 541–570.

Gergen, K. J. (1994). *Realities and relationships: Soundings in social construction*. Cambridge, MA: Harvard University Press.

Gergen, K. J., Gergen, M. M., & Barrett, F. (2004). Dialogue: Life and death of the organization. In D. Grant, C. Hardy, C. Oswick, & L. Putnam (Eds.), *The SAGE handbook of organizational discourse* (pp. 39–60). London: Sage.

Hänninen, V. (1999). *Sisäinen tarina, elämä ja muutos [Inner narrative, life, and change]*. Tampere, Finland: University of Tampere.

Hargrave, T. J., & Van de Ven, A. H. (2006). A collective action model of institutional innovation. *Academy of Management Review, 31*, 864–888.

Heikkinen, H. (2002). *Draaman maailmat oppimisalueina: Draamakasvatuksen vakava leikillisyys [Drama worlds as learning areas: The serious playfulness of drama education]*. Jyväskylä, Finland: University of Jyväskylä Studies in Education, Psychology and Social Research.

Jarnagin, C., & Slocum, J. W., Jr. (2007). Creating corporate cultures through mythopoetic leadership. *Organizational Dynamics, 36*, 288–302.

Johnstone, K. (1981). *Impro: Improvisation and the theatre*. New York: Routledge.

Josendal, K., & Skarholt, K. (2006). Communicating through theatre: How organizational theatre engages researchers and industrial companies. *Systemic Practice and Action Research, 20*, 65–76.

Kemmis, S. (2001). Exploring the relevance of critical theory for action research: Emancipatory action research in the footsteps of Jürgen Habermas. In P. Reason & H. Bradbury (Eds.), *Handbook of action research* (pp. 94–105). London: Routledge.

Kemmis, S., & McTaggart, R. (2000). Participatory action research. In N. K. Denzin & Y. S. Lincoln (Eds.), *Handbook of qualitative research* (pp. 567–606). London: Sage.

Kemmis, S., & Wilkinson, M. (1998). Participatory action research and the study of practice. In B. Atweh, S. Kemmis, & P. Weeks (Eds.), *Action research in practice: Partnership for social justice in education* (pp. 21–36). London: Routledge.

Kolb, D. A. (1984). *Experiential learning—Experience as the source of learning and development*. Upper Saddle River, NJ: Prentice-Hall.

Lämsä, A.-M., & Sintonen, T. (2006). A narrative approach for organizational learning in a diverse organisation. *Journal of Workplace Learning, 18*, 106–120.

Lester, R. K., & Piore, M. J. (2004). *Innovation—The missing dimension.* Cambridge, MA: Harvard University Press.

March, J. (1991). Exploration and exploitation in organizational learning. *Organization Science, 2*, 71–87.

Marshak, R. J., & Grant, D. (2008). Organizational discourse and new organization development practices. *British Journal of Management, 19*, 7–19.

Meisiek, S. (2002). Situation drama in change management: Types and effects of a new managerial tool. *International Journal of Arts Management, 4*(3), 48–55.

Meisiek, S. (2004). Which catharsis do they mean? Aristotle, Moreno, Boal and organizational theatre. *Organization Studies, 25*, 797–816.

Meisiek, S., & Barry, D. (2007). Through the looking glass of organizational theatre: Analogically mediated inquiry in organizations. *Organization Studies, 28*, 1805–1827.

Mezirow, J. (2000). Learning to think like an adult: Core concepts of transformation theory. In J. Mezirow & Associates (Eds.), *Learning as transformation: Critical perspectives on a theory in progress* (pp. 3–33). San Francisco: Jossey-Bass.

Mienczakowski, J. (1995). The theater of ethnography: The reconstruction of ethnography into theater with emancipatory potential. *Qualitative Inquiry, 1*, 360–375.

Mienczakowski, J., & Morgan, S. (2001). Ethnodrama: Constructing participatory, experiential and compelling action research through performance. In P. Reason & H. Bradbury (Eds.), *Handbook of action research* (pp. 176–184). London: Sage.

Mienczakowski, J., Smith, R., & Sinclair, M. (1996). On the road to catharsis: A theoretical framework for change. *Qualitative Inquiry, 2*, 439–462.

Neelands, J. (1990). *Structuring drama work.* Cambridge, UK: Cambridge University Press.

Nissley, N. (2010). Arts-based learning at work: Economic downturns, innovation upturns, and the eminent practicality of arts in business. *Journal of Business Strategy, 31*(4), 8–20.

Nissley, N., Taylor, S. S., & Houden, L. (2004). The politics of performance in organizational theatre-based training and interventions. *Organization Studies, 25*, 817–839.

Oddey, A. (1994). *Devising theatre a practical and theoretical handbook.* London: Routledge.

Oswick, C., Anthony, P., Keenoy, T., Mangham, I., & Grant, D. (2000). A dialogic analysis of organizational learning. *Journal of Management Studies, 37*, 887–901.

Palmer, I., & Dunford, R. (2008). Organizational change and the importance of embedded assumptions. *British Journal of Management, 19*, 20–32.

Pässilä, A. (2012). *Reflexive model of research-based theatre—Processing innovation at the crossroads of theatre, reflection and practice-based innovation activities.* Doctoral dissertation, Lappeenranta University of Technology, Finland.

Pässilä, A., Oikarinen, T., & Kallio, A. (2013). Creating dialogue by storytelling. *Journal of Workplace Learning, 25*(3), 159–197.

Pässilä, A., Oikarinen, T., & Vince, R. (2012). The role of reflection, reflection on roles: Practice-based innovation through theatre-based learning. In H. Melkas & V. Harmaakorpi (Eds.), *Practice-based innovation: Insights, applications and policy implications* (pp. 173–191). Dordrecht, The Netherlands: Springer.

Reissner, S. C. (2008). *Narratives of organisational change and learning making sense of testing times.* Cheltenham, UK: Edward Elgar.

Rhodes, C. (1996). Researching organizational change and learning: A narrative approach. *The Qualitative Report, 2*(4), 17. Retrieved from http://www.nova.edu/ssss/QR/QR2-4/rhodes.html

Schechner, R. (1988). *Performance theory.* London: Routledge.

Schein, E. H. (1999). *Process consultation revisited: Building the helping relationship.* Reading, MA: Addison-Wesley.

Schiuma, G. (2011). *The value of arts for business.* Cambridge, UK: Cambridge University Press.

Schreyögg, G., & Höpfl, H. (2004). Theatre and organization: Editorial introduction. *Organization Studies, 25*, 691–704.

Taussig, M., & Schechner, R. (1994). Boal in Brazil, France, the USA: An interview with Augusto Boal. In M. Schutzman & J. Cohen-Cruz (Eds.), *Playing Boal: Theater, therapy, activism* (pp. 17–32). London: Routledge.

Taylor, P. (2003). *Applied theatre: Creating transformative encounters in the community.* Portsmouth, NH: Heinemann.

Van de Ven, A. H., & Poole, M. S. (1995). Explaining development and change in organizations. *Academy of Management Review, 20*, 510–540.

Van de Ven, A. H., & Poole, M. S. (2005). Alternative approaches for studying organizational change. *Organization Studies, 26*, 1377–1404.

Van de Ven, A. H., Rogers, R. W., Bechara, J. P., & Sun, K. (2008). Organizational diversity, integration and performance. *Journal of Organizational Behavior, 29*, 335–354.

Weick, K. E. (1979). *The social psychology of organizing.* New York: Random House.

Weick, K. E. (1995). *Sense-making in organizations.* London: Sage.

Weick, K. E., & Quinn, R. E. (1999). Organizational change and development. *Annual Review of Psychology, 50*, 361–386.

Creative Space in Organizational Learning and Leadership: 21st-Century Shapeshifting

13

Shaun McNiff

I have spent four decades leading what can be "creative spaces," studio groups where people come together with a common commitment to support creative expression and learning. My goal from the start has been the making of environments that inspire and act upon people in creative ways and help them do things that they cannot do alone (McNiff, 2003, 2009). For nearly the same length of time, I have worked in leadership roles at colleges, universities, and other organizations where the environments, albeit known for creativity, learning, the generation of knowledge, and innovation (Meusburger, 2009), are distinctly different domains from the creative space of the studio. Whereas the creative space is defined by its openness to new relationships and connections to all forms of experience, even the most creative organizations are characterized by divisions of many kinds, described in this chapter as silos.

I have explored the subject of creativity and learning in groups and communities (McNiff, 1998, 2003, 2004) and keep seeing the major differences between the two kinds of spaces that I refer to below and the roles I play in each. I have come to realize that I actually thrive on different kinds of environmental challenges and the practical discipline of twenty-first century shapeshifting, taking on varied personas while integrating separate domains to further group creation and learning. Whereas the mythological shapeshifter is a person who literally changes into other forms, the idea is used metaphorically in the following pages to demonstrate the dynamics of experimentation and change that characterize all aspects of the discussion. This chapter's recommendations for organizational learning are made on the assumption that other people benefit as I do from greater exposure to new and wide-ranging experiences. There are no doubt continuities to my behavior, style, values, and goals in all of these settings, but the dominant sense that I have when operating in the two

S. McNiff (✉)
Lesley University, 29 Everett Street,
Cambridge, MA 02138, USA
e-mail: smcniff@lesley.edu

A. Berthoin Antal et al. (eds.), *Learning Organizations: Extending the Field*,
Knowledge and Space 6, DOI 10.1007/978-94-007-7220-5_13,
© Springer Science+Business Media Dordrecht 2014

environments is literally one of moving between different worlds, shaped by the missions, intentions, and desired outcomes that determine the nature of each organizational structure. My way of leading an organization, conducting meetings, solving problems, and interacting with people might be perceived by community members as more "creative" than I might realize, especially when compared to more traditional leaders, but from my perspective the overall atmospheric qualities characterizing the arts studios and university governance are distinctly different. However, the core principles of artistic action manifest what I try to achieve in both domains—for example, transforming conflict, not knowing the end at the beginning, building upon spontaneous gestures, placing things in new relationships, and developing a unique style. As a shapeshifter, the artist/leader plays different roles that are nevertheless informed by consistent qualities of the creative process. Rather than simply accept divisions of experience, which are often what can be called mental constructs, I try in this chapter to find points of possible intersection. As Rudolf Arnheim (1904–2007) emphasized in his writings, which I apply below to organizational settings, we humans find it easier to identify differences and split experiences rather than pursue more complex relationships (Arnheim, 1996, p. 3). As individuals and as members of organizations, we tend to stay within clearly defined comfort zones, thus avoiding the challenges of shapeshifting.

Because Arnheim's psychological writings on spatial forces in artistic compositions and architecture relate closely to the goals of this series of books on Knowledge and Space originating in his native Germany, I would like to bring him into the discourse. His thoughts about the creative tensions between centers and peripheries, chaos and order, splits and integrations, and other dynamics that ultimately seek a functional whole offer a valuable theoretical underpinning to my efforts to describe practical experiences within the contrasting realms I call organizational silos and the creative space. I try in this contribution to describe the respective powers of these environments, reflect on why they operate in different ways, and explore how they might interact more productively with one another.

Everything I do in my various professional roles strives toward interaction among different domains and the making of creative spaces, and therefore I must declare this bias at the start. Because my experience in organizations both as a participant and leader often serves as a foil to creation, I have learned to embrace the difficulties as formative forces. I have discovered how the inevitable resistance to creative transformation is the gateway, an indicator of where people need to go, and the work that has to be done (McNiff, 2009). In the organizational realm a further appreciation of the reluctance to transcend separation can lead to the creation of a more creative and viable common pulse.

The Power of Silos

In promoting the process of integration in the arts, professions, education, and organizational life, I have learned to respect the great power of disciplines, guilds, ideologies, and other forces that rival and constantly challenge creative and transformative learning processes within all kinds of institutions. These separations are manifestations of what can be called the silo principle, and it is a dominant influence that will not be leaving organizational and professional life any time soon.

Even groups and communities that commit themselves to creativity and learning are pervaded by silo phenomena, especially within many large organizations where decentralized and often internally competitive units have accounted for considerable growth, success, autonomy, and individual responsibility within the workplace. In the professions, specialization has similarly fostered growth and power. However, this success often leads to an absence of communication, collaboration, and learning between units together with the persistence of staunch commitments to holding and preserving domains and identities, behaviors that contradict the creative process that thrives on making new relationships between previously separate entities.

Within organizations some silos can be intensely creative, and they might be established in order to experiment with greater autonomy, generate ideas and products, or encourage cross-disciplinary work. But as an admitted idealist, especially in the realm of education where new learning and discovery need access to a breadth of resources and disciplines, I have always been inclined to support porous domains in which people welcome transit and ultimately see themselves as collaborators serving a common purpose. Although some functions within organizations may benefit from the silo effect, creative learning does not.

In navigating organizational spaces, I have learned repeatedly that the difficulties and obstacles that I face best inform the nature of the work that I do. I call this "creating from the hard places," the shadow side of creative expression and learning, which I have grown to appreciate as my most vital partner in creating (McNiff, 1998, 2003, 2007, 2008). As an advocate of integrative learning and the creative process, there is nothing in my experience that begins to match the challenges encountered by established domains, both inside and outside the person, which instinctively guard against, resist, and oppose all efforts to transform and shapeshift them into something different.

In keeping with this book's focus on spatial influences on learning, let me offer a vignette of how organizational forces manifest themselves in the world through corresponding physical forms. I was visiting Austin, Texas, to give a lecture for a conference held at the University of Texas. As I looked at the grand campus boulevards, the Texas Tower in the distance, the Memorial Stadium, and the massive and elegant campus buildings, I imagined the place as the survival of imperial Rome with a modern coliseum, and temples for the pantheon of individual deities honoring music, visual art, dance, drama, science, and other disciplines, each one markedly separate from the others and carrying a unique spatial persona. I was giving an address on "the poetic basis of depth psychology" and the use of all of the arts as ways of knowing at the conference center next to the Lyndon Baines Johnson Presidential Library. Looking out at the monumental spaces around me, I realized how my themes went contrary to the material structures of the site, whose architecture, physical space, and academic powers promoted separation versus mutuality. The university's master plan and space reflected the organization of education and professions everywhere.

In my work with art and healing I am well aware of the principle of correspondence and how external physical structures stimulate similar inner states (McNiff, 2004). In education and university life the dominant spatial patterns reinforce silos and separate domains of action and learning through every feature of their material beings. As Massey (1999, 2005), Meusburger (2009, p. 98), and many other geographers say, "place matters," and thus for those of us who foster cross-disciplinary learning it tends to function more as an antagonist than as an ally.

In 1974 I had founded a graduate institute and masters programs at Lesley University in Cambridge, Massachusetts, and one of the primary reasons why I selected Lesley as a site to establish education and therapy programs focused on integrating the arts and other disciplines was that the school did not have a history of separate arts departments. This lack of institutional separations and "turf" to be protected offered a relatively open field for the creation of something new. However, even in this place, committed to progressive programs and interdisciplinary cooperation, there were and continue to be numerous obstacles to reciprocal and cross-disciplinary creation and learning.

The new integrated graduate programs succeeded and took a prominent place within the university, but they essentially became new "disciplines" with distinct, separate, and often competing identities within the larger organization and community. The spatial and academic encapsulations were reinforced by budget and finance, physical facilities, the insularity of academic disciplines, group identities, the politics of boundaries, and many other forces that discourage creative integrations. Even within institutions where the leadership is fully committed to integrative and cross-school and departmental study, the partition of learning areas is a significant and formidable factor. Significant physical and psychological obstacles arise in relation to shapeshifting in both personal and spatial terms. If the structures of spaces are more amenable to multiple functions, role changes, and creative shifts, they can support corresponding effects on the people who work within them. In keeping with my belief that the creative process is outside in the world as well as inside the person, spatial factors can lead and support the creative process by establishing motivating forces.

The separation of spatial entities does manifest an archetypal tendency in human experience to acknowledge and celebrate multiplicity. Threats to creativity occur when the tendency to separate is driven by power and control motives and an emphasis on superficial differences that then prevent interplay and active participation in a larger field of learning. Hillman's (1989) "polytheistic psychology" underscores the importance of multiplicity within the person and life. Instead of encouraging fragmentation, he wants to give each of the aspects of a person or community its place, power, and beauty within a moving, episodic, and dramatic existence. Although Hillman treats the idea of integration with suspicion, I use the term to support multiplicity rather than what can become a tyranny of singularity, what William Blake called "single vision" (letter to Thomas Butt, November 22, 1802, as quoted in Keynes, 1956, p. 79), or the blending of varieties into homogeneity. In this sense integration is approached as a process, not as a fixed unity, as the very practice of imagination that Hillman and I advocate. It is the stage when the multiple players interact; when the moments of experience keep their autonomy while making something new together.

Within academic institutions language, too, plays a role in shaping space in conscious and subliminal ways by separating the core functions of an organization via the naming of distinct areas as divisions, centers, institutes, programs, and schools. Aware of these partitions and striving to further openness and access for both students and faculty, our university adopted the term "passport" for study and teaching in different areas. Although this metaphor has facilitated movement between domains, it also recognizes the spatial reality of border-crossing that too often characterizes the phenomenon of moving between disciplines and sectors of an academic organization in which the mission is, ironically, committed to social and personal change, new learning, and creation.

Silos flourish everywhere, even within institutions committed to collaboration. My experience suggests that new multidisciplinary creations can survive only if they themselves become new centers of practice that operate within the overall geography and ecology of an institution, competing successfully for resources that sustain the work. As the programs I have described complete four decades of operation, I can report that some logical areas of reciprocal study are still unrealized. This condition is reinforced by the politics of silos, whose representatives assert, not always accurately, that external government and professional regulations make it impossible to cross boundaries for the benefit of students and the people they serve. In response, I like to quote a farmer from Connemara region of Ireland who said to me in 1980, "You can't fence anything with wings."

Good and necessary ideas do continuously fly across borders, like "cross-over" artists, and make new things, but as I have learned, the natural structures of human behavior and systems do more to prevent than encourage this flight and then quickly establish the new things as separate spatial entities, arguably necessary for their growth and survival. Creative transformation is based upon making new relationships, joining previously separate domains, and fashioning entities and environments that meet the ever-changing demands of the world. Yet most physical environments and the people within them resist accepting the new, breaking habits, and changing even the most elemental movements in space.

As in organizations everywhere, I found that the new units needed their own space and the accompanying autonomy and responsibility in order to generate original "products" or programs, particularly when such units are a creative synthesis of previously separate entities. In order to help the new entity root itself and grow, it is separated from the dominion and established structures of the context from which it integrated previously separate features. Paradoxically, it then becomes a new silo that guards its turf.

Rather than wring my hands and fret about these obstacles to cross-border creations, I try to acknowledge them, even play with them, and work with their energy as a mode of transformation. Although I admire Nietzsche's (1883–1885/1917) call to "break up, break up" (p. 202) to create anew and recognize the process of destruction and breakthroughs in the creative process, I do not advocate "breaking" silos apart. As I hope to show here, they have their place in organizations and consciousness. I am committed to making them more receptive and open to what exists outside through learning and new knowledge, more flexible and appreciative of how they can be strengthened through collaborations with other domains, more responsive to the needs and interests of the people they serve, and more secure about themselves, for it is the fear of losing their places in the world that drives the more negative and restrictive forms of silo behavior. Also, "silos lack scale" (Aaker, 2008, p. 12), so organizations have self-interest in minimizing their dominance especially with respect to areas that negatively impact the image, growth, and sustainability of the whole.

I have discovered that resistance is natural when a person is asked to move beyond familiar terrain and even more so when that person is invited to embrace uncertainty (McNiff, 2009). As my colleague Hugh O'Doherty at the Center for Leadership at Harvard's John F. Kennedy School of Government says, people are "hard-wired" to resist these invitations for change (personal communication, March 16, 2007).

Yet the power of silos, in the sense of both personal and organizational selves, and the ingrained reluctance to relax them in education and professional practice cannot go unchallenged, for they contradict the dynamics of creative imagination, transformative learning, and health, all of which thrive on the free and open circulation of different energies within a person and organization. If the advancement of the self, defined by its relationships to other phenomena, is dependent on the cultivation of what Winnicott (1971) called the "potential space" between a person and the environment (p. 100), then a compelling case can be made for learning that expands spatial perspectives.

The guaranteed persistence of forces opposing creative exploration and new learning serves as a reminder that creative spaces must be made anew in each moment of operation. Before reflecting further on ways to group and organizational learning, I would like to define my notion of creative space and how it is established.

Creative and Learning Spaces as Permeable Domains

A *creative space* is an environment, both inside and outside a person, that is distinguished by a sense of possibility, imagination, energy, discovery, and change together with conflict, mistakes, vulnerabilities, and imperfections that are welcomed as necessary partners. It is a thoroughly porous context in which boundaries are freely crossed, and it thus complements silos that tend to be more fixed and committed to containment.

In contrast to place, which is a distinct physical entity, spaces and especially my notion of creative space are perceived and thus psychological states. Because space is endless, distinctions such as inside and outside, distant and far, are relative and traversed by the movements of people (Arnheim, 1996, p. 49), who, as I like to say, can both physically and psychologically walk between worlds. In physical and psychological space they encounter features that either further passage or hinder circulation (p. 50; Meusburger, 2009, p. 112).

In keeping with the idea of Celtic thin places, creative spaces tend to be liminal, fluid, supportive of movement between domains and new formations rather than rigidly set and impenetrably walled, and they are receptive to the process of shape-shifting as described in this chapter. Imagination is a fundamental quality of creative space and classical definitions, beginning with Thomas Hobbes in the mid-1600s, present imaginal experience as a connecting force, an intermediate or middle realm where different faculties and elements join and make new forms (Akenside, 1744/1772; Coleridge, 1817/1907; Richter, 1973).

In creative spaces people are supported in doing unusual things, transforming what currently exists into something different, and making novel and lasting connections between previously separate entities. In this sense, creativity is a thoroughly spatial activity. It requires the ability to enter the unknown, to let go of preconceptions and plans, to be open to the unexpected, and to respond to difficulties, setbacks, mistakes, and tensions as opportunities for new learning.

Within the creative space, dissolutions of the familiar, habits, and predictable operations are often required as well as the ability to make oneself vulnerable and even appear foolish in taking on a task whose end is not known at the beginning. As Heifetz and Linsky (2002) write, "No wonder people resist" when confronted with situations that can actually be "dangerous" and "risky" (p. 34). Arguably, all of the psychological qualities that have been discovered about creative space in group arts studio environments can transfer directly to organizational life. Yet most features of organizational experience are set up in ways that are contrary to these elements. The creative process tends to be marginalized because its emphasis on unplanned discovery is different from directive behavior, preordained strategic directions, controls, linear authority, avoidance and actual policies and procedures against conflict, the preference that even creative types have for clear goals, the necessity of meeting standards for production, and the solidity and relative permanence of places of operation—that is, silos (McNiff, 2006, 2007, 2008). However, an organization cannot sustain its productivity and move forward unless it constantly encourages original actions and useful innovations.

In many settings leaders create and workers implement. In creative spaces leaders support co-creation and transparently model the willingness to engage difficulties, engage uncertainty, and risk change. The idea of the leader as a keeper of a creative space of experimentation and learning, as the person responsible for cultivating a total environment that derives its powers and direction from what people, and silos as groups of people, do within it, can be totally aligned with productivity. In fact, it is arguably more in sync with the complex spaces and worlds in which we work today. When I was being trained in group therapy years ago, my supervisor kept stressing how one can never assume that a collection of people sitting together in a room "is a group." He felt that groups need to be created through the work they do together and the commitment of individual members to one another. The same applies to creative spaces, which I see as an even more fragile and perishable phenomenon than a group. In my experience, creative space must be recreated every time I meet with people with the goal of furthering expression. We can never take it for granted as a given entity, and it requires constant care.

I liken the loss of creative space to the natural process of breath that comes and goes. It is lost in order to be regained. After each gathering, the particular moment of creative space ends. When we participants meet again, the group must renew the qualities that make an environment creative.

Although the defining qualities of creative space are more psychological than physical, architecture and design can further creative activity, learning, collaboration, and movement across silos. However, perfectly designed and ideal physical environments can be thoroughly noncreative and even repressive. Everything depends upon what people do with the places that they are given; how they infuse them with values and human interactions. Having worked in many hundreds of settings, which generally have presented physical obstacles, I can affirm that the creative spirit and learning may flourish in impoverished places.

Creative space is furthered by what I call dreaming with what we already have, seeing things more deeply and with great appreciation for their unique qualities. This sensitivity is the perceptual alchemy of the artist who sees in novel ways. Attitude and the ability to change perspectives are core elements of the creative space. The most ordinary things can be sources of illumination when we pay careful attention to them. Bachelard (1958/1994) felt that all images of spaces, from grand landscapes to the most apparently ordinary household things and elemental facets of physical matter, evoke a "psychic state," the quality of which depends upon one's receptivity and responsiveness to them in the moment that they appear (p. 72). We reliably see how tending to small and humble places in an organization can generate effects with the potential to expand from micro- to macrospheres.

I like to describe how depth is on the surface of everything waiting to be seen. Deep-down is right now, the present moment permeated by potential depths inviting perception. In this respect solitary aesthetic contemplation of people, physical spaces, and configurations of objects contribute to a more comprehensive spatial imagination. Artists regularly describe themselves as witnesses who discover the self in the external objects they examine.

The qualities that I find most fundamental to making creative space include giving careful attention to other people and the immediate environment. In my studio sessions group members practice the discipline of witnessing others as they express themselves, and this process can transfer directly to organizational life. Quality and effectiveness are determined by whether or not people can make a particular moment, as it is happening, the most important one in their lives. If we are distracted, not fully present to the other person risking self-expression, the space becomes fractured, fragmented, and unsafe. We need to step outside our individual silos of consciousness, concentrate completely on the present field of action, and then feel free to let it go so we can open to the next.

Of course, creative space can be established by a solitary person interacting with an environment, but in my practice I find that its power is considerably augmented by the supportive presence of others who generate a "slipstream effect," an environmental circulation of creative energy, which tends to carry us further and deeper than we can go alone (McNiff, 2003, pp. 37–54). This dynamic perhaps accounts for the historical occurrence of centers of creativity in particular places. Practice with others helps the person internalize the creative space and learn how to make it alone, a contemplative skill that characterizes the work of creative artists and thinkers.

Safety is created by the support and attention of others. It also requires responses, preferably creative ones that sustain the process of expression and maintain the flow and cohesion of the space. Studio participants respond honestly, transparently; convey what they think and feel but without judgment of others; pay close attention; take risks in doing new things; enter uncertainty; and listen.

The discipline of presence is a pervasive quality of creative space. People can be physically situated in a room but mentally and emotionally in a very distant place. This condition again reinforces the psychological basis of creative space. In my practice I also find that the studio participants and I can go much farther and deeper when we slow things down, pay attention, take pauses, and act in more mindful ways. This principle of action, which originates in the group arts studio, is perhaps the one that applies most consistently to organizational experience, where I encourage people to take a breath when emotional expressions move too fast. Listening and receptivity are arguably even more important than expression and initiative, but in the ultimate sense every human encounter, even on the most minimal stage of action, contains all of these elements. It is generally not easy for people to act in this way that contrasts to the most ingrained habits of everyday life and the workplace, so the skills generally need to be practiced repeatedly and learned.

Perhaps nothing is more effective in building creative and safe learning environments than the process of a person taking a risk to do something completely new and unknown and then receive the full attention and support of group members. When working with people in the area of creative expression, I have observed a common fear of appearing foolish or strange; the feelings even approach terror when people are offered the opportunity to present themselves in new ways with their bodily, vocal, poetic, or visual expressions (McNiff, 2006). To help people in my studio groups relax self-consciousness and inhibitions to expression, I suggest that they try to stop thinking about themselves as the locus of the creative force. The same idea applies to the workplace, where fellow employees can help one another see how misleading and egocentric it is to think about creation as purely self-initiated rather than "respond" to what the environment presents.

I ask people to imagine *being in the creative energy of the world* rather than viewing creativity as something exclusively inside themselves with all of the attendant responsibilities and controls. As soon as they are able to see creativity as something that is both inside and outside the person, a significant burden is lifted. They shift from a self-centered focus to an exploration of how to tap into the energy and contents of the surrounding space and allow themselves to be carried by the streams of an environment. The challenge of expression thus shifts to one of being receptive and responding to what is already present rather than thinking that something has to be made, and initiated, from nothing. In the latter context the inexperienced or frightened person naturally feels a vacuum inside, with nothing in particular to bring forward, or the fear might arouse a sense of pandemonium and inner chaos instead of a perception of how the mythic Pandora, "all-giver," held a vase of bounteous gifts.

To deal with either the feelings of nothing inside or brimming with "too much," I encourage participants in my studio groups to start expressing themselves with elemental movements, to repeat gestures and let variations emerge naturally. As an organizational leader, I encourage similar actions by inviting inhibited people to give a spontaneous response to what they see happening around them no matter how insignificant it may seem—an observation or suggestion that becomes a starting point for a new conversation.

By using the most basic expressions of the body, with every art medium from dance to painting and writing, the work in the studio becomes very palpable. You cannot fail, I say, as long as you move with authenticity and purpose. I stress the importance of "good enough art" and try to help people relax the grip of inhibitions. The same principles apply to behaviors in organizations. Often, the people who have difficulty speaking or offering ideas have important insights if we can find ways to access essential things sans all the pretense that too often shapes communication. When studio participants fear immobility or try to do too much and panic, I draw attention to the breath and encourage slow and rhythmic movements together with pauses. The aesthetic significance of these expressions and the overall safety and energy of the space is reinforced by others who act as witnesses and who ultimately respond with expressions of their own as described above. The creative space thus becomes an ecological interplay of movements and gestures through which value is determined by the ability to see and appreciate what is happening before us. The lessons and applications to self-understanding, creativity enhancement, and community development flow from this process of experimentation, which constantly reinforces the power of attitude, perception, trust in unplanned expression, and close attention to others.

Most people who are given the opportunity to express themselves in the presence of others tend to prepare what they are going to do before they do it, so it is generally not easy to become part of something that "will carry us." I say to groups that the only thing that you can do wrong is start to plan what you do. Feeling an intention, a purpose, and a desire for expression is fine, but as soon as we explicitly script action, the intelligence of spontaneous gestures is neutralized. Of course, people are all apt to imagine and play out various scenarios in advance, as a way of preparing and channeling energy, but when performing, I emphasize letting go of plans in order to meet what will emanate from the present moment.

This experimentation with spontaneous discovery can complement the often exclusive focus on planning that permeates organizations today. Without questioning the value of plans, it is possible to learn how there are intelligences that operate outside their frameworks.

Trust the Process: An Artist's Guide to Letting Go (McNiff, 1998) grew from the resistance that I encountered in working with teachers and other leaders who expected training in the creative process to be predictable and replicable, outcomes that contradict how the end is not known at the beginning of creative discovery. Over and over again, I see that if people establish a safe and creative space and then let go and immerse themselves in the essential movement of creative expression, it will take them where they need to go.

However, I find that obstacles and forceful resistance to this type of openness are everywhere, even in the most ideal spaces, and, as I have emphasized above, they may have a necessary role in all aspects of creativity and learning inside and outside organizational settings. People seeking to know creative expression need to deepen understanding of its counter principles. And the key element that defines whether or not a space is transformative is whether or not it allows and supports the open engagement of these difficulties, the dark substances and uncertainties that always accompany deep learning and change, and what I call creative space. We humans can learn to find meaning in what first seems worthless or perhaps even disturbing, and rather than see ourselves as victims, we can remake our relationships with sources of affliction (Levine, 2009) that can become the most potent and reliable force of creative shapeshifting.

My suggestion to the organizational world is that experimentation with the arts and creative expression may offer the most penetrating and complete, albeit unlikely, space for learning about the deepest aspects of leadership, human vulnerability and potential, creative discovery, community collaboration, productivity, and positive navigation among the complexities and contradictory tensions of institutional life. Although what participants and I do within the creative spaces of an arts studio often differs from tasks and responsibilities of organizational work, the domains have much to learn from one another. The distinct qualities of each can further appreciation for the other and their ultimate collaboration.

Tensions Between Centers and Peripheries

Rudolf Arnheim's writing about the psychology of spatial relationships in the arts can further the understanding of the creative tension between silos and creative spaces. As we come to understand the distinct powers of each domain, we gain a deeper sense of their potential interplay. Although known for his emphasis on order and balance, Arnheim felt that formative creative tensions are at the core of everything new and productive. He observed how chaos theory in physics and other studies of nonlinear processes inform the search for "a more complex sense of order in the irregular" (personal communication, September 11, 1994). His theories offer fresh perspectives on leadership and creative space.

In 1988 Arnheim published *The Power of the Center*, which distills core concepts from his previous works on art and visual perception (1954), architecture (1978) and ways in which physical structures contain expression and act upon people who perceive them (1971). These "fields" of activity in their infinite variety involve interplay, what Arnheim (1988, p. 3) described as connections between the internal experience of a person's perception and external phenomena or structures that carry expression within themselves. In *The Power of the Center* he describes this dynamic as an exchange between "centric and eccentric systems" (p. vii), palpable "spatial relations" (p. 3), which manifest core psychological dynamics.

Arnheim (1988) describes a center as "a focus of energy from which vectors radiate into the environment; it is also a place upon which vectors act concentrically"

(p. 13). Since every person is a center of activity, together with "every visual object, be it a patch of paint or a building" (p. 52), it follows that organizations are themselves centric systems that are, in turn, composed of many more centers of action and perception. Arnheim describes how, as the center's "vectorial field spreads into the surroundings, sufficient space is needed to give this energy as much free play as seems desirable" (p. 52).

Experience at the perceptual level naturally establishes centers of focus, what Arnheim (1988) calls "centers of energy" (p. 13), which can be distinguished from physical centers and midpoints in particular places. The center derives its power from the tension generated through its interactions with other forces radiating from the peripheries of perceptual fields. As he reflected upon these spatial dynamics in the visual arts, Arnheim realized how the forces of centricity and eccentricity corresponded to human experience, "namely, the spread of action from the generating core of the self and the interaction with other centers in the social field" (p. ix) and how "trying to find the proper ratio between the demands of the self and the power and needs of outer entities" (p. ix) was played out whenever artists in varied media developed compositions. After describing how "deviation from the center enriches the dynamics of visual shape" (p. 119), Arnheim suggests that the same dynamic exists in other spheres of human behavior where the center is simultaneously held with variations playing off it. This spatial juxtaposition characterizing successful artistic compositions can be contrasted to compressed and tightly enclosed structures that similarly correspond to human behaviors and difficulties within organizations. Analogizing spatial relations to experience, he concludes,

> Soon enough, however, the self-centered individual or group is compelled to recognize that its own center is only one center among others and that the powers and needs of other centers cannot be ignored without peril. This more realistic worldview complements the centric tendency with an eccentric one. (Arnheim, 1988, p. 2)

To the extent to which centers are created by tensions within environments, their own ongoing viability and creativity may be threatened when formative tension decreases. They become self-immersed and lose the interaction with what Arnheim (1988) calls eccentric forces (a fitting synonym for creative space) that help renew and enhance their functions. As mentioned above in relation to the ongoing renewal of creative spaces, organizations might consider the extent to which they are or are not regularly replenishing and shapeshifting themselves.

Applications to Leading and Learning

Arnheim's conclusions about spatial dynamics and the reflections presented in this chapter about the characteristics of creative space suggest that organizational leadership and learning need to complement the natural centric tendency with sustained efforts to help people appreciate and understand other sectors of activity inside and outside the organization. For example, successful athletes see the whole field of play while also concentrating on the immediate things that they are doing and the people with whom they are interacting. In descriptions of skilled players, an attribute frequently mentioned is the ability not only to see the field as it presently is but also to sense what will happen next, to anticipate the emergent action. In organizational life the ability to perceive and understand the whole field of experience, what might be described as the institutional perspective, is uncommon. It is easier—and perhaps even more natural, as Arnheim (1996) suggests—to view space from personal vantage points: "everything is seen, first of all, in perspective" (p. 430). Adoption of an institutional or environmental point of view, one that differs from what is given directly by the human senses, includes the viewpoints of others, and may involve a certain degree of discomfort, is cultivated through practice and learning.

All too often, leaders tend to be thoroughly centric, operating exclusively from their personal centers of power and viewing situations only from their own standpoints or the position taken by a group of like-minded associates. Everyone has experienced organizations in which only the leader is allowed to create, with the rest of the staff, even senior members, implementing the initiatives. However, the issue is complex in that the leader who creates alone can establish highly successful organizations staffed by people more than willing to perform assigned functions. These expectations are often placed on centric leaders who strive to serve their communities and who are not necessary grouped with the narcissistic-omnipotent types that lead in this way. Effective solo creators are very good at knowing their fields of play, and they often see beyond the immediate context, like the athletes mentioned above, and envision emergent conditions not seen by others. They are also willing to take on responsibilities and conflicts that most people avoid. As with silos, this kind of leadership might work at opening the field of creation to others in order to become more sustainable.

Leadership that welcomes contributions from the eccentric spheres never abandons centric functions and responsibilities. It entails the reciprocal and interactive dimensions described as characterizing creative space and shifts between centric and eccentric realms. In contrast to how the creative space of the centric leader is restricted to the personal sphere, where it may often function ingeniously, opening to others requires a more lateral field of creation. The potential dynamics can be challenging when people do things that leaders do not support or when the latter have to "sacrifice" personal positions in deference to others. Also, expecting, even inviting, others in the organization to become involved in the creative process is, as described above, often met with considerable resistance and discomfort, and these combined tensions for both leaders and community members suggest why the centric model is more common.

To people committed to more inclusive participation, I have learned to say that the best way for them to support the creativity of others is to affirm expression without judgment and to combine that affirmation with the discipline of listening and paying close attention to what these others feel is fundamental to success. It is just as important, perhaps essential, to understand the viewpoints of adversaries and those who disturb one's sense of the organizational field. They are part of the whole mix and may sometimes be viewed as assets that can help achieve common goals.

This more lateral approach to leadership is in complete sync with my description of the creative space, a realm based on giving attention and support to others within an ever-widening field of relationships. It is a remarkably simple and yet profoundly challenging task that can become an ongoing educational and community-building priority with strategies designed to fit the unique needs of different settings. One of the best ways to learn how to practice it is to "start where you are," as contemplative teachers advise, and attempt to see the most immediate things, people, and yourself anew and with a deeper aesthetic and functional appreciation. In leading, I try to sustain both big-picture and small-scale goals together with centric and eccentric perspectives. I repeatedly discover how important it is to make sure there are relevant and easily understood objectives for the whole organization. But on a daily basis it is the more immediate and mundane interactions with people that can shapeshift a community in ways that exceed preliminary expectations. I learn repeatedly, through achievements and shortcomings, how subtle interactions with colleagues create this force of transformation or further resistance to it. Sensitive actions and affirmations of others, when combined with the principles and goals discussed above, continuously build and rebuild creative space.

References

Aaker, D. (2008). *Spanning silos: The new CMO imperative*. Boston: Harvard Business School Press.

Akenside, M. (1772). *The pleasures of imagination: A poem in three books*. London: W. Bowyer and J. Nichols. (Original work published in *The Poems of Mark Akenside*, 1744)

Arnheim, R. (1954). *Art and visual perception*. Berkeley, CA: University of California Press.

Arnheim, R. (1971). *Entropy and art: An essay on order and disorder*. Berkeley, CA: University of California Press.

Arnheim, R. (1978). *The dynamics of architectural form*. Berkeley, CA: University of California Press.

Arnheim, R. (1988). *The power of the center: A study of composition in the visual arts*. Berkeley, CA: University of California Press.

Arnheim, R. (1996). *The split and the structure: Twenty-eight essays*. Berkeley, CA: University of California Press.

Bachelard, G. (1994). *Poetics of space* (M. Jolas, Trans.). Boston: Beacon. (Original work published 1958)

Coleridge, S. (1907). *Biographia literaria* (J. Shawcross, Ed.). London: Oxford University Press. (Original work published 1817)

Heifetz, R., & Linsky, M. (2002). *Leadership on the line: Staying alive through the dangers of leading*. Boston: Harvard Business School Press.

Hillman, J. (1989). In T. Moore (Ed.), *A blue fire: Selected writings of James Hillman*. New York: Harper and Row.

Keynes, G. (Ed.). (1956). *The letters of William Blake*. New York: Macmillan.

Levine, S. (2009). *Trauma, tragedy, therapy: The arts and human suffering*. London: Jessica Kingsley.

Massey, D. (1999). Philosophy and politics of spatiality: Some considerations. In *Power-geometries and the politics of space-time* (pp. 27–42). Hettner-Lecture: Vol. 2. Heidelberg, Germany: Heidelberg University Department of Geography.

Massey, D. (2005). *For space*. London: Sage.

McNiff, S. (1998). *Trust the process: An artist's guide to letting go*. Boston: Shambhala Publications.

McNiff, S. (2003). *Creating with others: The practice of imagination in art, life and the workplace*. Boston: Shambhala Publications.

McNiff, S. (2004). *Art heals: How creativity cures the soul*. Boston: Shambhala Publications.

McNiff, S. (2006). The terrifying beauty of creating anew. *POIESIS: A Journal of the Arts and Communication, 8*, 100–103.

McNiff, S. (2007). Empathy with the shadow: Engaging and transforming difficulties through art. *Journal of Humanistic Psychology, 47*, 392–399.

McNiff, S. (2008). Creating with the shadow: Reflections on Stephen K. Levine's contributions to expressive arts therapy. In E. Levine & P. Antze (Eds.), *In praise of poiesis: The arts and human existence* (pp. 20–31). Toronto, Ontario, Canada: EGS Press.

McNiff, S. (2009). Creative space. In S. McNiff (Ed.), *Integrating the arts in therapy: History, theory, and practice* (pp. 166–177). Springfield, IL: Charles C. Thomas.

Meusburger, P. (2009). Milieus of creativity: The role of places, environments, and spatial contexts. In P. Meusburger, J. Funke, & E. Wunder (Eds.), *Milieus of creativity: An interdisciplinary approach to spatiality of creativity* (pp. 97–153). Knowledge and Space: Vol. 2. Dordrecht, The Netherlands: Springer.

Nietzsche, F. (1917). *Thus spake Zarathustra* (T. Common, Trans.). New York: Boni and Liveright. (Original work published in German 1883–1885)

Richter, J. P. (1973). *School for aesthetics* (M. R. Hale, Trans.). Detroit, MI: Wayne State University Press. (Original work published 1804)

Winnicott, D. W. (1971). *Playing and reality*. New York: Routledge.

The Klaus Tschira Foundation

Physicist Dr. h.c. Dr.-Ing. E. h. Klaus Tschira established the Klaus Tschira Stiftung (Klaus Tschira Foundation) in 1995 as a not-for-profit organization conceived to support research in the natural sciences, mathematics, and informatics and to foster public understanding of these sciences. Klaus Tschira's commitment to this objective was honored in 1999 with the "Deutscher Stifterpreis," the prize awarded by the National Association of German Foundations. Klaus Tschira is a cofounder of SAP AG in Walldorf, one of the world's leading companies in the software industry.

The Klaus Tschira Stiftung provides support mainly for research in the natural sciences, mathematics, and applied informatics and funds educational projects at schools and universities. The resources are largely used for projects initiated by the foundation itself. It commissions research from institutions such as HITS (Heidelberg Institute for Theoretical Studies), formerly known as EML Research, founded by Klaus Tschira. HITS focuses on new theoretical approaches to interpreting the rapidly increasing amounts of experimental data. In addition, the Klaus Tschira Stiftung invites applications for projects that are in line with the central concerns of the foundation.

The seat of the Klaus Tschira Stiftung is Villa Bosch in Heidelberg (Fig. 1), the former residence of Carl Bosch (1874–1940), the Nobel Prize Laureate for Chemistry. Carl Bosch, scientist, engineer, and businessman, joined BASF (Badische Anilin- & Soda-Fabrik) in 1899 as a chemist and became its CEO in 1919. In 1925 he was appointed CEO of the then newly created IG Farbenindustrie AG, and in 1935 he became chairman of the supervisory board of this chemical conglomerate. In 1937 Bosch was elected president of the Kaiser Wilhelm Gesellschaft (later renamed as the Max Planck Gesellschaft), the premier scientific society in Germany. Bosch's work combined chemical and technological knowledge at its best. Between 1908 and 1913, together with Paul Alwin Mittasch, he solved numerous problems in the industrial synthesis of ammonia, drawing on a process discovered earlier by Fritz Haber (Karlsruhe), who won the Nobel Prize for Chemistry in 1918. The Haber-Bosch process, as it is known, quickly became the most important method of producing ammonia—and remains so to this day. Bosch's research also influenced

A. Berthoin Antal et al. (eds.), *Learning Organizations: Extending the Field*,
Knowledge and Space 6, DOI 10.1007/978-94-007-7220-5,
© Springer Science+Business Media Dordrecht 2014

Fig. 1 The Villa Bosch (© Peter Meusburger)

high-pressure synthesis of other substances. He was awarded the Nobel Prize for Chemistry in 1931, together with Friedrich Bergius.

In 1922 BASF erected a spacious country mansion and ancillary buildings in Heidelberg-Schlierbach for its CEO, Carl Bosch. The villa is situated in a small park on the hillside above the Neckar river and within walking distance from the famous Heidelberg Castle. As a fine example of the style and culture of the 1920s, Villa Bosch is considered one of the most beautiful buildings in Heidelberg and has been declared a protected cultural site. After World War II, it served as a domicile for high-ranking military staff of the United States Army. Thereafter, a local enterprise used the villa as its headquarters for several years. In 1967 Süddeutsche Rundfunk, a broadcasting company, established its Heidelberg studio there. Klaus Tschira bought Villa Bosch as a future home for his planned foundations toward the end of 1994 and had the building restored and modernized. Combining the historic ambience of the 1920s with the latest infrastructure and technology, Villa Bosch reopened in new splendor in mid-1997, ready for fresh challenges. Seminars and conferences are held today in the auditorium of the Villa Bosch Studio.

The former garage, located 300 m west of the villa, now houses the Carl Bosch Museum Heidelberg, founded and managed by Gerda Tschira and dedicated to the memory of the Nobel laureate, his life, and his achievements.

Fig. 2 Participants of the symposium "Learning Organizations" at the Villa Bosch in Heidelberg. (© Thomas Bonn, Heidelberg)

This book is the result of a symposium entitled "Knowledge and the Economy," which took place at Villa Bosch (Fig. 2).

For further information contact:
Klaus Tschira Stiftung gGmbH
Villa Bosch
Schloss-Wolfsbrunnenweg 33
D-69118 Heidelberg, Germany
Tel: (06221) 533 113, Fax: 533 599 113
www.klaus-tschira-stiftung.de

Index

A
Academy of Management, 190
Action
    coordinated, 164–166
    participatory action research, 195,
        210–212
    setting, 192
Advanced management practice (AMP),
    135–138
Aesthetic
    distancing, 204
    learning space, 208–210
Affiliation, 59, 62, 63, 71, 72, 74, 78, 80–82,
    111, 114
Age, 59, 60, 63, 64
Airport, 11, 23, 25
Alienation, 151, 207, 213
Allocation, 93–94, 96–99
    power, 51
AMP. *See* Advanced management
    practice (AMP)
Antipathy, 78, 80, 81
Apple, 88
Apprentice, 36, 40, 41, 183
Architecture
    School of Architecture
        and Planning, 7
    space, 106
Arts
    artful capabilities and
        competences, 185
    artful creation, 185, 186
    artful process, 188
    artistic capabilities, 185
    artistic interventions, 9, 11, 177–196
    artist-led interventions, 181–183
    artist placement group, 182
    based actions, 203, 204, 206
    based learning practices, 203
    forms, 179, 190

Attention, 3, 6–8, 10, 17, 19, 22–24, 31, 35,
    44, 49, 57, 65, 72, 73, 75, 93, 99, 105,
    120, 131, 132, 136, 160, 165, 179, 189,
    191, 193, 194, 205, 206, 217, 230–232,
    235, 236
Attractiveness, 4
Austin, Texas, 225
Austria, 180
Authority, 2, 5, 6, 21, 52, 53, 60, 63–65, 138,
    163, 165, 169, 229
Autonomy, 24, 87, 120, 225, 227

B
Ba
    mental ba, 32–34, 37–39, 42–46
    physical ba, 32, 33, 37, 39, 42–46
    virtual ba, 30, 32, 33, 46
Basho, 46
Beta video, 49
Beuys, Joseph, 183
Biosensor, 89, 91, 93–96
Bonn, 89
Boundary, 85, 155
Brazil, 166, 170, 189
Brundtland Commission, 170
Buzz, 86, 87, 98

C
Cambridge, Massachusetts, 226
Case study, 11, 18, 22–24, 54–55, 65, 86,
    98, 99, 204, 205, 210–214,
    216, 218
Catalyst program, 181
Center, 1–4, 6, 35, 58, 61, 88, 94, 98, 107,
    161, 164, 186, 206, 224, 225, 227, 228,
    230, 233–235
Centrality, 3, 6, 186
Centralization, 3, 5, 71, 72, 166

A. Berthoin Antal et al. (eds.), *Learning Organizations: Extending the Field*,
Knowledge and Space 6, DOI 10.1007/978-94-007-7220-5,
© Springer Science+Business Media Dordrecht 2014

Child mortality, 157
China, 166
Civil society
   bureau, 165
   declaration, 169
Co-authorship, 115, 117
Codes, 9, 39, 42, 117–119, 132, 139, 177
Cognitive conservatism, 72, 78
Command, 49–65, 72, 75, 203
Commission on Sustainable Development,
      167, 170
Communication
   patterns of communication, 104
   technologies, 3, 5, 158, 165
Community
   community of blood, 40
   community of practice, 5, 8
   community of spirit, 40
   community order, 34, 35
   community-order perspective, 30, 31
Competence, 5, 44, 45, 131, 168, 185, 209
Competition, 5, 31, 43, 55, 166
Complexity, 26, 76, 104, 106, 129, 139
   organizations, 5, 18, 129, 203
Conference center, 107, 225
Conflict, 9, 26–27, 31, 74, 79, 85, 86, 90,
      92, 96–99, 138, 140, 148, 149, 166,
      169, 171, 180, 218, 224, 228,
      229, 235
   management, 74
Consensus formation, 71, 77, 78
Consultants, 55, 57, 149, 178, 179, 183, 188
Contact system, 3
Context, 2, 4, 6, 7, 9, 11, 17, 19, 26, 29, 31,
      33, 40, 45, 50, 55, 74, 86, 87, 93,
      96–98, 104, 105, 117, 129, 133, 137,
      143, 145, 150, 158, 159, 161, 162,
      166, 170–172, 179, 186–190, 195,
      205–208, 210, 214, 216, 217, 227,
      228, 231, 235
Control
   promotive control, 71, 73–75, 80, 81
   restrictive control, 71, 72, 74, 75, 77–82
Conviction, 49–65
Coordination capability, 76, 80
Co-presence, 87, 96, 98, 113–116, 121–123
Cornelsen Verlag, 182
Corporate network, 4, 64
Creativity
   creative space, 9, 12, 223–236
   creative transformation, 224, 227
Culture
   clash, 178
   cultural norms, 85, 88

strangeness, 85
tension, 88, 90, 91, 98
Customer
   complaints, 92, 95
   service, 59–62

D
Debugging, 77, 94–95, 97
Decision-making, 3, 5, 56, 71, 74–76, 78, 79,
      82, 132, 158, 162, 163, 210
Denmark, 180, 184
Deutsche Bahn AG, 183
Developer, 91, 92, 94–97, 118
Dialogic scripting, 206, 213
Differentiation, 6, 44, 88, 147, 149–152,
      154, 186
Diffusion
   contagion diffusion, 65
   diffusion of knowledge, 4
   hierarchical, 50
   innovation diffusion, 52–53
Dislocation, 96–98, 131, 139, 140
Dissonance, 9, 86, 90, 99
Distance
   cognitive distance, 85, 99
   cultural, 86, 90
   multidimensional distance, 88
   physical distance, 9, 85–88, 99
   relational distance, 9, 85–100
   topological distance, 59
Diversity, 26, 85, 97, 106, 205, 207, 218
Division of labor, 4, 19, 52
dm-drogerie markt, 183
Domain, 5–7, 11, 70, 192, 193, 223–233
Dramaturgy, 206, 207

E
EA Generali, 180
Earth Summit, 162, 163, 167
Eccentric spheres, 235
Economic geography, 85, 86, 98, 99, 104
Educational achievement, 3
Embeddedness, 104, 116–121, 159, 194
   embedded routines, 161, 163–164, 170
Emigration, 151–153, 155
Engineering manager, 211
Enterprise resource planning (ERP), 11, 17–27
Environment
   environment, 103, 227, 230
   psychology, 4, 7, 105
   sustainability, 157
Equilibrium, 30, 147, 148, 153

ERP. *See* Enterprise resource planning (ERP)
ERP systems, 17–27
Error, 70, 71, 78, 82, 92, 95, 191, 231
Estrangement, 207
Ethnography
    exploration, 36–38
    interviews, 89, 90
    methods, 89, 107
Eurogroup consulting, 182
Exchange
    spirit of exchange, 30
    task-oriented exchange, 79
Experience, 5–7, 10, 17–27, 33, 34, 40, 41, 46,
        52, 60, 75, 76, 78, 79, 82, 86, 95, 130,
        132, 135, 138, 140, 144–146, 151, 155,
        159, 160, 164, 177, 183, 187, 188,
        191–193, 195, 205, 208, 209, 214–216,
        223–227, 229, 231, 233–235
    imaginal experience, 229
Experiment, 4, 11, 46, 80, 89, 90, 92–94, 97,
        137, 159, 161, 167, 171, 177, 180–183,
        186, 191, 192, 195, 203, 223, 225, 229,
        232, 233
Expertise, expert, 5, 7, 19, 37, 39, 41, 44, 60,
        91, 93, 96, 114–117, 122
Externalization, 2, 29, 43

F
Face-to-face
    contacts, 3, 5, 19
    interaction, 27, 96, 113
Field theory, 146, 150, 155
Finance, 23, 57, 59–61, 64, 69, 73, 93,
        166, 226
Financing for Development Conference, 168
Finland, 211
Firm, 4, 6, 11, 18, 49–57, 59–61, 65, 69, 73,
        75, 87, 89, 92, 100, 153
First mover advantage, 49
Fluidic cell, 95
Forestry industry, 10
Fragmentation, 8, 226
France, 11, 22, 41, 182, 195
French Proximity School, 88
Frozen images, 208, 212

G
Gendered dynamics, 137
Geneva, 158, 165, 166, 168, 169
    Geneva Summit, 168
Geography, 1, 2, 4, 7, 85, 86, 98, 99, 104, 122,
        192, 227

geography of the firm, 4
human geography, 7, 122
Germany, 1, 11, 54, 55, 64, 79, 89, 107,
        154, 224
Gift theory
    exchange, 34, 38, 39, 42
    reciprocation, 35
Global-exchange approach, 30
Global governance, 158, 159, 163, 167
Global pipeline, 87
Governance, 3, 30, 35, 157–159, 163,
        165–167, 169–171, 224
    mode, 30
Group-analytic concept of relatedness, 130

H
Habitus, 148, 150–153
Handbook of organizational design, 1
Harvard, 1, 2, 228
Hau
    hau-ba model, 29–46
    hau theory, 30–31
Headquarter, 3, 9, 11, 18, 25, 34, 87, 157
Heuristic concept, 98
Hierarchy, 2, 10, 23, 44, 50, 53, 55, 56,
        59, 60, 62, 63, 65, 71, 72, 147,
        150–152
Holistic perspective, 203
Hub model, 87
Human relations approach, 105
Hypomania, 144, 145

I
IBM, 51
Identity, 3, 30, 34, 39–42, 45, 51, 72, 78, 82,
        94, 170, 171
    oriented reasoning, 72, 78
Ideology, 17–27
Illumination, 230
Imagination lab, 183
Imaginative thinking, 204
Informal relations, 50, 55, 56, 59, 63, 65
Information
    acquisition, 78, 103
    exchange, 79
    information and communications
        technologies, 96
    overload, 70
    pathology, 70, 71, 78, 79
    processing, 69–71, 78, 79, 82
    processing capacity, 71
    technology, 17

Innovation
  biography, 88
  bottom-up innovation, 51–52
  conflict, 86, 98
  controversial innovation, 49–65
  diffusion, 52–53
  promoters, 53, 54, 60, 63, 64
  top-down innovation, 50–52, 60
  types of innovation, 50
Interaction
  dynamic, 90–98
  researcher–researcher, 93–94
  researcher–user, 95–96
  variables, 74, 91
Intermediary, 19, 22, 40, 179, 181, 182, 190
Internalization, 2, 29, 44, 45, 148, 151
International Institute of Management
  (WZB), 1
International Telecommunications Union
  (ITU), 164, 165, 170
Internet Corporation for Assigned Names
  and Numbers (ICANN), 166
Intervention technique, 206
Interview, 10, 23, 26, 36, 38, 40, 55–57, 60,
  65, 73, 75, 77, 89–91, 93, 94, 107, 179,
  182, 183, 187, 193, 194
Israel, 2, 11, 144, 145, 147, 151
ITU. See International Telecommunications
  Union (ITU)

J
Japan, 2
Johannesburg, 164, 168, 171
Joint ventures, 8

K
Knowledge, knowing
  bodily knowing, 191
  exchange of knowledge, 3, 31, 113, 114
  explicit knowledge, 29, 43, 89
  growth of knowledge, 69, 80
  intraorganizational relations of knowledge
    exchange, 56
  knowing your place, 151–152, 155
  knowledge creation, 2, 11, 29, 35, 86, 88,
    99, 103, 113, 192, 203, 204, 208,
    210–213, 216, 217
  knowledge environment, 1–12
  Knowledge, forms of, 178, 186, 191
  knowledge practice, 86, 92, 95–97, 99
  knowledge production, 3, 82, 99
  knowledge-sharing, 4, 29–31

knowledge transformations, 29, 33, 43, 46
knowledge work, 4, 37, 38, 69, 82, 91, 92,
  96, 98, 99
pharmacists' leadership program,
  137–139
sources of knowledge, 18, 24–27, 87
strategic knowledge community, 30
tacit knowledge, 39, 43, 46, 86, 210
transfer of knowledge, 3, 29
ways of knowing, 186, 192, 194, 195, 225

L
Laboratory, 89, 93–99
Learning
  double-loop learning, 178
  feedback learning, 161, 167
  feedforward learning, 161, 164, 169, 171
  group learning, 103, 138
  groups, 135, 136, 138–140
  learning flows in organizations, 186
  learning (or not) from reality, 22
  learning from screens, 17–27
  learning-in-organizing, 130
  learning lab, 184
  organization, 104, 130, 149
  polyphonic learning space, 203, 204
  processes, 3–5, 8, 9, 11, 18, 106, 121, 130,
    150, 184, 208, 209, 216, 225
  reflective, 159, 160
  trajectories, 184–186
  unsuccessful, 8
Lesley University, 226
Life space, 9, 144–147, 149
Luxury products, 23
Lyndon Baines Johnson Presidential
  Library, 225

M
Management
  abstract, 19, 22, 26
  controller, 23–25
  intervention, 56
  learning, 129, 132, 135, 139
  promoted innovation, 53
  real time, 22
  research, 10, 106, 194
  senior, 51–53, 60, 62, 65
  through computers, 18
  top-down, 9, 211
  top manager, 5, 6, 57
Market
  orientation, 50, 56–65

Massachusetts Institute of Technology (MIT), 1
Maussian exchange rules, 31
Maussian gift, 31, 42, 45
    microcycles of gifting, 42–45
Measurement
    application, 94–97
    test, 92–97
Memory, 30, 34–39, 41–45, 132, 159–161, 169, 216
Metaxis, 208–209, 216
Microsoft, 18, 88
Migration, 151–153, 155
Milieu, 3–5, 178, 192
Millennium Development Goals, 157
Mimesis, 208
Mixed methodology, 65
Mobility
    of objects, 97
    professional, 87, 98
Monocentrism, 94
Monterrey, 168
Multistakeholder, 158, 159, 161–162, 164, 166–171
Myopia, 160

N
Narrative, 77, 204–208, 210, 214, 215, 217
National Symposium on Habitability, 191
Nested workflows, 93
Network
    formal, 53, 54, 59, 63–65
    network, 53, 59, 63, 65
    Situational organizational network analysis (SONA), 65
    social network analysis, 50, 56, 65, 107
    supplier, 8
New York, 157
NGO, 159, 162, 165
Nonstate actors, 158, 159, 162–164, 167–170
Nonstate sphere, 158
Norms, 57, 85, 86, 88, 151, 152, 160, 162, 163, 171
Not-Invented-Here-Syndrome, 160
Novelty, 49
Novo Nordisk, 180

O
Office
    configurations, 103–123
    decentralization, 3
    location, 3
Operationalization of variables, 106

Operational manager, 23–25
Operator, 19, 37, 38, 77, 214, 215
Ophthalmological engineering, 11, 50, 54–55, 64
Opportunity costs, 96–98
Organization
    behavior, 1, 6–8, 52, 103–123, 139
    change, 49–54, 64, 65, 186, 187, 206
    communities, 30
    culture, 53, 65, 87, 103, 110, 178, 179, 182, 183, 190
    dynamics, 129, 139, 140
    ecology, 50
    enquiry, 104
    environment, 104, 184
    events, 203, 204, 206, 216, 218
    humanistic dimension of the organization, 203
    identity, 51
    innovations, 11, 22, 49–54, 56, 57, 60, 62–65
    intermediary organization, 179, 181, 182, 190
    memory, 34, 159, 161
    organizational learning, 1–12, 99, 103–123, 129, 130, 134, 135, 139, 140, 143–155, 158, 160, 161, 177–196, 203–218, 223–236
    practices, 50, 51, 56, 65, 136
    spaces, 10, 177–196, 225
    temporary, 7, 8, 11, 157–172
    theater, 214–216
    theory, 4, 12
    the unconscious in organizations, 129–141
    units, 49, 51, 53, 61, 99
    unlearning, 1
Overspecialization, 71

P
Pair-programming, 118
Participant observation, 10, 34, 89, 90, 92
Patterns of change, 11, 149–151, 155
Peer-reviewing, 92
Perception
    modes of perception, 20–22
    perception of time, 21
Performance evaluation process, 23, 25, 26
Performative narration, 207
Periphery, 4, 6, 51
Philosophical perspective, 3

Place, 2, 4–6, 8, 12, 20, 30–33, 35, 42, 46, 62,
    89, 90, 93–95, 98, 106, 111–113, 118,
    120, 122, 123, 130, 134–136, 138, 140,
    144, 145, 151–155, 163, 180, 191, 206,
    208, 209, 211, 216, 217, 225–228,
    231, 233
Policy, 106, 157–159, 162–164, 166, 167,
    190, 193
    intergovernmental policy process, 159
Polycentrism, 96
Poverty, 157
Power
    asymmetries, 52
    authoritative, 53
    geometries, 6
    relationships, 71, 207, 208, 210, 214
Private sector, 109, 157, 158, 168, 169, 177
Privileges, 9, 52, 184
Process analysis, 39
Professional skills, 5
Programmer, 19
Proximity
    physical, 86, 87, 112
    relational, 85–88, 98, 104
Psychic state, 230
Psychology, psychologists, 2, 4, 7, 105, 178,
    225, 226, 233
    polytheistic psychology, 226
Psychopathology, 144
Public sector, 109, 177

Q
Quality management, 61, 626
Questionnaire, 55, 65, 73–76, 80–82

R
Rationality, 19, 34, 71, 183, 203,
    205, 210
Reformation, 151, 153–155
Region, 2, 3, 5, 51, 132, 147, 149–152, 154,
    163, 227
    regional development, 3
Relatedness, 130, 134, 135, 139, 140
Relational reality, 145–146
Relation, relationship
    energizing relationships, 52
    interorganizational relations, 100
    relational perspective, 49
    relationships between space and
        organizations, 106
    supervisory relations, 115

Reporting system, 23, 25
Representation
    abstract representation, 8, 18, 20, 27
    representation of authority, 5
Reputation, 4, 5, 58, 91, 93, 97
Research
    integrated R&D network model, 87
    research and development (R&D), 55,
        59–61, 64, 69, 87, 88, 96, 99, 203, 204,
        209, 211
    research-based theater (RBT), 11,
        203–218
    researcher-user interaction, 95–96
    research institute, 107–115, 117,
        120–122
Resistance, 9, 44, 50–52, 54, 56, 57, 65, 77,
    92, 95, 131, 195, 224, 228, 232, 233,
    235, 236
    institutional resistance, 52
Rio de Janeiro, 162, 170
Rivalry, 71
Role-play scenes, 214, 218
Routine, 18, 22, 92, 180, 184
    routine behavior, 18
Rules, 9, 31, 33, 34, 50, 52, 86, 88, 89, 98,
    148, 150–154, 160, 162–164,
    167–170, 210

S
Sales
    salesman, 215
    sales unit, 9
SAP, 18–20, 22–24
    SAP xRPM, 18–20
School, 7, 52, 88, 132, 135, 136, 144, 145,
    151–153, 179, 182, 189, 190,
    226, 228
Science
    science studies, 7
    scientification, 17
    scientific atmosphere, 114
    scientific reputation, 5, 91, 93
    scientist, 91, 92, 117
Screen, 18–20, 27, 70, 118
Scripting, 206, 213, 214
SECI
    SECI matrix, 32, 33, 38, 39, 42,
        44, 45
    SECI model, 9
    SECI spiral, 39, 44–46
Secrecy strategy, 53
Semantic differential, 74

Sense-makers, 203
Sensor system, 11, 89, 92, 93
Separation, 6, 224–226
Service, 59–64, 99, 131, 177
   length of service, 59, 60, 63, 64
Shapeshifting, 223–236
Shared beliefs, 86
Shifting cognitive gears, 154
Silo, 225, 227, 228
   silo phenomena, 225
Social field, 146–148, 152, 234
Social phenomena, 143, 145, 154, 155
Social system, 5, 6
Sociology, 2, 8, 145
Software interfaces, 26
Solidarity, 109, 110, 112–117, 121–123, 135,
   157, 167
Sony, 49
South Africa, 166
Soviet Union, 154
Space
   communicational space, 207
   generic function of space,
      110–112, 122
   polyphonic learning space, 203
   polyphonic spaces, 9
   relative space, 2, 132
   social space, 9, 11, 143–155, 208
Spain, 182
Spatiality
   dynamic spatiality, 88, 98
   spatial concentration of knowledge
      and power, 3
   spatial context, 4, 105
   spatiality of science, 3
   spatial patterns, 6, 98, 99, 226
   spatial turn, 7, 105, 192
Spearman-Brown formula, 74–76
Stakeholder, 166, 168
Standardization of practices, 22
Storyteller, 206, 207, 215–217
Strategy
   strategic alliances, 8
   strategy orientation, 61
Structure
   structural controversy, 50
   structural hole theory, 53
Subculture, 52
Substantialist thinking, 145
Surveillance, 22, 165
   panoptic surveillance, 22
Switzerland, 183
System's operators, 19

T
Task-oriented effort, 72
Technology
   technological change, 177
   technology orientation, 56–59, 61
Telecommunication, 3, 5, 164, 166
Tension, sociocultural, 85–100
Theater
   Boalian theater, 205
   philosophy of theater, 207
   research-based theater, 11, 203–218
   theater-based interventions, 181
   theater techniques, 204, 206,
      207, 216
   theatrical pictures, 212–214
Theoretical physics, 107, 113, 115, 122
Throwntogetherness, 130, 134, 135,
      139, 140
TILLT, 181
Time
   time frame, 19, 31, 162
   time-spatial conflicts, 92, 96–99
   time-spatial tensions, 85–100
Trade secrets, 10, 40–42
Trainee, 55
Transaction, 86
   transaction costs, 86
Transformation, 29, 30, 32, 34, 37, 38,
      42, 43, 46, 69, 130, 134, 149, 151,
      153–155, 180, 184, 193, 224,
      227, 236
Trust, 42, 85, 190, 210, 215, 232
Tunis, 158, 166, 171
Tutor, 40, 41, 132

U
Uncertainty, 5, 81, 85, 138, 140, 160, 161,
      196, 228, 229, 231
Unconscious, 9, 11, 129–141
UN Economic and Social
      Council, 168
UN Environment Programme, 163
UN General Assembly, 163, 164
UN headquarters, 157
UN High Commissioner for Human
      Rights, 163
Unilever, 181
UN Internet Governance Forum, 163
United Kingdom (UK), 11, 22, 181, 182,
      186, 189
United Nations, 9, 11, 157, 170
United States, 1, 12

University, 1, 4, 5, 12, 69, 78, 107, 109, 111, 120, 224–247
UN World Summit on Environment and Development, 162

V
Valence
    negative valence, 147
    positive valence, 147
VHS, 49
Virtual communication, 27
Visibility, 105, 109, 121

Visual display, 18, 19

W
Weickian tradition, 205
Workplace
    shared workplace, 19
    workplace environments, 104, 105, 109, 110, 112
World Summit on the Information Society (WSIS), 158, 159, 161, 162, 164–171
Worldviews, 86, 151, 203, 205–207, 214–217
WZB (Social Science Research Center Berlin), 1

Printed by Printforce, the Netherlands